THIRD EDITION

ADVERTISING
CONCEPT AND COPY

GEORGE FELTON

W. W. NORTON & COMPANY

NEW YORK • LONDON

For Karen, who never says, "That's nice, dear."

For information about permission to reproduce selections from this book, write to Permissions, W. W. Norton & Company, Inc., 500 Fifth Avenue, New York, NY 10110

For information about special discounts for bulk purchases, please contact W. W. Norton Special Sales at specialsales@wwnorton.com or 800-233-4830

Book design and composition by Gilda Hannah
Manufacturing by Four Colour Print Group
Production manager: Leeann Graham

Library of Congress Cataloging-in-Publication Data

Felton, George, 1947–
   Advertising : concept and copy / George Felton.—Third edition.
      pages cm
   Includes bibliographical references and index.
      ISBN 978-0-393-73386-0 (pbk.)
1. Advertising. I. Title.
      HF5823.F43 2013
      659.1—dc23
                          2013004842

W. W. Norton & Company, Inc., 500 Fifth Avenue, New York, N.Y. 10110
      www.wwnorton.com
W. W. Norton & Company Ltd., Castle House, 75/76 Wells Street, London W1T 3QT

2 3 4 5 6 7 8 9 0

CONTENTS

How this book is organized, and why

If you're new to the book, you'll see that I've divided it into three parts. The first two sections correspond to a natural sequence in the solving of an advertising problem: first you create a strategy, then you execute it. The last section offers suggestions for making those executions memorable.

Part 1, Strategy, operates on the premise that the selling idea beneath an ad's surface determines its success. You get that good idea by researching your product, understanding who buys it and why, and studying the marketplace in which it competes. In doing those things you'll discover the problem that your advertising must solve, you'll find the strategic approach that best solves it, and you'll be able to write the creative brief that focuses this strategic thinking into specific advertising objectives.

Now, how to put that strong selling idea into action? How to express it? Part 2, Execution, examines the tools at your command, from the elements of print advertising—headlines, visuals, copy—to the wide variety of media and advertising genres available to you. These are the means by which you turn strategic thinking into real-world effectiveness. Thus the movement of the first two sections: What are you going to say? How are you going to say it?

Part 3, The Toolbox, is what it sounds like: a place to find problem-solving tools. Here I discuss basic principles of creativity and follow that with techniques that advertising professionals have used, over and over, to produce attention-getting, persuasive work. I hope you'll try these techniques when the blank page or screen looms too large. They're more specific and therefore more helpful than the earnest advice we give ourselves and get from others to "think."

As a copywriter, you're expected not only to write well but to think well—generating unusual, provocative ideas, visual as well as verbal ones. How this is done is a great mystery, of course, and no book can tell you enough. But especially in Part 3, The Toolbox, I've tried to give you the best advice I can find on developing your creativity. After all, that's what you're selling.

What I've kept and what I've changed

I've rewritten this book to make it better, examining each section and each sentence with an eye toward improving it. I've kept what's good, cut what's weak, and updated everywhere. Most obviously, I've updated the ads themselves. Although principles of persuasion don't change, the look and language of ads certainly do, and there's nothing more exciting than fresh work. (That said, great ads are timeless, which is why I'm reprinting some classics, too.)

I've added a lot of new material, beginning with the chapter Telling Stories. Advertisers, especially copywriters, are often called brand storytellers but rarely told what that means, so I've tried to explain the term, at least as I understand it. Telling Stories should help writers find, develop, and deepen the narratives inherent in the brands they represent.

You could say that storytelling is everything in branding, but you could say that voice is, too. How a brand talks may be the essence of copywriting. That audible personality precedes and determines the voice of any given ad or ad campaign, so I've expanded chapter 9, Establishing Voice, to explain how to create a brand's personality with words.

I've written a new chapter, Interactive Advertising and Social Media, as new media often change how copywriting works, what ads are, and who's in charge. In this chapter, I explain and resolve all digital issues. Just kidding. But I do try to say useful things about how to think and write in digital, interactive environments. Since the exact forms of doing so change nearly by the hour, I've tried to concentrate on truths that transcend this or that platform. I've also expanded my discussion of nontraditional and guerrilla advertising, as so much of the best advertising isn't exactly advertising but is something else, something less commercial and more interesting.

My advice about slogans, theme lines, and naming has become its own chapter. I felt the need to say more because they're so often the crux of the matter for writers. They also demonstrate the principles of persuasion briefly enough that we can get a good look at them.

Throughout, I've tried to make *Advertising: Concept and Copy* a writer's book. How does the language work? How can we use it to persuade?

Acknowledgments

Writing a book may seem the most solitary of tasks, and in some ways it is, but it is also the labor of many hands and minds.

I want to thank the companies, advertising agencies, and design studios whose work I have borrowed. Many people let me interrupt their already busy lives, then hunted through the back of their minds or the deep reaches of hard drives to find ads I requested, and often to suggest ones I hadn't. Many of them also helped me acquire the permissions necessary to show these ads to you. I am in debt also to the clients, creative directors, art directors, copywriters, designers, photographers, and illustrators—among them Columbus College of Art & Design (CCAD) alumni Christopher Cole, Steve Stone, Mark Suplicki, and Crit Warren—who thought up this brilliant work in the first place. It's the best thing in here. I'm equally indebted to the many people whose insights and ideas I quote in this book. They have thought it and said it better than I ever could, and the book is richer for their presence.

I thank my students at CCAD, whose energy and ideas got me started on this book in the first place. I also thank my colleagues in advertising, design, and liberal arts at CCAD for their insight and support. Bruce Hager of CCAD's terrific IT staff came to my aid happily, readily, and I'm sure way too often, solving digital mysteries with his own kind of magic. I thank the College for granting me a sabbatical, which has given me the time to finish this edition, time for which I am grateful.

Many people at Norton helped make this book real. They include editorial assistant Libby Burton, editor Andrea Costella Dawson, copy editor Jacqueline Decter, and assistant editor Ben Yarling. In ways large and small, they carried the book not just forward but upward.

Gilda Hannah, the book's designer, has made of it a handsome thing—no small task, given the often obdurate materials and myriad changes in text and illustration. She performed, page by page, one compositional feat after another. The cover designer, Michael Quanci, has created a striking piece of graphic art. I hope the book lives up to it.

Without the encouragement and skill of my editor, Nancy Green, who liked *Advertising: Concept and Copy* when she first saw it and has now expertly guided it through two editions, this book simply would not be.

Finally, I thank my wife, Karen Thomas, whose love and patience have sustained me through this project, and sustain me always.

GEORGE FELTON
Columbus, Ohio

PART ONE
STRATEGY

"We place a lot of importance on strategy. It's not worth anything to be creative if you're not going to make that turnstile turn. Creative and strategy are so integral, one depends on the other."
—JEAN ROBAIRE, art director, Stein Robaire Helm

A great ad is a wonderful thing; it's why you love advertising. But what you're looking at is only half of what's there, and the part you can't see has more to do with that ad's success than the part you can. Before those surface features (the terrific headline or visual or storyline or characters or voiceover or digital dexterity or whatever) can work their wonders, the ad has to have something to say, something that matters. Either it talks to real people about real needs, or it speaks to no one. To make great ads, then, you have to start where they start: with the invisible part.

1 · Creating an Advertising Strategy

To do well what should not be done is to do badly.
—THEODORE LEVITT

First things first

Probably the greatest danger you'll face as a copywriter is trying to solve the problem, whatever it is, too fast. You'll rush for a selling argument or a new media solution or for headlines themselves before making sure they work. And since great advertising does require a twist (you can't just put clichéd ideas in clichéd places), it's tempting to play with language and imagery right away, trying to create some "pop," usually with puns, double entendres, and other jokes. But cleverness is useless if you're saying something beside the point. Until you discover the real reasons that people buy this or that good or service, or identify with this brand instead of that brand, you create ads for no one.

So great advertising really begins with the grunt work, the legwork, digging around in the issues, getting up to speed on the product and brand, working to know enough even to begin playing with idea and language.

If, for example, you're trying to persuade teenagers not to drink and drive, writing headlines like "Don't drive yourself to drink" or "Don't take the car for a spin if your head's spinning" or "How can you stay in a single lane if you're seeing double?" is a waste of time. The real problems of drinking and driving are elsewhere. Why, in the face of repeated warnings and omnipresent advertising against it, do many young people still drink and drive? The answer isn't something you can come up with sitting around in search of a line. You can only discover it by researching the problem, its social and psychological dimensions. You've got to get out there and talk to some people and do some thinking.

Most don't-drink-and-drive advertising, sensibly enough, stresses the risk of death on the highway (fig. 1.1). But suppose, in your research, you discover that it's far more likely people will lose their licenses than their lives by drinking and driving. Suppose you also discover that many teens, young and strong, consider themselves almost immortal and are largely unable to imagine their own deaths. They can, however, understand the value of driving—seeing it as an essential initiation into adulthood—and they can feel the weight of peer pressure. Knowing all this, you may want to make a different argument (fig. 1.2).

Strategy versus execution

Ads and ad campaigns really have two parts: *what* you're saying and *how* you're saying it. The "what" is your strategy—the plan of attack, the big idea, the selling argument. The "how" is the execution of that strategy—the particular form it takes: the images, language, and media that you use. (Employing the battlefield distinction, some advertisers split these two into *strategy* and *tactics*.)

Looking at the ads opposite, one might say that the strategy of the first is: Don't drink and drive because you may die. The strategy of the second is: Don't drink and drive because you may live. Obviously these are fundamentally different propositions, different "whats," and each proposition could have been differently expressed, given a different "how," as well. People respond to both the underlying idea and its expression. Notice that the ads in figures 1.3 and 1.4, which look so different from the first two, really aren't. They express the same two ideas, but in new terms. They're different *executions* of the same two *strategies*.

When creating ads and ad campaigns, be smart at both strategy and execution. Often it's easy to admire

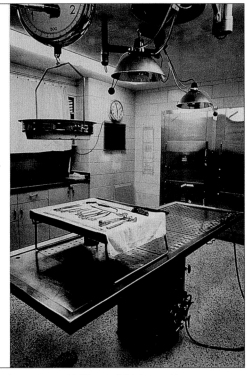

LAST NIGHT HE CELEBRATED MIDTERMS. TODAY HE HAS THE FINAL EXAM.

Drinking and driving, or even riding with a driver who's been drinking is dumb. And there's never a reason good enough to change that.

DON'T DRINK AND DRIVE.

1.1. A reasonable advertising strategy for the teen-age drinking and driving problem.

If the thought of losing your life doesn't keep you from drinking and driving, imagine losing your license.

1.2. Perhaps strategically even stronger, this ad directly understands its audience.

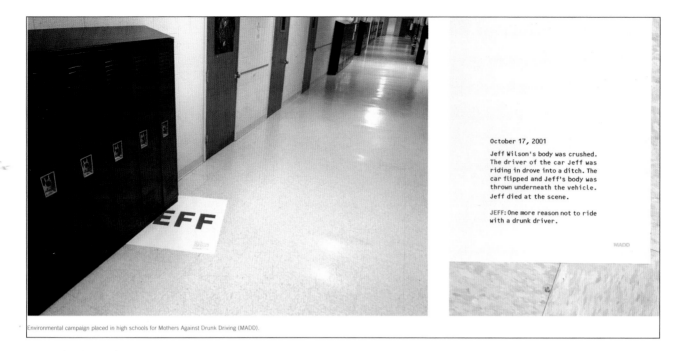

October 17, 2001

Jeff Wilson's body was crushed. The driver of the car Jeff was riding in drove into a ditch. The car flipped and Jeff's body was thrown underneath the vehicle. Jeff died at the scene.

JEFF: One more reason not to ride with a drunk driver.

MADD

Environmental campaign placed in high schools for Mothers Against Drunk Driving (MADD).

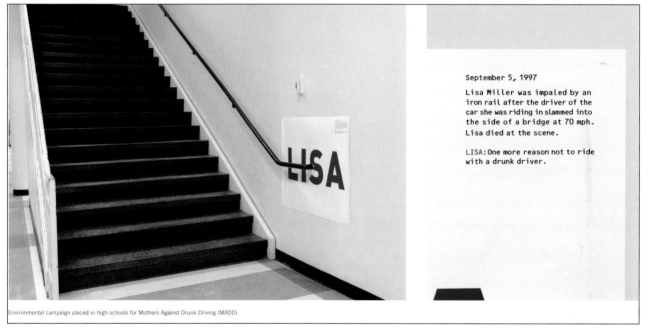

September 5, 1997

Lisa Miller was impaled by an iron rail after the driver of the car she was riding in slammed into the side of a bridge at 70 mph. Lisa died at the scene.

LISA: One more reason not to ride with a drunk driver.

Environmental campaign placed in high schools for Mothers Against Drunk Driving (MADD).

Above
1.3. As an advertiser, you'll need not only to develop a strategy but to express it in different ways. Here the first underlying strategy—don't drink and drive, you'll die—receives a different execution. These posters were placed in significant places in a high school: LISA impaled on a handrail, JEFF slid under a locker, with copy blocks detailing how they had died in drunk-driving accidents.

Opposite
1.4. These two nontraditional ads speak to their audience, not about dying but about living with a drunk-driving incident. In the bar stunt, patrons were handed an outrageously high bill (up to $73,000), which, as they gasped and looked more closely, detailed the medical expenses for a drunk-driving accident. The second ad, a kind of grim theater, understands the social stigma of a drunk-driving conviction. As part of the British government's road-safety campaign THINK, this drunk-driving offender had to stand under a 7-foot-tall beer glass at Paddington Station in London.

To watch the $73,000 bar tab video, go to fig. W-1.4.

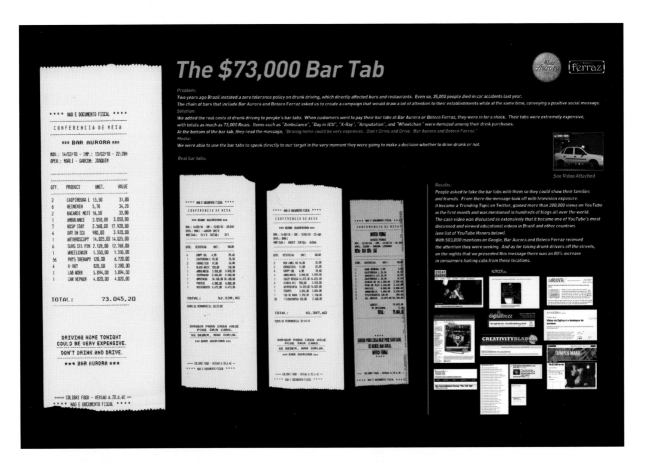

the clever "creative" on an ad's surface, for example, the well-crafted, parallel headline on the kids-in-the-backseat ad, their wonderfully worried looks, Mom's irritation, the point of view of the camera—all of it— and think that those make the ad great. But what also makes that ad great is the idea behind it: What if you live?

> "Advertising based on a sound strategy but executed poorly is as dull as another snowy day in January. Advertising executed brilliantly but based on a weak strategy may be entertaining—but it won't work. So you have to do the whole job, not just half. Strong strategy. And strong execution."
> —RON ANDERSON, executive vice president, Bozell & Jacobs

How to create strategy

To develop a strong strategy, you need to understand three things: the product, the consumer, and the marketplace.

1. The product. What are you selling, really? This can be something more and different than it might at first appear. It's certainly something about which you need to know more than you do right now.

2. The consumer. Who are you selling to, exactly? Have you located those people who are your best market? How well do you know them? The key to selling products is understanding people's relationships with them, what they want from them. What needs and motives does your product address? What problems does it solve?

3. The marketplace. How do your brand, its products, and its advertising fit into the array around them? No sale occurs in a vacuum; there are probably other products and brands like yours, and your category has been advertised to consumers before. They've seen it all and used it all. How will your brand stand out in the marketplace? Why should consumers choose it instead of a competing brand?

Those are all interesting questions—and all related: you can't locate your target market until you know what you're selling exactly, but you can't know what exactly you ought to promise until you locate a target market and decipher its needs. Nor can you create an effective strategy until you analyze the marketplace positions your client's competitors occupy and successfully differentiate your client's product and brand from theirs.

Sorting through all this isn't easy, and each advertising situation will prove different from the one before it, too, so your job never reduces to a formula. Your goal is to understand the parts of the advertising scenario so well that you see how they fit together— to know enough to create advertising that works, that talks to real people about real needs. You'd like to convince a teen-ager, perhaps for the first time, that "Don't drink and drive" isn't simply someone else's slogan. It's what he or she truly believes—because of the advertising you created.

2 · Researching Your Client's Product

One thing I try to do is know everything that is possible to know about a brand when I work on it. When you dig deep into a brand, really do a big archaeology on it, you find out why it was created in the first place, why they named it what they did, what the dreams of the founders were, why it comes in the kinds of packages it does, why the logo looks the way it does—you find truths and values that have probably gotten buried under creative trends through the years. So I'll do things like go back and look at old advertising they did decades ago, before bullshit crept into our business. This helps you discover the truth, and when you can build creative work around some kind of truth, it's much more powerful, and substantial.

—JEFF WEISS, creative director, Amster Yard

Write about the product. In the greatest, soundest, most creative advertising, the theater revolves around the product. Ask yourself what makes the product 'tick.' How does it fit into people's lives? How does the competition fail or disappoint? What's its 'personality' in the marketplace? Advertising that isn't really about the product is almost always self-indulgent crap.

—CLIFF FREEMAN, founder, Cliff Freeman & Partners

In truth, advertising starts with consumers and what they want, but in practice, advertising starts with your clients, who have a product—a good or service—with which they'd like help. You are called in initially to do something for a client's product.

Steep yourself in information

Become an expert in your client's product and its category. Get overinformed. I once knew a student who wanted to sell Aloe & Lanolin soap to her classmates as a course project, but it never occurred to her to find out what aloe and lanolin were, exactly, and what they were doing together in a bar of soap. As you might guess, her success was limited.

Let this be your model instead. Before creating their legendary ad campaign for the original Volkswagen Beetle, the creative team at Doyle Dane Bernbach first headed for the manufacturing plant in Wolfsburg, West Germany, to do their homework. Says William Bernbach: "We spent days talking to engineers, production men, executives, workers on the assembly line. We marched side by side with the molten metal that hardened into the engine, and kept going until every

part was finally in place. . . ."[1] And only through this effort did they find their selling proposition, the VW as an "honest" car—simple, functional, and incredibly well made. Whenever you see reprints of these classic VW ads, study them, not only because the ads are great, but because each ad shows so clearly the homework required to think it up. Read enough VW ads and two things will happen: (1) you'll learn a lot about the cars, and (2) you'll want one. Sufficient testimony to the power of that campaign. (See fig. 2.1.)

How to learn about your client's product

1. If possible, use it: wear it, eat it, drive it, drink it, bathe with it. Try its competitors, too. Nothing replaces first-hand experience.

2. Become its student. Learn what's in it, how it's made, who makes it, how it works, what its history is, all those things. Read the brand's website; Google the brand; check out its presence in social media; gather brochures, annual reports, and other collateral.

3. If there are local dealers, ask them about your client's brand and its competition. How to

2.1. Too many ads fail to find the drama in the product, "borrowing" interest from elsewhere instead. The original VW ads, however, made the car itself *consistently* interesting, a remarkable feat in a campaign that ran from 1959 to 1977.

Volkswagen's unique construction keeps dampness out.

For years there have been rumors about floating Volkswagens. (The photographer claims this one stayed up for 42 minutes.) Why not?

The bottom of the Volkswagen isn't like ordinary car bottoms. A sheet of flat steel runs underneath the car, sealing the bottom fore and aft.

That's not done to make a bad boat out of it, just a better car. The sealed bottom protects a VW from water, dirt and salt. All the nasty things on the road that eventually eat up a car.

The top part of a Volkswagen is also very seaworthy. It's practically airtight. So airtight that it's hard to close the door

without rolling down the window a bit.

But there's still one thing to keep in mind if you own a Volkswagen. Even if it could definitely float, it couldn't float indefinitely.

So drive around the big puddles. Especially if they're big enough to have a name.

sell a Honda? Ask a salesperson at the showroom how he or she does it.

4. Find out what consumers think about the brand, product, and category. Word of mouth, actual information from real humans, is crucial, yet copywriters too often fail to ask for it. Cultivate sources who understand their own consumer behavior, who can talk about shampoos for a while, or smart phones. How do they choose among Herbal Essences, Bumble and bumble, John Frieda, and all the rest? Do they prefer iPhones or Androids? Why? What's their favorite snack food, beer, fast food, car? Did they like the Levi's "Go Forth" campaign, and

have they looked at Levi's because of it? Go online to epinions.com, amazon.com, brand-centric blogs, and other sites where people are talking about their experiences with brands and products. Listen.

5. Don't just focus on the brand; learn about the product category, too. If you're selling Centrum, find out about vitamins: search the Web for health information. A sentence like "Your body misses eight crucial vitamins every day" can apply to Centrum as easily as to any other brand, right? Not only can the category serve as a source of information for your client's brand, but you may end up selling the category rather than the brand (see "Generic claim" in chapter

5). And no matter what, you need to know why consumers have the product itself in their lives, what it does for them, and how it does it.

6. Visit a library, by going online or actually walking into one. Google and Wikipedia are wonderful resources, but libraries have it all: encyclopedias (often a good first stop—how does soap work?), dictionaries (what's aloe? what's lanolin?), audio and video material, bibliographies and indexes—for example, Business Source Complete, ProQuest, and EBSCOhost—plus many other searchable databases otherwise unavailable to you.

We're so habituated to online searches that we forget that there are still books, useful ones, sitting there quietly in libraries—books on your subject (whose bibliographies often provide leads), books that, even if written years ago, may still be definitive. Let's say you're researching a package design problem. Thomas Hine says in *The Total Package*'s bibliography, itself abundantly helpful, that "even though it's more than sixty-six years old . . . Richard B. Franken and Carroll B. Larabee's *Packages That Sell* probably remains the fundamental text on the development of the marketing dimensions of packaging."[2] How would you know about that book, or even Hines's book, if you let Google serve as your only research guide?

But best of all, libraries have real, live reference librarians, people with graduate degrees in knowing what's where, experts waiting to be called upon. Call upon them. I always do. They're terrific resources. Explain your project, say what work you've done, ask nicely for help, and watch them cut a path for you through the wilderness (fig. 2.2).

Study the competition

Not everyone is buying your client's product. Find out what they're buying instead.

Right

2.2. IBM is so large and diverse that general claims of excellence would accomplish little. This campaign instead highlighted one project after another to prove excellence rather than simply claim it. The headlines employed reversal and opposition to intrigue readers, but the copy's specifics sealed the deal. You can't use facts like these until you find them. The moral? As David Ogilvy put it, "Do your homework."

Ⓢ For more ads in this campaign, go to fig. W-2.2.

2.3. City buses face strong competition from cars, but they do hold a trump card.

Two key issues

1. Who is your client's competition, exactly? Usually you assume it's competing brands. But it may not be other brands so much as other ways consumers satisfy the same need—in other words, the indirect competitors. For example, Hallmark and American Greetings are direct competitors of each other, but they also face text messages, e-mail, Facebook, Twitter, phone calls, and even personal visits as indirect competitors. Each is a delivery system for feelings; they're all media for the consumer's "sentiment message."

If your client's brand dominates its category, study indirect competitors, especially since they present challenges you may be overlooking.

As testimony to the power of indirect competitors, a consortium of hotels created advertising aimed not at competing hotels and bed-and-breakfasts but at other ways people connect with friends and family. One magazine ad showed a grandfather holding his grandson's hand at the beach with this headline: "It's awfully hard to spoil someone over the phone."

So ask yourself who are the major players, both direct and indirect, with which your client's product competes. Assess their strengths and weaknesses. Where does your client's product fit in the array? And what competitive benefit does it offer that they don't (fig. 2.3)?

2. What product category(ies) should your client's product compete in? This corollary of the first question can also be answered too quickly. If you're selling Wheaties, you may assume you're just competing with other cereals. But there are other categories you might want to compete in as well: Wheaties is a kind of vitamin; it's a snack food for the healthy-minded; it's a breakfast, not just a cereal. So remember to ask what product categories you can compete in and which ones are best. (For more on turning competitive position into the entire advertising strategy, see "Positioning" in chapter 5.)

The Snickers "Not Going Anywhere for a While?" campaign was created when ad strategists realized that Snickers was competing less against other candy bars than against other snacks, snacks people ate when they couldn't sit down to a meal—things like a peanut butter and jelly sandwich, a slice of pizza, or a bag of chips.[3] A more recent Snickers campaign used the same insight—that sometimes people can't eat a meal but they need to eat—expressing it another way with the theme line "You're not you when you're hungry."

Ed McCabe once wrote an ad for Vespa motor scooters that showed one sitting in a garage beside a car, with this headline: "Maybe your second car shouldn't be a car." He saw the wisdom in selling Vespa as a better car instead of a better bike. Similarly, a diamond retailer, realizing that the competition included more than other diamond merchants, wrote an ad with this headline: "Women don't cry when they open lingerie." And the copywriter for the ad in figure 2.4 took the idea of competing product categories beyond the literal (beaches) to the abstract (vacations).

It can be clarifying to ask your client this question: "What business are you in?" Then, together, think through the answer. If Apple had considered itself in the computer business rather than the digital communication business, imagine how limited its product line—and success—would have been. Threadless is an online T-shirt retailer, but that's not the business it's in, according to Mig Reyes, lead interactive designer:

2.4. These Florida beaches realize they compete not just with other beaches but with other vacations.

196 MILES NORTH EAST.

THERE'S A SCREAMING CHILD WAITING IN LINE FOR A ROLLER COASTER.

2.5. One good reason to buy this brand: not all chickens are created equal.

"At Threadless, we're not about putting designs on T-shirts. We're about championing the underdog designer."[4] They do that by inviting designers to submit designs, site visitors to vote for their favorites, and everyone to enter contests where T-shirts help causes worldwide. For Threadless, T-shirts are where things start rather than end.

Identify what you're looking for in your research

"Interrogate the product until it confesses."
—ROB KITCHEN, creative director, CDP, London

If you let your research remain open-ended, you'll accumulate a pile of information but never get anywhere. Save time by knowing what you're looking for and what you're not.

1. Don't get hung up in corporate this and earnings that. You're looking for information about this product that makes it worth buying, maybe even worth believing in. It's not a lump of wet clay, so look for features, particularities, whatever makes it more than a commodity, and whatever distinguishes it from its competition (fig. 2.5). What's in it? What does it do? (My Quaker Oats canister tells me, loud and clear, that "Oatmeal helps remove cholesterol!" and, with my numbers, I'm listening.) How is it made? Real slow? Real fast? At high temperatures? By whom? European artisans? The latest robotic wonders? Where is it made? Why there? Use the reporter's questions to help you generate material: who, what, when, where, why, and how.

2. What do people have against your client's product? What's its greatest liability? Why doesn't ev-

Don't wait
until someone
says, "your money
or your life,"
to remember
they are two
separate things.

citi

Live richly.

A member of citigroup

www.citi.com

He who dies with the
most toys is still dead.

citi   Live richly.

A member of citigroup

2.6. Most credit lenders are eager to sell the supposedly limitless possibilities spending creates. This campaign instead focused on its limitations, finding an argument no one in their category was making: we're here to help you manage money better, not just spend it. A responsible credit lender; now there's a contradiction in terms. Good zig in a world of zags.

erybody use it? Maybe the nut your advertising needs to crack is objections people have to the brand. The original Volkswagen campaign, for example, took one supposed deficit after another (small size, unchanging looks, putt-putt engine, ugliness, etc.) and turned each into a virtue.

3. What's its greatest strength? Does it share that virtue with its competitors or own it itself? Is there an argument for this product category no one is claiming? Could you make that claim? Doing so, finding a "hole" out there in the marketplace, can be easier than you think—and a powerful way to differentiate your client's brand from everyone else's (fig. 2.6).

4. How does your client's product fit into consumers' lives and culture? Is your product associated with any rites of passage, life transitions—like birth, graduation, marriage, retirement, and so on? Is it tied—or could it be—to major cultural issues like self-improvement, health, environmental concerns, recommitment to education, emphasis on the family, and so on? As Alex Bogusky and John Winsor of ad agency Crispin Porter + Bogusky argue, "Success starts by making it a habit to push against your definition of where the product begins and where it ends."[5]

5. What are the values of your client's brand? What does it believe in besides just making, say, a tasty burrito? Chipotle's mission statement is "Food with integrity," about which they say: "Food with integrity is our commitment to finding the very best ingredients raised with respect for the animals, the

environment and the farmers." This sentence alone gives you places to start telling the brand's story.

Remember: products are rarely simply themselves; they're also complex symbols, markers for larger psychological states, social roles, and cultural meanings. What yokes your client's product to consumers' lives?

Much of this information is divined, systematically analyzed, and then sold to advertisers by market research firms, but much is also available by simply paying attention to trends as they manifest themselves around you. Read newspapers, magazines, and blogs, follow online discussions and people on Twitter, watch TV and movies, listen to what's said by radio talk show callers and by people on the street, on buses, standing next to you in line. We all have pop culture antennae; the good ad writers keep theirs up.

Obviously I'm suggesting a lot of research here. You'll know by the nature of each project and its timeline how much you can realistically expect of yourself. Sometimes you'll have to do a quick study of your client's product and its competitors. Other times you'll be able to analyze more of the field. You can't be expected to do all this research all the time, but the more you do the better. It will pay you back.

Translate features into benefits

Let's say you've done your homework. You now know all sorts of things about the product—its manufacture, ingredients, moving parts, founding father and mother, everything. But it's all inert data until you make it matter to consumers, and you do that by promising benefits, not just enunciating features.

Here's the distinction. Unless it's a commodity, like salt or sugar, whatever product you're selling has aspects that one might call features: a key ingredient, an algorithm that selects songs for a radio playlist, a lubricated strip above the blade, one-third the calories of the regular brand, no caffeine, extra caffeine, timed-release deodorant capsules, biodegradability, free online support, a hatchback, an angled brushing head, more dealers than the other guys, and on and on. In other words, every product has certain parts, ingredients, things it can do, conditions associated with it, that taken together make it what it is, make it, in Theodore Levitt's terms, not just a "generic product," the thing itself, but an "augmented product," a whole cluster of attributes that add value.[6]

But features alone won't sell a product. They're just things hanging off a product. The real question is, what do consumers get out of them? Learn to ask, of any product fact or feature, "So what?" Who cares? Can or does this matter to the consumer? What's the payoff? Link benefits to features. Complete the argument.

Using previous examples, you can see that one-third fewer calories means people can have their cake and eat it, too. A hatchback lets people load up their gear quickly and easily. Timed-release deodorant capsules mean a person won't be embarrassed by wetness and odor, appearing unflappable and cool all day long. Free online support means those who bought the product can relax in their ignorance, feel good about their choice, and realize they're not alone with complicated technology. No caffeine means people are taking care of themselves, not to mention being "safe" by following a trend. Now all these neutral features have been expressed as benefits, too, so people can see what's in it for them.

Remember this marketing maxim, simple but profound: people don't buy ¼-inch drill bits; they buy ¼-inch holes. As Theodore Levitt points out, people don't really buy gasoline either: "They cannot see it, taste it, feel it, appreciate it, or really test it. What they buy is the right to continue driving their cars."[7] When ad great Claude Hopkins was advertising patent medicines in the early 1900s, he realized that "people were not buying medicine, they were buying results," so he pioneered the idea of the druggist's signed guarantee.[8] This habit of mind—seeing products from the benefits end—seems obvious, but it's amazing how often ad writers overlook it when planning strategies and creating ads (see figs. 2.7 and 2.8).

Translating features into benefits is the central gesture of advertising. You are saying to consumers, "The product has this feature, so you get this benefit." Advertisers have become more subtle over the decades about this proposition, and both feature and benefit can be more abstract than concrete. Nevertheless, translating features into benefits remains fundamental to selling anything. Let's watch Apple demonstrate with copy from its website:

> iCloud automatically downloads any new music purchase to all your devices over Wi-Fi—or over 3G if you choose. Which means you can buy a song from iTunes on your iPad at home, and find it waiting for you on your iPhone during your morning commute. All without having to sync.

More copy, about another Apple product:

> iPad is one big, beautiful display—9.7 inches of high-resolution photos, movies, web pages, books, and more. LED backlighting makes everything you see remarkably crisp, vivid, and bright. Even in

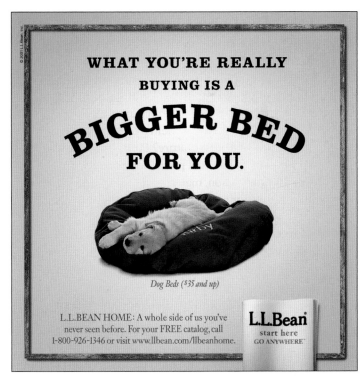

2.7. Who said the doggie bed was about the dog? Always look for the real consumer benefit of a product; it may not be what you think.

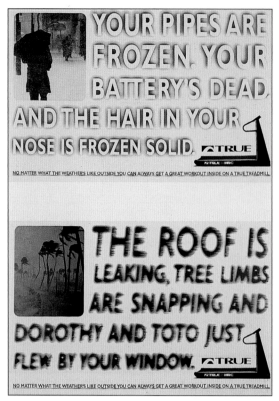

2.8. Most home workout equipment is sold with product features, tech-talk, and glistening abs, ignoring one obvious—and powerful—benefit people seek from home equipment: the right to stay home. As the subhead puts it, "No matter what the weather's like outside you can always get a great workout inside on a True treadmill."

places with low light, like an airplane. And there's no wrong way to hold iPad. It's designed to show off everything in portrait and landscape, so with every turn (even upside down), the display adjusts to fit. Because it uses a display technology called IPS (in-plane switching), it has a wide, 178° viewing angle. Hold it up to someone across the room, or share it with someone sitting next to you, and everyone gets a brilliant view.

You can see how consistently Apple's copywriters connect features to benefits without making the sales pitch feel heavy; the writing is so specific that readers can see what's in it for them, and the prose style is friendly and clean. It's the verbal equivalent of Apple's product design. Study Apple's copy whenever you need to revisit fundamentally strong copywriting.

MANY THINGS ARE FEATURES

All this focus on features may feel old school, and if you think of features in the most narrow, hardware-ish way, it is. But remember that a brand's image is a feature, too, one that people will often pay plenty for (status benefits, quality benefits, etc.). The product's story—its history and cultural fit—is another feature. So, too, is a brand's tradition of customer service (Nordstrom comes to mind) or its emotional connection to people's lives (Pillsbury, Coca-Cola, and many more

brands are about feelings as much as facts). As figure 2.9 shows, features don't even have to be things. And, as figures 2.10 and 2.11 prove, features don't have to be exotic or unusual either.

Ernie Schenck, vice president and creative director at Hill Holiday, provides an excellent overview of what you're trying to do and why:

> I think our job, particularly today, is first to be able to recognize a story—and then to be able to relate it in a meaningful way. And every brand has a story. . . . I start out by looking at everything the client has, wading through a volume of information, most of which is completely useless. I'm talking about primary research, secondary research, everything. It's a pain to look through it. But if you do the due diligence, you will almost always unearth some wonderful nuggets of information that may begin to reveal the plot-line behind the brand.[9]

As Schenck points out, copywriters are storytellers, so much so that I'll devote a chapter to storytelling. But let's take things a step at a time. Translating features into benefits requires an understanding of consumer motives. What do people want from the material world? How many needs do they really have? Let's take a closer look at consumer psychology.

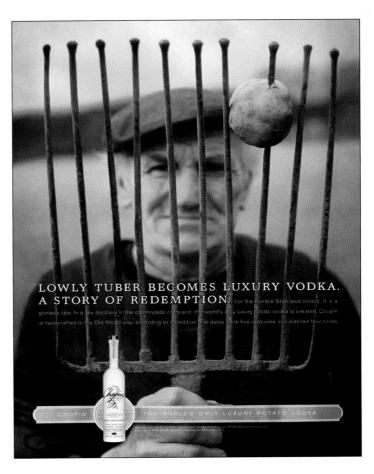

LOWLY TUBER BECOMES LUXURY VODKA. A STORY OF REDEMPTION. For the humble Stobrawa potato, it is a glorious tale. In a tiny distillery in the countryside of Poland, the world's only luxury potato vodka is created. Chopin is handcrafted in the Old World way, according to a tradition that dates back five centuries, and distilled four times.

Opposite
2.9. Avoid feature myopia. A feature doesn't have to be some physical part of your product, something mixed into or hanging off it; it can be any differentiating aspect of your brand's story. It can, for example, be a channel of distribution. Here the Wondergro line of lawn care products differentiates itself on the basis of being sold only in garden stores—by professionals, in other words, not by the hit-and-miss help found in giant retail outlets.

Right top
2.10. Ads that have done their homework don't have to sound like it, the copywriter droning on beside the desk. This ad is selling a product feature, and a humble one at that, the potato. But the ad is intriguing and visually dynamic. It's not boring, and you shouldn't be either. Make the truth interesting. We'll listen.

Right
2.11. Can a lowly price point be made interesting? This radio spot answers the question.

 Listen to the radio spot at fig. W-2.11.

SAMTRANS RADIO
:60
"GEORGE WASHINGTON"

MUSIC: Battle Hymn of the Republic

VO: General George Washington.
       The first president of the United States.
       The father of our country.
       Couldn't tell a lie.
       Had wooden teeth.
       Wore a wig.
       Dressed himself in frilly shirts.
       Wore tight knickers with white stockings and black patent leather shoes.
       George Washington.
       His face plastered on one dollar bills, the most used currency in the entire world.
       The man.
       The myth.
       The legend.
       And now the ticket on a SamTrans bus.
       Ride anywhere in San Mateo county for one George Washington.
       A dollar.
       A buck.
       A greenspot.
       Anywhere that SamTrans goes from Palo Alto to Daly City.
       First he crossed the Delaware.
       And now San Mateo County.
       Love your country.
       Be patriotic.
       Ride SamTrans.
       Call 1-800-660-4BUS.

3 • Understanding Consumer Behavior

> If you want to build a ship, don't drum up people to-gether to collect wood and don't assign them tasks and work, but rather teach them to long for the end-less immensity of the sea.
>
> —Antoine de Saint-Exupéry,
> *The Wisdom of the Sands*

Remember that marketing's central idea, as Theodore Levitt phrases it, is that "people buy products . . . in order to solve problems. Products are problem-solving tools."[1] Remember, too, that products may solve any problem from a physiological one all the way up to a psychological, social, or even spiritual one, and of-ten several at once. So, for example, when people buy clothes at Banana Republic instead of at Walmart, they are meeting the civilized need to cover themselves, certainly, but they aren't stopping there. They're also choosing to buy *insurance*—fashion insurance. They will pay more for these clothes because they want to reduce the perceived social risk of wearing the wrong ones.

Maslow's hierarchy of needs

This idea that a product can solve more than one prob-lem at the same time owes much to the psychologist Abraham Maslow, who posited in human beings a "hi-erarchy of needs" ascending from the physiological to the psychological. He argued that people are driven to fulfill them all, although lower-level needs must be met before one can attempt to satisfy higher-level needs.[2] Here is his hierarchy:

1. Physiological needs: hunger, thirst, warmth, pain avoidance, sexual release, and others
2. Safety needs: housing, clothing, financial and physical security
3. Love and belongingness needs: social ac-ceptance and personal intimacy (Maslow argued

that much of mankind's frustration stemmed from inadequacy in this area, since lower-level needs had been met. People can often say that they have eaten enough or own enough clothes, but who can say, "I am loved enough"? It isn't surprising, therefore, that the greatest number of consumer goods appeal to this level of need.)
4. Esteem needs: feelings of adequacy and achievement, approval, prestige, social status
5. Self-actualization needs: the need to under-stand, cognitively and aesthetically; the ultimate integration of the self and realization of one's highest inner potential

As you see when you look at advertising, most prod-ucts intersect Maslow's ladder at more than one point. Even as apparently simple an act as having friends over for pizza involves three levels of Maslow's hier-archy: physiological needs, love and belongingness needs, and esteem needs. People feed their bodies, bond with others emotionally, and perform some work on their social status; and they do it all by means of that innocent-seeming, double-cheese-and-pepperoni pizza.

Climb Maslow's ladder

"Search for some way to relate the tiny, constricted world clients live in to the larger, sunnier world people actually care about. Deodorants aren't about keeping dry, they're about being loved. Computers aren't about getting more work done,

A hearing aid can improve a lot more than your hearing.

⊜Starkey
Your hearing is our concern.

3.1. Smart advertising finds the strongest benefit, not simply the most obvious one. A hearing aid's highest possible benefit is more than just better audio, yes?

they're about power. Cars aren't about transportation. Food isn't about hunger. Drink isn't about thirst. And so on."

—STEVE HAYDEN, president,
Ogilvy & Mather Worldwide

Rarely do people buy products simply for their minimal satisfaction of the lowest-level need; therefore, as an ad writer, always think about climbing the ladder: in addition to a product's obvious solution to a need, what else is at stake? Always ask yourself, what is the *highest possible benefit* I can claim for this product? And realize that such ladder climbing is smart. In a culture as surfeited with competing material goods as America's, many products can satisfy lower-level needs, so consumers often differentiate among them on the basis of what else those products can do (see figs. 3.1, 3.2, and 3.3).

For example, the durable slogan for Jif peanut butter ("Choosy Moms Choose Jif") sails right past the promise of satisfying the physiological need of hunger

(everyone already understands that peanut butter fills stomach cavities) and promises to fill the higher-order needs of love, nurturance, and maternal competence. After all, those really are the psychological and emotional values at stake when a mother buys food for her children. Moreover, since peanut butter is a prepared food—a convenience food, really—rather than something Mom made herself, do you see that also embedded within that phrase is forgiveness for buying it, the assurance that such a food choice is more than convenience, or other than convenience: buying Jif, far from being a labor-saving option, really reflects well on Mom. Do you see the promise there? Jif has climbed the ladder.

Nike doesn't just sell stylish, durable athletic gear. With phrases like "There is no finish line," "I can," "Make yourself," and the core slogan, "Just do it," they sell the transcendence of sweat, self-actualization through the testing of the self. Rockport doesn't simply promise well-made shoes; it writes headlines like "Shoes that help you live longer" and discusses in the

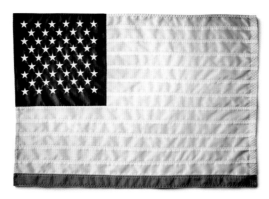

PLEASE DONATE BLOOD.
DON'T LET SUPPLIES GET ANY LOWER.

THE BLOOD CENTER
OF SOUTHEASTERN WISCONSIN, INC.

3.2. Here giving blood is linked to a benefit even higher than helping another person: helping a whole country full of people.

3.3. The benefit of a successfully shipped package has to do less with the package than with the person or company that sends it. The maintenance or enhancement of that person or company's reputation and professional acumen is what's for sale, not package delivery itself.

copy the health-enhancing virtues of walking. Even Rockport's simple campaign theme line "Be comfortable. Uncompromise. Start with your feet" relates the product to a cultural trend (increased casualness in public places), while tying the benefit to issues larger than arch support.

Stouffer's makes frozen meals, but a larger problem Stouffer's claims to help solve is the disintegration of the family. How can Stouffer's possibly claim that? By emphasizing that the family that eats together grows stronger together. In a campaign using the theme line "Let's fix dinner," Stouffer's selected six families, each with problems of divorce or some other difficulty or dysfunction, and asked each one to have regular family dinners. Campaign creative director and writer Laura Fegley of JWT/New York explained, "Instead of just telling parents to have more family dinners, we wanted to show them all that could be gained by getting everyone to the table. And more importantly, that it was doable with real families living busy, messy lives."[3]

Stouffer's created a website, posted videos of the families on it, and used social media to let the families show others the unifying power of dinner together. Visitors to the Stouffer's "Let's fix dinner" website could "Meet the McClearys" or "Meet the Bensons" and so on, learning about each family, its problems, and the role regular dinnertimes played in rebuilding or sustaining that family. This campaign climbs the ladder.

So does a South African TV spot for the stolen vehicle recovery system Tracker (fig. 3.4). The ad demonstrates that what's at stake is not just a car but the whole of human life. It makes the case by having the courage to show life's heartache as well as its joy; this is not the unearned, and therefore unconvincing, happy-happy-joy-joy of most advertising. The spot arrests viewers' attention and adds emotional depth by presenting a woman's life backwards, spooling it in reverse from old age all the way back to infancy, the moments of her story focused in the back seats of cars that have carried her safely through life. The spot ends at its logical beginning, the moment Tracker helped recover a stolen car and rescue her as a baby. Accompanied by Brandi Carlile's bittersweet song "The Story," the scenes have such poignancy and surprise that it's hard to watch the spot without being moved. The video was compiled entirely from still images; the unusual visual changes and rhythms accentuate life's significant moments, dramatizing how much, not how little, is at stake. Sensational advertising.

Become sensitive to the problems being solved by a product; they are often more various and rise higher up the ladder than you might think. Consumers are looking not for a product that will do the least for them but for one that will do the most.

3.4. A stolen vehicle recovery system can recover much more than the car.

Ⓢ Watch the spot itself and a "making of" video at fig. W-3.4.

3.5. DayOne sells products and support for new parents. What's the highest possible benefit? What's really for sale? The picture and headline ("The weight of the world—8 lbs. 4 oz.") tell us everything we need to know.

A shopping list of needs

Maslow's hierarchy is so brief that a more specific catalog of needs (and products associated with them) can be helpful. This list, not a hierarchy but a horizontal array, is from Robert Settle and Pamela Alreck's *Why They Buy: American Consumers Inside and Out.*[4]

1. Achievement: the need to perform difficult tasks, exercise one's skills
[Professional tools, sports equipment, any skill-providing service: computer training, physical training, college courses, and so on. The Army slogan "Be all you can be" and Black & Decker's "How Things Get Done." A Girl Scouts campaign, "Where Girls Grow Strong," issued the following challenge in one ad: "Cleopatra ruled Egypt when she was 18. What are you doing?" Another ad said, "There is no couch potato badge." A Nike ad for women's running shoes put it this way: "Someone who is busier than you is running right now."]

2. Independence: the need to be autonomous, have options, be different
[Fashion makes this appeal; cars do, too. Hair care items "let you be you." Lots of products promise separation from the milling herd. Virginia Slims cigarettes

linked themselves to women's rights with "You've come a long way, baby" and, later, "Find Your Voice." Saab's slogan urged consumers to "Find your own road." Apple invited people to "Think different."]

3. Exhibition: the need to gain public attention, show off, be noticed
[Clothing, fashion, accessories, even hair styles help assert the self. So, too, do big things like cars and homes. An ad for Sotheby's Realty used this headline: "An exceptional home is simply a frame for an exceptional life."]

4. Recognition: the need to be highly regarded by others, to be held up as a good example
[Many "badge" items symbolize this; so does getting a college degree, joining socially valuable organizations, or climbing any highly visible ladder. *The Economist* magazine encourages readership with headlines like these: "Would you sit next to you at dinner?" and "The edge of a conversation is the loneliest place on earth."]

5. Dominance: the need to exercise power over others, direct and supervise, have influence
[Any power item, from a big car or house to a pesticide or detergent that has punch. Oxy 10, a pimple cream targeting teenagers, closed a TV ad with this:

"Exert control over *something*." The following line promises another kind of control: "There are some things money can't buy. For everything else, there's MasterCard." Verizon Wireless invites people to "Rule the Air." Dial for Men body wash uses the slogan "Take back the shower." One print ad's headline: "Mark your territory"; another's: "18 fluid ounces of pure shower caddy dominance."]

6. Affiliation: the need to be closely associated with others, the need for relationships
[Joining the Army, joining anything, fills this need. Personal care items, breath mints, and toothpaste facilitate closeness with others: "Aren't you glad you use Dial? Don't you wish everyone did?" Head & Shoulders shampoo put it more starkly: "You never get a second chance to make a first impression." For decades, AT&T encouraged people to "Reach out and touch someone." A liquor ad for Father's Day said, "One father. One day. One whisky. Better get two glasses." Epson makes office equipment; their slogan's pun does double duty, addressing both affiliation and dominance: "When you've got Epson, you've got a lot of company." The line invites people to regard Epson as widely used and powerful—"a lot of company" in both senses of the term.]

7. Nurturance: the need to provide care for others, to have and protect (fig. 3.5)
[Child care and pet care products; gardening; cooking, cleaning, and housekeeping; volunteer or charity work. Big Brothers Big Sisters says, "It takes a good man to make a good man. Be a mentor." A number of ecologically minded groups have used "One Earth, One Life, One Chance" to encourage people to care for the planet.]

8. Succorance: the need to receive help from others, be comforted, be encouraged and supported (fig. 3.6)
[Anything that functions as a care-giver: personal services, especially those that work on the body, limousines, salons, spas, counseling services; anything that "pampers" us. Schwan's Home Service has used this headline: "Research shows that 95% of housewives could use a housewife." American Furnishings describes its products as "Nesting Materials for the Great American Home." Sounds cozy to me.]

9. Sexuality: the need to establish and develop one's sexual identity, be sexually attractive, give and receive sexual satisfaction
[It would be quicker to list the products that *haven't* used sex to sell themselves. Appeals to sexuality *do*

3.6. They're not called "pets" for nothing: people nurture them. But they return the favor.

3.7. Some people like high-octane stimulation.

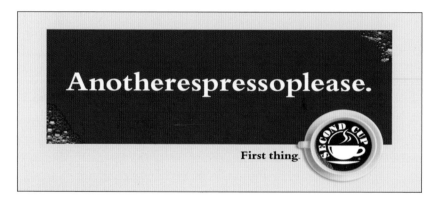

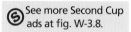

3.8. Other people do, too.

See more Second Cup ads at fig. W-3.8.

3.9. A cluster of benefits: diversion, novelty, succorance, sexuality. A great headline, too.

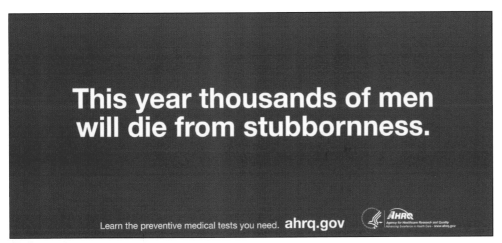

3.10. This paradox encourages men (and those who love them) to learn what's behind the headline.

make sense, though, for gendered products, fragrances, fashion, lingerie, anything linked to dating and romance. Norwegian Cruise Line used the following headline in print and TV advertising: "There is no law that says you can't make love at 4 in the afternoon on a Tuesday."]

10. Stimulation: the need to stimulate the senses, pursue vigorous activity, engage the mind and body, stimulate the palate, be active (figs. 3.7 and 3.8) [Sporting goods, health clubs, restaurants, amusement parks, even bubble baths and fabric softeners. PlanetOutdoors.com tells people to "Get on. Gear up. Get out." The TV series *Survivor* promises vicarious thrills with the tagline "Outwit. Outplay. Outlast." Outdoor gear company The North Face claims of its Summit Series, "We test on humans," a clever way of linking the product line to extreme outdoor challenges.]

11. Diversion: the need to relax, have fun, escape from routines, be entertained (fig. 3.9) [Vacations, amusement parks, sports, and so on. Corona beer encourages people to "Find your beach." Coca-Cola invites them to "Open happiness." Sony PlayStation makes it clear where the fun is: "Live in Your World. Play in Ours." A print ad for Harley-Davidson motorcycles asked, "Ever get lost in your own garage?"]

12. Novelty: the need to alter routine, be surprised, acquire new skills, have new and different experiences [Travel, education, movies, books. The North Face tells people to "Never Stop Exploring." Microsoft asked, "Where do you want to go today?" Norwegian Cruise Lines claimed, "It's different out here."]

13. Understanding: the need to comprehend, teach and learn, discover patterns, make connections (figs. 3.10 and 3.11)

3.11. The University of San Francisco is a Jesuit institution, whose values are a significant part of an education there. These two ads wittily express the benefit.

[Self-improvement courses, education in all its forms, movies, books, and other sources of information and instruction. Butler University's slogan "Challenge your mind—change your world." An Apple slogan, which also appealed to the need to achieve, was "The power to be your best."]

14. Consistency: the need for order and cleanliness, to control uncertainty and avoid ambiguity, make accurate predictions
[All cleaners, repair services, maintenance items; "matched" goods, organizers. The Holiday Inn told travelers "The best surprise is no surprise." "Always Coca-Cola" suggests this brand's reassuring constancy in people's lives. The Container Store didn't think their surge in sales after 9/11 was a coincidence. Here's their vice president of marketing: "Our customers want to get control, and when they can't control the world around them, they turn to things they can control."[5]

15. Security: the need to be free from fear, feel safe and protected, avoid accidents, acquire assets (fig. 3.12)
[Insurance, burglar alarms, investments, all safety equipment. AC Delco's slogan encourages people to specify its brand of auto parts: "If you're not asking for it, you're asking for it." A Volvo headline states the car's selling proposition succinctly: "Pay more for a car and live to see why." For decades, American Express credit card advertising warned consumers, "Don't leave home without it."]

Examining the list, we see, for example, that many need–product connections can easily be made: Why buy a smoke alarm? Security. Why go to college? Understanding. Why buy household cleaners? Consistency.

But such easy connections can be simplistic. The smoke alarm, for instance, may also signal indepen-

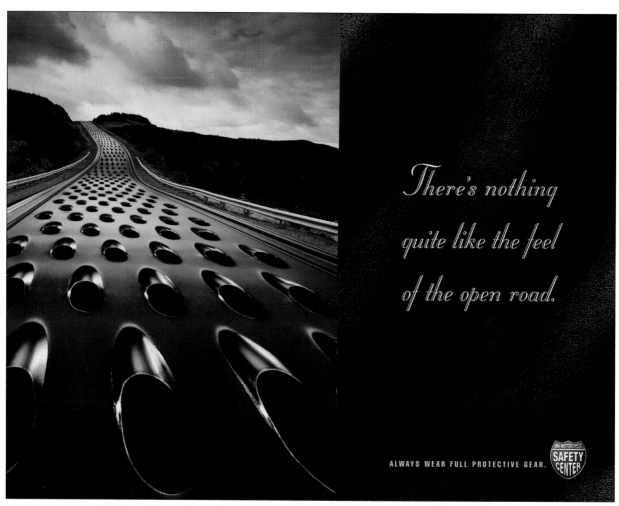

3.12. A graphic visual metaphor and punning headline combine to make the case for motorcycle safety.

Gibson PURE

LYRICS. WASTED TIME BETWEEN SOLOS.

3.13. This Gibson ad understands the multiple needs of the adolescent American male—achievement, independence, exhibition, recognition, affiliation, and stimulation—and shows how a guitar can help.

dence, especially if you're living on your own for the first time. It may express affiliation if all your friends agree that no reasonable person should be without one. If you're a parent and put one in the baby's room, it becomes a form of nurturance. If you buy several and put them in many places, you could be expressing a need for consistency. If you're a landlord, you might buy them simply to comply with property statutes, for whom the alarms provide legal security. And all these people may be responding to more than one motive (fig. 3.13).

When you're trying to sell a product and begin listing benefits, from most important to least, you immediately ask yourself, "Important to whom?" The list varies, depending on who's buying. Let's find out who is.

4 · Analyzing the Marketplace

There is no future for products everybody likes a little, only for products somebody likes a lot.
—Laurel Cutler, VP-consumer affairs,
Chrysler Corporation

The principle of market segmentation

"If you're not thinking segments, you're not thinking."
—Theodore Levitt

Fewer and fewer products are sold today via a *total market approach*, that is, by creating one product and one argument for all humanity—"One Size Fits All" thinking, if you will. Sophisticated production techniques allow many product and packaging variations, and the Internet individualizes people's relationships to products, so one size no longer need fit all. Plus, mass media have so splintered that broad-beaming an advertisement on major TV networks, for example, is often an inefficient and imprecise way to reach potential users. And given the heterogeneous lifestyles, media use, and consumption patterns in this country, a mass audience rarely exists.

So you will usually be selling via market segmentation strategies, that is—by creating separate selling arguments to separate segments or target markets of potential consumers, frequently with separate versions of the product.

Sometimes your advertising problem will present a fairly well-defined target market. You'll be asked to write recruitment materials for a college, and you gain a good sense of who might come simply by looking at the students already there. Or you'll be asked to create a website for a local soccer club or fantasy football league, and you'll get to know those people, too. Other times you'll be asked to sell a product with a less firmly established target market; part of your creative task then will be to locate and define a likely segment. You'll

need to understand your target audience well enough to tailor an argument just for them.

Methods of segmentation

"People don't really want to be different. They just want to be the same as certain kinds of people."
—Don Peppers, head of new business development, Chiat/Day

How do marketers find relatively homogeneous groups of people with similar product needs? There are many possible *segmentation variables*, those dimensions by which market segments can be defined, but you can think of all of them as grouping (and separating) people on the basis of either who they are or how they behave.[1]

DEMOGRAPHICS

Usually you begin by targeting product or category users. (For example, if you're selling running shoes, you target runners. If you're selling Wheaties, you target cereal eaters.) Then you further define the market through those physical attributes, including socioeconomic and cultural variables, commonly known as *demographics* and including such indexes as population size and shifts; gender and age; geographic location and mobility; income and expenditures; occupation and education; race, nationality, and religion; and marital status and family status.[2]

Every person is a sum of such parts, and if you think about yourself, you'll see that not only can you be so defined, but lots of your buying behavior is a di-

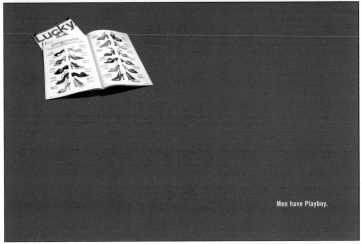

4.1. Here two shopping magazines demonstrate the defining power of a demographic by talking differently about the same impulse. Many products not intimately related to sexual differences have been successfully "genderized," including cigarettes, shavers, deodorants, diapers, beverages, radio stations, and cable TV channels.

rect result of one or a combination of these characteristics. If, for example, you're a twenty-year-old college student, think of the things you are interested in and buy as a consequence. If you live in San Diego instead of Minneapolis, consider how the geographical differences dictate everything from clothing to leisure activities to utilities use to food and so on. If you're a single, thirtysomething, working woman, look at how many of your product needs spring directly from such circumstances. The images in figure 4.1 indicate that gender alone can determine not only what to sell but also how to sell it.

Marketers track demographics the way fishermen track schools of fish, and for the same reason. In fact, one marketing maxim, employing the same metaphor, says simply, "Fish where the fishing is good." With obvious relationships to consumer behavior, demographic data do indeed tell marketers where to drop their lines by indicating what the buying patterns are, how they're concentrated, and where they're headed.

Consider age. Each age brings with it certain needs, tastes, preferences, role-related behavior, and disposable income, all of which help determine what is bought.[3] Levi's Dockers, for example, were created because marketers realized that the Baby Boomers, that large cohort of consumers born between 1946 and 1964, had outgrown their jeans, both literally and metaphorically: they needed more room and wore jeans less often but could find nothing to fill the need. Dockers—mid-priced, casual, stylish-but-jeans-inspired—understood the aging of the boomers and spawned a whole new category of men's fashion as a result.[4]

PSYCHOGRAPHICS

As important as they are, however, demographics alone often prove insufficient as a way of locating target markets and of explaining and predicting consumer behavior. A demographic segment may include various consumer patterns; various demographic segments may contain the same consumer pattern. Run-

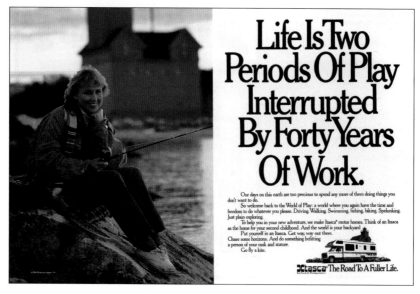

4.2. Demographics and psychographics combined: these ads target the upscale gray market (many of them "empty nesters"), understand what they're thinking, and tie recreation vehicles to the lifestyle change.

ners, for example, share certain product choices, yet they cut across many demographic segments. A forty-year-old single male with an income of $90,000 may be a plumber, a college professor, or an airline pilot, each with an obviously different lifestyle and consumption pattern. The "green revolution," the environmental concern that has affected so many attitudes toward product use, can't be measured by demographic indexes at all. People haven't changed quantitatively; they've changed qualitatively, in their attitudes.

Thus to demographics must be added *psychographics*—people's attitudes, opinions, and habits; their personality traits, lifestyles, and social class. Think of psychographics as the opposite of demographics: not the outside of one's life, but the inside. And think just how much those insides have been

changing over the years—the continual redefinition of women, men, and sex roles in this society; the rise of alternate lifestyles (and people's changing attitudes toward them); the psychological effects of single parenting and latch-key childhoods; the "post-literate" but visually sophisticated mindset of many young people; the rising health consciousness of recent decades; the demand for convenience across almost all product categories—the list is both endless and ever-evolving. You can see how much consumer behavior is tied up with these factors. Since people express their values and realize their lifestyles with the things they buy, employing psychographics helps define target markets, create profiles of targeted consumers, and determine advertising strategies themselves (fig. 4.2).

BUYING BEHAVIOR

You can also separate consumers into groups by how they think about and use products themselves—by how people behave with them, if you will.[5] The major behavioral indexes are discussed below.

Occasions

When people buy or use something can be a means of market segmentation. Think of popular holidays—Mother's Day, Father's Day, Valentine's Day, Thanksgiving, and so on. Each gift-giving holiday becomes a way to segment a market. Rites of passage do, too. People give computers to high school graduates, rings at weddings, gifts for birthdays, anniversaries, and the like. Even certain times of day or year require purchases: a camera for a vacation, snacks for late at night (Wendy's: "Eat Great, Even Late!"), coffee in the morning ("The best part of waking up is Folgers in your cup").

Retailers hold grand openings, anniversary sales, going-out-of-business sales, you name it. TGI Black Friday, a mobile app, consolidates retail deals for the day after Thanksgiving, America's busiest shopping day ("shop smarter and faster"). Events—the New York City Marathon, for example—are opportunities for sponsorship and advertising (banner along the route: "Five boroughs. Two caplets. Tylenol"). There are many, many ways you can sell something by tying it to an occasion (see figs. 4.3 and 4.4).

You can even invent an occasion, as American Express did by creating Small Business Saturday, a day that the brand hopes will become, like Black Friday, an annual shopping holiday after Thanksgiving. AmEx, extending its reach, wants to support small business owners by encouraging consumers to shop with them that day.

Benefits sought

What people seek in a product varies, and you can create market segments by appealing to those varying needs. Toothpaste marketing used to be a classic case of benefit segmentation: if people wanted fresh breath, they bought Close-Up; if they wanted fewer cavities, Crest; white teeth, Ultra-Brite; no chemicals, Tom's of Maine; no pain, Sensodyne; and so on. Today, toothpaste marketing remains an exercise in benefit segmentation, but each brand hopes to devise enough formulas to cover all possible market segments. There are forty-one configurations of Crest alone, from exotica like Crest Baking Soda & Peroxide Whitening

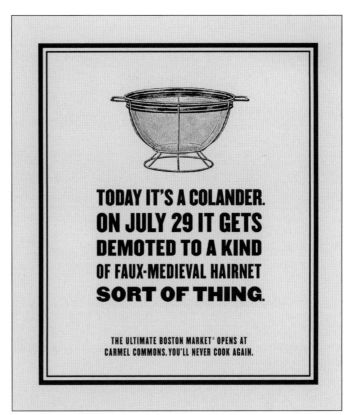

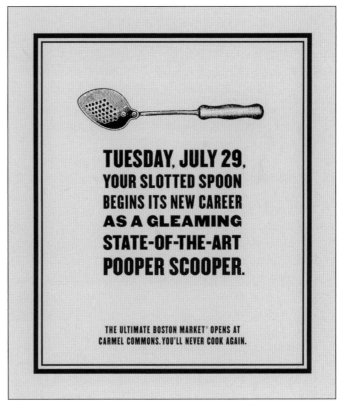

4.3. A very clever way to announce the opening of the "ultimate" Boston Market. This campaign whimsically suggests that the food's so good people will "never cook again." Time to find new uses for all that stuff in the kitchen.

THIRTY PEOPLE ON YOUR LIST?

THIS COULD TAKE MINUTES.

L.L.Bean

start here
GO ANYWHERE.

L.L.Bean's tradition of great holiday gifts is within easy reach at our website.
To order, go to www.llbean.com or call 1-800-543-9071.

4.4. Here L.L.Bean presents itself as one solution to a busy gift-giving season.

with Tartar Protection Striped Toothpaste and Crest Sensitivity Clinical Sensitivity Relief Extra Whitening Toothpaste (yes, that's its name) all the way back to the brand's single-minded beginning, Crest Cavity Protection Toothpaste—Regular.

Ask yourself what benefits consumers seek from your client's product, and create target markets accordingly. Low price may be a benefit some people seek. Or good service.

Usage rate

If you consider your own buying habits, you may notice that you are always running out of milk but rarely replenish the six cans of pop at the back of the refrigerator; that you have the latest audiophile gear, but your most complicated kitchen appliance is the can opener; that you buy a new car every three years but would never own a motorcycle. In brief, of all the products out there, you buy only a small number; and within that small number, you consume a lot of some things but a lot less of many others. In short, you're a heavy user of some products, a light-to-moderate user of others, and a non-user of far more products.

So is everyone—a truth that leads to targeting these various consumption levels, segmenting markets on the basis of usage rate or user status. Are your

target customers non-users of a product, ex-users, light users, first-time users, moderate users, heavy users? People in each segment tend to be similar. Sell one way to a light user, another way to a heavy user. Many strategies target the heavy users for the obvious reason that those people account for the bulk of sales in a product category. In fact, a marketing rule of thumb, the "80/20 rule," says that in many categories 20 percent of the market consumes 80 percent of that product: roughly 80 percent of all the beer is drunk by 20 percent of all the beer drinkers, 80 percent of all the ketchup is used by 20 percent of the ketchup users, and so on.

Although such percentages vary, for many categories there is a heavy user who can be profiled, then targeted. By seeking to locate and understand those consumers, marketers hope to fish where the fishing is really good. But even good spots can be too heavily fished, so marketers often target the light-to-moderate user (and occasionally the ex-user or non-user) since those markets, frequently ignored, have less competition. Carving out a larger percentage of a smaller segment can often be more profitable than getting only a small percentage of a larger one.

Loyalty status

Find out who the brand-loyal users are. What unites them? What separates them from others? What unites those loyal to another brand or to no brand? Consider creating appeals to each. (See fig. 4.5 for an ad that appeals to members of the club.)

Readiness stage

Are your target consumers ready to buy, unaware of the brand or product category, informed, interested, what? Intersect them, wherever they are (fig. 4.6).

Attitude toward product

Perhaps people's attitudes, from negative to positive, toward the product or brand divide clearly enough that different ones can be targeted. For example, in introducing Silk soymilk to a broader audience, its advertisers had to figure out consumers' "stuck points," the attitudes toward soymilk that were holding them back. One was a sense that soymilk just couldn't taste good, so an ad in the campaign said, "First time tasters rave, 'It doesn't suck.'" (See fig. 4.7.)

Segmenting markets is rarely a clear-cut choice among demographics, psychographics, or the behavioral indexes; rather, these indexes are combined to

SOMEWHERE ON AN AIRPLANE A MAN IS TRYING TO RIP OPEN A SMALL BAG OF PEANUTS.

Give us life at ground level, rolling along the endless highway on a Harley-Davidson: 100% depressurized. Just sunlight on chrome. The voice of a V-Twin ripping the open air. And elbow room, stretching all the way to the horizon. Maybe you too think this is the way life ought to be lived. Time to spread some wings. 1-800-443-2153 or www.harley-davidson.com. The Legend Rolls On.

4.5. This ad isn't positioning one way to travel against another so much as it's ridiculing non-bikers. It invites Harley-Davidson loyalists (and aspirants) to bond over the freedom of the road. A wonderful headline, don't you think? It makes flying seem so small minded, such a cramped, pathetic idea.

target and profile a product's likeliest consumers. The Dockers marketing example mentioned earlier combined the age/gender demographic (25- to 40-year-old men) with psychographics (the mindset—casual and jeans-oriented) and benefit sought (comfort) to determine the right advertising message. (See fig. 4.8 for another example of a brand combining indexes in order to say the right things to the right people.)

What can you do?

Short of taking a course in market research, subscribing to a market research firm's data, or becoming a market researcher yourself, you may assume that there's no realistic way to generate and combine psychographic, demographic, and buying behavior information. And to some extent you're right. But no matter how sophisticated such research becomes, it still remains simply the *assertion* of buying categories by people thinking about consumers; it's not revealed, inscrutable Truth. So you, too, can think about who's out there buying your client's product and how many kinds of "whos" there might be.

First let's look at a real-world example. Chiat/Day/ Mojo, at the time Nissan's ad agency, used psychographic segments of new-car buyers created by a market research firm to help it devise strategies.[6] The study

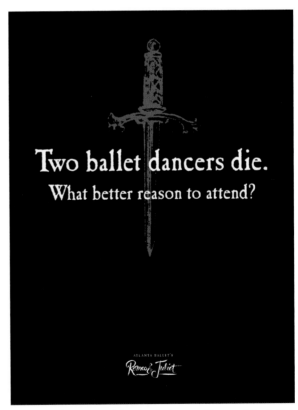

Two ballet dancers die.
What better reason to attend?

ATLANTA BALLET'S
Romeo & Juliet

4.6. This ad targets people who don't normally attend the ballet by making a joke they'll appreciate. And the joke's wit suggests that the evening might be more fun than they thought.

4.7. Getting people over that first speed bump.

For additional ads in the campaign, go to fig. W-4.7.

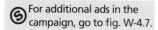

If you don't try it, fear wins.

All natural, lactose free, high in protein, with a surprisingly good taste. *C'mon. Don't be so stubborn.*

Silk
ORGANIC PLAIN
SOYMILK
CALCIUM

postulated six consumer categories on the basis of people's attitudes toward cars and the "driving experience."

Gearheads, the true car enthusiasts, actually work on cars and are mostly male, blue collar. They are the most likely to believe that the car they drive says a lot about them. They love sports cars, both domestic and Japanese.

Epicures, the largest group, like fully equipped, comfortable cars, are looking for style and elegance, and represent the second-highest percentage of women and the highest household incomes, $100,000 or more. They especially like convertibles.

Purists, the youngest group, are skeptical and not brand loyal but like driving and love sports cars. They represent the high concentrations of laborers and Asian Americans.

Functionalists are conservative homeowners, often with children, who want sensible, fuel-efficient transportation. They buy small to mid-sized domestic cars.

Road-Haters, tied with the epicures as the largest group, are safety conscious, strongly prefer large domestic cars, don't enjoy driving, and represent the highest share of women, the highest ages, and the lowest incomes.

Negatives are uninterested in cars, regarding them as necessary evils, hassles. They're the most educated, with large incomes, and frequently buy small foreign cars.

You can see that these categories really are just assertions (who knows for certain how many kinds of new-car buyers there are?). But they combine psychographics and demographics in ways that may jibe with your sense of who's out there (see fig. 4.9). You can also see that if you're Nissan, this is helpful material. You can target as many segments as you feel you have cars for, and you can create advertising that talks about those cars in ways that fit the needs of the targets. You can also use this material to change the kinds of cars you make, another virtue of good research.

SPEAK THE AUDIENCE'S LANGUAGE

"To know whom to write for is to know how to write."

—Virginia Woolf

Consider the following ads and note how well they know whom they're written for—how well they understand and locate, by their language and thought, highly specific market segments. This one, which appeared in London newspapers in 1900, was written by polar explorer Sir Ernest Shackleton:

Men Wanted for Hazardous Journey. Small wages, bitter cold, long months of complete darkness, constant danger, safe return doubtful. Honor and recognition in case of success.

Response was overwhelming and immediate. The ad worked because it understood exactly what certain men wanted to hear, and said it to them clearly, simply, and powerfully.[7]

Here is another ad, written ninety years later, and placed in men's magazines. It, too, understands what a certain market segment wants to hear and says it to them. Notice how precisely a particular person is evoked—the appeal combines demographics (male, thirty-plus, upscale, urban) with psychographics (a particular lifestyle motive for running). The ad, a spread for Nike, shows a small figure running in downtown San Francisco, with these words as both headline and copy:

He's fat and he's soft and he's wearing your clothes and he's getting too old and he was born on your birthday and you're afraid that if you stop running, he'll catch up with you.

A Nike Bauer Hockey poster targeting hockey-loving teenagers had the following headline/copy:

Be the one to steal the draw, to scrap in the corners,

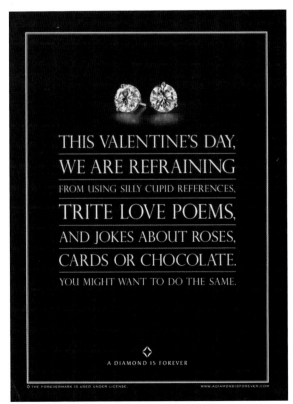

4.8. Demographics, psychographics, and occasions combine to create the selling arguments.

Ⓢ To see more diamond ads, go to fig. W-4.8.

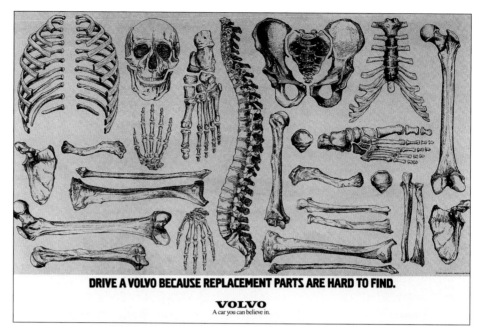

4.9. Volvo targets road-haters; Porsche, epicures.

to roof it, to rush it and not get a roughing, to crush the crease, to red-face the net keep, to snipe from the blue.

I don't understand a word of this. But I don't play hockey or watch it either. The poster speaks to its core audience in a code only they understand. What better way to convince them that Nike Bauer is the authentic hockey brand? Don't claim it, prove it. And keep outsiders out while you're at it.

See figures 4.10–4.14 for more ads that understand who they're talking to.

THINK LIKE THE MARKET SEGMENT

"If you can't turn yourself into your customer, you probably shouldn't be in the ad writing business at all."

—LEO BURNETT, founder, Leo Burnett agency

It's easier to sell a product if you actually know some-

4.10. Think like a parent, and you'll get more Cub Scouts. Another ad said, "Ever gaze at your child and wonder: Shouldn't he have more grass stains on him?"

4.11. People identify with their cities. Why not invite Milwaukeeans to share, with a smile, part of their city's heritage?

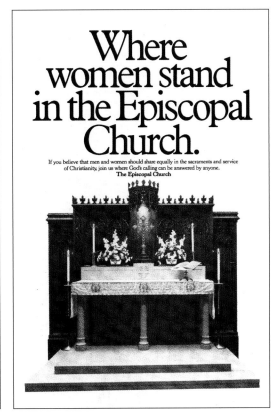

4.12. This aggressive campaign for the Episcopal Church realized that more than one kind of person was missing from the pews, for more than one reason. Ads targeted specific segments of potential churchgoers by addressing lifestyles and needs.

Ⓢ See other ads from this campaign at fig. W-4.12.

one who is part of its target audience. If, for example, you're selling golf equipment and you've played the game and know golfers, then you can become them in your mind while making ads. If you're selling baseball games, you'll know who's in the stands (fig. 4.15). If you're selling newspapers, you'll know who reads them and when (see fig. 4.16).

One difficulty occurs when you must imagine an audience with which you have little experience: a different subculture or ethnic group, any audience a long way from you—maybe you're an undergraduate in New York City writing ads that sell farm equipment, or someone who's never taken more than a snapshot selling photography gear to pros. What to do? If possible, locate and interview someone who is a part of the target. Find the websites, blogs, and magazines of that profession and read them. Study photography ads to see what the issues are, what the selling arguments are, how the language works, what the slang is. You cannot write a good ad for a target audience until you become a surrogate member of it. If you aren't born into it, then you must join it through empathy and effort. You must think and talk and want like your audience.

Another difficulty arises with business-to-business advertising: you must imagine not one but two audiences, and neither of them is a person. For example, you're asked to write advertising from a home construction firm to an architectural firm seeking to convince the latter that the former is the builder to choose. Even in this instance, however, the trick is to forget the firms and to simply become two people: a guy who builds houses talking to a guy who designs them. (Business-to-business advertising is examined more completely in chapter 14.)

What market segmentation means to you

"[Aiming your advertising] is the same as hunting quail. You look up when a covey takes flight, and you think you'll hit something by just pulling the trigger. But you discover you have to choose a target—or you won't hit anything. Trying to sell anything to everyone isn't a strategy. It's wishful thinking."

—HAL RINEY, founder, Hal Riney & Partners

Segmenting the market clarifies things. You understand what motivates each targeted segment of con-

86.3% of college students surveyed had a less than 1-in-17 chance of remembering the exact number of college students surveyed who could recall without looking the percentage given at the beginning of this sentence by the time they reached the end of it.

Just a reminder that cramming for finals will only do so much.   *Get a good night's sleep.*

http://www.nsa.net/celestial/seasonings.html

4.13. Ever stayed up too late for an exam and found your mind swimming around like this one? Celestial Seasonings quietly sells Sleepytime tea by bonding with college students. As the copy line counsels, "Just a reminder that cramming for finals will only do so much. Get a good night's sleep." Here a product that might have been sold as "relaxing" is wisely given a sharper focus. A series of such ads, each matching a tea with a target audience, would be stronger than any number of more generic ads. People look up when their names are called.

4.14. "Tobacco Contains Radioactive Lead" is spelled out with cups on a high school fence, a common way teens create public messages. By delivering the fact in this form, the ad calls out the name of its core audience, encouraging them to act similarly. As the slogan/call to action puts it: "Knowledge is contagious. How you spread it is up to you. Infect truth."

4.15. Since the Chicago Cubs play most of their games in the afternoon, not at night, these ads target business people already in the city, using language familiar to the working crowd.

You're going to read this no matter what. It's true. It doesn't matter what's written here. You're going to follow it through to the end. Every last word. And to prove it, here's the word cabbage written nine times in a row – cabbage, cabbage, cabbage, cabbage, cabbage, cabbage, garage, cabbage, cabbage. Did you see the word, garage? Of course you did, because you read every word. And even if you didn't, you're now going back to find the word 'garage'. See. Told you so. But fret not. You're not reading every word because this ad has you spellbound. No. It's probably because you couldn't find a Metro to read. And so you're stuck reading this, and cabbage eight, no, nine, wait, ten times.

metr⊕

News worth sharing.

4.16. This ad works because it understands the psychology of its audience (newspaper readers) and the exact situation they find themselves in: on a subway car or bus, with nothing to read. Not anymore.

sumers, what they go to the product for, and what language they speak. If, however, you never decide on target markets and instead try to sell everyone in a language that offends no one—the "8 to 80" perplex—if you never place a particular person before your mind's eye when creating ads, then diffusion and blandness will undo you.

So never content yourself with addressing fuzzy somebodies at best or demographic nobodies at worst, thinking, for example, that you are sufficiently precise if you say that your advertising is "aimed at women 25–45." (Imagine for a moment the variety within those demographics. It could vary all the way from the young woman sitting beside you in a class to your mom.)

Instead, locate a particular person in your mind's eye: your brother, your grandmother, the computer geek you know. Can you make that person laugh? Can you get inside with the right talk and the right imagery? Try.

5 · Defining Strategic Approaches

Start with strategy. We try to begin with a strategy that feels different, that immediately defines the client and sets them apart. If the strategy isn't doing that job, the creative probably won't do it either. Your gut usually tells you when you've found a good strategy—it seems obvious, even though it wasn't obvious before. Like, "Why didn't I think of that before," or "Why isn't anybody else doing that?" Then you start to get a little nervous that somebody's probably working on that strategy right now. That's a good feeling, it usually means you're onto something that's right.
—MIKE SHINE, copywriter and creative director, Butler Shine & Stern

If I were to say—in three words—what all good ads do, I'd say: "Dramatize the benefit." Advertisers differ, however, in what they consider the benefit in need of dramatizing—sometimes it's a product's feature or a marketplace position, other times a problem solved or a state of mind achieved.

Also, since ads sell a product to a consumer, ad writers can choose to emphasize one or the other. Thus, you can think of advertising approaches as residing on a continuum from product-oriented strategies, on the one hand, to consumer-oriented ones on the other, from hard product to soft lifestyle. You could also say that the approaches range from rational to emotional—product-oriented arguments frequently appealing to reason, the consumer-oriented approaches often stressing the emotional qualities of life with the product.

How many kinds of strategic approaches there are depends on who's counting. Here's my count; others, of course, will differ.

Product-oriented
 1. **Generic claim:** sell the product category, not the brand.
 2. **Product feature:** sell a product feature; appeal to reason.
 3. **Unique selling proposition:** sell a benefit unique to the brand.
 4. **Positioning:** establish a distinct and desirable market niche.

Consumer-oriented
 5. **Brand image:** create and sell a personality for the brand.
 6. **Lifestyle:** associate the product with a way of life.
 7. **Attitude:** associate the product with a state of mind.

When you artificially separate the flow of advertising, all categories—including these—are false, their distinctions neat in type but messier in reality. Many ads borrow from several of these categories; other great ads can't be lodged in any of them. When you're making ads, use the idea of categories, but don't be bound by it. Don't worry over which you're using so much as this: Is what you're doing working?

Product-oriented strategies
First, let's examine strategies that emphasize the thing for sale rather than the person who might buy it.

GENERIC CLAIM
Selling one of the principal benefits a product category delivers—fast headache relief for aspirin and other pain relievers, water-borne relaxation for cruise lines, clean clothes for laundry products, and so on—is probably the most widely used advertising strategy. Many ads simply make a generic claim, associate the brand with that claim, then count on the cumulative power of advertising and association, as well as the

5.1. These brands make generic claims—the optical retailer offers good-looking glasses, the small car promises economy—but they do so energetically. The strength of the execution (rather than the singularity of the strategy) is what makes these ads distinctive.

Celibacy isn't always a choice.

Designer eyewear 40-60% off everyday. FOR EYES

Why gas stations sell food.

Civic Hatchback
HONDA

memorability of a strong execution (fig. 5.1) to link the principal benefit with that brand. They do this even though competitors can (and do) make the same argument and deliver the same benefit.

Selling the product category, not the brand, makes even better sense if your client's product has a dominant share in a market. Your client's main competitor is consumers themselves—their levels of usage—more than other brands. As marketing consultants Jack Trout and Al Ries advise, "When you own the pie, you should try to enlarge the pie rather than try to increase the size of your slice."[1] Arm & Hammer thus needs to sell the idea of baking soda, not its brand. Likewise, Campbell's doesn't need to sell its brand but the generic product; the Campbell's slogan

"Soup is good food" encouraged consumers simply to eat more soup.

New products (like digital video recorders and HDTV) also needed at first to sell the basic argument (why buy a DVR? why get HDTV?) before worrying about brand differentiation (fig. 5.2).

PRODUCT FEATURE

Ask yourself why people buy your client's product. If their choice is largely rational, a sifting among product distinctions (most hardware, large and small; durable goods; high-ticket items), and your client's product truly has distinctions that matter, then sell them. Focus not on generic product benefits but on competitive ones. Appeal to the logical choice based on sensible differences among brands. Consider the ads in figure 5.3. Gary Knutson, creative director at Howard, Merrell & Partners, explains the campaign: "Every other manufacturer was selling sunglasses as fashion statements. We simply zigged when everyone was zagging, and spelled out product features that made Costa Del Mar sunglasses superior."[2]

This strategy can work in competitive markets, where you're fighting to distinguish your client's product from others, and it can work whenever why people buy is at least partly a rational decision. You can emphasize either the product's specific virtue or the consumer's problem being solved—or both, as does this headline for an Acura coupe underneath a picture of the car in action: "Could your heart benefit from the use of another 24 valves?"

UNIQUE SELLING PROPOSITION

If you can fill in the following sentence for your client's brand, then you're making a Unique Selling Proposition: "You should buy a ____ because it's the only one that ____." You're telling consumers that if they want this feature/benefit, the only place they can get it is from your brand.

Rosser Reeves, an American advertiser of the

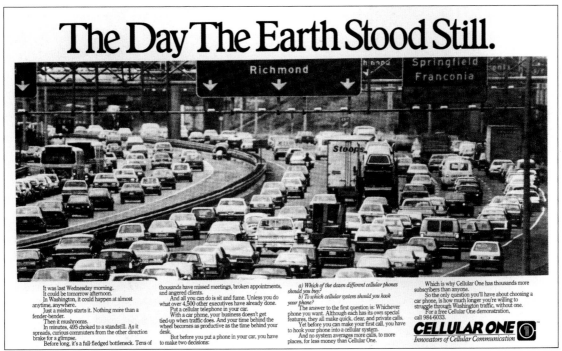

Top and above
5.2. Pioneering ads for cellular phones, like this traffic jam ad from 1985, made the generic claim. As the market grew and became competitive, ads focused on differentials, like better service or lower rates, as did this "bad example" ad from 1995.

Imagine dangling a bowling ball from the earpiece.

The lengths to which we go to ensure the lasting quality of Costa Del Mar sunglasses are legendary.

But there is certainly nothing more impressive (some might say outlandish) than our metal frame stress test.

This consists of attaching a *twenty-pound free weight* to the temple of every fiftieth pair of frames.

If they can survive this, we feel fairly confident that your American-made Costa Del Mar sunglasses will live up to their weighty responsibility as a lasting investment.

Costa Del Mar

If your store doesn't carry them, patronize better stores.

Why half the time spent making our glasses is spent polishing them.

Cheap sunglass frames may be painted or coated in some fashion. This finish invariably wears off with use. By contrast, American-made Costa Del Mar sunglasses are *polished* to a natural sheen by tumbling the frames in *teakwood chips* for six days.

To some, this may seem a bit extreme. But then, when you spend the other half of your time making the finest lenses available, wouldn't it be a shame to skimp on the frames that surround them?

Costa Del Mar

If your store doesn't carry them, patronize better stores.

5.3. If you've built a better product, tell people about it. In this campaign, great headlines dramatize distinctive and relevant product features, and great copy makes the case.

Most cheap sunglasses — and an appalling number of expensive ones — are made with nylon frames. The nature of this material is that it has a "memory."

By contrast, American-made Costa Del Mar frames are made of top quality *Zyl*

(cellulose acetate). When you twist Zyl, it doesn't fight back. Which means, unless your ears are somewhere on your elbows, your Costa Del Mars will retain your perfect fit.

Costa Del Mar

If your store doesn't carry them, patronize better stores.

For the name of a better store nearest you, or to order direct, call 800-221-0484. In Florida 800-447-3700.

Why a well-made pair of sunglasses has no memory.

1950s, built his career on the idea that the best way to sell things was by making what he called a "Unique Selling Proposition" (USP), a specific promise of benefit unique to the brand, one that the competition either did not or could not claim. So, for example, M&Ms "melt in your mouth, not in your hands," an argument implying that its competitors failed to do so. This singling out of some specific aspect of the product and then basing an ad campaign on it was predicated on the buying public's willingness to be-

lieve that products do indeed differ from one another, that a given brand can deliver something that others can't (fig. 5.4).

For decades, Folger's emphasized that its coffee was "mountain grown." All coffee is mountain grown, but Folger's said it first, thus appearing to make an argument unique to itself and owning territory in consumers' brains as a consequence. (This first use of a generic feature by a brand is sometimes called a *preemptive claim* instead of a USP. You are preempting

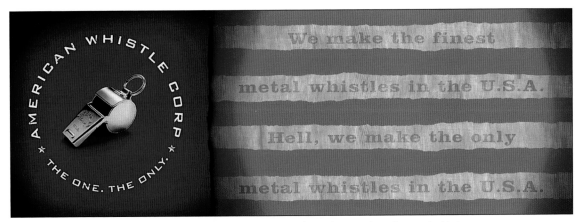

5.4. USP advertising: as the slogan says, this is the one, the only, metal whistle.

Ⓢ See another whistle ad at fig. W-5.4.

its use by competitors even though they, too, could have made the same claim, had they thought of it first.)

Although it's often true that technological parity now makes it difficult to create and maintain a hardware differential, products whose selling argument is a USP are still out there. Apple, for example, has always emphasized hardware/software uniqueness in selling its computers and digital products, from the very first personal computer to Cube, iMac, iPod, iTunes, iPad, iCloud, and beyond. The argument is that only an Apple is an Apple.

Nonetheless, product-oriented USP advertising has given way over the decades to softer, brand-image, style- and feelings-oriented advertising. People are still willing to believe that brands differ from one another, but the differences have shifted from those of technology and hardware to ones of emotion and relationship. John Hegarty of London's Bartle Bogle Hegarty thinks trends have moved past the USP to, first, the "Emotional Selling Proposition," where how people felt about a brand was what made it unique (see fig. 5.5), to the "Irrational Selling Proposition," from the 1990s onward, where only fun, odd, often absurdist campaigns registered with ad-drenched consumers (think of the ads for Lee Jeans featuring the Buddy Lee doll, for example, or of the funny, ironic, behind-the-scenes sportsworld created by ESPN's advertising).[3]

POSITIONING

"The true nature of marketing today involves the conflict between corporations, not the satisfying of human needs and wants."

—AL TROUT and JACK RIES, *Marketing Warfare*

The advertising world owes *positioning* to Trout and Ries, who developed the concept in a series of articles and later a book.[4] Simply stated, positioning is the perception consumers have of a product, not unto itself, but relative to its competition. Products are "positioned" in consumers' minds, each being given an evaluation, a definition, a niche, in the product inventories they maintain. Consumers condense their estimate of each product into one simple (and often permanent) perception and create hierarchies of similar products.

For example, among detergents, people consider Tide all-American, all-purpose; Cheer is all-temperature; Dreft is soft, for babies' things; Dash is the budget brand; Fab combines a softener with the cleaner; Bold is the enzymes cleaner; and so on. To be successful, a brand must carve out for itself an identity that's not only distinct (a handle by which people can recognize it) but also viable (one for which they'll buy it).

The power of positioning

"The starting point must be a distinct point of view. Bernbach taught us that if you stand for everything, you stand for nothing. That's why the essence of positioning is sacrifice—deciding what's unimportant, what can be cut away and left behind; reducing your perspective to a very sharp point of view."

—KEITH REINHARD, chairman, DDB Needham

Positioning is a marketing idea so strong that entire campaigns can be based on it. Even though the slogan hasn't been used since the early 1990s, many people still remember 7-Up as "the Uncola," a pure example of the power of positioning; they were asked to buy it for what it wasn't. Pepsi's slogan "The Choice of a New Generation" sought to reposition Coca-Cola as the drink of old folks, while Coke's "The Real Thing" and "Coke Is It" campaigns tried to position it as the only authentic cola. (Many slogans and campaign theme lines are simply crystallized position statements. See the advice on writing slogans and theme lines in chapter 17.)

Positioning strategies are essential when products are new, since those products occupy no place whatsoever in consumers' minds. How you position them has much to do with their success. If your client's product is simply a "me-too" product, then its chances for survival are poor. Roughly 20,000 new products are intro-duced in America every year, and 90 percent of them fail: a killing field.[5] Discovering and then expressing a distinct, competitive position thus becomes a major goal of your advertising. Alex Bogusky and John Winsor of Crispin Porter + Bogusky say this about positioning: "If you're not quietest, fastest, lightest, which is to say if you can't figure out a way to become an absolute, then move on."[6]

Positioning can also determine advertising strategy when your client's product is not the category leader. After all, there is nowhere to go but up. If the product is a strong #2 or #3, say, you may want to go right after the leader. The key is finding a weakness inherent in the leader's strength (figs. 5.6 and 5.7).

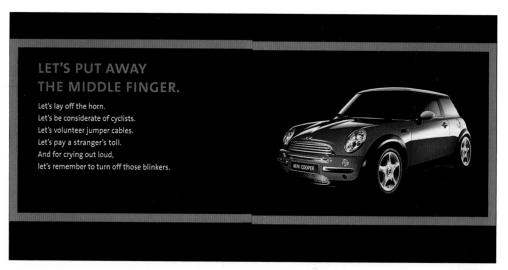

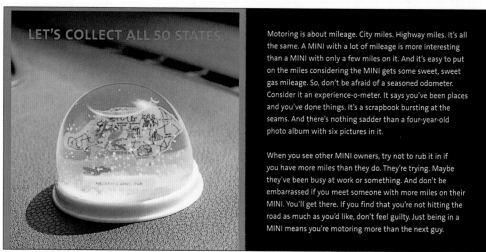

5.5. MINI advertising presents both a Unique Selling Proposition and Hegarty's Emotional Selling Proposition. MINIs are unique partly because of hardware but also, and just as important, because of the emotional connection they invite people to make with them. People can buy a lot of small cars, but they'd only feel quirky, cool, and ready to say "Let's motor" in a MINI.

As Trout and Ries argue, "What the leader owns is a position in the mind of the prospect. To win the battle of the mind, you must take away the leader's position before you can substitute your own. It's not enough for you to succeed; others must fail. Specifically, the leader."[7]

Key positioning questions

What position does your client's product now occupy?

What positions do the competitors' products occupy?

What new position should your client's product occupy? How do you want to modify its current position?

What strategy should your advertising adopt as a consequence?

In the battle between Target and Walmart, two big-box retailers, Target has positioned itself as the "designer" big box by featuring products designed especially for Target by Michael Graves, Sonia Kashuk, Mossimo, Todd Oldham, Philippe Starck, and others. Walmart could have recruited their own roster of designers, essentially claiming "me, too," but, instead

5.6. *Sporting News* takes on the market leader, *Sports Illustrated*, whose definition of sports can be pretty broad.

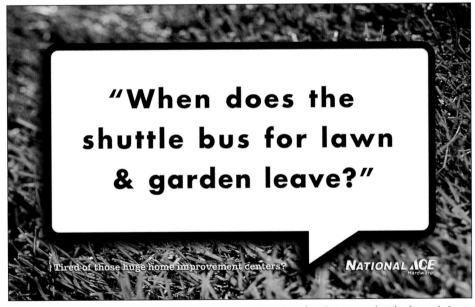

5.7. Ace positions itself against the big-box megastores by going after their strength. What's good about the big boxes—a million things—is also what's bad—a *million* things. Good for selection, bad for feet.

(S) For additional ads in both campaigns, see figs. W-5.6 and W-5.7.

they've decided to flank Target's position by staking out different territory: Walmart wants to be seen as the "greener, more sustainable" big box, an argument that also addresses what people most hold against the company, that it doesn't care about the environment. So, if successful, the new positioning will do double duty: separate Walmart from Target and reverse a consumer negative.[8]

While many campaigns are based on positioning, its greatest value to you may be as an *idea*, an indispensable index by which to gauge the product and its relationship to the competition. You may never make positioning a dominant advertising strategy, but you should never be ignorant of the product's place in consumers' minds. How they regard it, especially relative to similar products, is essential information. No product is position-less.

Consumer-oriented strategies

Instead of focusing on the thing you're selling in your ads, you may want to go beyond hardware to what surrounds it. There can be a lot for sale out there.

BRAND IMAGE

"Image means personality. Products, like people, have personalities, and they can make or break them in the market place. The personality of a product is an amalgam of many things—its name, its packaging, its price, the style of its advertising, and above all, the nature of the product itself. Every advertisement should be thought of as a contribution to the brand image."

—DAVID OGILVY, founder, Ogilvy & Mather

David Ogilvy is generally credited with developing the idea of brand-image advertising, and each of his great campaigns from the 1950s—Rolls Royce, Schweppes, Hathaway shirts, and others—established a consistent style and sensibility that, once begun, were maintained. Brand-image advertising is not the selling of specific product features, elements intrinsic to the object itself, but instead the selling of the object's aura, its personality, those aspects extrinsic to it that make up its (self-created) image.

All ads, regardless of strategy, contribute to a brand's image, so in this sense all advertising is brand-image advertising. If a brand has no image, then it's got a bad ad agency. Thus, discussing the *strategy* of brand-image advertising becomes tricky,

since image is always at issue. But in this instance let's use the term to mean a strategy focused on the personality of a brand. When people look at that product's advertising, they realize that they're being asked to buy into a personality, not an argument. That's the distinction.

"When a customer identifies with the personality of a product, and finds its behavior attractive, he transfers that personality and behavior to himself by buying and using that product. It's like putting on a badge and wearing it proudly."

—KEITH REINHARD, chairman, DDB Needham

What, for example, differentiates Reebok from Nike, Coca-Cola from Pepsi, BMW from Lexus? Primarily their advertising symbol systems. Each makes a good product; none is so advanced that its technical merit alone distances it from its competition. In consumers' rational minds, they realize that as an object, each is substantially equivalent to its major competitor(s). Since the product is intrinsically similar, the extrinsic brand image of the product, communicated through its advertising (often called advertising's "added value"), becomes the meaning customers seek. The differentiated systems of language and design in which the products reside are what customers buy. And they are happy to do so (figs. 5.8 and 5.9).

Ogilvy makes this comment:

Take whiskey. Why do some people choose Jack Daniel's, while others choose Grand Dad or Taylor? Have they tried all three and compared the taste? Don't make me laugh. The reality is that these three brands have different images which appeal to different kinds of people. It isn't the whiskey they choose, it's the image. The brand image is 90 percent of what the distiller has to sell.[9]

And so it is with many products: most of what they have to sell is symbolic. Consider using this strategy when your client's product is in a parity situation or when the product is almost a commodity: cigarettes, beer, liquor, cologne, soap, and so on (for which a unique feature or rational argument is often hard to find). Brand-image advertising is also a good idea for *badge products*, those items whose names are visible,

NOBODY EVER GOT A BLISTER BUILDING A WEB SITE.

There aren't many jobs that require a guy to be just as tough as he is smart. The same mix of brains and brawn you put into your work, we put into your tools. Milwaukee. Nothing but heavy duty.

5.8. I've never held a Milwaukee tool, but the visual and headline ("Nobody ever got a blister building a Web site") have already convinced me that no job's too tough for it.

whose identities are socially obvious (clothes, cars, etc.), unlike socially invisible products (canned goods hidden in cupboards, detergents stored in the laundry room, etc.). Other products, invisible themselves, that contribute to people's social esteem—personal care items, for instance—can also be sold via brand image.

If you think that's a long list, you're right. Brand-image advertising pervades so many product categories and has become so ubiquitous that in many ways it has won the how-to-advertise war. Lee Clow, chairman of TBWA\Chiat\Day, explains why:

> You have to connect with consumers. Brands are like people, and the personalities you create for brands, the likability, the "I like spending time with those guys," has to open the door before anyone will visit your Web site. They'll ultimately want the informational side of [your message], but you have to make them like you first, before they want to spend time with you and hear what you think about this, that and the other thing.[10]

Right
5.9. Coffee may be like liquor: a lot of what people are tasting is in their heads. Looking at this ad, I can taste a coffee that's rich, deep, and steeped in New Orleans tradition. Where am I getting these ideas? Brand image.

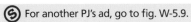 For another PJ's ad, go to fig. W-5.9.

★ ★ ★ OUR ★ ★ ★
COFFEE
HAS BEEN THROUGH
A DEEP ROAST,
SLOW GRIND AND
THE SPIT VALVES
of some GREATEST
of the
MUSICIANS of OUR TIME.

5.10. Here the product accompanies an adventurous way of life that the target audience aspires to. By seeming indispensable to such a lifestyle, the brand becomes an incremental way of achieving it.

How to create brand-image advertising

1. Study the image advertising created for other brands, such as Nike, MINI, and Apple. What do you think of these brands, and what in their advertising has led you to think that?

2. Ask, what is the product or brand? What's a Volvo? What's a Timex? See what answer you get. Either create ads that express the brand's personality, or reshape the personality to fit the answer you seek.

3. Regard the product as a person; write up a profile of it as though it were a person, and study that. Dan Wieden, co-founder of Wieden + Kennedy, Nike's principal ad agency, calls Nike "complex, contradictory and genuine, like an interesting person, which is why people respond to it."[11] When asked what makes a great brand, Eric Spiegler, senior vice president at O'Leary and Partners, explains brand-as-person this way: "As simply as I can put it, a great brand understands me and vice versa. I want to hang out with it and it wants to hang out with me. I didn't say a great brand had good taste in friends."[12] (For

more on brand personality, see the discussion of voice in chapter 9, since personality comes so directly from the way a brand talks.)

4. Pay attention (as much as a copywriter can) **to the design and typography of the campaign,** how the graphic elements look and feel. Design and type are also powers behind brand images. Style is substance with brand-image advertising.

LIFESTYLE

"Brands have become so similar to one another that the real leverage in the advertising is no longer the content of the product but the placement of the product in the consumer's life."

—BARBARA S. FEIGIN, research director, Grey Advertising

"I had my first kiss while I had a bottle of Coke in my hand. . . . Coca-Cola isn't about taste; it's about my life."

—CHARLOTTE BEERS, former CEO, Ogilvy & Mather

Closely related to brand-image advertising is another approach that emphasizes not product hardware but consumer states of being—an approach one might call *lifestyle advertising*. Rather than creating an image of the brand itself, it creates an image of the consumer, making him or her, in effect, the product. The viewer is shown a desirable state of being, to which the product is appended.

Lifestyle advertising is what it sounds like: ads show a desirable way of living and simply insert the product into it. Such advertising expresses the highest possible benefit because rather than arguing a narrow product advantage, it implies a large personal improvement. The lifestyle shown is one the viewers can have, or begin to have, if they buy the product that seems to be its indispensable accessory (figs. 5.10 and 5.11).

Remember: the idea is that the target audience doesn't so much see the product (in fact, many such ads barely show it at all) as they see what it must be like to own it. When creating this kind of advertising, don't regard the product as some piece of hardware with features and USPs, some thing over there. Regard it as a necessary complement to a way of being; and then use imagery that you think communicates this atmosphere—these psychological benefits, this alternate reality, if you will, that can be the audience's if it uses the product.

ATTITUDE

Attitude advertising is advertising in which tone of voice is so dominant that it becomes what's for sale. Usually the attitude is the brand's—part of its personality, the "tone of voice" part—and it can be so dis-

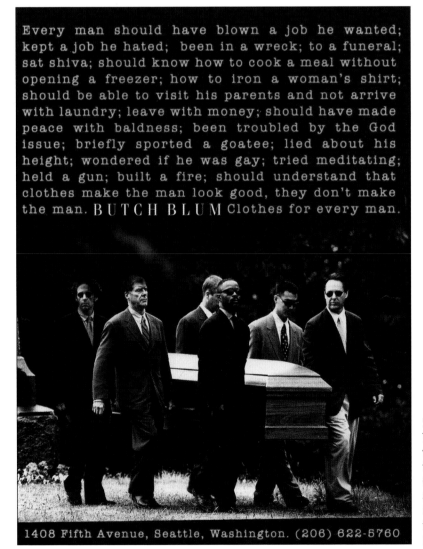

Every man should have blown a job he wanted; kept a job he hated; been in a wreck; to a funeral; sat shiva; should know how to cook a meal without opening a freezer; how to iron a woman's shirt; should be able to visit his parents and not arrive with laundry; leave with money; should have made peace with baldness; been troubled by the God issue; briefly sported a goatee; lied about his height; wondered if he was gay; tried meditating; held a gun; built a fire; should understand that clothes make the man look good, they don't make the man. B U T C H   B L U M Clothes for every man.

1408 Fifth Avenue, Seattle, Washington. (206) 622-5760

5.11. Lifestyle as deathstyle. This ad takes a man's last trip with his buddies and uses it to sum up the meaning of life. Clothes are mentioned only at the end—Butch Blum is a Seattle clothier—and then only to dismiss them. Great copy. Powerful work.

tinctive that it runs the advertising. Nike may have initiated this attitude-is-everything approach when it began the "Just do it" campaign in the mid-1980s. Assuming responsibility for consumers' physical—and by implication, spiritual—health, Nike raised the pitch of its admonitions. Bold type and bold people looked up from the page or from their workouts and scolded folks for being their usual, sloppy selves. "Just do it," the ads warned, and as one of the players added, "And it wouldn't hurt to stop eating like a pig, either." "Ouch. Yes, ma'am," people seemed to say, as they sprinted out the back door wearing Nikes.

But attitude advertising doesn't have to be finger-in-the-face aggressive. Think of MINI's "Let's motor" campaign, which is driven by a sweet but spunky, sociable but iconoclastic voice. Every ad brings this same attitude to life on the road and invites consumers to share it by buying a MINI. Consider, for example, the headline and part of the copy for a magazine ad: "Small thought #7: How is it that dogs can stick their heads out of moving cars? Have you ever tried that? It hurts. Hurts bad. . . . But for some reason, dogs can take it. And they love it. But humans get to steer. So it all evens out." This attitude—a sense of pleasure in the small things and fun behind the wheel, a sweet blend of whimsy and adventure—is the essence of MINI's advertising. Consumers read their way from one ad to another, always encouraged to share the mindset. That's finally what's for sale: a great big box of attitude, with a lovely little box of car inside.

ABC created an all-type print campaign that aimed to distinguish its TV network from all the others by expressing an ironic attitude toward people's too-heavy TV use. Tongue-in-cheek ads recognized and then "celebrated" the TV-centric, couchified life. Here are three of the ads:

If TV's so bad for you, why is there one in every hospital room?

Before TV, two World Wars. After TV, zero.

Don't just sit there. Okay, just sit there.

Sometimes, though, brands adopt the audience's point of view. The attitude is the consumer's rather than the brand's. Attitude ads become a corollary of lifestyle advertising, perhaps its next development: the symbolic simplification of a complete narrative into its one purest emotion. A long-running Miller High Life beer campaign used headlines that sounded like the attitude of a middle-aged, unpretentious beer drinker. Here are four of them:

Who cares what's in a hot dog.

Would the man who invented artificial turf care to step outside?

No callus too thick.

Can someone please tell me why baldness is regarded as a problem?

Often it's hard to say whether the attitude is coming from the brand or from consumers because the brand seems to be agreeing with their inner speech. Their attitude is its attitude is their attitude. As essayist and social critic George W. S. Trow put it, "The progress of the advertisement is toward the destruction of distance between the product and the person who might consume the product."[13] See figure 5.12 for a brand whose attitude comes from it and its core consumer.

Regardless of whether you're considering attitude as a part of brand image, consumer lifestyle, or both, it can be central to the ads you create. Ask if an emotion or attitude is part of what's for sale. Maybe it's the brand's attitude toward its competitors or toward the culture or toward users or nonusers of the product. A clever student ad from Brainco for Godiva Premium Ice Cream, an upscale product, says simply, "Waiting for a sale? How amusing," with the slogan "Cold. But rich." Now there's an ice cream with attitude.

Or maybe the attitude in question is one people have toward the product category or about your client's brand or about the social circumstances that surround using that product. Create ads whose tone of voice, whose mindset, becomes the argument. A campaign for Timberland sold outdoor gear by opposing it to the indoor life that consumes most office workers. Headlines sounding like Zen epigrams pointed out the desiccated life of the corporate indoors. One ad showed an EXIT sign in a hallway, with the headline "This is not a sign. It is a calling." Another ad showed an open elevator and said, "The elevator. Yet another box within a box designed to take you to a box." On a stark photograph of an empty, fluorescent-lit meeting room: "Frustrations grow best in artificial light." The implication? A spiritually centered life awaits, if one simply develops the right attitude. (For an example of a brand's attitude springing right up from the ground, see fig. 5.13.)

Alive, a weekly city paper, wanted to position itself

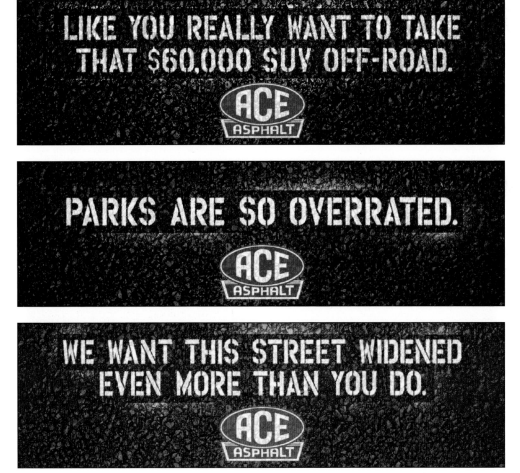

5.13. Can blacktop have an attitude? It can now.

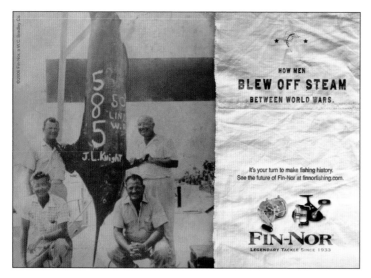

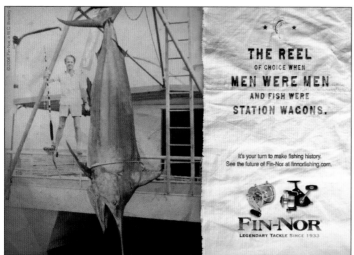

5.14. Fin-Nor fishing tackle, a venerable brand, had lost its place in the market. This campaign sought to reestablish the brand's position by tapping into its legacy, re-creating its big-fish, big-fisherman history. Here brand image becomes positioning.

as the source of information for what to do and where to do it (slogan: "Music, art and culture in Columbus"). So it ran a bus card campaign with headlines like these: "You in the MINI, yes. You in the mini-van, not so much" and "You on the Vespa, yes. You on the crotch-rocket, not so much." *Alive* didn't just claim it was an arbiter of the social scene. It proved it through its attitude.

Why has attitude advertising become so crucial? For the same reason that its cousin, brand-image advertising, has. Jeff DeJoseph, executive vice president of brand planning at J. Walter Thompson, explains:

[Because] in a whole variety of categories there's nothing to say about the product. The actual competitive differences are ever so slight. Many brands have parity status. And consumers are bombarded with exponentially more messages. So there's no reason to select a brand other than how you affiliate with it, how you feel about it. It's not the fact of the brand, it's the emotion you attach to the beer or the car or the jeans.[14]

Strategies as a continuum

When you're creating ads, it's not a case of either-or: either you use this kind of strategy or you use that one; either you sell product features or you create a feelings-oriented brand-image campaign. These categories are really more a continuum than a rigid set of mutually exclusive approaches. In fact, given the unending discussion about whether people buy with their heads or their hearts, it's best to neglect neither reason nor emotion. Focus on one, but include the other. This Web copy from the Danish clothing brand Only is talking to teenage girls about a dress and nicely entwines product specs with emotional benefits: "A charming and enchanting summer dress with girlie details, short sleeves and a spring band in a classic empire cut style. Will ask for tender kisses and soft cuddling on your behalf." As Rosser Reeves put it, "The best theoretical objective is to surround the claim with the feeling."[15]

Also remember that although you may be working on only a small part of a large campaign or creating only a few ads for your portfolio, in the real world ads are parts of campaigns and function in concert to accomplish more than one aim. Some ads will establish the campaign theme so that other ads, operating within that theme, can be product specific. Ads can, and usually do, blend strategies (fig. 5.14). These categories are yours to use. They are suggestions for thinking—not binding, separate entities.

Take what you've learned and mix thoroughly

To create great advertising, you must examine product, competition, consumer behavior, and target markets. But don't simply weave your way through them impressionistically. Combine them into a plan of action, a strategic document in which you summarize the research and decide what your ads must accomplish. Write a creative brief. Let's see what needs to be in it.

6 · Developing the Creative Brief

With all the noise, infinite brand touch points and multiple marketing partners working for a common client, it's critical that creative briefs be exactly that: brief. Without a crisp, elegant statement to guide us and keep us honest, none of us stands a chance of pulling off what we get paid to do. If the next brief you see contains more than one idea or has to be explained to the team working on it, kill it. Or it'll kill you later.

—JOHN COLASANTI, president and managing partner, Carmichael Lynch

Setting the objective

It's easy to see the virtue of analyzing consumer behavior, defining target markets, understanding your client's product, and examining possible strategies; but it's easy to forget that a precise objective is as important as anything else. Some advertising problems may sharply define your objective, others will be looser, and, if you're working on ads for your portfolio, you'll have no objective whatsoever until you give yourself one.

A hearty endorsement—"This product is good, so buy it now"—might feel sufficiently precise. But unless you're creating reminder advertising, whose purpose may simply be to wave hello to the consumer, your advertising objective should be as specific as possible—utterance, not gesture. Otherwise you'll create advertising whose effectiveness can't be determined, partly because you've never asked what it ought to be doing.

> "There is nothing worse than a sharp image of a fuzzy concept."
>
> —ANSEL ADAMS, photographer

So what's a good objective? That's obvious: one that solves your advertising problem. What's your advertising problem? That's often not so obvious, but it is something your research should suggest. Information about consumer behavior, target market, product, and position in the marketplace—all the issues this book has been discussing—should be coming together to indicate what your advertising needs to do.

Maybe your client's product is new, so you need to generate awareness. Maybe the product isn't new, but it's got new, more convenient packaging or better flavor, so communicating that becomes your objective. Perhaps the product is on the downhill slope of its product life cycle, and you're trying to reverse its direction, or at least slow the slide, by proposing new uses, as Arm & Hammer did for its baking soda—encouraging consumers to put it in the refrigerator, sprinkle it on the carpet, use it on insect bites, on their toothbrush, in the washer, in the cat litter, and so on.

Maybe the market has leveled off, and you're trying to expand it, which is what diamond merchants did by introducing the diamond right-hand ring, meant to be a gift a woman gives herself for her accomplishments. This added another diamond to married women's fingers and raised the prestige—and price—of what had been called a cocktail ring. Maybe you want to change attitudes about your client's brand or product category (see figs. 6.1 and 6.2). Perhaps the client faces heavy competition, so you must communicate product superiority—by announcing a unique feature or creating a differential via a distinct brand image. Or you're targeting new markets, so you must create ads that speak their language and bind your client's product to their needs.

Who can say what your objective should be? That comes only from intelligent, creative analysis of everything in the product's force field. It's complicated, but you need to become simple and single-minded; distill all that you've learned into one advertising objective. Just what, exactly, do you want to communicate?

6.1. When Schwinn's product quality went south, the company needed to admit it. Casting the apology into tough talk and bike metaphor gave Schwinn an attitude that suggested they really had fixed their bikes.

6.2. L.L.Bean, known for its winter-worthy, no-nonsense clothing and gear, wants to be known for other seasons, too. Good use of opposition in the headline.

What one thing do you want the consumer to believe, or understand, or feel, or do about the product? Unless you focus on a specific objective, your ads will suffer from blurriness. Be an arrow, not an ink blot. As Norman Berry, executive vice president of Ogilvy & Mather, put it: "Vague strategies inhibit. Precise strategies liberate."[1]

Developing the creative brief

In its shortest form, your creative brief needs to answer just three questions:

What benefit are you promising, what's your selling argument?

Who are you making it to?

Why should they believe you?

And you can put that in a sentence or two:

Ads will target environmentally conscious users of household cleaners and persuade them that Murphy's Oil Soap cleans thoroughly without damaging the environment. Support will be that it contains no harsh detergents or alkalis: it's 100 percent pure vegetable oil.

Ads will target upscale women, ages 22 to 32, and persuade them that Limited Express clothing will help make them successful, professionally and socially. Support will be the creation of a brand personality: fashion-forward, self-confident, hip.

Typically, however, ad agencies flesh this out into a page or two, and so can you. Creative briefs often cover these areas:

Key Insight	These combine to
Advertising Problem	tell you what your
Advertising Objective	ads need to do.
Target Consumer	
Competition	These focus
Key Consumer Benefit	your approach.
Support	

The following sections explore each area.

KEY INSIGHT

Bill Westbrook, when he was corporate creative director at Earle Palmer Brown, began each of his creative briefs with "a single-minded statement that sorts out from all the information about product, market, competition, etc., the element that is the most relevant to advertising."[2] Many advertising strategists agree. Begin your strategic thinking by looking for the key fact or key insight (think of it as an Aha! moment). Why? Because it will cast the light by which to see the advertising problem you must solve.

Westin's "Heavenly Bed," for example, is an idea central to the hotel's advertising. It came about, says Tom Kelley, chief executive officer of design firm IDEO, after anthropologists (yes, they work in advertising and design, too) discovered that the bed was the problem hiding in plain sight for hotels.[3] If the bed's the problem, make the bed the solution, so all Westin visitors experience the now-iconic "heavenly" beds, pillows, and bedding.

Since the key fact can be less than obvious, or there can be several key facts, finding the advertising problem they point to can be tricky. The creative brief helps you think things through.

ADVERTISING PROBLEM

"We spend more time finding out what the problem is than we spend solving it. Most designers skip the 'identify-the-problem' step, they're so bristling with solutions, like puppies leaking everywhere."
    —STEPHEN DOYLE, Drenttel Doyle Partners

"People who think advertising is about writing good ads will be disappointed. Advertising is about solving problems for clients."
    —SUSAN GILLETTE, president,
    DDB Needham, Chicago

Once you've located that key fact or insight, what is it telling you? What is the product's biggest consumer-related problem? Let's say you're trying to get people, especially young people, to stop smoking. One key fact is that telling people that cigarettes are bad, which stop-smoking advertising has done for years, doesn't work. People know cigarettes are harmful, and still they smoke. Teenagers, especially, find authoritarian injunctions counterproductive. Telling them not to do something is often encouragement enough to do it. So the insight, the Aha! moment, from the American Legacy Foundation and its agency partners—Arnold Worldwide and Crispin Porter + Bogusky—was to give young people another authority figure against whom to rebel: Big Tobacco. The argument of the **truth**®

6.3. Ironies of tobacco industry malpractice were highlighted in the fictional (but factual) upside-down Crazyworld. Said Mike Howard, one of its creators, "With the Crazyworld campaign, we wanted to leverage [teen-agers' strong sense of right and wrong] and show young people a world in which most business-es are held to one set of rules and standards, while Big Tobacco operates in a parallel universe in which their actions are relatively devoid of consequence."

youth smoking prevention campaign became, then, not "Stop smoking" but "Don't Let Big Tobacco Get You." Cigarettes aren't the enemy as much as are to-bacco's corporate honchos who play people for suck-ers by telling them lies. In other words, the strategy is to make Big Tobacco the bad guy, not cigarettes or parents

A related insight is that if cigarette brands are cool,

truth better be cool, too.[4] And so it is. Crazyworld, one of many creative executions from the **truth** cam-paign, posits a world gone mad, where up is down and wrong is right, as a symbol of the "logic" of to-bacco advertising (fig. 6.3).[5] Another creation, Shards O' Glass, a faux company satirizing cigarette manu-facturers, claims on its website, "Our goal is to be the most responsible, effective and respected developer of glass shard consumer products intended for adults. Our Shards O' Glass Freeze Pops are the nation's top-selling frozen treats containing glass shards. Little wonder, considering all we put into them! . . . And remember, Shards O' Glass Freeze Pops are for adults only." (See fig. 6.4 for two ads from a campaign using the theme line "Infect the knowledge. Spread **truth**.")

ADVERTISING OBJECTIVE

Given the problem, what should your objective be? What effect do you want to have on the consumer? An advertising objective is really a communication objective: what you want people to understand, believe, or feel about the product. (You can't set marketing tasks for yourself—like improving sales by 20 percent—since these can be realized only by the entire marketing effort operating in an economic climate, not by advertising alone.)

For example, American Standard, makers of toilets and sinks, faced this problem: a marketplace misperception was limiting sales. "We had to make this product seem not-so-standard. A lot of people felt American Standard was fine for airport restrooms, but not for 'my house.' It wasn't considered special," explains Kerry Casey, Carmichael Lynch's executive creative director.[6] The advertising objective became to persuade consumers that American Standard cared about bathrooms—their bathrooms. The ads Carmichael Lynch created were witty and beautiful and featured great-looking bathroom fixtures, all to change that marketplace perception of the brand (see fig. 6.5).

TARGET AUDIENCE

To whom do you want to communicate this message? Which product users will you target? Define the target audience more specifically than simply demographically, just with numbers. What about psychographics—lifestyle and attitudes? Can you create a profile of the consumer you're addressing?

6.4. This idea—an ad within an ad (an ad that's a photograph of magazines opened to magazine ads)—encouraged teens to remove the ads from magazines and put them in public places or to do what the photographs suggest: go to newsstands themselves and open magazines to these **truth** spreads. In effect, the campaign said to teens, "Do something with this; pass it on." These ads, created by Arnold DC in 2001, are an early instance of interactive print. The agency often considered the work to be a "viral" campaign before "viral" became a marketing tactic.

6.5. Personifying the bathroom made American Standard very much at home in many customers' houses.

IT'S SEEN YOU
NAKED
IT'S HEARD YOU
SING

Your bathroom probably knows more about you than your own mother. So it's only fitting you make it the most wonderful room in the house. Call us and we'll send you a free guidebook overflowing with products, ideas and inspiration. 1-800-524-9797. *American Standard*

COMPETITION

Where does your client's product fit in the marketplace? How is the product perceived now, and how do you want it to be perceived? What product category should it compete in? Who are its competitors, both direct and indirect? Assess their strengths and weaknesses.

Graceann Bennett, managing partner/director of strategic planning at Ogilvy Chicago, believes that "at the root of every game-changing idea is a good enemy" and that "great brands push against something." She suggests using this three-part planning sequence to help you think your way toward an advertising strategy: First, what idea or circumstance is your client's brand pushing against or should it push against? Second, what, as a consequence, should the brand stand for? And third, can you create for this stance a succinct call to arms? She gives these examples:[7]

Target
Up against: You have to be rich to afford good design.
Stands for: Democratization of design.
Expression: "Design for all."

Nike
Up against: There are real athletes and the *rest* of us.
Stands for: There's an athlete in each of us.
Expression: "Just do it."

Bennett's agency was responsible for Dove's Campaign for Real Beauty, created to move Dove from the soap category to the beauty category, the strategy being to position the brand against the rigid and often painful definition of female beauty created over the decades. Here is how Dove's argument breaks out:

Up against: The overall beauty category claim: "You are broken, and we will fix you," which has lowered women's self-esteem.
Stands for: Widening the definition of beauty.
Expression: Real beauty comes in all shapes, sizes, and colors.

You certainly don't have to use Bennett's three-part approach to strategy, but it's an interesting variant on positioning and may help you find your way. Try it and see.

KEY CONSUMER BENEFIT

If the objective is what you want to happen, the benefit sees it from the target audience's point of view. What benefit does the product deliver; what problem will it solve?

Here is how Evan Fry, co-founder of Victors & Spoils, sees the brief, especially this part of it: "I like a simple brief; one page. Personally I like to frame it as, what's the one thing you'd like the target [to] take away from seeing the finished work? I like that question because it keeps people on track and, oddly, it frees you up. It forces you to think about [the consumer's] mindset. It's an efficient question."[8]

SUPPORT

Now, prove it. If you promise a benefit, what's your evidence? Support that claim.

Sometimes creative briefs also address two other areas. They include a tone statement, explaining the feel the ad writer envisions for the campaign. Whimsical, no-nonsense, aggressively competitive, off the wall? Voice and tone are crucial. What's best for the product, target audience, and advertising problem?

Creative briefs may also identify mandatories and limitations. For example, Bill Westbrook includes in his creative strategy "any restrictions or client data which are necessary to a clear understanding of creative direction including legal cautions, carry-over of a successful slogan, items of line to feature, type of casting acceptable and corporate tags."[9] Usually you cannot simply start over with a clean slate but must deal with advertising and branding constraints already in place. Taking the advertising in the direction you want it to go without rupturing current consumer perceptions in the process, making the transition toward your goals a seamless one, is often your real-world task.

Try to say all this in one page. Remember that the essence of your brief is simply:

What benefit are you proposing?
To whom?
Why should they believe you?

The categories above suggest areas to cover, but there's no one way to write a brief, except thoughtfully. The creative brief below, written for a diamond ad campaign, demonstrates one method of organizing the material.

Figure 6.6 shows two of the ads created from this brief. Christopher Cole, its art director, says, "Mark [copywriter Mark Wegwerth] and I focused on talking to men from a man's point of view. Up to that point most ads for engagement rings would talk to men, but from the woman's point of view. Both Mark and I had purchased engagement rings within a year of making these ads, so we were very much in the frame of mind of the target audience."[10]

CREATIVE BRIEF[11]

Client: **Diamonds Direct**

What is the business objective?
To source a greater share of business from local competitive jewelers—both big-box retailers and specialty stores—in shopping malls.

How can advertising help accomplish this objective?
By demonstrating that Diamonds Direct is a prestigious jeweler that sells quality engagement rings at a reasonable price.

Who is the target consumer?
Men who are getting married for the first time.
Age: 23–32

Buying an engagement ring is one of the larger purchases a man will make. His future wife, her family, and friends will evaluate him based on the choice he makes. This leads to fear that he will make a mistake. At this stage of life most men do not have a great deal of disposable income, so they do not want to pay too much.

Getting a good deal will also mean he will have more money available to purchase a larger, higher-quality stone, which will in turn impress his mate. The fear of paying too much for a ring is potent, in some cases more potent than the fear of choosing the wrong ring.

Men will typically talk to friends and family, research diamond quality and contemporary ring designs, and, having settled on a type of ring they want to buy, will then factor in cost as part of their decision-making process. A premium-quality diamond jeweler that promises the right ring for less than its competitors would be a welcome ally in the process that men navigate when purchasing an engagement ring.

What do we want them to know about us?
That Diamonds Direct has high-quality engagement rings at a price they're prepared to pay.

Why will they believe this is true?
Diamonds Direct is not part of a large retail chain located in a shopping mall, so they can sell their product with less mark-up than their competitors.

6.6. Funny, simple, and painfully true. Other headlines were "Asking her used to be the hard part" and "Maybe commitment isn't what men are afraid of."

As David Fowler, executive creative director at Ogilvy & Mather, points out, "It is infinitely helpful to realize that in advertising, as in life, there is no grand map that everyone is privy to except you. We are all muddling forward, through the fog."[12]

Nonetheless, it can help to see the maps with which agencies have "muddled forward." Here is one from Goodby, Silverstein & Partners:

1. Why are we advertising at all?
2. What is the advertising trying to do?
3. Who are we talking to?
4. What do we know about them that will help us?
5. What is the main thought we need to communicate?
6. What is the best way of achieving this?
7. How do we know we're saying the right things in the right way?
8. Executional guidelines.

The Richards Group has used a similar sequence for its briefs:

1. Why are we advertising?
2. Who are we talking to?
3. What do they currently think?
4. What would we like them to think?
5. What is the single most persuasive idea we can convey?
6. Why should they believe it?
7. Are there any creative guidelines?[13]

Final advice

"The quality of the solution depends entirely on how well you state the problem."
—CRAIG FRAZIER, illustrator/designer

Sometimes creative people mistakenly think that the brief is at best a perfunctory outline, a simple condensation of the obvious, and at worst a straitjacket against good ideas. But neither is true. The genuine complexities of the marketplace are what make this strategic document so essential, and they're also why thinking one through requires intelligence and marketing savvy.

PART TWO
EXECUTION

"The truth isn't the truth until people believe you; and they can't believe you if they don't know what you're saying; and they can't know what you're saying if they don't listen to you; and they won't listen to you if you're not interesting. And you won't be interesting unless you say things freshly, originally, imaginatively."

—WILLIAM BERNBACH,
founding partner, Doyle Dane Bernbach

You've done your homework: you now know your client's brand inside out, the strengths and weaknesses of the competition, and where everybody fits in the marketplace. You've studied the target consumers, too—their wants and needs—and translated product features into meaningful benefits. You've examined the kinds of strategies available to you and formulated your own. You know what argument you're making, to whom, and why. In short, you're as armed and loaded as you're ever going to get. Now it's time to put that hard-earned creative brief into play. It's time to create eye-popping, drop-dead ads. How to do so?

7 · Telling Stories

Stories are the most basic tool for connecting us to one another. . . . People attend, remember, and are transformed by stories, which are meaning-filled units of ideas, the verbal equivalent of mother's milk.

—MARY PIPHER, clinical psychologist

The human brain is hard-wired to turn information into narrative: heroes, villains, victims, plots, solutions.

—CARL POPE, executive director of the Sierra Club

As an advertising writer, you will often be called a brand's storyteller, and for good reason. People need narratives to make sense of their lives, to shape experience so that it means something instead of nothing. Because stories testify to what people believe, they like to hear them over and over. And brand stories matter as much as any others; in a consumer culture they may matter even more.

Uncover the story

Once you think of yourself as a brand's storyteller, then all your product research is less to find stray factoids than to dig into that brand's history and reason for being, the narrative that accompanies it. Starting out, you may not know what that story is. Or it may have gotten buried, chopped up, skewed, or lost over the years. But in your research you'll discover a story worth telling. And what you learn will give you more than enough details to fill that story in and carry it forward.

What's a story?

Let's unpack *story*, a term that gets tossed around without much agreement on what it means. A story is a narrative, a series of events that happen over time to someone or to a number of someones; it is character(s) in action. A story is not just a product differential or marketplace position or brand raison d'être. It may use these to create stories, stories may be hidden inside these things, but "The only pain reliever with Xylocaine" is not itself a story. It's a differentiating

product spec. BMW's "The ultimate driving machine" isn't a story either, just a slogan, a positioning statement. It's a claim that stories might prove, though, and stories have done just that. One of the renowned early forms of branded entertainment was *The Hire*, a series of short movies starring Clive Owen as The Driver. Each movie put a BMW through a lot of hard driving inside a mysterious, fast-moving tale. The movies turned the slogan from just a claim into action that proved the claim. (See fig. 7.1 for another selling argument transformed into a story.)

What are a story's elements?

As you remember from fiction or film classes, *stories*— novels, short stories, movies—have parts: plot, characters, setting, theme, symbols, style, and point of view. Each can play a role in the meaning of your brand; each can prove instrumental in how your brand enters consumers' minds and stays there. Let's examine them one at a time.

PLOT

More than just a story, what you're really looking for is the *plot* of the story. Here's a famous distinction between the two:

"The king died and then the queen died" is a story. "The king died and then the queen died of grief" is a plot.

—E. M. FORSTER, *Aspects of the Novel*[1]

Plot is a story's engine: it drives events by transforming chronology into drama. And *conflict* drives plot: someone wants something, and another person or force stands in the way. The protagonist has an antagonist. Conflict is how any story moves forward.

What conflict is inherent in your brand? From what struggle did it emerge? Or from what struggle does it rescue people? In short, what's its plot? (See fig. 7.2.)

How many plots are there?

Joseph Campbell, in *The Hero With a Thousand Faces*, thought there was only one: the quest, in which "A hero ventures forth from the world of common day into a region of supernatural wonder: fabulous forces are there encountered and a decisive victory is won: the hero comes back from this mysterious adventure with the power to bestow boons on his fellow man."[2] (See fig. 7.3.)

Robert McKee, screenwriting teacher, agrees:

In essence we have told one another the same tale, one way or another, since the dawn of humanity, and that story could be usefully called *the Quest*. All stories take the form of a Quest. For better or worse, an event throws a character's life out of balance, arousing in him the conscious and/or unconscious desire for that which he feels will restore balance, launching him on a Quest for his Object of Desire against forces of antagonism (inner, personal, extra-personal). He may or may not achieve it. This is story in a nutshell.[3]

Six durable plotlines

If one story seems too few, here are basic plots you may also remember from literature classes (notice how each, in its way, is a quest). One of them might already be or could become the driver of your client's brand. (Please forgive the sexism of "man" in what follows. "People" won't work, nor will flip-flopping "man" and "woman." I'm stuck with "man," I'm afraid. Apologies all around.)

1. Man against nature. People need help just to survive. Lots of help. Insurance companies defend people from life's ill winds: hurricanes, tornadoes, fires, and floods. All outdoor gear (The North Face, Patagonia, Timberland, Coleman, Nike ACG) helps people prevail against the wilderness; the enemy is mountain terrain or river ice or some other obstacle out there, even rain (headline on a Rockport hiking

7.1. eCampus.com claims that it sells "Textbooks and stuff. Cheap," a solid selling argument. How can it become a story instead of just a claim? By finding someone who hasn't heard of the company but needs it, then playing out the consequences. Here a college student, desperate for money, goes to the usual source: his parents. But the twist is that . . . well, you'll see.

Ⓢ Watch the TV spot at fig. W-7.1.

The images show an eight-panel storyboard:

1.
2. FROST BANK
GREW UP IN TEXAS.
3. WE WERE RAISED ON
TEXAS VALUES.
4.
5. RESEARCH SUGGESTS
THAT OUR WAY OF BANKING
6. MAY NOT WORK EVERYWHERE.
7.
8. Frost Bank
WE'RE FROM HERE.

7.2. Every plot needs a villain. Here the villain is New York City itself. The bank's friendly representative faces indifference, impatience, even hostility as he tries simply to engage people in conversation. What better way to dramatize the down-home qualities of Frost Bank, and, by implication, Texas's values against those of the urban East, than with this fellow, shunned for being friendly?

Watch the TV spot at fig. W-7.2.

IF THEY CAN FLY IN IT, YOU CAN HUNT IN IT.

AMMUNITION THAT WORKS AS HARD AS YOU DO.

A day like this will have most hunters hunting for the next bowl game on television.   Leaving the two of you with all the birds.

7.3. My father raised bird dogs and hunted pheasants. Had he seen this ad, he would have recognized himself in it—a perfect moment in a small, but true, variant of the quest of the hero.

boot ad: "We could make them less expensive. God could make rain less wet"). Land Rover's story has always been man, elegantly equipped, against nature (fig. 7.4). Three prints ads demonstrate the brand's argument:

> Remember the $34,000 you were saving for a rainy day? (Range Rover in the rain)
>
> Who says you can't buy your way out of trouble? (Range Rover climbing a rocky hill)
>
> It gives new meaning to the term upward mobility. (Range Rover going up a 45-degree incline)

But beyond outdoor challenges, think of basic needs like food, shelter, clothing, and protection against disease and infirmities of all sorts. People live inside an all-too-permeable—and vulnerable—skin.

Does your brand save people from an otherwise harsh, short life? Tell that story.

2. Man against society. Things didn't get easier once people came in out of the rain. Society creates its own kind of rain. Has your brand helped people triumph over communal and cultural difficulties? Has it gone up against misguided societal assumptions? Dove's Real Beauty campaign, for example, fought against this culture's rigid, unrealistic stereotypes of what women should look like. Even as in-

If you can't swim, drive.

DISCOVERY

LAND-ROVER

THE ALL NEW DISCOVERY SERIES II

7.4. Another Range Rover ad with a similar visual says, "We brake for fish."

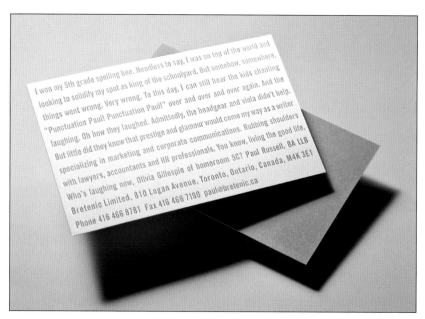

7.5. A marketing writer tells his man-against-society backstory—or, in this case, child against elementary school. Conflict leads to sweet revenge.

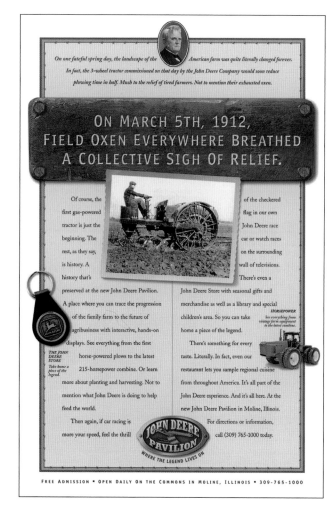

7.6. The John Deere Company has, well, John Deere behind it, an innovative fellow with interesting stories to tell. This one's about the commissioning of the first three-wheel tractor.

nocuous a brand as Tupperware countered society's notion of how and where to sell things, introducing home parties as stores—a pioneering use of social networking—and women as income-earning business people—an early moment in the story of women's liberation. (For another example, see fig. 7.5.)

Many brand stories use a subset of man-against-society: **the man or woman who saw (or the brand that saw) things differently.** Tell the founding myth about the person who created the brand in order to eliminate a societal blind spot or improve upon "it's always been done this way" thinking. King Camp Gillette, who in 1901 founded—what else?—The Gillette Safety Razor Company, fought against the assumption that shaving blades had to be permanent, which meant that, when dull, they had to be taken to a sharpener. Considering this a waste of time, he invented the world's first disposable blade. Ever since, Gillette's story has been how their research-and-development wizards keep gaining the edge over people's recalcitrant beards, body hair, and bad ideas, one shaver after another, many named futuristically: Atra, Trac II, Sensor, Fusion, Mach 3.[4] (See fig. 7.6 for the tale of another man who saw things differently.)

3. Man against man. The duel, the conflict between the hero (protagonist) and his enemy (antagonist), drives many stories. Pepsi was created to counter Coca-Cola's market stranglehold and has been locked in combat with it ever since. Apple computers go head to head with PCs; recent advertising personified the competition as two fellows—the cool

Apple guy one-upping the bumbling, pretentious (but envious) PC guy. Insurance companies like to talk about fighting against double-dealing competitors, the red-tape guys (the headline on a Liberty Mutual ad showing a storm-damaged house: "In the history of repairs, red tape has yet to fix anything."). Lawyers tell similar stories. Can you make, has the brand made, the struggle against a villain its story?

This category also has a subset, one that could be called **The Little Engine That Could** or **David and Goliath**. You know these plots. There are lots of little-engines-that-could whose stories need telling (VW Beetle and Avis famously developed two such story-lines). More recently, MINI and Smart Car have seen themselves as David to most other cars' Goliath. Microbreweries happily bring slingshot and stone to the fight against beer behemoths. If your brand is the "little guy," tell its story. People are in your corner already.

4. Man against himself. Isn't much of life a war within? People wrestle with their own inner demons: sloth, ignorance, gluttony, anger, insecurity, any of a multitude of bêtes noires. They fight to lose weight or gain peace or quit yelling or get smarter or learn to love or . . .

Crispin Porter + Bogusky created advertising for Domino's Pizza that grappled with a difficult truth: Domino's made a lousy pizza. The campaign showed the chefs and everybody else going to war (against their former selves and ways) to build a better pizza. Ads featured disaffected consumers being surprised at their doors by pizza-bearing delivery guys who wanted them to try Domino's again. The Domino's attack on itself is a bold stroke, and not a common one, but there is a story waiting to be told every time a brand utters the phrase "new and improved."

Think of the things created and sold to save people from themselves. Perhaps your client's brand intends to do that or already does. If so, tell the stories of people's inner weaknesses or demons and the deliverance the brand offers. (See fig. 7.7 for whimsical takes on one of man's wars with himself.)

5. Man against machine. Apple was "the computer for the rest of us." Prior to Apple, computers were either huge, incomprehensible things whirring away inside business empires or else smaller but no more friendly beasts. Apple shrank the big ones, demystified the rest, gave them a human touch ("hello," the first Mac screen said in cursive script), and ushered computers into people's homes and lives. Initially, Apple was the protagonist against IBM and other corporate

monoliths. Now, as Apple has broadened into many consumer electronics, it's Apple against technological difficulty, Apple against the status quo.

OXO designs kitchen and household tools that are easier to use ("Tools you hold on to"). That's a product differential, not a story, but there are stories inside it. People's battles with kitchen tools and themselves are endless: hands too little or too big, left-handedness in a right-handed world, peelers that don't, graters that won't. The brand's plot is partly man versus himself (his inadequate reach), but mostly it's man against machine. OXO asks the basic questions: why should our tools hurt our hands, and why don't they work better? Fittingly, OXO began when its originator, Sam Farber, watched his wife, Betsey, who had arthritis, struggle with kitchen tools. The brand was born in pain.

What damnable machine or technological mess is making life more difficult than it should be, and is your client's brand the solution? Tell that story.

6. Man against fate. Are people destined to spend their years in penury and despair? No, they are not. Self-help organizations, lawyers, financial services, government, religion, and education all promise to help people change destiny's big picture. State lotteries offer people a long-shot chance to defy fate. Lots of branded things have gone to war against the ravages of time and chance. Can people beat cosmic forces? They can try. Maybe your client's brand can help.

How many plots are there, really?

Although the six plot lines just discussed cover a lot of ground, how many plots there are is anyone's guess. Many durable stories come from myth and folklore and include Killing the Beast, the Ugly Duckling, and the dark stories gathered by the Brothers Grimm, including Cinderella, Hansel and Gretel, Rapunzel, Snow White, and Little Red Riding Hood. All such tales tap into deep human impulses and needs, which is why they've been told and retold over time.

Your job is to find new particulars in old stories. David Fowler, executive creative director at Ogilvy & Mather, New York, advises, "Instead of just writing ads, stop and think about the story you want to tell. Consider how others have told it before you. Then tell it once more, new."[5]

CHARACTER

Many brands have CEOs, founding mothers and fathers, a family or group who created the thing. Many of these characters, long dead, live on through brand

7.7. Conserving water is something people know they should do but often don't—conscience losing to habit. How to convince people to win this inner battle? Deliver the argument lightly, as do these short stories—quick little sketches with characters, setting, and plot. They say serious things unseriously, a smart way to get people to listen to difficult truths. In the first two spots, grass proves how dumb it is by failing to recognize a distinctive sound and by failing to recognize an unusual water source. In the second two ads, flowers show what happens when they've had a little too much water.

🅢 To watch the four TV spots, go to fig. W-7.7.

names: Schick, Sears, Ben & Jerry's, Schlitz, Heinz, Bausch and Lomb.

Ma Boyle, the president of Columbia sportswear, has been turned into a character. Perdue chicken for decades used the cranky old chicken farmer himself, Frank Perdue ("It takes a tough man to make a tender chicken"), to personify the rigor of that brand's approach to raising chickens.

If the people behind a brand are quirky or significant, let them help tell its story. Two brands of ice cream in my town differentiate themselves by means of the people behind them. Graeter's ice cream has been hand made by the Graeter family since they emigrated to Cincinnati from Bavaria in the mid-1800s. The brand's website and posters on the walls of their stores tell me all about the French pot process, the hand churning, and the original market at the foot of Sycamore Hill. Another brand of ice cream, Jeni's, has Jeni Britton Bauer behind it, a young woman whose art school background has found expression in her designer ice creams (Vanilla Cedar Wood, Goat Cheese with Cognac Figs, and Sweet Corn & Black Raspberries, among other unusual flavors). Here is a bit of Jeni's voice and mission from the brand's website, Jeni's Splendid Ice Creams:

> We create ice creams we fall madly in love with, that we want to bathe in, that make us see million-year-old stars. We devour it out of Mason jars, coffee mugs—whatever we can get our hands on. Handmade American ice cream = Bliss with a big B. Every single thing we put in our ice cream is legit. Generic chemist-built ice cream bases and powdered astronaut-friendly gelato mixes? No, ma'am. We build every recipe from the ground up with luscious, Snowville milk and cream from cows that eat grass. With that exquisite base, we explore pure flavor in whatever direction moves us at any moment, every day, all year.

See figure 7.8 for the Web page itself.

Both brands interest consumers in who is behind them. People think of these founders when they think of their ice cream. And since the founders have become characters, their stories give the brands life. Are there characters who, in telling your brand's story, can become part of it (see fig. 7.9)?

SETTING

Setting is a powerful force in many novels and films;

7.8. Jeni tells about her ice cream—how it's made, who makes it, and what binds her crew together. Quirky details and a singular voice combine to differentiate the brand.

think of Joseph Conrad's jungle in *Heart of Darkness*, the moors in Emily Bronte's *Wuthering Heights* and Arthur Conan Doyle's *The Hound of the Baskervilles*, the apocalyptic landscape in Cormac McCarthy's *The Road* (both his book and the movie). Place can exert the force of character.

Is the "where" of your brand important to its story? It is to Hewlett-Packard. The garage in which HP was founded is a legend told and retold by HP itself. It is to Pepperidge Farm, which started in Margaret Rudkin's kitchen on her family property in Fairfield, Connecticut. Decades of advertising have created of it a mythical place, a pre-mass-merchandised Eden in which white, horse-drawn wagons and old-timey trucks drive the bread to market. Corny? Yes. Comforting? Also yes. Would you want a hip, "edgy" bread? (See figs. 7.10 and 7.11 for two more brands whose stories involve place.)

STYLE

Style is the brand's voice. Every powerful brand comes wrapped in a distinctive one. (See chapter 9 for how to develop voice.)

7.9. The U.S. space program has been a hero's quest if ever there was one. How to tell the story? Find the characters who shape its themes, then use paradox to draw readers in.

SYMBOLISM

A *symbol* is a central image or thing in which is condensed much of a story's meaning (symbols in literature, we remember, include such items as Ahab's whale, Hester's "A," T. J. Eckleburg's billboard eyes in *The Great Gatsby,* and the lighthouse in Virginia Woolf's *To the Lighthouse*). Symbols in brands include things as various as Prudential's Rock of Gibraltar, the red umbrella of Travelers insurance, Nike's swoosh, the little bluebird of Twitter, and Dos Equis beer's "The Most Interesting Man in the World"—each of which carries much of the brand's meaning in compressed form. So, too, do a brand's color palette, typography, and every other aspect of its graphic presentation.

As a writer, you'll watch those graphic decisions being made by the visual thinkers you're working with more than you'll make them yourself. But you'll be expected to be a good critic and occasionally a direct contributor. You'll certainly be expected to put language up against visual ideas.

Find one central image around which to wrap the story

Brand strategist Tom Himpe gives this advice (he's talking about stunts, but his advice applies to storytelling):

> Another crucial element in making sure the media picks up a story is imagery. . . . Images condense all dramatic elements around a theme into one striking visual that invites the viewer to read about it. In terms of PR, imagery is the easy way into a story, making even the least accessible and most difficult stories attractive to a wide group of people. . . . The more complex and unattractive the story, the more important it is to try and speak the visual language that everyone understands.[6]

Greenpeace is good at doing this, Himpe says, creating dramatic and memorable visuals by placing their little rubber boats up against much larger tankers and Navy vessels. It's the story of David and Goliath.

What condensed image might contain your client's brand story? (Watch a sign become a symbol in fig. 7.12.) An image containing elements in tension—for example, Greenpeace's big versus little—is probably strongest because it expresses a conflict.

POINT OF VIEW

Point of view in film and literature means the literal point of view (first, second, third, limited, omniscient) from which the story is told. You can apply the term in similar ways to brand stories. What is the authorial point of view toward the product, its benefits, its audience? Most advertising uses first person ("we," "our") and second person ("you," "your") to keep things personal, the essential relationship being expressed in this sentence structure: "We, the brand, speak warmly with you, the consumer, about your needs and how we can fulfill them." But speakers for brands are increasingly consumers themselves. Their points of view help shape the brand's point of view. That's one reason many brand voices sound identical to the voices of their core consumers.[7] (See fig. 7.13 for an ironic use of the consumer's point of view.)

THEME

Theme is the brand's core argument for itself, its position or differential (BMW's "The ultimate driving machine"). The stories inside that theme, which is often lodged in the slogan, are what advertisers need to tell and encourage consumers to tell. A brand without a theme isn't long for this world.

When you're developing a brand's theme (should that assignment come your way), you need to put the argument on the head of a pin. Study the subtitles of books of narrative nonfiction, which at their best demonstrate the art of a theme concisely and energetically expressed. Here are a few nonfiction titles, followed after the colon by their subtitles:

Always On: How the iPhone Unlocked the Anything-Anytime-Anywhere Future and Locked Us In

The Devil in the White City: Murder, Magic, and Madness at the Fair That Changed America

Brain Bugs: How the Brain's Flaws Shape Our Lives

7.10. This is where Evian's bottled water comes from and how it's created—a dramatic setting and a differentiating story, especially since many competitors simply filter or distill city water.

Here Comes Everybody: The Power of Organizing Without Organizations

Your job, when you work on a brand's theme, is similar to that of book marketers: boil its meaning down into one core proposition—an argument or idea that's different, succinct, and compelling. Given these challenges, why not take a cup of coffee and a notebook to a bookstore?

7.11. The University of San Francisco has much to offer, part of it right there in the name.

7.12. Frost Bank's claim of Texan friendliness is condensed into one simple gesture.

To see the TV spot, go to fig. W-7.12.

Invite your audience to help tell the story

"Instead of trying to manage your company's relationship with its customers and their culture, think instead about being their voice inside the walls of your company."

—ALEX BOGUSKY and JOHN WINSOR

With interactive advertising, your client's brand can create a shape that consumers fill and a storyline that they carry along. Subaru, for example, invites brand loyalists to recount true-life stories about the durability (the brand differential) of Subarus. "Dear Subaru" campaign ads were essentially testimonials in which loyalists shared affectionate, often quirky stories of life with their Subaru. One owner recounted how her car outlasted its key; another owner found the family Subaru surrounded by ten curious goats on a trip through Utah, snapped a picture of the encounter, and thereby created one of the many testimonials in the "Dear Subaru" campaign, whose theme line, appropriately, was "Love. It's what makes a Subaru, a Subaru."

How short can a story be?

Stunningly short, according to this anecdote about Hemingway. When asked to write the shortest story ever, he supposedly jotted on a napkin, "For sale: baby shoes, never worn." Though the anecdote is probably apocryphal, Hemingway did value economy—what he left out of his stories often mattered more than what he put in, and some of his stories say a lot in only a few pages.

Here's another writer who thinks that a story can be stunningly brief:

> We used to tell a story at J. Walter Thompson that illustrates the power of stories. It goes like this: The Amish have an excellent reputation for making top quality products. It so happened that a family in a town close to an Amish community had to find homes for a litter of kittens. They put out a sign that said "FREE KITTENS." For an entire week no one stopped. Then they changed the sign to "FREE AMISH KITTENS." The litter was gone in a day.
> —JAMES PATTERSON, novelist, former chairman, J. Walter Thompson, North America[8]

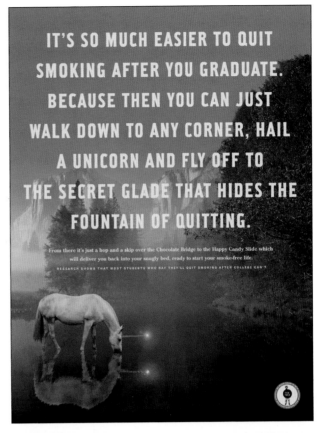

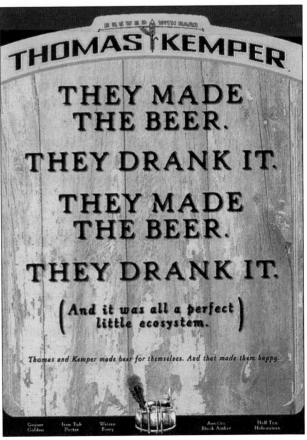

Right top

7.13. This ad satirizes the kinds of stories people, especially college students, tell themselves when they're trying to quit smoking. After the headline, the ad continues, "From there it's just a hop and a skip over the Chocolate Bridge to the Happy Candy Slide which will deliver you back into your snuggly bed, ready to start your smoke-free life," followed by a voice that clears the air: "Research shows that most students who say they'll quit smoking after college can't."

Right

7.14. Repetition announces and enacts this brand's story. By positing two fellows almost reluctant to sell their beer, the ad creates a micro-microbrewery story, neatly summarized at the end: "Thomas and Kemper made beer for themselves. And that made them happy." To buy the beer is to break up this "perfect little ecosystem," of course, so the final argument—and the brand story's subtext—is one's ability to obtain that which is unobtainable. The narrative, smartly conceived and succinctly expressed, creates a strong position in a market filled with microbreweries.

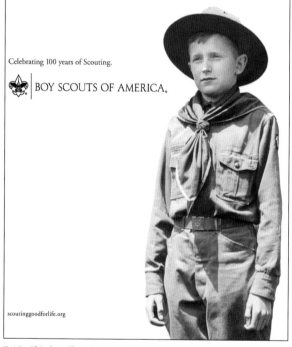

FOR 100 YEARS, OUR NATION HAS STOOD ON THE SHOULDERS OF GIANTS.

TINY, NECKERCHIEFED GIANTS.

Celebrating 100 years of Scouting.

BOY SCOUTS OF AMERICA.

scountinggoodforlife.org

7.15. This headline is a very short story. Or to put it another way, it's like a zipped file: over a century of stories is compressed in it. All a copywriter needs to do is double-click the file.

One word can't quite be a story, but it can suggest one, don't you agree? Reading the word "Amish," people can almost see the life these kittens were born into and the values that surrounded them. Rationally, a kitten's a kitten, but "Amish" carries a lot of freight, implies a lot of backstory. To pick one of those kittens is to take that story home, too. (See figs. 7.14 and 7.15 for other short short stories.)

The power of brand storytelling

I said earlier that brand stories often matter more than other stories in our culture. Natalia Ilyin, designer and writer, explains the role of designers (and copywriters, since they do the same thing with words) in creating these stories:

> As designers, we create ideal mental worlds, inhabitable worlds of imagination, and we make them seem real to everyday people. . . . If we are not actively involved in laying the cozy woolen throw upon the wicker chair [she'd been reading an L.L.Bean catalog, with its myth of the North Woods], we are passively involved. We design the identifiers of the product that lies upon the chair, we design the chair. We are part of the great storytelling machine of our culture. We are not nihilists. We are believers. We push Heaven.[9]

The power of storytelling is immense. Your ability to spot a story, and to tell it, will enrich your work as a copywriter perhaps more than any other skill. Journalist Bill Moyers cast the value of storytelling into long relief: "Once in East Africa, on the shores of an ancient lake, I sat alone and suddenly it struck me what community is. It is gathering around a fire and listening to someone tell us a story."[10]

Find the human story in your brand, tell it, and watch people gather around the fire.

8 · Thinking in Words and Pictures

What I really like to do is have people think, to challenge people. We put the dots out there and you connect the dots. You participate in the advertising, that's what we like to do.
—RICH SILVERSTEIN, co-founder,
Goodby, Silverstein & Partners

Advertising is a relationship between language and imagery: words are tied to pictures. There are complications and exceptions, of course. In TV and video a soundtrack accompanies a series of images. In direct mail and e-mail the words frequently dominate, even exclude, the visuals. And in radio there are no visuals at all (except in listeners' heads, where there can be plenty). But fundamentally, the rhetoric of advertising involves some relationship between showing and saying: show people a picture, moving or still, then say something about it. Or say something, then show a picture about it.

Achieve synergy, not redundancy

Try to create a relationship—tight, almost molecular—between words and pictures. The word *synergy* has been applied to the desired effect between what you say and what you show.[1] (When two or more elements combine to achieve a total effect greater than the sum of their individual effects, they are synergistic; so too are great headline/visual combinations.) Each ad in figure 8.1 shows how its two halves—headline and image—can depend so utterly on each other that neither makes sense by itself, and their combined impact is stronger than a simple totaling of effects.

You can't always write an ad in which word and image depend that completely on each other. But you can avoid the Dumb Ad, which shows something and then says the same thing. Such redundancy flattens ads, makes them boring and too clear, and gives consumers nothing to do but bear up under the repetition. People

don't want to see an ad that says "Giant savings!" and shows a giant-sized product. But if it says "Giant savings!" and shows a little, bitty picture of the product, then things get more interesting, don't they? That's the key principle. Create some tension between word and image.

So get in the habit of asking, "If I say thus and such, what will I show? If I show thus and such, what will I say?" And never content yourself with merely repeating in words what you show. Following this rule isn't easy, but you'll know it when you do. William Butler Yeats talked about the sound a poem makes when it finishes: like a lid clicking shut on a perfectly made box.[2] Your ad should make a similar sound when you get just the right fit between headline and visual.

Let the consumer do some of the work

"In baiting a trap with cheese, always leave room for the mouse."

—HOWARD GOSSAGE, quoting the short story writer Saki

One way to hear box lids shut is to let the consumer do some of the work. The problem with Dumb Ads is that their redundancy belabors the point. Smart ads leave room for consumers to do something, and in the moment when they confront this not-quite-instantaneously-clear ad, they become involved. In figure 8.2, for example, readers look at an apparently incomprehensible headline but then quickly enough resolve it. This little do-it-yourself moment is a kind of pleasure. Readers are being respected for their intelligence and

8.1. Quintessential examples of synergy in a headline/visual. In each ad, the headline and visual depend so much on each other that neither one makes sense by itself.

given a chance to put it into play. They snap the lid shut themselves.

Combine overstatement and understatement

You can create synergy between headline and visual by combining understatement with overstatement. If your visual is wild and obviously excessive, then back off verbally. And vice versa. In other words, don't shout twice. This juxtaposition of loud and soft, big and little, really snaps that box lid shut (fig. 8.3). And it works as well in TV and video as it does in print—run one kind of soundtrack over another kind of imagery. If the car is undergoing a torture test, speak quietly about the "modest testing procedure" or play "Singin' in the Rain."

OVERSTATEMENT

Consumers have been hyped so much ("Greatest offer ever!" "Unbelievable performance!" "Spectacular savings!") that such exaggeration no longer works, if it ever did. But intentional overstatement (hyperbole) can work; it can "prove" the product benefit without your having to prove it, get a laugh or a smile in the process, and create enough ripple on the page or the screen to get consumers' attention.

A law firm wanted to position itself as eager to work for small clients. With the line "No case too small," what to show? How about one of those tags from comforters, blankets, and mattresses—you know, the ones that say, "UNDER PENALTY OF LAW THIS TAG NOT TO BE REMOVED"? That became the whole ad: the torn tag and the line "No case too small." (Notice how

8.2. Leaving room for the mouse: Acela, Amtrak's high-speed rail service, cleverly announces one benefit of getting from point A to point B on the train. The ad puzzles for a moment, and in that moment the reader is caught.

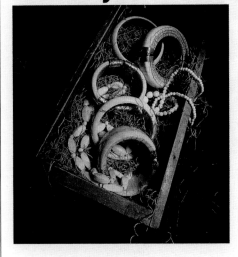

How do you fit five elephants in a box?

First find someone who'll do the killing. Arm him with a machine gun and an axe. Send him off to slaughter elephants. Pay him for the tusks. And ship them away to be carved into bracelets and necklaces.

The African elephant is being driven from the face of the earth for the sake of consumer demand for ivory trinkets. In just 10 years, the population of African elephants has been more than halved. If this rate of killing continues, the African elephant could be extinct in just 25 years. The killers and the people who pay them don't care about elephant deaths. They don't hear the world's outrage. They just want money. They're the people we must stop.

Please join World Wildlife Fund's Elephant Action Campaign. Help us put these killers and the people who finance them out of business. Your donation of $15 or more will help us support increased anti-poaching patrols. And supply equipment to those rangers who are already in the field – desperately trying to stop the sense-less slaughter of one of the world's great species.

Time is running out. 143 African elephants are dying every day. So their tusks can be turned into jewelry. You can stop this. Before it's too late. Call 1-800-453-6100 to make a donation.

8.3. Strong, ironic relationships between headline and visual: one funny, the other tragic.

quiet that headline is.) The ad is funny and persuasive, at least of the law firm's claim to take on small cases. It "proved" the point, without ever getting into the land of belief—or, these days, disbelief.

How to overstate? Find your product's benefit and over-exaggerate it. What's the strongest thing you can think of, especially out of category? Or find its ideal user (or nonuser) and exaggerate him or her. Or find a hyperbolic image or headline for the worst possible consequence of not using the product. Pick the point you want to make and then blow it out the top. Exaggerate that claim to ludicrous extremes. Put your claim or benefit in a "It's so . . . that . . ." or "If it were any more . . . , it would . . ." format, and voila!—there's your hy-

perbole. You can run the exaggeration in your headline or in your image. And once you've shouted, back off in the other half of the ad.

Usually, if not always, you're making a joke and sharing a wink with the consumers. They don't "believe" the claim literally—they're not being asked to—and that's why it works (see figs. 8.4–8.6).

UNDERSTATEMENT

Don't over-exaggerate things; under-exaggerate them. Say or show less than the situation calls for. Consider this example from real life: after a tornado leveled a town, one family spray-painted a sign on the garage door of what was left of their house: "Just another

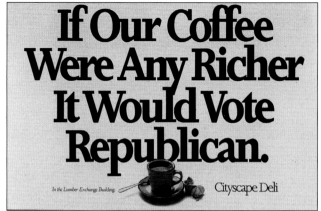

8.4. Exaggeration becomes a kind of truth telling.

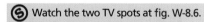

8.5. Whimsical hyperbole: a bottled water becomes its own hors d'oeuvre.

8.6. First Bank's mobile alerts inform customers if there is suspicious activity on their bank accounts. These two TV spots dramatize that benefit by overdramatizing the problem: the "suspicious activity" is both way out of category and over the top. Then the benefit enters quietly, typographically: "Know about trouble before it happens. Mobile Alerts." Nice combination of loud and quiet, crazy and sane.

Ⓢ Watch the two TV spots at fig. W-8.6.

Oh my, no helmet.

BRAIN INJURY ASSOCIATION OF WISCONSIN

8.7. The headline states the last thought that would occur to most people seeing the ad. But because it states the first thought of the ad's speaker, it demonstrates the monomaniac's true belief—and readers find themselves impressed by his conviction. The joke makes its point.

weekend with the grandkids." That's the saving sense of humor in intentional understatement. Do the same thing with your ad: write a dry line that kicks.

How to do it? Give yourself a crazy visual and then ask, "What's the quietest comment I could make about it?" Or if you write an outlandish headline, then undercut it with the visual.

If you start with a visual about which there appears to be only one thing to say, consider saying something else (fig. 8.7). For example, if you're selling dental floss or toothpaste, you may show an old guy with no teeth. But then what to say? The obvious choices would be things like "Do you want to be this guy?" or "Don't let this happen to you!" But they're too obvious. What else could you say? "Relax. Baby food tastes better than it used to." "Think of the time you'll save not chewing." Or "Smile. No more dental bills." If, on the other hand, you show a smiling person with beautiful teeth (probably the visual cliché of the toothpaste genre), provide an alternative meaning: "Too bad he didn't use Crest." And explain in the copy that his teeth only look okay.

Learn to look at any visual and say not the expected thing, but something off to the side, especially something that intersects your client's product or brand.

For more on comic misdirection and the art of the headline, see chapter 16, How to Write a Headline.

Emphasize one idea per ad

Always pick one selling idea and let it dominate the ad. Even though you'll often be tempted, don't try to say several things at once. Your readers or viewers will simply get confused, and you'll dissipate the power of one thought driven home. Chip and Dan

Heath use this metaphor in *Made to Stick*: "When you say three things, you say nothing. When your remote control has fifty buttons, you can't change the channel anymore."[3]

A Vancouver advertising agency, Rethink, provides another helpful metaphor with its "Ping Pong Ball Theory":

It's simple. If we were to throw one ping pong ball at you across a table, you'd probably catch it. If we were to throw five balls at the same time, you probably wouldn't catch any of them. Most advertising messages have at least five ping pong balls. We strive to keep our messages single-focused, with just one ping pong ball per ad. This means there's a far greater likelihood that our message will be seen and absorbed.[4]

You *can* sell more than one idea at a time, if you make them feel like one idea, if you roll them together in the carpet. In the following headline the copywriter connects two different selling ideas —the car is sporty yet sensible—with a psychological metaphor, making two arguments seem like one:

A sports car for both sides of your brain. The half that's seventeen, and the half that's retired and living in Miami. (Subaru SVX)

For years Miller Lite beer promoted itself via the slogan "Tastes great, less filling," attempting in that phrase to say two things at once. Secret deodorant created a theme line that has driven the brand for over fifty years: "Strong enough for a man, but made for a woman." Two ideas again, but rolled together nicely.

The questions are these: do consumers hear you (or are you just making noise)? And do they believe you (or are you claiming too much to be credible)?

How to write a headline

Who knows how you write one besides just basically think it up? I'll give you techniques and suggestions, but finally you're alone inside your own head.

One way to jump-start yourself, though, is to write down in a straightforward way your advertising strategy, the promise you plan to make to the consumer—the benefit(s) of the product, the problem(s) it solves. What's your selling argument? Say it as many ways as you can. This is your starting point, conceptually. These arguments are *what* you want to say; they're probably not *how* you want to say it yet.

You can be wrong at this level (that is, by choosing the wrong strategy), but if you're making the right appeal, then the problem with most of your sentences is that they're not stoppers—they're too flat, too bald, too boring, too blah. No one will be compelled to consider them. So take each one and try to say it another way; spin it sideways, heat it up. Get that idea in readers' faces, push it, use slang, take chances. Wrestle that reasonable idea out of its middle-of-the-roadness and into the ditch. Ogilvy & Mather's Steve Hayden puts it this way: "To me, the secret of advertising is to make an irrational presentation of a rational argument."[5]

The benefit has to be on-strategy, but its expression has to be a little twisted, lateralized, freed from cliché, or made more specific, more interesting. The dead clichés are usually right there in the middle, the first things you think up. Keep going. With this technique you must still supply the necessary wit and ingenuity, of course, but at least you have given yourself a method of operating and clarified your task.

Remember: always try to express the selling promise as a consumer benefit; see it from the consumer's point of view. For example, in a contest for a membership to Scandinavian health spas, the big headline was "Win Yourself a Brand New Body." The smaller subhead explained, "Enter for a Free 1-Year Membership." That's the way to say it. Why sell just a membership when you can express the benefit so much more powerfully? The big promise dominated, as it should, with the subhead or copy clarifying the offer.

As you discover when you work on advertising problems, you often lose the selling idea in the act of trying to express it creatively. There's a continual struggle between being on-strategy and being clever. Each wants to pull you away from the other. Your job as a thinker and problem solver is to keep both in mind, to spin the strategy without losing hold of it. As though to indicate this truth, the two most common rejections of your ideas will be "I don't get it" and "I've seen it before." In other words, it's either too weird or too obvious. That's why the great ones don't come easy.

VISUAL ADVICE

You can show almost anything, of course, but here are the most frequently used visual approaches:

1. Demonstrate the product in use. If it's got some motion or drama, show it (fig. 8.8). Show it being spread on something, handled through the turn, driven into wood, repelling water, or otherwise demonstrating what it does. In an unusual promotion, a detergent brand sent a box of its detergent through the mail, wrapped in a white T-shirt. Recipients were invited to use the detergent to clean the now-dirty T-shirt. Simple and surprising.

2. Show the product itself, unwrapped or still in its package. Great importance rests, in this case, on what you say about the product. One technique is to be metaphorical: talk about the product in terms of something else; express its benefit via language usually associated with something else (see fig. 8.8 again) For a discussion of this popular, powerful headline approach, see chapter 23, Verbal Metaphor.

3. Present a close-up of some critical part of the product. Show the springs on Nike Shox, the three stripes in Aqua-Fresh toothpaste, and so on. This is a sensible strategy for any feature-oriented approach (fig. 8.9).

4. Emphasize a visually interesting aspect of the product story. Maybe it's the unusual plant it's made in, the founding city or founding father or mother, the valley where it's grown, a piece of historical data that captures the consumer's mind and eye.

5. Emphasize not the product but a person connected to it. This person may be a celebrity, an authority figure or expert, someone from history, a pop culture icon, even an invented character like Tony the Tiger or the Keebler elves (see fig. 8.10; see also chapter 19, Testimonials: The Power of Personality, and the voice discussion in chapter 9, Words I: Establishing Voice).

BOILING WATER REMOVES IMPURITIES.
LIKE YOU, FOR EXAMPLE.

8.8. Conveying the motion and drama of the product—in this case, white water rafting. The headline is a terrific example of verbal metaphor, talking about the product in language people associate with other contexts. Another headline in the series: "Water gives life. Occasionally it takes some back."

Italy gave us the Mafia. They also gave us these. Let's call it even.

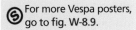

8.9. A Vespa campaign showed cropped shots of the scooter, emphasizing its Italian styling heritage. Great headline, too: "Italy gave us the Mafia. They also gave us these. Let's call it even."

ⓢ For more Vespa posters, go to fig. W-8.9.

6. Highlight the benefit of using the product. Show the payoff, the result, of using the product. Or show the negative consequences of not using the product (see fig. 8.11), usually less clichéd and therefore more interesting.

7. Go a step further and show the lifestyle the product helps create. Beyond the white teeth and smiles there is a desired lifestyle. Show this state of mind, this attitude or way of being that the product engenders. (Or, again, show the unhappy state of mind of the nonuser.) This is a good visual technique for brand-image/lifestyle advertising.

8. Use split-screen imagery. Try this-versus-that: before and after; a comparison with the competition, or among versions of the product itself, or with something unexpected (see chapter 20, Two-Fers).

9. Show not the product but some modification of it, a transformation or metamorphosis that is visually arresting and communicates the selling idea (see fig. 8.12). Or go further and show a metaphor for the product or service, something dissimilar that stands for its benefit. (For further discussion of

He's got user-friendly products.

He's got freezer-space solutions.

He's got nothing on besides
a toque and a handkerchief.

Whenever your needs are, the Doughboy can help. Take, for example, Pillsbury's new Scoop Easy drop Biscuit dough. It saves you time and labor. You just scoop, drop and bake. Best of all, the result looks and tastes just like it was made from scratch. And because Scoop Easy has a five-day refrigerated shelf life, it frees up valuable freezer space. To find out what the Doughboy can do for you, call 1-800-767-5404.

There's a lot the Doughboy can do. (Pillsbury)

8.10. Pillsbury wanted to expand its presence in the food service industry, so it literally walked the Doughboy into a big freezer as a way of saying the company belonged there. The slogan advances the argument: "There's a lot the Doughboy can do."

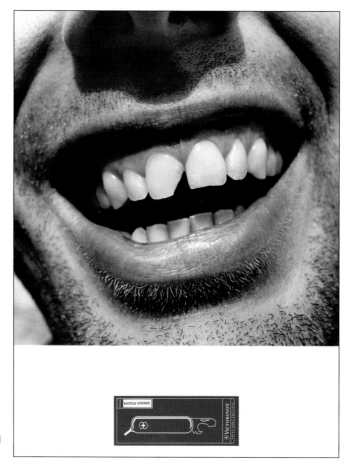

8.11. Demonstrate the benefit of using a product by illustrating the liability of not using it.

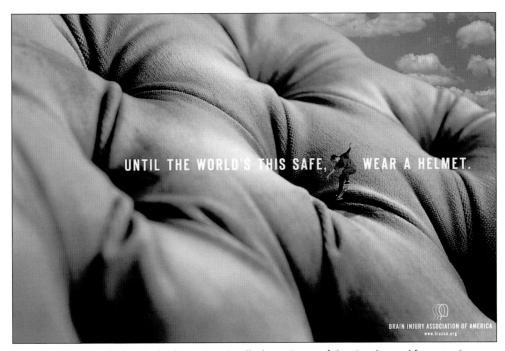

8.12. Metamorphosing the landscape is a visually dramatic way of showing the need for protection.

these techniques, see chapter 22, Visual Metaphor.)

10. Remove rather than add. Crop the image, show only part of the product, boil a complicated narrative down to its simplest aspect, suggest rather than state—reduce, reduce, reduce. That Vespa ad (fig. 8.9) crops a motor scooter. The poster in figure 8.13 crops a play.

11. Show nothing. Use all type instead. If you say it well enough, you're done. Besides, letting the viewer supply the visual leaves room for the mouse. The travel service Expedia.com put up this outdoor board: "Imagine not seeing this ad for two whole weeks."

12. Walk away from the product. While it makes sense to start visual thinking with either the product or its happy user, you can land in Clichéville that way and never get out. Try to walk away from the product—go toward things associated with it, or consequences of it, or conditions that lead to it. Yet another way to leave room for the mouse (see figs. 8.14–8.16).

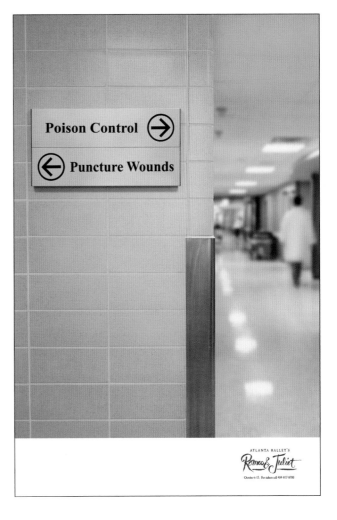

Right
8.13. This ad looks like anything but what it's for. An apparent photo of a hospital hallway, it both crops the play and updates it, moving it out of time and place. Hip humor brings Shakespeare closer to the audience.

WE NOW CARRY BABY PIRANHA.

9218 West Oklahoma   the Fish Factory   Phone 414/546-2201

8.14. More interesting, and more suggestive, than looking at a fish, don't you think?

8.15. One consequence of taking too long a shower.

HEADLINE ADVICE

The best headline ideas will arise out of your own approach, both strategic and visual. Nevertheless, try these suggestions:

1. Consider command headlines. You generate commands by using the imperative form of the verb, with "you" understood: "Join the army"; "Visit the zoo." Commands make readers pay attention because someone is verbally pointing a finger, demanding a response (fig. 8.17). So don't say, "People should discover the Bahamas" or "Discovering the Bahamas." Say, "Discover the Bahamas." Nike didn't say, "Just doing it," did they?

2. Ask questions. "Are your feet happy?" "Have you looked at your wife lately?" Questions have rhetorical power. They come up from the page, out of the radio, or off the screen in a way a statement doesn't, getting in the viewer's face, making the viewer deal with them. When you want a response from someone in conversation, you ask a question. Hey, have you fallen asleep? (See? It works here, too.)

3. Add "how" or "why" to a headline to increase its pull and bond it to the visual.

BLAH:

We put six airbags in the Audi A4.
   (visual of open airbag)

BETTER:

Why we put six airbags in the Audi A4.
   (visual of a loving, happy moment between husband and wife)

"How" and "why" also draw consumers into the ad by promising inside knowledge:

How to tell if your house has termites.

Why you should spend $200,000 on a DePauw education.

4. Let the consumer know, one way or another, "This ad's for you." David Ogilvy once wrote, in his elegance, that a print ad's "headline is 'the ticket on the meat.' Use it to flag down the readers who are prospects for the kind of product you are advertising. If you are selling a remedy for bladder weakness, display the words BLADDER WEAKNESS in your headline. . . . If you want mothers to read your advertisement, display MOTHERS in your headline. And so on."[6]

Writing in 1963, Ogilvy now sounds dogmatic and dated, but he's still correct. The message does not have to be in the headline, however, nor must it be as literal-minded and obvious as Ogilvy implies. In the decades since then, people have become sophisticated consumers of public messages. Lots of elements besides the ad's language can be the ticket on the meat. In print it might be the images themselves, the typography, or the design of the page; on TV and online video it might be the editing rhythms or the soundtrack; in radio the sense of humor or just the tone of voice. But it's got to be there. I only look up when someone flags me down, when someone calls my name, and so do you.

5. Decide whether you need to shout. Other traditional advice has been to name the brand in the headline (or use great big product shots or large logotypes to identify the ad's commercial point) or repeat the brand name endlessly in radio and TV spots. This is another "rule" that's not always wise, necessary, or graceful. How prominently—visually or verbally—to emphasize the product's name in the ad should be approached situation by situation. You want to sell the product, but shouting is not often the best way.

6. Consider how long the headline needs to be. As long as it needs to be to say itself, not one word longer. The tendency is to keep headlines short, although it's always possible to find a great long one.

8.16. Showing white clothes to demonstrate a detergent's cleaning power is clichéd and boring. Why not show a more surprising consequence: an eye whose pupil is constricted from looking at *very* white clothes?

The classic is, of course, Ogilvy's seventeen-worder for Rolls-Royce:

> At 60 miles an hour the loudest noise in this new Rolls-Royce comes from the electric clock.

Since that headline was written in 1958, you may argue that people won't read that many words anymore. But here's a headline written in 1997 for Adidas swimwear. It accompanies a photo of a woman, swimming laps:

8.17. A command form of the verb, not to mention a terrific way to dramatize the product's benefit.

Assault someone, you get five years. In hockey, five minutes. Is this a great game or what?

Deep down, they're really good kids. They're just dealing with a lot of stress right now. So why not bring $5 and a valid college I.D. to the Fairgrounds Coliseum this Friday or Saturday at 7:30 and watch some talented young men try to walk the straight and narrow. And, if they slip up and commit an act considered a felony in most states, well, a little time in the corner should straighten them out. You naughty boys.

For more information, call 488-8000.

One selfish lover, three late trains, two disastrous meetings, one irate boss, two large bills. The weight I lose in the pool.

Here are two headlines written in 2011 for Raise the Roof, an organization helping homeless children and teenagers. They encourage people to get their priorities straight:

A lost cat wanders the street and the neighbourhood is alerted. A homeless 16-year-old wanders the street and people really hope they find that cat.

You see an abandoned chair on the street and you think "It has the potential to be something beautiful." You see a homeless youth on the street and you think "Don't make eye contact."

The real trick is to say what you want to, then tighten it. Don't limit your ideas by presupposing that you must have teensy ones or be terse. For example, a tongue-in-cheek headline for a minor league hockey team, the Columbus Chill, could have been written this way:

If you assault someone in America, you'll get five years in prison. But if you assault someone in

hockey, you'll only get five minutes. So is this a great game or what?

The actual headline, however, didn't waste a word (fig. 8.18). Feel how much stronger it is?

7. Use both internal and end punctuation on headlines. Most ad writers use periods to close headlines (and often slogans), even when they aren't complete sentences. Periods add a sense of certainty and authority to the fragment or phrase.

8. Use subheads frequently. Whenever they need it, finish headlines with more straightforward subheads. For example, Columbus State Community College put this headline on outdoor boards: "Take Columbus State home with you," an interesting but unclear offer. The subhead resolves matters: "Over 300 online courses." Communicate completely with your audience. "Oh, they'll get it when they read the copy" is almost never a good excuse for an ambiguous, teaser headline in print advertising, and there's no excuse for any headline/subhead combination that still doesn't make enough sense (unless ambiguity is part of your strategy). An ad should work both fast and slow; that is, a scanner should get something from it—at least the selling idea—and a true reader should get more—the complete story.

9 • Words I: Establishing Voice

> The only thing that makes writing good is giving it our voice, our own personality. Writing is always an act of faith in your own character.
> —ANNA QUINDLEN

What Anna Quindlen says is as true for companies as for people. They speak most authentically when there is no gap between who they are and how they talk. So, who are they? That's your first job as a copywriter: understand the character of your client's brand. Find out who you're representing.

Discovering who is talking precedes the words themselves and determines them. The literary critic M. H. Abrams, discussing Aristotle's theories of rhetoric, said this: "An orator establishes in the course of his oration an *ethos*—a personal character which itself functions as a means of persuasion; for if the personal image he projects is that of a man of rectitude, intelligence, and goodwill, the audience is instinctively inclined to give credence to him and to his arguments."[1]

Advertising is a form of public speechmaking, and whenever people see it, they confront a speaker delivering a persuasive message. Even if that message has no literal spokesperson, it always has a consciousness, and people's response to this frequently invisible but everywhere apparent speaker becomes central to the success of the message and the brand behind it. Consumers are never just buying a product; they're buying an *ethos*, too. Do they like this person or don't they? Are they interested in this sensibility or aren't they? Do they want to bring this person home with them or not?[2]

So whenever your client's brand talks with consumers—whether on the company website or in an annual report, app, blog post, tweet, e-mail blast, hang tag, package copy, T-shirt slogan, piece of street theater, banner trailing behind a plane at the beach, or simply the joke on a napkin in the store—no matter what that message is, or where it appears, it should represent the brand's personality and speak with the right voice.

None of it should get written without first consulting a higher authority. And that higher authority is the brand itself.

In talking about this sensibility, I am, of course, talking about brand image. You've noticed how an advertising agency creates a persona for a company and its products and then maintains it through the years. (*Persona*, Latin for the "mask" once worn by classical actors, is another good word for this created self, the speaker people hear and the personality they sense through a brand's language and imagery.)

For example, Volkswagen's classic ads from 1959 through the 1970s, created by Doyle Dane Bernbach (DDB), seemed to have a self-deprecating, funny, modest-but-self-assured persona—people almost felt as though they'd enjoy having lunch and some laughs with the VW person, whoever he was. People also felt that the mind behind the car was the car's argument for itself: rational, practical, intelligent, whimsical, but ultimately serious.

In 1998 with VW's introduction of the New Beetle, Arnold Communications faced a tough challenge: reinvoke that original Beetle persona while moving it forward. Arnold needed to remind Baby Boomers how much they'd loved their Bug, but the agency didn't want younger audiences to dismiss the New Beetle as a Geezermobile. Sell nostalgia but be contemporary about it, that was the task—and live up to the greatness of the original DDB campaign in the process.

The original Beetle persona had to reappear, as though back from an extended vacation and as hip as ever. "It's tonal. You can't mess up on voice," said art director Alan Pafenbach, one of the campaign's leaders.[3] The new advertising took the graphic simplicity of the original campaign (sans serif typography and lots of

9.1. The voice of the New Beetle.

white space) and intensified it: there was no copy in the print work, just a snappy headline, and no visual context for the car, just its silhouette in white space. Arnold Communications reprised the original witty voice while updating it to address improvements to the car and changes to the culture since the 1960s. And the car now had an additional benefit for sale: not just utility and reason, but nostalgia (fig. 9.1). The ugly car had long since become cute. Terrific, headline-driven print ads cited improvements while making gentle fun of the original Beetle's weaknesses:

Comes with wonderful new features. Like heat.

The engine's in the front, but its heart's in the same place.

Or invoked Baby Boomers' nostalgia:

If you were really good in a past life, you come back as something better.

If you sold your soul in the '80s, here's your chance to buy it back.

But spoke to younger generations, too:

Digitally remastered.

Is it possible to go backwards and forwards at the same time?

TV spots did cool stuff like show a silver Beetle zipping and bouncing in white space inside the TV frame, with this closing line: "Reverse engineered from UFOs." (Music soundtracks from German alt-rock bands added a contemporary feel to the voice.)

The ads invoked the past but spoke in the present tense. They looked back and leaned forward at the same time.

In short, the advertisers for both Volkswagen Beetles created a personality by which consumers could identify the brand and relate it to themselves. All great brands not only create a strong image for themselves but also manage it, modifying its characteristics to match changing circumstance and purpose. The New Beetle had the same personality as the old one; it had just been updated for new times and new audiences.

According to David Martin, founder of The Martin Agency and a strong proponent of sustaining successful brand images, "Personality is a buoy, not a dead weight. Great brands are built over a long period of time with advertising that is faithful to product personality. . . . Brand personality is permanent. Lose it and lose the franchise."[4]

How to build a brand personality

QUESTIONS TO ASK

1. What image of the brand already exists?

2. Is it the right one for the brand? Does it fit the target market? The brand's position in the marketplace? The times?

3. What modifications, if any, do you want to make to that image? (Do you also want to change the brand's positioning or target market?)

4. What voice is the best expression of this brand image?

5. How will you use this voice to communicate brand objectives? In other words, how will the brand's persona make specific selling arguments? How will he or she say them?

WAYS TO FIND ANSWERS

Read the brand book
Sometimes you'll inherit the brand's personality and be asked simply to carry it forward. The best way to do that is to ask to see the brand book or standards manual. If you're lucky, there will be one. (If you're luckier, there won't be one, and you'll be asked to write it.) These things vary from slim to hefty, but they spell out what the brand's elements are and how they're to be handled. Topics usually include the brand's color palette, typography, imagery, and logo treatment, but also things you'll be especially interested in like personality, voice, and mission statement. A brand book, if one exists for your client, is essential reading (fig. 9.2).

Write the brand book
You may be asked not to continue a brand's personality, but to change it. Or you may be creating work for your portfolio, in which case the personality of the brand is yours to choose. The best way forward in these cases is to write the brand book yourself, at least those parts that help you figure out who the brand is and how it should speak. Here are suggestions:

1. Write a mission statement or manifesto.
2. Write a slogan.
3. Pick five adjectives.
4. Write a profile.
5. Talk like that person talks.

Write a mission statement or manifesto
"Over the years, we've kind of formalized how we believe iconic brands are created—and the first piece involves understanding what a brand truly believes, as opposed to what it makes or sells."
—LEE CLOW, TBWA\Chiat\Day

All right, what does your client's brand believe in? Besides making kitchen utensils or distilling whiskey or selling lawn fertilizer, what does the brand stand for? What's its highest calling? Create a pithy paragraph or a list of principles that your brand embodies, wants to embody, or could embody. Climb the ladder. What does it value? What is its reason for being? Make these complete thoughts, too, not just words or phrases like

9.2. Rather than specifying voice, this brand book demonstrates it. Reading the copy, you familiarize yourself enough with its voice to carry it forward.

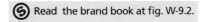 Read the brand book at fig. W-9.2.

WE'RE FOR DOGS. SOME PEOPLE ARE FOR THE WHALES. SOME ARE FOR THE TREES. WE'RE FOR DOGS. THE BIG ONES AND THE LITTLE ONES. THE GUARDIANS AND THE COMEDIANS. THE PURE BREEDS AND THE MUTTS. WE'RE FOR WALKS, RUNS AND ROMPS. DIGGING, SCRATCHING, SNIFFING AND FETCHING. WE'RE FOR DOG PARKS, DOG DOORS AND DOG DAYS. AND IF THERE WERE AN INTERNATIONAL HOLIDAY FOR DOGS, ON WHICH ALL DOGS WERE UNIVERSALLY RECOGNIZED FOR THEIR CONTRIBUTION TO THE QUALITY OF LIFE ON EARTH, WE'D BE FOR THAT TOO. BECAUSE WE'RE FOR DOGS. AND WE'VE SPENT THE LAST SIXTY YEARS WORKING TO MAKE THEM AS HAPPY AS THEY'VE MADE US.

9.3. *Dogma* was a call-to-arms for Pedigree's employees, meant to inspire them to embrace the brand's new mission.

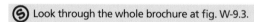 Look through the whole brochure at fig. W-9.3.

"honesty" or "transparency." What about honesty? In what ways? "Transparent"? How so? To whom? Push your thinking.

For example, Pampers could say that it makes the world's driest diaper for babies, and that may be true. But a higher purpose might be that the brand helps children grow. The dry diaper is just one means to that end. A brand that believes in things beyond simply a well-made product gives itself bigger thoughts to inhabit, bigger corporate possibilities to pursue, and bigger responsibilities to accept. The brand, as a consequence, can own more psychological space in consumers' minds. By believing in more things, it becomes more worth believing in.

Here is the clothing company Patagonia's mission statement: "Build the best product, cause no unnecessary harm, use business to inspire and implement solutions to the environmental crisis." That sentence has risen well above merino wool and nylon shells.

Lee Clow and his people at TBWA\Chiat\Day faced this issue of brand mission when they won the Pedigree dog food account. Who were the people at Pedigree, and what did they believe in besides making dog food? Clow and his people needed to locate (even to help create) that brand's true character. They analyzed the product, brand, company, employees, consumers (both dog and human), everything. Only by

doing so could they hope to speak in the right voice.

During the process, Chiat created an internal document for Pedigree employees and stakeholders, *Dogma*, that presented and celebrated the new point of view (fig. 9.3).

If you were given nothing but the "we're for dogs" paragraph, you could write Pedigree copy from it because you know where the brand's heart lies and how its voice sounds. You also know or can guess how Pedigree might put these beliefs into action: build dog parks, lobby for a national dog holiday, support dog adoption, and so on. In that paragraph, you have a microcosm of the brand and its potential.

Once you understand a brand's core values, you can begin to talk in ways that represent the brand. You won't be stuck in the spot copywriters sometimes find themselves: trying to say something clever for this or that ad, spinning out jokes in search of a point and a voice. Save yourself from that hot seat by knowing the brand's mission before attempting to execute it.

Write a slogan

Slogans may seem so simple and interchangeable that writing one won't get you far, but if you can lodge the right argument and voice in a slogan, you will have found the brand's Rosetta stone. Pedigree brand dog food's slogan used to be "Developed with vets, recommended by top breeders." Contained in that line was an entire approach to the dog food business. As a crystallized mission statement, it focused on experts (vets and breeders), health and nutrition, and, subtly, purebreds more than mutts.

TBWA\Chiat\Day, after it won the Pedigree account, replaced that slogan with "Dogs rule," a line that changed everything. The voice went from sober-minded and clinical to colloquial and fun. The key concern switched from who endorses the food to why people owned dogs—and the answer was simple: because they loved them like crazy. The new slogan captured what Clow called "the emotional high ground" of owning a dog. Start there, TBWA\Chiat\Day advised Pedigree, and so they did (fig. 9.4).

Once the voice was established in branding documents like *Dogma* and in the slogan "Dogs rule," everything else followed. Inside the company, employees were encouraged to bring their dogs to work and take them on customer calls, employees received health insurance for their dogs, and their dogs' pictures were put on their business cards. Outside the company, Pedigree recorded people's dog stories and posted them on the company's website (dogsrule.com), encouraged people to upload pictures of their dogs to add to the "million dog mosaic" also being assembled on the website, and organized nationwide dog adoption drives. In New York City, Pedigree put a pop-up dog store and adoption center in Times Square, for which they created guerrilla advertising—placing dog shapes in New York's Central Park that said on their sides, "Wish I was here. But I'm not. Come visit me and other great shelter dogs at the Pedigree Dogstore on 46th and Broadway." TBWA\Chiat\Day creative di-

rector Chris Adams, one of the Pedigree campaign's creators, summarized the brand's new mission: "We have become a brand not just about the food but everything that makes the world better for dogs."[5] (See fig. 9.5 for TV spots in the "Dogs rule" campaign.)

This Pedigree rebranding demonstrates the value of manifestos, mission statements, and slogans. You can't talk a certain way until you know who's talking and what about. When you're searching for a brand's voice, take the time to write a manifesto of core principles (or a mission statement with some bite), then condense those principles into a slogan, a call to arms, whether you use it or not. Work hard on how you say these things. If you find the right principles and say them the right way, you will have created the brand's voice and set its compass.

Pick five adjectives

A similar way to find a brand's voice is to collapse your thinking about that brand into a handful of words or phrases, five or so, that sum up its personality. Don't be generic: "passionate" (how so?), "friendly" (who isn't?). Pick specific words and define them if you need to.

A clutch of adjectives may sound too insubstantial to sum up a company, but they don't have to be. Here, for example, is the description of the personality of Resource Interactive, a digital marketing firm, from its CEO, Kelly Mooney: "Our voice should be sophisticated but not inaccessible, funny but not hilarious, contemporary but not slick, friendly but not down-home, smart but not smart-aleck."[6] If someone handed you that sentence, with its well-chosen distinctions, you'd know how that person should talk.

The brand book for my school (Columbus College

9.4. A simple, strong marketing position (how could other brands have missed it?), expressed just as simply and strongly.

of Art & Design) says, "Our brand personality articulates how we should look, feel, and sound," then characterizes it with six words, each briefly defined:

Purposeful (poised, practical)
Intense (driven, focused)
Innovative (pioneering, problem-solving)
Inspired (passionate, motivated)
Collaborative (curious, nimble)
Clever (stimulating, canny)

Even though these words are pretty high up the ladder of abstraction, you could gauge, as a writer, whether you're staying inside the brand's personality, couldn't you?

Think of "pick-five-adjectives" as a style guide in miniature, a list any writer could consult to write in that brand's voice.

Write a profile

Still another way to find a brand's voice is to think of the brand, not as a few adjectives, but as a whole person. If this brand were a person, who would it be? Describe who the brand is now—if you're not changing it—or who you'd like it to be—if you are changing it. A variant is to profile the core consumer or brand fan.

Either way, answer questions like these: Is the brand a man or a woman, can you say? Old? Young? A parent? What does she like to talk about, and what does she avoid discussing? What ethnicity is he? A churchgoer? Liberal or conservative? J. Crew or Jay-Z? Death Cab for Cutie or early Black Sabbath? What does he hope no one knows? Where has he volunteered? What's in her fridge? What does she think about finance or food or cars or whatever your prod-

1

2

3

5

4

9.5. Pedigree's overarching TV spot, the mission-statement ad, is "We're for Dogs." By establishing the brand's position, it enables Pedigree to address specific issues within the big idea: for example, that older dogs need special nutrition and that every dog deserves a home. In all Pedigree TV spots from this campaign, the emotional connection people have with dogs is front and center. Viewers *feel* these spots as much as watch them.

Ⓢ Watch these three Pedigree TV spots at fig. W-9.5.

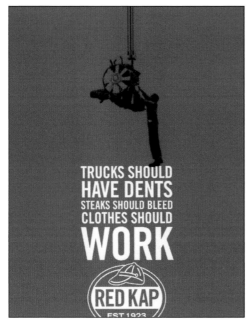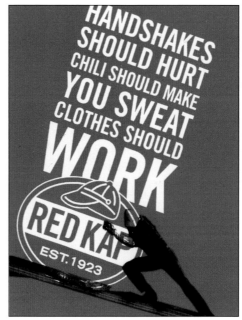

9.6. A straightforward voice of the working man and woman: no qualifiers, no ambiguity. Things may be screwed up, this voice says, but they don't have to be, if people would do the right thing. Hearing the voice, I can imagine the clothes. The brand's website extends this point of view by inviting loyalists to enter a Work Week Done Right contest and to submit Red Kaptions, short calls-to-arms about doing things right (e.g., "Tell people you work without saying a word").

uct category is? Did she live for a year in Paris or never get out of Millersburg, Ohio? Does he shoot the rapids and jump out of airplanes or collect stamps and first editions? Warren Buffett rich or working-stiff poor?

Design writer Nancy Bernard shows how to write a profile:

> Young, male, been to college, hates pretension, likes toys. Will probably always be young at heart; wickedly witty, but never mean; liberated: lets his girlfriend drive on the way TO the pub; does his bit for the world by being friendly; likes rap, techno, and indie music, of course, but isn't above playing Petula Clark, loudly, with the windows down; comfortable, casual dress—with the occasional twist; loves great design and engineering, but is turned off by conventional status symbols; makes everything his own.

She then asks, "How do I know this guy so well? Because he's been talking to me consistently for about a year. He's MINI Cooper—let's motor!"[7] If you look at the MINI ads in this book and elsewhere, or go to the brand's website and read awhile, you can hear this person clearly. (If you look into a MINI driving by, you

may even see him.) Bernard's profile reveals the man behind the voice and inside the car.

Talk like that person talks

If you're not working backward like Bernard was, look at your profile and try to hear this person speak. How does he or she talk (fig. 9.6)?

Consider questions like these: Is he a nonstop talker or tight lipped? Ironic or straightforward? Does he prefer short sentences or long ones? Big words or small ones? Are there words he wouldn't say? Words he'd probably say? Would he swear? Is she friendly and warm, or analytical and cool? Does she use fragments, contractions, and colloquialisms? Does she tell jokes? What kind?

When you're thinking about the words your brand uses, consider, as always, the differing connotations among words that denote the same thing. If the brand is fashion, for example, watch how word choice defines that brand's position: "stunning" doesn't mean "gorgeous," and neither says what "hot" does. Which word the brand prefers says a lot about who it is. Even something simple like a sign-off says plenty: "thanks" is chummier and more off-hand, perhaps less full a compliment, than is "thank you." Something is always at stake. Every word counts, often out loud.

It may help you focus to ask what pop culture figure, movie star, or movie character reminds you of your brand. Maybe that person and your brand talk similarly. Clint Eastwood, as Dirty Harry, pointed guns at bad guys and said things like "You've got to ask yourself one question: 'Do I feel lucky?' Well, do ya, punk?" And "Go ahead, make my day." A bank better not use that snarl, but a state lottery might have fun with it.

Who, in our culture's parade of personalities, sounds the way you want your brand to sound? If you were repositioning Keds to a younger audience and looking for a relaxed voice, you might ask whether Zooey Deschanel would more likely wear Keds than, say, Lady Gaga. If so, then think about how Zooey talks and use some of her persona to inform yours.

When you're creating your brand's voice, be sure also to examine the personalities of the main competitors. You want, as in positioning, to create a personality for your brand distinct from those with whom you compete. Who is out there? How do they talk? How can you speak differently?

To create space for itself in a crowded field, an unknown brand of coffee put a strong personality into words and took that to market. Hear in the sidebar (opposite page) how the copywriter, Bryan Judkins, gave the brand its voice and see the brand's attitude in figure 9.7.

A FEW GOOD VOICES IN YOUR HEAD

> "The intent of a piece of copy is to project the client's identity, not the writer's."
>
> —Howard Gossage, copywriter and advertising innovator

The best copywriters know how to sound like people other than themselves. And they need to, since no two clients are identical. Throwing your voice, assuming the personalities of other people, is a skill you can develop. Study the language and speech rhythms of people different from you. Read novelists and short story writers, poets and screenwriters. Hear how writers create distinct voices, separate sensibilities. Acquire voices. They'll come in handy.

A brand often uses several voices: the corporate voice on the website; more casual Twitter, Facebook, and blog voices; and sometimes the particular voices of secondary characters, like the president (Zappos' CEO is busy on Twitter) or other people inside the company, real or invented. Duke the dog, Bush Beans' mascot, is on Facebook. Target has created a manic super shopper, the Christmas Champ, who has her own TV spots and online videos, Twitter account, YouTube presence, and absurdist microsites. She's over the top but in a funny, friendly, Target-y way, which is as it should be. Creating a number of personae within a brand can be a good way to express its various selves. But the voices, however many there are, should perform in concert, become a kind of choir.

Apple has at least two tones of voice: the helpful, upbeat, here's-how-it-works-and-what-it-does-for-you voice that people encounter on Apple's website but also the transcendent, inspirational voice, the big-picture voice of "Here's to the Crazy Ones." (If you've never seen this ad, Apple's original 1997 "Think Different" TV spot, look for it on YouTube. It features famous rebels from history and great copy, spoken by Richard Dreyfuss. It will give you chills, make you proud to be a human, and spur you to do more with your life—no small trick for one TV spot.)

Copy: Writing "all the little words"[8]

As we've seen, before you ever write a word of copy, you need to understand the overall voice and stance of the brand. Not until they are resolved can you write effective copy. Once you start to write copy, however, you'll make a pleasant discovery: you already know how, for the simple reason that you've already done it.

HOW COPY IS LIKE FRESHMAN COMPOSITION

You probably took a college composition course in which you wrote essays. Copy is really nothing more than English Composition 1: nonfiction prose written to support an argument. In a print ad, for example, the headline and visual advance the argument, and the body copy justifies it. Although well-written copy does differ from the prose of a well-written essay (and I'll discuss those differences soon), the similarities far outweigh the differences. Good writing is good writing. Period.

If you apply what you learned in freshman composition to your copywriting, you'll be fine. Let's recall those principles of good prose your English professor taught you:

1. Voice: The writing has a natural, authentic sound, free of clichés.

2. Details: The writing is full of specifics; it's particular, not vague.

Wrapping a brand in language: Bryan Judkins talks about creating Ugly Mug's voice

Ugly Mug coffee, a small coffee roaster in Memphis, had an unusual name and nothing else. It wanted to compete with major brands, each of which had a place in people's minds and on the shelf. What to do?

The short answer turned out to be, hire Indianapolis ad agency Young & Laramore—specifically, copywriter and creative director Bryan Judkins. He and his colleagues created a brand almost entirely with words, bringing a voice and attitude up out of nothing.

I asked Bryan how he found this voice and these words.[9] He answered in two ways: first, by replicating the voice and approach of the package copy; then, more traditionally, by answering my questions.

Before reading either answer, take a close look at some of the package copy and posters for Ugly Mug (fig. 9.7).

THIS COPY…

IS WRITTEN FOR THE WORKING STIFF, NOT THE PLAIN STIFF * MAKES NO PROMISES BUT PLENTY OF GUARANTEES * NEVER BLINKS * IS TO BE TAKEN SERIOUS-LIKE * SIMULTANEOUSLY TALKS WITH A STRUT AND A SAUNTER * INVIGORATES THE SENSES AND OPENS THE PORES * CAN BRING A GROWN MAN TO HIS KNEES AND THE TOUGHEST BROAD IN THE ROOM TO TEARS * STANDS TALL AGAINST THE GUTLESS SWILL THAT PASSES FOR INSPIRATION THESE DAYS * WAS CONCEIVED, WRITTEN AND REWRITTEN WITHIN EARSHOT OF THE HEARTBROKEN DESPERATION OF TENNESSEE BAND, LUCERO * CAN IMPREGNATE A BARREN MULE * IS A LITTLE BIT CRAZY, AND THERE'S NOTHING YOU CAN DO ABOUT IT * IS YOUR ROSEBUD, YOUR VALHALLA, YOUR LOST ARK, YOUR GOLDEN MONKEY, YOUR CHINATOWN. PLEASE READ RESPONSIBLY

Q: Why that voice?

A: Two reasons. First, it became apparent that the grocery store coffee shelf is kind of overwhelming. You can get a little intimidated by all the pretentious coffee terminology and a little exasperated by the sameness of it all. So a bold, unpretentious premium coffee was bound to stand out. Plus, the brand arrived at our desks with the name Ugly Mug, and although we flirted briefly with renaming it, we agreed that it's the sort of name that guides your thinking. Why fight it? An ugly attitude. Makes sense for a drink that either (a) you drink to wake up in the morning when confronting the fact that you have to get up and get going; or a drink (b) you drink for energy, to get out of a slump, to get things done and stop f-ing around.

Q: How do you develop a personality for a brand?

A: Well, it's sort of a combination of the goal—what do we want people to think based on the strategy, in this case, that this premium coffee had more attitude and less frou-frou pretension—and trying to capture ideas around that. Then, frankly, you just try to say interesting or funny things in an interesting or funny way. There's a part of the process that is less about the dictates of the research, and more about what you know about the world and what you know about people and what they think is funny, and what the competitors are or aren't saying, and you're just trying to make sure people don't forget they saw the work.

Q: What's your advice on throwing your voice in service to a client?

A: It isn't a science. Think of what you'd find interesting. Then find an interesting way to say it on the client's behalf. As a writer you probably invent little rules for yourself, little guidelines or guardrails to keep yourself from making your writing sound like another product, or like other work you've written. Sometimes you're obliged to write those guidelines down for a style manual or something, but other times you just use your horse sense to make sure you're still talking like THAT client. It's a lot like a novelist or screenwriter composing for a certain character—you just get the sense of what that character would or wouldn't say. A brand is a lot like a character who's expected to behave consistently, within a believable range of personality. If they stray outside that personality, they start to sound lobotomized. Also, as a person who appreciates culture in general, you know what's old/hack/cliché and you keep your character/client from saying that stuff at all costs. And then you just apply the lessons of the strategy to that character. It sounds a lot more erudite than it actually is. So does that last sentence.

For Ugly Mug, we spoke in a slightly acidic tone, not unlike coffee itself. If we weren't channeling the voice of someone just waking up and not yet having their first cup of coffee, we were channeling Ugly Mug's hometown of Memphis. Positioning Tennessee as the mighty opposite to Seattle and Ugly Mug Coffee as the remedy to the rampant fancification of all we hold dear. Another thing: It's always easier to move the cursor to the right with the appropriate soundtrack. So to add a little steel to the spine of these words, the Memphis punk-country band Lucero was never not in earshot.

9.7. Ugly Mug branding: voice as attitude as coffee.

To see more packaging and advertising from the campaign, go to fig. W-9.7.

MORNING PEOPLE. THEY BEGIN THE **DAY** WITH A SEEMINGLY **BOUNDLESS** SUPPLY OF ENERGY AND PLUCK. **LUCKILY** FOR THE REST OF US, THEY USUALLY **SLOW DOWN** BY AROUND ELEVEN O'CLOCK, AT WHICH POINT THEY'RE PRETTY **EASY TO PICK OFF, SWAT DOWN,** AND CRUSH THE **HOPE OUT OF.**

UGLY MUG COFFEE CO.
Memphis, Tennessee U.S.A.

WHO IS THIS **PERSON** I WAKE UP NEXT TO **EVERY MORNING?** COMPLETELY **UNRECOGNIZABLE.** CERTAINLY NOT THE SAME **SWEET,** CARING WIFE I WENT TO BED WITH. **NO,** THAT **WOMAN** IS **GONE.** AND FOR THE **PASSINGEST** OF **PASSING MOMENTS,** I'M **OPEN** TO THE **CONCEPT** OF **ALIEN ABDUCTION.**

UGLY MUG COFFEE CO.
Memphis, Tennessee U.S.A.

THIS COFFEE...

HAILS FROM **MEMPHIS,** THE SEATTLE OF **SOUTHWESTERN TENNESSEE** ✦ SHOOTS STRAIGHT, **BUT** KNOWS HOW TO TALK ITS WAY OUT OF A FIGHT ✦ **CAN PROP** TIRED EYES OPEN BETTER THAN **TOOTHPICKS** ✦ TASTES **LIKE COFFEE,** NOT SOME KIND OF CANDY CORN VANILLA FANTASY WORLD ✦ **HELPS YOU** GROW BIG AND **STRONG** ✦ WILL **TOUGHEN UP** YOUR SELF-IMAGE ✦ CAVES TO NO MAN ✦ CAME FROM **MEMPHIS** WITH A **DOLLAR** AND A **DREAM** ✦ IS RICH **ENOUGH** TO PLANT FLOWERS IN ✦ **REMINDS US** OF A TIME BEFORE THE DOUBLE MINT MOCHA DECAF SKIM LATTE **RULED** THE EARTH ✦ IS **ROASTED** IN THE **CRADLE** OF **ROCK 'N ROLL,** WHERE OTIS AND ELVIS GOT THEIR START ✦ ISN'T PICKED BY SOME **GUY** NAMED JUAN WITH A SOMBRERO AND A DONKEY…IT'S PICKED BY RAUL. RAUL DRIVES A SECOND-HAND PLYMOUTH AND UNDERSTANDS YOUR NEED FOR FINE COFFEE ✦ IS **MEANT TO BE DRANK, NOT "EXPERIENCED"** ✦ HAS KNOWN **MORAL INDIGNATION** ✦ IS **THE ORIGINAL** ENERGY DRINK ✦ NOT ONLY WAKES YOU UP, BUT **SLAPS YOU AROUND A BIT,** JUST TO MAKE SURE YOU DON'T **SNEAK BACK** TO BED ✦ **IS READY** TO HEAR YOUR **CONFESSION** ✦ **KNOWS GOOD LOOKS** WILL ONLY GET YOU **SO FAR** ✦ IS OUR **GIFT** TO YOU ✦ **WAS PURCHASED, ROASTED** AND **PACKAGED** WITH A LITTLE SOMETHING WE LIKE TO CALL **INTEGRITY** ✦ SPEAKS WITHOUT RESORTING TO FAUX EUROPEAN WORDS. **EXCEPT FAUX** ✦ IS AT THE FOREFRONT **OF THE MUTINY** ✦ BREWS DARK AND RICH LIKE THE **FERTILE SOIL** OF THE MISSISSIPPI RIVER ✦ IS MORE **ROCKABILLY** THAN POP ✦ CAN FLY A CROP DUSTER LOWER AND FASTER THAN ANYONE HERE ✦ IS ROASTED WITH AN EYE **TOWARDS GREATNESS** ✦ MUST **NEVER FALL INTO** THE **WRONG HANDS** ✦ DOESN'T SO MUCH **PERCOLATE** AS IT DOES **RABBLE-ROUSE** ✦ LEAVES BEHIND A TRAIL OF **BLACK GROUNDS** AND **BROKEN DREAMS** ✦ INSPIRES PRESIDENTS AND MADMEN ✦ IS LIKE A **LULLABY IN REVERSE** ✦ **UNDERSTANDS YOU.** MAYBE **TOO WELL** ✦ IS **YOUR** FAVORITE COFFEE'S **FAVORITE COFFEE** ✦ ✦ INFUSES THOSE WHO DRINK IT WITH **SUPERHUMAN VIGILANCE** ✦ **TWANGS** LIKE A STEEL GUITAR ✦ RIDES TALL IN THE SADDLE ✦ BRINGS **STRENGTH** TO THE WEAK OF **SPIRIT** AND **HOPE** TO THOSE **WHO TRULY NEED IT.**

UGLY MUG COFFEE CO. Memphis, Tennessee U.S.A.

3. Style: Form matches content: the prose is not overwritten. It's stylistically graceful, with strong, clear sentences and well-chosen language.

4. Thesis: The writing has one central, unifying idea. It hangs together.

5. Organization and structure: The writing develops this idea in some order; has a beginning, middle, and end; and coheres throughout.

That's a familiar list, isn't it? The first item on the list—voice—is so important that I'll spend the rest of this chapter analyzing it and save the others for the next chapter.

VOICE

As I discussed earlier, *voice* is the brand's personality as expressed in language. Every ad and corporate communication should be true to that personality, the brand's tone and point of view. No renegades, no stray soldiers.

> "In your natural way of producing words there is a sound, a texture, a rhythm—a voice—which is the main source of power in your writing."
> —PETER ELBOW, from *Writing without Teachers*

Voice is so crucial to writing that in a sense it's everything. As you remember from freshman composition, all good writing has a sound—the human, expressive rhythm that animates it. Good writing sounds like someone particular uttered or thought it. If your language has no sound or rhythm, it's dead, and so is your ad.

But even after you've established a brand's personality, its voice can be difficult to talk about for several reasons. For one thing, you can't point to it exactly. It's just there, *among* all the words. For another, it's made up of myriad things: the words you choose (and the words you avoid), the sentences you write, the amount and kind of detail you use, what you're talking about, what your point is, how you organize the writing, who you're talking to. Almost every choice you make as a writer plays a part in creating the voice of the copy—the sense readers get, when they read it, of living speech. Throughout this discussion of good writing, remember that I'm always talking about voice, too.

Analyze the voices of ads

Let's look closely at some advertising copy to see if it's possible to isolate the characteristics that make up a

So, you're hanging ten in Maui or you're just stepping into your hot tub. Fine. You'll need a few things. First, you'll need a solid rubber outsole for traction. Then you'll need a spandex upper for breathability. Like gills, sort of. And you'll definitely need some wacky colors to make the fish think you're one of them. In short, you'll need NIKE Aqua Socks. Remember: when the going gets wet, the wet go Hawaiian.

9.8. Nike's distinctive voice perfectly matches product with target audience.

voice, the parts that combine to create a reader's intuitive sense of the speaker. Consider, for example, this copy for an ad for Nike's water socks (fig. 9.8):

Headline:
Hawaiian shirts for your feet.

Copy:
So, you're hanging ten in Maui or you're just stepping into your hot tub. Fine. You'll need a few things. First, you'll need a solid rubber outsole for traction. Then you'll need a spandex upper for breathability. Like gills, sort of. And you'll definitely need some wacky colors to make the fish think you're one of them. In short, you'll need NIKE Aqua Socks. Remember: when the going gets wet, the wet go Hawaiian.

How to characterize this voice? It's hip and flippant,

9.9. A more sophisticated voice works well for a more expensive product and an older, more urbane target audience.

CIVILIZATION IS ADVANCING AT A STATELY 18 KNOTS.

Long before reaching your destination, you will experience a sense of having arrived. Such is life aboard our newest ship, the intimate *Royal Viking Queen*, and her larger, more stately companion, the elegant *Royal Viking Sun*.

Here, all that has made sailing Royal Viking Line so wondrous over the years is heightened as never before. Consider mingling with learned experts in World Affairs. Or collecting secrets of aquatic life from the Cousteau Society.

Elsewhere, guest chefs the likes of the renowned Paul Bocuse will provide exquisite nourishment for areas found somewhat south of the mind.

We do not wish to prod, but if this ROYAL VIKING LINE appeals to your sense of adventure,

there is no better time to experience it all than now, as we depart for 165 charmed ports including the storied waters of Europe. Your travel agent has particulars, or call 1 (800) 457-8599. We look forward to seeing you on board.

---

but it's got some steel, too. The tone is authoritative, telling readers what to do, what's cool, but doing so with jokes. It's clearly a variant of the Nike voice ("Just do it") that consumers have been hearing for years.

How do I know all this? The authoritative tone comes from the repetition of the near command, "you'll need," which doesn't allow room for disagreement; but the voice lightens that tone by mixing in whimsical allusions ("to make the fish think you're one of them," and so on). Also, the language contains slang ("hanging ten," "sort of," "wacky"), contractions ("you're," "you'll"), and sentence fragments ("Fine." "Like gills, sort of."), all of which produce a very informal, almost chummy tone. By beginning in the middle of a thought ("So"), the copy implies an already formed relationship; it seems to know the reader. The closing, clever twist on the cliché adds to the sense of a witty hipster. Finally, the diction (word choice) is unpretentious, so the voice is that of a peer—a fun but knowledgeable older brother, perhaps. Altogether, a perfectly created voice, given the advertisers' sense of this product, the Nike audience, and the Nike campaign theme. Here, as elsewhere, they're telling consumers *how* to just do it.

By contrast, look at the ad for the Royal Viking Line (fig. 9.9). Consider some of the copy:

Headline:
Civilization is advancing at a stately 18 knots.

Copy:
Long before reaching your destination, you will experience a sense of having arrived. Such is life aboard our newest ship, the intimate *Royal Viking Queen*, and her larger, more stately companion, the elegant *Royal Viking Sun*.

Here, all that has made sailing Royal Viking Line so wondrous over the years is heightened as never before. Consider mingling with learned experts in World Affairs. Or collecting secrets of aquatic life from the Cousteau Society. Elsewhere, guest chefs the likes of the renowned Paul Bocuse will provide exquisite nourishment for areas found somewhere south of the mind.

The copy obviously implies an older, more genteel speaker and audience. The implied distance between the two is greater also. This is not chumminess. How can you tell? The sentences are more sophisticated, and so are the words. There are almost no fragments and no slang, no contractions. With adjectives like "wondrous," "exquisite," and "renowned," the copy is more intent on evoking a mood, an upscale one at that. Each element, from the self-congratulatory paradox of the opening sentence to the unusual details (the Cousteau Society, chef Paul Bocuse, even the unnecessary initial caps on "World Affairs"), helps accentuate the copy's "we are the best" attitude. The tone is self-assured, precise, authoritative, but at the reader's service. It sounds like this cruise will cost a lot, but consumers will have an elegant time. The voice perfectly embodies the kind of experience Royal Viking is selling.

You can simply *hear* how each piece of copy creates its own unique persona, can't you? Explaining the differing effects requires analysis, but clearly the right speaker is presenting each product, and each voice rings true. That's the goal: to sound like a real person, not an edifice of polished prose. As Elmore Leonard says, "If it sounds like writing, I rewrite it."[10] Here's how copywriter Steve Hayden, vice-chairman of Ogilvy & Mather Worldwide, puts it:

> I look for body copy that's written with care, for copy that strikes the imagination. I look for phrases like, "Most people come back from vacation with little more to show for it than tiny bars of stolen soap." You know, how did that get into the ad? But it's that occasional application of wit that lets you know you're still alive. I look for surprises that say there's a human being behind this, as opposed to a corporation. And I look for that ability to project a human quality. To communicate one-on-one.[11]

Two points. You don't create copy by analyzing it; you create copy by throwing yourself into a voice. But you do improve copy by analyzing it, and that requires a sensitivity on your part to what aspects of the language are creating what effects. Become a good critic of voices. It will help you rewrite your own.

Write in the first and second person

To write well, you must become the sound of someone talking—not literally your own self, but the self of the seller: the corporation or the person talking to consumers in the ad and for the brand. If you just write logical, institutional prose that *assembles* the case for a product, prose without someone inside it, then you're missing the essence of good writing. It must project a personality, a living voice, and that's always an "I," whether your copy uses one or not. As Thoreau said, "We commonly do not remember that it is, after all, always the first person that is speaking."[12] He wasn't talking about ad copy, but he could have been.

So prefer the first person ("I" and "we") and the second person ("you") to the third person ("it," "they"). Don't say what "they're" doing at Nike for people and "their" problems. Say what "we're" doing at Nike for "you" and "your" problems. How will "our" products serve "your" needs? Copy that pulls the reader close this way is much more intimate and effective than stiff, third-person prose. Try to sound like speech, or at least very warm thought.

The two preceding examples of ad copy use "you" and imply "we." (The Royal Viking's "her" is, of course, the feminine pronoun sometimes used for ships. This pronoun not only tells readers that each ship has a distinct personality but also adds a touch of formality—a good idea, given the cruise line's upscale product.)

Decide who's talking

Who are you going to be in this ad? There are several possibilities:

1. Be the company. Usually you'll assume the company's voice and make nice. Sometimes you'll sound best-friendly, other times more distantly pleased-to-be-having-a-conversation friendly. But whether you throw your arm over the consumer's shoulder or not, you usually try to be sociable. After all, if you want to talk people into something, being friendly is a reasonable approach. (Both the Nike and Royal Viking ads adopt the company's point of view and make nice.)

But you don't have to smile. As I've illustrated elsewhere, Nike can be stern, telling people things they should do, acting as their self-improvement conscience, their tough-love coach. Many public service ads (for and against causes or issues) shame readers with caustic sarcasm or with pointed, impatient tones, wagging their finger at human sloth, selfishness, or stupidity. Ads for products can also surprise by getting right in the reader's face (see fig. 9.10) or by inviting the reader to get in someone else's face (see fig. 9.11). So you don't have to wear a big grin and say a big howdy to sell something.

2. Be the consumer. Don't address your readers, *become* them. Climb inside their heads and see things their way instead of making nice corporate talk. What are they saying and thinking about life around them and the products in it? What shape are they in? How can your client's products help them out and help them get their feelings out? And remember, consumers come in many variants: the heavy user, reluctant user, ex-user, non-user (see figs. 9.12 and 9.13). There are all kinds of potential, former, or current audiences

9.10. Selling people things by insulting them.

KISS IT GOODBYE IN THE REGISTER CLASSIFIEDS. 284-8141.

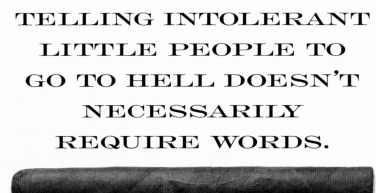

TELLING INTOLERANT LITTLE PEOPLE TO GO TO HELL DOESN'T NECESSARILY REQUIRE WORDS.

THE CIGAR BAR AT ARTHUR'S

9.11. Selling people things by inviting them to insult others.

9.12. The voice of the extreme non-user; his vitriol inversely and hilariously suggests the value someone might find in the *Village Voice*.

There's a story in every Boks.

8.29.92

Another summer spent bagging, dusting canned goods... When be back next summer, I groceries, scanning bar codes, the manager asked if I'd couldn't keep a straight face.

BOKS Reebok

Call 1-800-843-4444 for the store nearest you.

9.13. An example of an ad whose voice is the consumer's, not the corporation's. A lifestyle and attitude are for sale; the implication is that the shoes either accompany them or help make them possible.

whose inner voices are waiting for you to use. Jack Supple, managing partner and president of Carmichael Lynch, offers good advice:

> Don't say it; be it. You need to become one with your target audience. Use their voice. Talk as the target talks. If you're talking about Harley-Davidson, be a Harley person. If you're talking to Schwinn riders, you better be a Schwinn rider. . . . It's like this: In the end you're telling one of your best friends about another one of your best friends.[13]

3. Be both the consumer and the company. In a lot of ads it's hard to say who, exactly, is speaking. The headline or voice-over could be something consumers are saying to themselves, but it just as easily could be the company reading their minds and agreeing with them. Not a bad place to locate the voice of your ad. How can consumers disagree with themselves? And how can they ignore this product, especially if it's saying right out loud what they're thinking as they pass by its ad (fig. 9.14)?

4. Be the voice of some other player in the scenario. It's easy to assume that an ad's voice has to be either the company's or the consumer's. After all, they're the two most obvious players in the drama. But consider supporting players, too—from people (friends, parents, or children of the consumer; passers-by) to props (the product itself, a competing prod-

uct, or any of the various elements in the scenario). If you're selling running shoes, for example, think about the dog accompanying the runner; the sidewalk on which she runs; the weather in which she runs; the cars, trucks, and mud puddles she avoids; her legs; her feet; even her shoelaces. Every selling situation has lots of potential participants. Any of them could become the voice of the ad, and many memorable ads owe their originality to just such an unusual point of view (fig. 9.15).

How to decide which voice to use? Let your strategy help you decide: what's the best way to express your selling argument? If you're selling shoes that feel good, maybe you should let feet do the talking. If you're selling shoes as part of a lifestyle, the way Reebok was (fig. 9.13), overhearing their owner makes sense. If you're selling shoes as well-made things, interview the shoemaker and see if his voice can run the ad. As writer Tracy Kidder says, "Choosing a point of view is a matter of finding the best place to stand, from which to tell a story. The process shouldn't be determined by theory, but driven by immersion in the material itself."[14]

Decide how that person is talking about the product
Most ads sound like they're in love with what they're selling. But this can easily be overdone: the features are said to be great, the product marvelous, and the offer nothing short of astounding. Hype (unearned

YOUR JOB STINKS.

YOUR LOVE LIFE STINKS.

THE GUY IN THE CAR NEXT TO YOU STINKS.

IT DOESN'T GET ANY BETTER THAN THIS.

This is escapism. This is accelerating as the road clears and the CD drops into the slot and U2's "Streets With No Name" begins. This is cranking it. This is leaving work early on Friday afternoon. This is the Clarion Car Audio 5770 CD AM/FM Stereo CD Player. This is a removable chassis, single DIN unit that fits almost every car that's been around since you've been around. This is no skipping CDs, regardless of how hot or cold it gets. This is 108 watts of power served up the most efficient way known to mankind: 4 channels each delivering 27 watts respectively. This is Clarion's Magi-Tune™ FM reception system that eliminates "picket-fencing" interference and locks in weak signals without crowding from stronger adjacent channels. This is sex. This is purple haze. This is rock 'n' roll. Call Clarion at 1-800-487-9007, Dept. IN for more information. This is free.

clarion
CAR AUDIO
THERE IS NO SOUND BARRIER™

9.14. Attitude and lifestyle ads frequently adopt the consumer's point of view. They don't address the consumer; they *become* the consumer. People are, in effect, overhearing themselves. Company and consumer have merged.

9.15. Rain and suede are personified, the coat's feature (washable suede) being dramatized by the encounter between the two. Neither the consumer nor the company is speaking here. Who is? Hard to say. The weatherman as romancer?

9.16. An example of the attention-getting power and persuasiveness of a voice that understates rather than overstates its endorsement of the product.

overstatement) is a real turn-off—unless you wink about it. Experiment with other relationships toward your client's product: undersell it, oversell it (with that wink), be flippant, be modest, make fun of it, wonder why people would buy it, point out its limitations. An unusual attitude about what you're selling can get you past the clichés and unbelievability inherent in adoration of product.

An ironically overstated or understated attitude toward the product lets you say more than one thing at a time, provides readers or viewers the richness of more than one meaning, and gives them a little work to do: you leave room for them to get involved.

> "*All* interesting attitudes are complex."
> —WALKER GIBSON, *Persona*

Irony occurs when there's a difference between what you say and what you mean. Everyone uses irony (and its cousin, sarcasm). People will watch a LeBron James 360-degree slam dunk and say, "Not too bad." They'll sit in gridlock on the freeway and say, "I love this city." Why do people like these comments better than obvious, literal ones? Because they express a more complicated attitude toward the subject and

the person speaking. Such comments create more than one meaning simultaneously, and they create of the speaker someone smart enough to be of two minds about a single topic. With LeBron, people are saying "great shot," but they're also implying that he's so good he should do that, and they're preserving their own cool by acting unfazed. They're getting extra mileage out of one comment. Thus the value of irony: richness.

In an age inundated with hype, you're wise to think about your copy's attitude toward its product and brand. Can you find an attitude more interesting than "This product is fabulous. Buy it now and be the happiest person alive."? I bet you can (fig. 9.16).

Remember, too, that with most advertising you're creating a relationship between words and pictures. So, just like the ironic comment about LeBron's basketball shot, you can make ironic comments about your ad's images. You create a more complex voice— and your attitude toward the selling argument becomes subtler—when the image is *more* than the usual, the comment *less* so (or vice versa). Although this chapter has been focusing on the words in an ad, remember that an ad's voice is really the entire rhetorical package: language plus image. The whole ad has a voice, and you can use all the ad's elements to create it (fig. 9.17).

Keep your voice free of clichés

The best voices sound distinct, singular. One way they do so is by avoiding clichés, whether those particular to advertising or general to the language. You probably remember from your freshman writing course that *clichés*—overused words, expressions, and ideas—are bad: they flatten the prose, numb the reader, and make your voice sound like borrowed clothes look. They are you at your least individual, least interesting, most plagiaristic. So if you find yourself writing a phrase that sounds too familiar, too slick, especially one that tumbles out too fast, cross it off and look for another way to say the same thing.

One problem with copywriting, however, is that the language that defines advertising's territory, the phrases that constitute its meanings, are themselves clichés: "buy now and save," "new and improved," "state of the art," "now with even more cleaning power," "take advantage of this special offer," "for a limited time," "be the first to," "introducing a revolutionary way to," "complete satisfaction or your money back," and so on.

Of course, advertisers *do* want people to buy now and save, they *do* promise more power in this new formula, they *are* introducing a new product. But the language with which these arguments are made is itself so clichéd and corrupted that what ad writers have to say and how they say it have merged into one big cliché in many consumers' minds. Indeed, advertising may have more and more overused clichés than any other field. Consumers see advertising all the time, too, which only accelerates the speed at which fresh language decays into cliché.

It's a content and a form teetering on bankruptcy. The fact that as an advertiser or copywriter you must go in there one more time, make the same argument but make it with enough originality to escape the dead zone of consumer disbelief—this is the great challenge of advertising writing.

Mark Fenske puts the problem succinctly: "People know way too much about ads to let themselves be directly affected by one."[15] Which doesn't mean that you should avoid making ads altogether, though there's much to recommend creating things that aren't (see chapter 24, Postmodern Advertising, for a discussion of ways to get past ads).

Consumer resistance to "the pitch" does mean, at the least, that you write something better than ad copy. You need a real human voice talking about real human truths. Your enemy is clichés—both of language and idea.

How to avoid clichés

Writing well when there are so many clichés around almost seems to require a new dictionary. And to the extent that your voice is un-adlike, to the extent that you can sound not like an ad but like a person, an *interesting* person, so much the better. Sometimes you can avoid a cliché simply by inverting or otherwise modifying its expression. Lots of headlines and clever lines of copy result from twisting a cliché, as Nike did with "when the going gets tough, the tough get going": "when the going gets wet, the wet go Hawaiian" (see fig. 9.8). So don't shun clichés outright; but

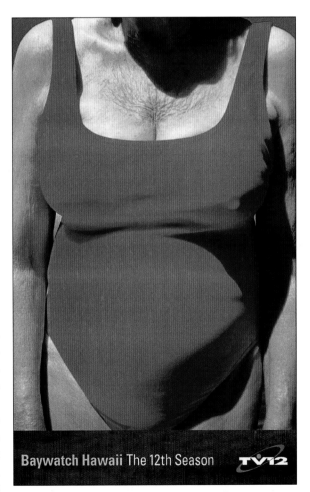

9.17. Ads have a voice even if there isn't a headline. How to comment on yet a twelfth season of *Baywatch*? Why not use a visual that humorously overstates the implications?

9.18. Sometimes it helps to avoid clichéd approaches to "cause" advertising—earnest pleas to idealism—by creating instead a voice that seems to smile through the apocalypse.

There are no hammers.
There are no nails.
But that's okay.
There's no lumber,
either.

Look at it this way: at least you won't need a building permit. What you will need is plenty of determination.

Foresight. The ability to look beyond very real hardships and obstacles and discern a greater good: that of empowering others, of helping them become self-reliant. It might mean teaching people how to raise new shelters. Or how to raze old ones. In every case, it will mean replenishing the most important resource a person can have: their dignity. And you thought construction wasn't a noble profession. **Peace Corps.** The toughest job you'll ever love.

be certain that if you do work with one, you tweak or twist it.

My best advice is the same as what's given in freshman comp courses: recognize and replace clichés in your own writing, and read, read, read good prose (in this case, copy). Copywriters know how many land mines are buried in the fields they must traverse; read the good writers to see how they get across.

For example, the copy for a Peace Corps ad could have sounded like this:

Become a Peace Corps volunteer and help those less fortunate than yourself. Bring your energy to an underprivileged nation and watch it bloom where there was desert. Bring smiles to the people as you teach them how to use modern methods of agriculture, develop healthier sanitation, and find hope in the future. Become your own best self by helping people help themselves.

By contrast, figure 9.18 presents a Peace Corps ad that knows about the clichés of volunteerism. So it features something else instead: ironic commentary about just how impossible the job may be. The attitude here is the hook: not overstated idealism but wise-guy cynicism (the first line of copy: "Look at it this way, at least you won't need a building permit."). Thus the voice is richer than that of most ads because it's more complicated, of two minds: the Peace Corps experience may be both rewarding *and* nightmarish. There is wisdom in this voice, and it wins readers over by transcending clichés.

Find your voice

"The larger one's repertoire of selves, the more wisely one can choose an effective voice in a given situation."

—WALKER GIBSON, *Persona*

The two best ways to learn to write better are, simply enough, to read and write. As I mentioned earlier, study good copywriters like a fiend. Study ads online and in newspapers and magazines, follow people in social media who think well about marketing and advertising. Analyze the work in the advertising annuals and read the copy in the design annuals. Eye-opening annuals include the *One Show Annual*, the British *D&AD Annual*, the *Art Directors Annual*, and those from *Communication Arts*. Get in front of the design and advertising magazines. I recommend *Communication Arts*, *Lurzer's Int'l Archive*, *Graphis*, *Print*, *HOW*, and the magazine for students *CMYK*. *Adweek* and *Advertising Age* cover the business side of advertising—trends, themes, issues.

Don't limit your reading to copywriting. The human voice—in all its variety—is the one you need to hear in your inner ear. Read Steve Martin, David Rakoff, Maureen Dowd, Ian Frazier, David Foster Wallace, Billy Collins, Joan Didion, George Saunders, Susan Orlean, Carl Hiaasen, Jonathan Safran Foer, Nora Ephron, David Sedaris, Michael Lewis. Read *Time* or *Newsweek*, *Wired*, *Rolling Stone*, the *Onion*, the *New York Times*, the *New Yorker*. Open Studs Terkel's books and hear people talk. Assimilate speech, from formal and literary down to funky and street-smart, because all copy comes out of these voices. You re-create the vernacular when you write copy, becoming the people's voice, their human sound. The rhythms and words you need are out there in print (as well as in music, movies, bumper stickers, and everywhere else). Stock up.

Here are two quite different people who make the case for reading:

It's hard for me to believe that people who read very little (or not at all in some cases) should presume to write and expect people to like what they have written, but I know it's true. If I had a nickel for every person who ever told me he/she wanted to become a writer but "didn't have time to read," I could buy myself a pretty good steak dinner. Can I be blunt on this subject? If you don't have time to read, you don't have the time (or the tools) to write. Simple as that.
—STEPHEN KING[16]

I read a lot. Mostly history, biography, one-off little weird things. After all, I'm a writer; I don't know why anybody thinks a writer shouldn't read.
—KEITH RICHARDS of the Rolling Stones[17]

Stylistically, the closest cousin to advertising copy is journalism, so attend especially to the voices of good journalists. Consider, for example, this little bit of Bob Greene, writing an obituary for the wrestler Buddy "Nature Boy" Rogers:

Nature Boy had the greatest speaking voice. He sounded like confidence squared. He walked with a strut even when he walked with a cane. Two strokes last month killed him. The last time I was in south Florida, I took him and his wife to dinner at an Italian restaurant called Casa Bella. He seemed to have a little trouble reading the menu. Maybe his eyes were going bad. I didn't mention it. Some things you just don't do.[18]

Greene's diction (word choice) is common, so he sounds real; he puts in details, so readers see things; and his sentences are straight-line American vernacular, subject + verb + object, so they make reading easy. Readers simply follow someone talking out loud. There's an authenticity to it. You wouldn't want to sell a Cadillac with this voice, but there are plenty of no-nonsense products for which it would work. (And all you've got to do is open a copy of *Architectural Digest* to hear how you'd sell a Cadillac.)

Also you've got to write regularly yourself to get better; exercise that writing muscle. No one gets much better just by watching. Try to write every day. Begin copy assignments with freewriting (rapid, uncensored stream-of-consciousness writing). As E. M. Forster said, "How do I know what I think until I see what I say?"[19] You've got to get the words out there before you can do anything with them. Quick free writings push you past writer's block and begin to show you what you have to say.

Remember: the essence of good advertising language is its human sound. Your first job is to get the consumer's attention, and your next job is to convince him or her that this corporate announcement aimed at thousands, if not millions, is really a nudge of the elbow from one friend to another.

10 · Words II: Writing Well

You may be a technology geek, you may have great desktop production skills, you might be a crack strategist and business nerd, but if you're calling yourself a writer, you should be a strong writer first; you should be reading all you can and writing for all you're worth. If doing that doesn't appeal to you, maybe you should pursue some other creative path.

—TERESSA IEZZI, editor, *Advertising Age's Creativity*

These days, there is way too much emphasis in the schools on integrated thinking. Instead, let's teach our junior copywriters how to write. Integration can be taught easily on the job.

—JOE ALEXANDER, group creative director,
The Martin Agency

Voice is critical to writing well, but it's not alone. Let's examine the other items from your English professor's list of principles:

1. Voice.

2. Details: The writing is full of specifics; it's particular, not vague.

3. Thesis: The writing has one central, unifying idea. It hangs together.

4. Organization and structure: The central idea is developed in some order; there is a beginning, middle, and end, and the writing coheres throughout.

5. Style: Form matches content: the prose is not overwritten. It's stylistically graceful, with strong, clear sentences and well-chosen language.

Detail, detail, detail

While no "rules" of writing are absolutely and always true, this one comes close: good writing is concrete and specific; bad writing is abstract and general. Do you remember your freshman composition instructor always asking for more detail? You needed to point to things, put them in your writing, so that your audience knew what you were talking about. You had to hang your ideas on something besides thin air. This obligation to support generalities with specifics holds true in body copy. A well-chosen detail is more persuasive than a multitude of vague claims of superiority. Consider the advice of ad great Claude Hopkins: "The weight of an argument may often be multiplied by making it specific. Say that a tungsten lamp gives more light than a carbon and you leave some doubt. Say that it gives three and one-third times the light and people realize that you have made tests and comparisons."[1]

WHENEVER POSSIBLE, REPLACE GENERALITIES WITH SPECIFICS

Here's an example from advertising. A VW poster about the safety of Jettas could have said this:

Driving is full of danger and potential danger. There are many distractions, various kinds of inattention, and other obstacles to safe traveling. Some drivers aren't attending to the task at hand; others have started off before they're ready. Everyone faces the uncertainties of intersections, the potential obstacles presented by animals on the road, even occasional life-threatening hazards just beyond the road's edge . . .

Do you see how these are, at best, quasi-details, not real details? As readers, we're floating above the road in clouds of abstraction and generality.

Here is the actual VW poster, with its ground-level details:

On the road of life there are broken traffic lights, outdated eyeglass prescriptions, and rearviews being used as shaving mirrors. There are 16-year-olds steering two-ton SUVs and armadillos wandering aimlessly onto interstates. And there seems to be some general confusion about the rules of a traffic circle. There are also pedestrians who like to read the morning paper while crossing the street and mattresses held loosely to car roofs by folks who never learned how to properly tie a half-hitch. And then there are icy patches of road that run alongside oak trees and those people who think red lights carry a five-second grace period. Come to think of it, the road of life can be a pretty unpredictable place. But we'll keep trying to make that road a little safer, as long as there are **passengers and there are drivers.**

It's easy to use "details" if you simply grab the ones that come readily to mind, which will be clichés, obvious and old. The writer of this Jetta ad looked hard and remembered well. Just the phrase "16-year-olds steering two-ton SUVs" probably didn't arrive in a first draft; the writer might have written the more general "teenagers driving SUVs." But "steering" is so much better than "driving," isn't it, with its not-quite-in-control connotation? "16" says just how new and inexperienced the driver is, and "two-ton" weighs in ominously as a contrast to "16." A strong phrase in a paragraph full of strong details. I don't know what a "half-hitch" is, but I'm glad it's in here; it helps me imagine a precarious mattress. "Outdated eyeglass prescriptions" is such a little thing, but a true one, and it sure beats "old people who can't see well," a more immediately available "detail," don't you agree?

This paragraph is easy to admire, hard to emulate. My shortest advice about how to get fresh detail into your work is this: pull up a chair; work past the easy, vague stuff. But here is some longer advice.

DRAW FROM YOUR RESEARCH

What works when you're researching your client's product also works when you're writing about it. Go back through the facts you discovered on the company and product—awards and honors won; the most intricate but essential part in the machine; the most distant place from which the company procures a part, or the farthest-flung user of the product; where, when, and how the CEO fell in love with the company's product; who he or she studied under; examples of corporate dedication. (Do the chefs grow their own herbs right outside the kitchen? Is the water recycled through filters every twenty minutes? Do the engineers—as Ogilvy discovered when researching Rolls-Royce—listen for axle whine with a stethoscope?) Look for particularities that you might use in the copy.

Deciding which details to use depends on the purpose and scope of the copy you're writing. If it's a website or brochure, a lot of details might be useful; if it's a single ad, online or in print, the headline/visual concept will obviously narrow and direct your writing. Focus on the details that support the ad's concept; save the rest for elsewhere. Regardless of which details you end up using, however, the point is always the same: specifics give density to your copy—weight, realism, and reader interest. They make whatever story you're telling more believable.

Just as copywriters look to the classic VW campaign from Doyle Dane Bernbach for other advertising virtues, they also see that it was a very specific campaign, citing fact after fact in its continuing argument for the Bug:

Headline:
After we paint the car we paint the paint.

Visual:
A VW bug body shell, freshly painted

Copy:
You should see what we do to a Volkswagen even before we paint it.
We bathe it in steam, we bathe it in alkali, we bathe it in phosphate. Then we bathe it in a neutralizing solution.
If it got any cleaner, there wouldn't be much left to paint.
Then we dunk the whole thing into a vat of slate gray primer until every square inch of metal is covered. Inside and out.
Only one domestic car maker does this. And his

cars sell for 3 or 4 times as much as a Volkswagen.

(We think the best way to make an economy car is expensively.)

After the dunking, we bake it and sand it by hand.

Then we paint it.

Then we bake it again, and sand it again by hand.

Then we paint it again.

And bake it again.

And sand it again by hand.

So after 3 times, you'd think we wouldn't bother to paint it again and bake it again. Right?

Wrong.

Some people think that product specs just don't cut it in copy anymore because all products are so similar as to make the specs irrelevant. But remember: detail can be of all sorts. Consider the following copy from an ad for Barney's New York, a clothing retailer. The campaign used the end of summer as impetus for buying fall clothes. The ad's visual was a full-bleed photo of an empty lifeguard chair at the beach, with the headline "SPF 0." The details in this copy aren't about clothing; they're about summer. And look at how specifically the copy remembers:

Blonde hair darkens.

Visine sales plummet.

Lifeguard whistles fall silent.

The signs are obvious.

Summer is over.

Once again baby oil is for babies.

Pool men take up roofing.

And towels migrate to bathrooms.

Slowly, the healthy glow is fading.

A milky luminescence returns.

But all is not lost.

You can still look good without a tan.

Come see the new Fall Collection. Barney's New York

You don't have to be writing huge chunks of copy to use detail, either. Even with a copy crawl, a little ant-line of words, you can say something rather than nothing. A trade ad for Wren, makers of housings and accessories for closed-circuit television, showed a surveillance camera with the headline "Giving you that creepy feeling of being watched since 1982" and this brief, but helpful, copy:

For fifteen years we've been making surveillance domes, globes, and camera mounts. That means saved inventory. Protected employees. And the occasional uneasy glance over a shoulder. Call 1-800-881-2249 to learn more.

Most first-draft copy is too vague, too thin. Readers just hear a pleasant, buzzing noise. Give them the rest of the story, whatever that story is, however quickly you have to tell it. Make their trip into your copy worth the trouble. Readers should know more after reading it than they did before. Rewrite it until they do.

USE PARTICULAR LANGUAGE

"Detail, detail, detail" doesn't simply mean bringing in facts. It also means being specific, not general, throughout the language. Find the best word, not just the most available one. Not "good" chocolate if "seductive" chocolate does more. Not "fabric" if it's "wool." Don't write "every zipper is well made" if instead you can write, as Timberland did for one of its coats, "every zipper is milled and tumbled smooth so as to not injure the leather."

Don't float above your subject; get down into its texture.

FIND THE RIGHT CONNOTATIONS

Connotation counts as much as denotation. You remember from freshman composition that the *denotation* of a word is its strict dictionary definition, and its *connotations* are the shades of meaning that surround it. Thus "smile," "grin," and "smirk" all denote the same thing, but each has a different shade of meaning, a different connotation. There are no synonyms. "Childish" and "childlike" denote the same state, but which would you rather be called?

The Timberland copywriters could have said the zipper was "manufactured," but wisely they added the sense of old-time, small-company methods with the word "milled." They could have said it was polished with "abrasives," but "tumbled smooth" sounds so much better I'd almost like it done to me. Both choices supply the right connotations to the same denotative facts.

Developing this feeling for words, turning them over in your mind before using them, is central to writing good copy. A few bad words can break the spell you're trying to cast. The pressure on word choice in the compressed space of body copy makes it similar to poetry—a high-wire act, grace along a narrow line.

The sound of a single bullet buzzed straight past my ear.

I didn't have to look at the rear-view mirror to know that Dubrov was back on our tail. Our only avenue of escape was through the street market up ahead.

The brightly colored patchwork of stalls rushed up to meet us as Johnson put his foot to the floor. A crate of watermelons exploded wetly against the car, the pink juice streaming across the windscreen.

I stole a quick glance in the mirror. Dubrov's gleaming black limo was getting closer by the second.

It was then that I sensed the first hints of acrid smoke. The stink of a grinding, dying engine.

Our car was going to go, and with it, all our chances.

And as the billowing smoke began to tear at my nostrils and burn my eyes, I realized that it was something much, much worse than an overheated engine. It was my

chicken pot pie burning in the kitchen, the charred, inedible victim of my engrossment in Mitsubishi's Home Theater with Dolby Surround Sound.

▲ MITSUBISHI
TECHNICALLY, ANYTHING IS POSSIBLE

10.1. This ad demonstrates the vivid, involving power of language itself. There are virtually no pictures in the ad, just copy. But we see, hear, touch, taste, and smell a lot, don't we?

CREATE IMAGES

An *image* is anything that appeals to one or another of the senses: sight, touch, taste, hearing, smell. Good writing puts the reader somewhere, and it does so largely through imagery. That's why "russet" is better than "potato" (the reader *sees* more), "sandpaper" is better than "rough" (he *touches* more), and "simmer" beats "cook" (she *hears* and *smells* more). Appeals to the senses are also conduits to the emotions. The more your readers see, touch, and so on, the more they feel. Images reach them.

Read the Mitsubishi TV ad in figure 10.1. The creative problem was how to *show* in print the power of large-screen TV. You can't really do that in print because you don't have the size and you don't have movement. So why not create an all-copy ad that shows, through its vivid language, what dramatic pictures are like? One axiom of good writing is "Show, don't tell." Look at how well this copy does that: things aren't referred to or labeled ("great," "terrible," "exciting"); they're brought right in. Readers experience them; readers have been shown, not told.

CONSIDER METAPHORS

Whenever you talk about one thing in terms of something dissimilar, you're using *metaphor*, and this is often a good idea—it makes what you're saying more clear and more vivid. Look, for example, at the metaphor in the Porsche ad's headline in figure 10.2. And

Imagine the stud fees we'd get if it was a race horse.

Since its introduction in 1974, the Porsche 911 Turbo has given birth to an entire generation of hopeful imitators. None of them even came close.

Considering these bloodlines, it should be no surprise that the new Porsche 911 Turbo is already being hailed as the next benchmark of contemporary supercars.

Made in extremely limited numbers, it combines the remarkable refinement of the new

generation Carrera 2 with the blistering performance of a 316-horsepower turbocharged engine, all wrapped in a legendary muscular body that has steadfastly defied imitation.

We invite you to come see it, along with our entire family of new Porsches. After all, if this is the head of the family, imagine how beautiful the offspring are.

10.2. The power of metaphor.

the copy develops the comparison between horse and car: "Since its introduction in 1974, the Porsche 911 Turbo has given birth to an entire generation of hopeful imitators. None of them even came close. Considering these bloodlines. . . ." The metaphor becomes a kind of detail; readers see the car as a thoroughbred, which is more vivid than "widely imitated," "quality craftsmanship," or other nonmetaphorical equivalents would have been.

The danger with metaphors? Without thinking, you can add other metaphors to the current one and create *mixed metaphors*, which are visual incongruities: "If he goes to the well one more time, he's going to get burned." That sort of thing. So comparing the Porsche to something else while also thinking of it as a horse—for example, saying "it's a piece of sculpture"—would be a mistake; readers' minds prefer one picture system at a time. Also with any metaphor you're taking a chance: maybe it's too weird, too cute, too clichéd, or—if overextended—too irritating. How many more times do you want the Porsche copywriter to mention horses in the ad? Not many, right?

Thesis

Copy is not a bunch of one-liners. It's not a Patton Oswalt or Steven Wright routine full of clever twists, catchy phrases, bizarre non sequiturs. (In this regard it differs from headlines, which often are like something out of a stand-up comedian's act.)

Just as an essay develops one main idea, or *thesis*, so too does copy. It follows from the ad's approach or thesis. Once you've figured out the ad's concept, you'll know what kind of copy to produce, and probably how much. Getting the copy right won't be easy—writing well is always hard—but you'll know what ought to be there. If you're selling children's toys because they help kids learn, then emphasize the educational, imaginative benefits of the toys. If, however, you're selling durability, then talk about rugged plastic and tough wheels, the indestructible little heart of these toys. Even though copy can be the place where you cite additional selling points—that's part of its function, after all—copy should have a dominant idea running through it, and that idea comes from the ad's concept.

Write your sentences in a straight line. Ask of each one, "Does this follow the thesis?" If not, is there a good reason, or have you just digressed? Look back at that VW copy; it was all about the paint job and nothing else.

Organization and structure

" 'Begin at the beginning,' the King said, very gravely, 'and go on till you come to the end: then stop.' "
—LEWIS CARROLL, *Alice's Adventures in Wonderland*

Like an essay, good copy has a beginning, a middle, and an end. Don't keep resaying the thesis; develop it.

BEGINNING

Think of the first line of body copy as the next sentence after the headline. That's why people read copy—to finish what the headline/visual started—so give them what they expect. What's the next thought after that headline? Say it. Follow directly from your lead. And pull hard. You either draw people into the copy with a strong beginning—or you lose them.

MIDDLE

The middle is where you put the selling facts; after all, people don't want more jokes, more one-liners at the headline level. They've gone to the copy for the fine print, as it were; they want details. Put them right here. Even though you may cite additional selling points, keep the ad's concept in mind; don't drop it altogether in the copy. Use its dominant idea as occasional language or imagery. Pull the ad's concept through the copy—not only to make the copy cohere with itself but to unify it with the ad's Big Idea.

Notice in the ad for L.L.Bean (fig. 10.3) how a "satisfy the customer" argument is made throughout the copy. Its point is single-minded and sustained: founder L. L. Bean's experience with his first boot taught him a lesson the company still observes. His story becomes its story, and readers leave the copy convinced of one thing: that L.L.Bean stands behind anything it sells.

END

The close is the place where you put the *call to action*. Much national brand advertising doesn't ask consumers to do anything more than consider the product. But retail ads (and increasingly all advertising) encourage a more active response: "Act now. Sale ends May 21," "Call our 800 number or visit our website for more information." The L.L.Bean ad invites customers to do exactly that: call the 800 number or visit the website to get a free fall catalog. Whatever you want the consumer to do, put it here, in the closing.

10.3. Copy sustains the headline's concept while delivering the specifics that complete it.

THINK OF COPY AS A THREE-PART STRUCTURE

Body copy should end rather than just stop. You want to create a sense of completion, a journey begun and satisfyingly concluded. One way to do this is to think of the headline, the first line of body copy, and the last line of body copy as a trinity—a unified, frequently clever, almost syllogistic summary of the selling idea. (It's handy, by the way, to think of two "last lines": the last line of your argument and what's often literally the last line—the call to action.)

Here's the three-part pattern in the L.L.Bean ad:

Headline:
The first boot he made lasted 2 weeks. The
    lesson it taught him has endured 89 years.

First line of copy:
Some lessons in life stay with you for a long time.

Last line of copy:
Today, you'll find the apparel and gear in our fall
    catalog considerably updated from those times.
    You'll also find the philosophy behind it un-
    changed.

You don't have to write copy this way, but it does work. Such symmetry is itself a kind of persuasiveness: the argument is reiterated but not repeated; the case *feels* closed.

ESTABLISH COHERENCE

So far I've been saying that copy should have one central idea that everything hangs from; it should be unified. But it should also appear unified, which means it must cohere. In addition to hooking up with the Big Idea, the copy's words, phrases, sentences, and ideas must hook up with each other. One writer called good prose a "nest of hooks," and that's a fine image by which to understand coherence. You shouldn't be able to pull any sentence out of the copy without bringing others with it (or without tearing a hole in the copy's sense). Everything should depend on everything else. Thus the relationship of the parts to the parts (*coherence*) is as important as the relationship of the parts to the whole (*unity*).

How to accomplish this? Lots of ways, but words that show relationships are essential. They link one element to another: "first," "second," "another," "and," "but," "so," "however," "above," "under," "last," "therefore," and so on. Pronouns deftly stitch one part to another, too: "The driver walked away from his car unhurt. *Its* airbag saved *his* life." Prepositional phrases, subordinate clauses, and other bits of language tie your meanings together for readers: "*In today's world*, who's safe? *As you know*, the police . . . " The repetition of a word or idea brings coherence, as does the repetition in parallel structures: "If a car is safe, its passengers are safe."

Put transitions up front in sentences so readers know where they're going. In other words, let the transitions steer them through your sentence, as, for example, "in other words" just did. As you write each sentence, keep the previous sentence in mind. Write every line *in response* to the one before it. Keep stitching sentences together (or go back later and do so).

Style

> "Have something to say, and say it as clearly as you can. That is the only secret of style."
>
> —Matthew Arnold, poet and critic

Copywriters shouldn't sound the same any more than essayists or poets should. But this does not mean that all approaches to style are equal. Nor does it mean that style cannot be taught or that it has no rules. Here are some stylistic fundamentals that good writers observe, no matter what they're writing:

1. Tighten and sharpen ruthlessly; never waste words.

2. Write with nouns and verbs, not adjectives and adverbs.

3. Write grammatically straightforward sentences.

4. Use concrete subjects and verbs. Avoid nominalization.

5. Prefer the loose style.

Most stylistic advice boils down to one rule: keep it simple. Use words and sentences no bigger than necessary to deliver the meaning (that is, never write to impress; write to say what you mean). Match form to content, language to idea.

In ways I hope to show you, all the preceding rules are interrelated; they're almost five ways of talking about the same problem.

TIGHTEN AND SHARPEN

> "You want to write a sentence as clean as a bone. That's the goal."
>
> —James Baldwin, novelist and essayist

Don't waste words. One thing you can always hear in great copy is all the words its writer *didn't* use, all the words left out, pruned away. Great copy is lean and like an arrow: it goes where it intends, no waste or wobble. Art directors (and readers) are in no mood for rambling discourses that leisurely visit the selling points.

As a guideline, write your copy to the best of your ability—and then cut it in half. While you probably can't eliminate 50 percent without cutting into muscle tissue, you'll be surprised by how much fat can go. When you strip your prose to its leanest, you'll notice a happy consequence: your voice sounds better—sharper, smarter, more persuasive. One benefit of cutting drafts is that you improve their sound. The VW copy quoted earlier serves as an example; it is so simple and unadorned, pure clear function, just like the car. William Strunk, coauthor of *The Elements of Style*, offers a good perspective on writing concisely: "Omit needless words. Vigorous writing is concise. A sentence should contain no unnecessary words, a paragraph no unnecessary sentences, for the same reason that a drawing should have no unnecessary lines and a machine no unnecessary parts. This requires not that the writer make all his sentences short, or that he avoid all detail and treat his subjects only in outline, but that every word tell."[2]

To tighten your work, reread it and ask of every word or phrase, "Do I need this?"

1. Have I said the same thing elsewhere in the sentence?

2. Is there a word I can substitute for a phrase? (For example, "it will not be very long before" can become "soon.")

3. Am I redundant? ("red in color," "visible to the eye," "new innovation," "final result," and so on)

4. Am I pompous, using more and bigger words than I need to?

5. Am I using the passive voice unnecessarily? ("After the car is painted, the paint is painted" is both wordy and impersonal. Wisely VW wrote, "After we paint the car, we paint the paint.")

6. Do I make meaningless distinctions? ("Are you the sort of person who likes the sport of golf?" reduces to "Do you like golf?")

7. How many of my words are just along for the ride, words that look like they're doing something but aren't? ("Honesty with people is a rare human quality that very few individuals possess" says no more than "Honesty is rare," which isn't saying much in the first place.)

You can eliminate a lot of wordiness simply by taking a pencil to it or hitting the delete key. You'll have to recast other sentences to tighten them. But either way, tightening is wondrous: watch the sentences get quicker, the writing start standing up.

Scrutinize your sentences, too. How many of them can go? Are you using two sentences to deliver an idea you could express in one? With body copy, check out your first few sentences. Are you taking too long to get started, just clearing your throat? Maybe your real first sentence is the third one. Mine often is.

> "When I see a paragraph shrinking under my eyes like a strip of bacon in a skillet, I know I'm on the right track."
>
> —Peter de Vries, novelist

Another piece of advice about editing yourself: the longer you can let a draft "cool," the more you can see the cracks in it. As time passes (an hour, a day, a month), the writing becomes less yours and more someone else's. Eventually it's just words on a page; you can hear and see them objectively. Editing can really get something done then. Try it.

WRITE WITH NOUNS AND VERBS, NOT ADJECTIVES AND ADVERBS

At first this seems to counter common sense: if copywriters are to be "descriptive" and "specific" in their body copy, what better way than by adding adjectives and adverbs? Don't they bring specificity to nouns and verbs? Yes they do, and copywriters need adjectives and adverbs. But it's possible to overindulge, clogging up the flow of sentences with modifiers at every turn.

Nouns and verbs are the two big powers. They run sentences, and you should let them run yours. Strong writers, whose work "flows," write with concrete nouns and verbs. They keep it simple and don't let too much modification stall the movement or muddy up the meaning:

> A weasel is wild. Who knows what he thinks? He sleeps in his underground den, his tail draped over his nose. Sometimes he lives in his den for two days without leaving. Outside, he stalks rabbits, mice, muskrats, and birds, killing more bodies than he can eat warm, and often dragging his carcasses home.
>
> —Annie Dillard, from "Living Like Weasels"[3]

You don't buy a car. The bank buys a car. Of course, if you had bought a Volvo two or three years ago, you'd have something today. You'd have a two or three year old Volvo. Which isn't bad to have. Because where three years is the beginning of the end for some cars, it's only the beginning for a Volvo.

> —Ed McCabe, Volvo copy

In 1941 millions of Jews were looking for ways to escape Nazi death camps. Gandhi recommended suicide. The movie *Gandhi* portrays the Mahatma as a saint. But an original article in the July *Reader's Digest* shows the advice of a saint can be hard to live by.

> —John A. Young, Jr., *Reader's Digest* copy

I needed a drink, I needed a lot of life insurance, I needed a vacation, I needed a home in the country. What I had was a coat, a hat and a gun.

> —Raymond Chandler, from *Farewell, My Lovely*[4]

It would be easy to screw up any of these by stuffing in modifiers. Let's ruin Raymond Chandler. Let's take his terse sentences and add adjectives, adverbs, and what's called *metadiscourse*. Metadiscourse is language that comments on what's being written, that addresses the reader or refers to the speaker or to the subject—as, for example, "for example" just did and as the opening phrase below, "to put it bluntly," does. Some metadiscourse—commenting on the comments—you need, but many writers fill every crack with it. Here is Raymond Chandler after his makeover:

> To put it bluntly, I really needed a stiff drink, I definitely could have used a great big chunk of whole life insurance, I needed in the worst way a quiet vacation somewhere, and, even more than all that, I really wanted another home, one hidden in the country away from the city's endless and difficult problems. But, unfortunately for me, just about the only things I had to my name, instead, were an old, tattered trench coat, a rumpled fedora hat, and a handgun that was, to be specific, 38-caliber with a snub nose.

All is lost, agreed?

It's easy to laugh at this exaggeration, but most writers realize that often enough they approximate it in their own writing. Find good nouns and verbs, then leave them alone.[5]

More about verbs

In *Diary of an Ad Man*, James Webb Young speaks with the voice of experience: "Don't praise the product. Just tell what it does, and how it does it, so that the reader will say: 'I must try that.' In short, go light on the adjectives and heavy on the verbs."[6]

Verbs hustle, weep, surprise, beam, tear, sear, shimmer, and shine; they can stick a finger right in your eye, split your heart open, or collapse into something you'd wedge in your hip pocket. Verbs (and verbals—words derived from verbs, like gerunds and participles) are the only words that *do* anything. Without them nothing happens, and with only general ones ("make," "do," "come," "go," "have"), not enough happens. So use strong verbs, and use them to express the action of an idea. That one Timberland sentence cited earlier offers "milled," "tumbled," and "injure." A lot happens. That determinedly simple VW paint-job copy offers basic but vigorous verbs—"paint," "bathe," "dunk," "bake," "sand"—and they're repeated until readers almost see the sweat of the workers.

Is-ness

Track down and replace excessive "is-ness" in your writing: too many uses of "to be" as the *main verb* ("is," "are," "were," "will be," "has been," and so on). "To be" is an odorless, colorless, actionless verb—just an equals sign, really. It's the weakest verb. If it's running the sentence by itself, you risk the word pile: a sentence with a bunch of upright things in it, all tottering into one another but not going anywhere.

Remember that "to be" often functions as an auxiliary verb, a helper, and that's fine. Thus the sentence "I am smiling because my hair is shining" really has two active verbs ("smile" and "shine"), so it moves, however quietly. "I am here but you are there and it is sad," that's is-ness. Try "I wilt here because you bloom there." See?

You can't eliminate "to be," nor do you want to. (I've been using it a lot in these sentences decrying its use.) Copywriters just rely on it too much. Verbs make sentences move; they animate the universe of things. Always examine your verbs to see if you've got your motor running.

WRITE GRAMMATICALLY STRAIGHTFORWARD SENTENCES

This is perhaps the trickiest challenge. Your sentences are your most complicated stylistic element. They're you. Everyone can locate a better verb and delete unnecessary words, but restructuring language use is a larger matter. Nevertheless, my advice so far has centered on simplicity, and all of it is interrelated. If you

find the right verb, you'll avoid is-ness. If you keep from overdosing on adjectives and adverbs, your writing will be tighter and sharper. It'll move and be readable. Now let's take this same idea of simplicity and apply it to sentences.

If writing good sentences has one first principle, this is it: "State who's doing what in the subject of your sentence, and state what that who is doing in your verb."[7] This sounds easy and obvious, but it isn't. Remember that a sentence, any sentence, is simply a way to say that some thing *does* something. Make sure that this thing (the real agent of action) is also your grammatical subject. And make sure that the real action is also the main verb. Lots of times copywriters put the true agent of action elsewhere than in the grammatical subject, and they stick the real action elsewhere than in the main verb. In other words, they hide what the sentence is saying, and they end up with a fuzzy style that nobody likes.

> The sensation of driving the Miata is pure enjoyment.

A bad sentence. Why? Its grammatical subject is "sensation," its main verb "is." Is the real meaning of this sentence "sensation is"? No. The real meaning is that people will enjoy driving the car. You've hidden the true subject and verb. The real agent of action is either "you" or "driving," and the real action is "to enjoy" or to have sensation. So if that's the real meaning, then put it into the grammatical subject and main verb:

> Enjoy driving the Miata.
> Driving the Miata will thrill you.
> Recharge your senses in a Miata.

Although the last example is the freshest, any of these is better than the original one. Now the agent of action and the action run the sentence; they're not hidden. If one of your sentences feels "blah," you may have the wrong noun and verb in charge. Ask yourself, "Who or what is the main actor in my sentence, and what's the main action?" Then get those two things, the real subject and verb, in their grammatically correct spots:

> BAD:
> A unique approach to outdoor gear by North Face has resulted in clothing that can be worn in any climate.

"Approach has resulted"? "clothing can be worn"? Are those the crucial meanings? Of course not.

Better:
North Face designs its gear so you can tackle any climate.

"North Face designs" and "you can tackle" carry your meaning more directly.

AVOID NOMINALIZATION

Copywriters often fail to match agents with subjects, actions with verbs because of something called nominalization. *Nominalization* involves making nouns out of verbs, and it's the way I killed that Miata sentence previously. "Sensation" is a noun, but it comes from the verb "sense." Likewise, "enjoyment" comes from "enjoy." Somehow or other, copywriters learn to sound formal and pretentious and educated by writing in a style that's heavily nominalized:

A determination of financial conditions facilitates re-evaluation of mortgage arrangements.

Do you mean that people should rethink their mortgage because rates have improved? Say so.

Much writing is dead because people fall in love with the pompous and the obscure. A nominalized style is like a crypt that entombs living speech. Let your nouns name real things, and turn your verbs loose. Don't lock them up in long, boring constructions. Get the real noun (often a concrete thing or a person) out there and give it the verb it deserves.

PREFER THE "LOOSE" STYLE

Keep your sentences simple and conversational. Make them easy to read. How?

Recast sentences that take too long to say. If you get tangled up in a sentence, back out and start over. It probably wants to become two sentences; you need to sequence what you're saying. Much of writing is simply starting into various constructions to see if they'll say what you want them to, like trying tunnel entrances.

Keep subjects and their verbs together. Put them early in the sentences, too, and add modifying material later—either to the ends of sentences, or in sentence fragments that follow. In other words, don't layer modifiers into the subject-verb mechanism; don't mess up the driveshaft.

Adding material to the ends of your sentences (rather than the beginning or between subjects and verbs) is called the *"loose" style*, and it's the American idiomatic voice: simple, straightforward, and adding to itself as it goes. Sentences written in the "loose" style are called *cumulative sentences*; that is, they state their idea right up front in the subject and verb, then add meanings and modifications as they go. They're easy to read, and they sound like you're thinking as you go, which you are. You approximate speech with constructions like these because you just keep talking, and as you talk, you tack new ideas, like this one, onto the end of your last phrase, as they occur to you, so you can go on forever if you feel like it. . . . See what I mean?

The sentences you want to minimize are complex ones with too much modifying material either embedded in the main clause or preceding it. (Check your grammar book under *periodic sentences* or *compound-complex sentences* for constructions to use sparingly.) For example, a sentence like this becomes difficult on the mind:

Although you seek a bank that has the sophistication to handle large accounts yet also has the flexibility to manage smaller ones, you may think that without investing in two separate institutions you're asking too much. . . .

I still don't know what this sentence wants to tell me; it's all preamble. Periodic sentences begin not with the main clause, but with subordinate clauses and phrases, so the sentences are coiled, delivering their full meaning only at the end. Readers have to hold everything in their minds' RAM until the payoff, and that's hard on their brains. Using some periodic sentences is fine, of course, but if you use too many—especially too many with embedded modifications—then your reader will flounder.

Let's recast that periodic sentence as loose sentences instead (and use parallelism in the last two of them):

You want a bank sophisticated enough to handle large accounts yet flexible enough to manage small ones. But you think you'll have to invest in two separate institutions. You think you'll be asking too much of one. . . .

See how this one is easier to follow and sounds more like someone talking?

How to use loose sentences for details

You will often use copy to cite product specs, to deliver the necessary detail, the rest of the product story. You can use loose structures to do this, simply adding details to the ends of sentences. The following professional writers show how gracefully —and clearly—the loose structure handles details:

> Every so often I make an attempt to simplify my life, burning my books behind me, selling the occasional chair, discarding the accumulated miscellany.
>
> —E. B. WHITE[8]

> He [Ken Kesey] wrote like he talked, antic, broad, big-breathed, the words flowing in a slangy, spermy, belt-of-bourbon surge, intimate and muscular, the rigors of the college wrestling mat somehow shaping his way of engaging the world in prose—you got a sense of a writer grappling with his subjects, pinning the story, the paranoia in his vision offset by the relish for the stage.
>
> —CHIP BROWN[9]

Each sentence is easy to follow: the first says, "I attempt to simplify my life," and the second, "He wrote like he talked," both straightforward subject-verb groupings. Then they pile up details off the end. Each sentence could have gone on almost forever, and the reader wouldn't get lost.

In copywriting this approach works well, too. You can be specific, but never let doing so overburden a sentence. Consider this example from the middle of some BMW copy:

> The driver, meanwhile, sits not in a mere driver's seat, but a cockpit—behind a curved instrument panel replete with vital gauges and controls, all placed for optimum visibility and accessibility.

Sentence fragments as the copy version of the loose style

Because copy sentences tend to be shorter than other prose sentences, often you will want to hang modifications off the end of a sentence as *fragments*. You punctuate them as separate sentences, but they're really part of the main thought that preceded them. Here's an example:

> So you need shoes and apparel that don't give up either. A shoe like the Air Cross Trainer Low from Nike, with the cushioning you need for running. The flexibility you need for aerobics. The stability required for court sports. And the fit and comfort your feet beg for regardless of where you tell them to go.

See how all these punctuated sentences are really fragments off the main assertion?

Fragments are almost essential to good copy

Copy is like one side of an intimate conversation, written down. Like the personal letter, it pulls the reader close. That's why sentence fragments (and short sentences) are so important to copy. Cutting off snippets of a sentence and writing sentences that are themselves snippets can provide the speed and openness you want. Well used, they become almost a hallmark of good copy. They focus the eye and mind. They're quick. They simplify issues and make things seem easy and convenient. Plus they sound conversational.

But don't go too far. If you chop up prose too much, it gets unclear and jumpy, too fragmented to make sense. So, like all good writers, use sentence fragments but only on purpose, when doing so helps the prose.

STUDY STYLE

> "The lyf so short, the craft so long to lerne."
>
> —CHAUCER

This discussion of style gets back, as it should, to writing well in general. I've been telling you all along that copy is simply good prose and that you've already had a course in that. But no one ever graduates from composition class. Everyone is a lifelong student of well-made sentences. Since you're a writer now, you should cultivate a writer's habits. In addition to learning by osmosis—reading good copy and good prose—study style systematically. One book you should always keep around is your grammar handbook from freshman composition. Handbooks vary; some are short, some are long, but they're all road maps of the English language, and you can't drive long or far without consulting one.

DECIDE HOW LONG COPY SHOULD BE

In the rush to cut into your copy and keep it simple, never forget that your goal is effective prose, not quick prose. How long is long? How short is short? Copywriter Alastair Crompton tackles that question:

The question, "How long should an advertisement be?" is the same question as "How long is a piece of string?" There is no rule. An ad is too short if it ends without saying the right things to make a sale. An ad is too long if it repeats itself, gets boring, stops giving facts and information, or uses two words when one would do.[10]

Since there is no "rule" about copy length, you must decide for yourself when that string is long enough. Determine how much more information your reader wants. Look to both your client's product and your ad's concept for the amount of copy you should write. If you're making a rational argument for the product because it's complicated—a car, a $2,000 racing bike—then a lot of copy makes sense. If, however, you're appealing to emotions with a brand-image strategy, and the product is one consumers *feel* rather than understand—a diamond, a cologne, clothing—then almost any copy may be too much. You must decide for yourself how much of the story is left to tell after you've found the concept and written the headline. There are no firm rules—I have in my office a fascinating diamond ad with several hundred words in it. On the other hand, a bike or car ad may use few words, or no words, relying instead on feeling or image and counting on other mechanisms (brochures, websites, apps, salespeople) to tell the rest of the story.

AVOID OVERWRITING

> "You come to your style by learning what to leave out. At first, you tend to overwrite—embellishment instead of insight. You either continue to write puerile bilge, or you change. In the process of simplifying oneself, one often discovers the thing called voice."
>
> —BILLY COLLINS, poet

One reason writing well is difficult is that it never reduces to formula; every good rule can be taken to a bad extreme. You can tighten too much and sound clipped and inhuman. You can sharpen too much and sound fussy. Your search for the precise expression can lead to thesaurus-writing—trading in your natural words for artificial ones—short for long, idiomatic for Latinate, real for bookish. Never write out of a thesaurus; in fact, try never to use one at all and you'll be a better writer. Only the words you own and know will work for you; you can't substitute elegant variations and still sound real. That's why reading helps you write; you

come into possession of a larger, more supple vocabulary the natural way.

Good prose must be particular enough to carry meaning but not so overwrought that it sounds like my previous ruination of Raymond Chandler: every noun with an adjective, every verb with an adverb, the whole thing overqualified until its voice lies buried under baroque ornamentation. And copy is especially easy to overwrite: you're making a case for something, you're persuading, and it's easy to push too hard, to hype instead of communicate. Plus you're often writing description. Adjectives and adverbs pop up, as they must, and verbs wither, since you're drawing a picture rather than telling a story. The prose overgrows into a thicket, strangling both your voice and the reader's interest.

How do you know when you've overdone it? By ear. Good prose is ultimately a matter of sound. Read your work out loud, hear it, especially with your target audience's ear. Would they like what you're saying and the way you're saying it? Are sentence lengths varied? Are long sentences mixed with short ones? Is there a good *rhythm* among them? While sentences are generally shorter in copy than in essays—ease of reading being such a priority—you don't want sentences so short as to sound staccato. Nor do you want them all the same length; one after another, they'll drone. Is your *diction* (word choice) precise enough to serve the argument but common enough to sound real? These balances are things you can hear; they're also things that improve with practice.

Here is an excellent demonstration from writing teacher Gary Provost of why you should vary sentence length:

> This sentence has five words. Here are five more words. Five-word sentences are fine. But several together become monotonous. Listen to what is happening. The writing is getting boring. The sound of it drones. It's like a stuck record. The ear demands some variety. Now listen. I vary the sentence length, and I create music. Music. The writing sings. It has a pleasant rhythm, a lilt, a harmony. I use short sentences. And I use sentences of medium length. And sometimes, when I am certain the reader is rested, I will engage him with a sentence of considerable length, a sentence that burns with energy and builds with all the impetus of a crescendo, the roll of the drums. The crash of the cymbals—sounds that say listen to this, it is important.[11]

10.4. How might you sell an in-essential item? By making it fun to contemplate. The retro design and amusing copy become their own little time travel. And just often enough the copy slips in a straightforward pitch for, yes, a potato clock.

How body copy is not like freshman composition

As you've seen, most of what makes an essay good also makes body copy good. Good copy is simply a variant of good writing. There are important distinctions in the variant, however. Here they are.

IT SELLS; IT DOESN'T JUST DESCRIBE

Copy is always selling something, a fact too many beginning copywriters forget. In researching the product and in employing the rules of freshman English, too many writers merely describe product specs. Description and analysis are fine purposes for many essays, but they are never the *purpose* of copy. You are making the case for a product, talking someone into wanting it or wanting more of it or trying it again after all those years ("Have you driven a Ford lately?"). Even when you're describing or analyzing

something, you're doing so to make it seem more appealing, or less complicated, or so well made that it must be bought. No matter what the prose's task seems to be at the moment, you are always a salesperson (fig. 10.4).

IT STATES THE BENEFITS, NOT JUST THE FEATURES

If you slide into product specs and forget that you should be selling instead, you will often write about *features* instead of translating those features into *benefits*. You and I have been here before. Remember, features belong to the product, but benefits belong to the people. Your copy will be "so what?" stuff until you show the advantages to be gained from all those features. This simple headline understands benefits: "California Closets. Because whenever you need something you'll know where it is."

BRAND-IMAGE COPY HAS ITS OWN RULES

Remember, however, that brand-image, lifestyle, and attitude copy describes and sells consumer *feelings*, not hardware. Many ads don't talk about products at all. Instead they resemble short stories, character sketches, or psychological counseling. So don't lock into thinking that ads must talk hardware. Body copy really sells the *idea* of the ad in words. So if the idea is the romance of the sea or the lifestyle of the person wearing a certain brand of clothing, then write that as well as you can.

Consider, for example, the Honda ad in which the station wagon is not described at all; the owner's lifestyle is (fig. 10.5). Instead of detailing product features, the copy narrates the changes in circumstance that the vehicle serves. (Notice the use of "you" to pull in the readers.) In following a life and its funny, endearing complications, readers not only identify with the owner but also appreciate, by implication, the capabilities of the Honda. Well-written lifestyle copy.

A final word: On rewriting

"There is no writing, just rewriting."

—JOHN UPDIKE, novelist

I could have put this in the headline chapter, too, because you can rewrite a headline all day long. But with body copy there are even more words to get right. Rewriting is not a curse visited on bad writers. Writing *is* rewriting. I often wish it were otherwise, but it isn't. I must write lots of drafts, go through a process every time, from fumbling and stupid and incoherent prose to something less so, until sometimes I arrive at good work. Occasionally I can write a headline or short copy block that comes out okay right off. Or sometimes it has to be okay because it's going out the door, no time to fiddle. But most things take me a few drafts. They'll probably take you a few drafts too: a couple just to cover the territory, then a few more to tighten and make it make sense, then a couple more to give it some grace. But even that "sequence" isn't true. Every piece develops differently, few come easily. So learn to accept this process as natural. Rewriting is the way of writing, and eventually it becomes the fun of it, too. Honest.

Literary critic Elizabeth Hardwick captures the universality of the rewriting life in the following comment:

Say, it is Monday, and you write a very bad draft, but if you keep on trying, on Friday, words, phrases,

One day you get married, have kids, get a dog and buy a wagon. So you start driving to day care. You drive to the baby-sitter's place. You drive to your parents'. And, according to your grandparents, you don't drive over to their house as often as you should. Then you start taking the children to preschool. Then to kindergarten. Then to grade school. You drop the kids off at swimming lessons, ballet lessons, trombone lessons and ice skating lessons. A week later, they drop the trombone lessons. You go to the beach one summer and to the lake up in the mountains the next. And you finally decide to go see the Grand Canyon. Your dog barks at all the gas station attendants along the way. You pick the kids up from soccer practices, which soon turn into basketball practices, which soon turn into baseball practices. Then come the football games, which they don't play in, but still need a ride to. And just when you're starting to feel a little like a taxi service, one of your little darlings walks up to you, smiles sweetly, and asks for the keys to the car. You might as well enjoy the trip.

The Accord Wagon ⊞HONDA

10.5. Good copy serves the ad's concept, whatever that may be. In this case, rather than detailing the features of the product, the copy details the lifestyle of its owner, demonstrating the wagon's utility in the process.

appear almost unexpectedly. I don't know why you can't do it on Monday, or why I can't. I'm the same person, no smarter, I have nothing more at hand. I think it's true of a lot of writers. It's one of the things writing students don't understand. They write a first draft and are quite disappointed, or often should be disappointed. They don't understand that they have merely begun, and that they may be merely beginning even in the second or third draft.[12]

Writing checklists

"Who casts a living line, must sweat."
—BEN JONSON, dramatist and poet

The basic writing exercise is simple and unvarying: write a draft and get criticism, from your own internal editor and from colleagues and clients. Keep rewriting until it sounds right, until it works. That's the method. No tricks, no shortcuts.

During that process check for the following things:

Checklist for body copy

1. The lead: Does it pull hard enough, make a quick enough and strong enough transition out of the headline/visual?

2. The middle: Does it say something new? Advance the story? Give details? Complete the argument? Or does it just make nice noises? (You don't have to write features and benefits copy, but be sure whatever you're doing is better.)

3. The close: Does the copy end rather than just stop? Does it pull things together? Does it provide a call to action, that second "last" line? What should readers do now that they've read your copy? Tell them.

4. Structure: Does the copy have a structure? Is the argument or story, however long or short, unified and complete? Does the first sentence follow from the headline/visual? Does the last line return to the first line and headline/visual? (You don't have to follow this pattern either, but remember that copy needs a shape and sense of resolution.)

5. Voice: Is the voice of the copy working? Does it match the headline/visual?

6. Clichés: Have you broken past clichés, both of English and of advertising?

7. Persuasiveness: Does the copy persuade or just describe? How convincing and motivating is it?

Checklist for the English language

1. Spelling and grammar: Is everything spelled and punctuated correctly? Are you gramatically correct? Or incorrect on purpose? (Apple's "Think different.")

2. Verbs: Look at the main verbs. How strong are they?

3. Alignment: Examine subjects and verbs, and align them with the agents of action and the action.

4. Transitions: Look at the transitions. Are there enough? Are they up front in the flow? Are there too many?

5. Sentences: Are they graceful? Varied? Rhythmic? Strong? Simple? How do they sound—not one by one, but all together? In short, does the copy "flow"? Have you connected thoughts and sentences so they sound like a single stream of speech, not a bunch of one-offs?

6. Tightening and sharpening: Have you tightened and sharpened the sentences? (Tightened: gotten as many words out of them as you can without drawing blood. Sharpened: replaced fuzzy, boring, general words with precise ones.)

6a. Editing: Have you edited ruthlessly? Gotten to a 1:1 ratio (the number of words you use exactly matches the ground you cover)?

7. Specificity: Are you as specific as possible? Do you invoke the senses (sight, hearing, touch, taste, smell)? Have you at least asked yourself whether you could?

8. Fun: Are you fun to read? Remember what an editor at the *Wall Street Journal*, Barney Kilgore, said: "The easiest thing in the world for any reader to do is stop reading."[13]

These are tough questions—and the reason all good copywriters read aloud (at least in their heads), solicit commentary, and then, invariably, rewrite.

11 · Interactive Advertising and Social Media

The Internet is inherently seditious. It undermines unthinking respect for centralized authority, whether that 'authority' is the neatly homogenized voice of broadcast advertising or the smarmy rhetoric of the corporate annual report.
—CHRISTOPHER LOCKE,
from *The Cluetrain Manifesto*

Both *social media* and *interactive advertising* define themselves. "Social media" refers to those aspects of digital media that are user-driven, platforms in which people share things (ideas, information, entertainment, almost any kind of content). Companies can jump right into the mix. "Interactive advertising" usually means digitally based, company-sponsored messaging that encourages viewers to respond, participate, even help create it.

But the distinction between interactive advertising and social media often blurs. The Internet *is* interaction; it's social by definition: a community of users, all talking to one another. Interaction is the essence of both online advertising and the use by brands of social media.

Early, not-so-good Internet advertising simply transposed existing forms onto the Web: print ads and outdoor boards became banner ads, and TV spots were dropped in, straight-up. People were still just watching. But Burger King's Subservient Chicken, to name one game-changer, was built on people typing commands to the man-in-a-chicken-costume and finding it uncanny that the Chicken could do what they said. This new, bizarre thing was fun to play with and more fun to pass along. As the Chicken demonstrated, interactivity begins when consumers opt in.

Digital vs. print-based thinking

The power of interactive advertising and social media might best be demonstrated by contrasting them with another medium, print.

I recently saw a magazine ad for a car whose headline was "Wipe that smile on your face," accompanied by a smiling, happy driver. The headline is a nimble enough reversal of the cliché, but the ad asserts something without proving anything. It has that empty cleverness associated with so much advertising copy.

Interactive advertising and social media, however, can prove that line true or false. The car company can find out if people really do wipe a smile on their face by giving trendsetters a car for a few weeks and letting them blog about it, smiles or no smiles. Or the company can film these people as they go about their driving lives and post their experiences online. Or it can sponsor a road trip, an obstacle course, a treasure hunt, a cross-country expedition, or any number of other driving experiences. The company can encourage site visitors to help direct these adventures, interact with the drivers, or comment on what makes them, the visitors, smile. In short, "wipe that smile on your face" can become a line with many meanings and ways to be put to the test. The brand can *prove* its "smile" claim by letting people enact it, debate it, interpret it, and assume control of it themselves.

One-way messaging, like that magazine ad, pales in impact with interactive approaches. It's not that a company shouldn't write such a headline, but that writing it doesn't do enough. The ad could, however, invite people to prove the line by visiting the car company's website and taking a virtual test drive (or involving themselves in other online options).

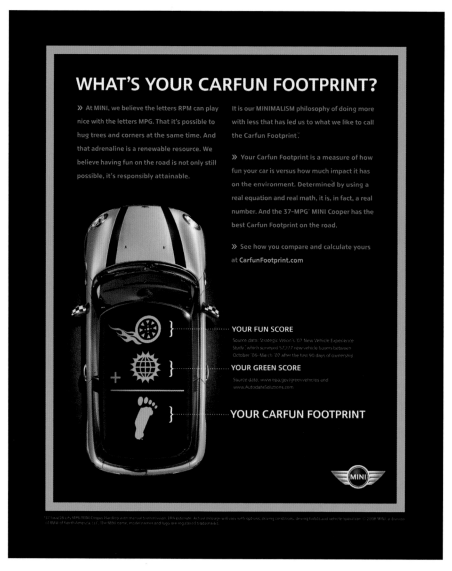

This MINI magazine ad (fig. 11.1) addressed the same issue as the "Wipe that smile on your face" ad: how much fun is this car? But instead of just talking about it, the ad tried to *prove* the fun claim. It gave consumers a way to determine how many smiles they were likely to have in a car by, if you can believe it, quantifying happiness—or, rather, quantifying the relationship between fun and environmental responsibility, an important criterion for any car.

Prospective car buyers could go to a MINI microsite and use a legitimate analytical method to determine a car's "carfun footprint," the ratio between having fun driving a car and taking care of the planet. This do-it-yourself idea had the MINI whimsy about it, and, more importantly, it made a kind of sense that puffery never will, while inviting viewers to interact digitally with the brand. It was a solid print ad that was also a

portal. Excellent, smart work, and very much a lesson in one page on how to move beyond print while not abandoning it.

What's an idea in interactive copywriting?

"Just making better ads won't get it. Marketing has to move beyond ad-making."

—Chris Wiggins, interactive creative director, Crispin Porter + Bogusky

Wiggins's comment applies to many areas of advertising but especially to interactive media because consumers can choose to involve themselves—or not. Unless a brand is interesting, even compelling, it is ghosted and gone. There are few captive audiences online.

Given people's disinclination to suffer through one-way advertising pitches, what to do? Here are guidelines for new media and the new consumer. Think of them as different ways of reaching the same goal: getting beyond one-way advertising.

1. Don't make ads; make "cool things." If people dislike advertising, give them something they do like. They'll be grateful.

2. Fit the message to the medium. Every medium wants to be used a certain way; the Internet is no different.

3. Make the cool thing a useful thing. Utility trumps all.

4. Synch the cool thing with the brand. Don't be interesting but commercially irrelevant; be interesting *and* relevant.

5. Synch the brand with people's behavior. Instead of going outward from the brand, go inward from consumers. Track back to the brand from what people are up to. What *are* they doing? What *do* they want or need?

6. Make social responsibility central to the brand. If your client's brand isn't helping make things better, why not?

7. If you do make ads, make cool ones. This has always been true, but it's true with a vengeance now.

DON'T MAKE ADS; MAKE "COOL THINGS"

The two largest obstacles you face trying to communicate with consumers are clutter (your message blends in with other messages) and fragmentation (people can be anywhere). Further, with interactive media, you start in a hole if you try to stop people from what they want to do. So broaden your ideas of advertising and communication. The best advertising is increasingly *not* advertising, but something else.

For advertising agency Crispin Porter + Bogusky, masters of new media, that something else is a "cool thing," something with legitimate value that people will seek out and pass along to others, that they'll find useful, entertaining, or both. A "cool thing," according to Chris Wiggins, can be a service, a physical object, an entertainment, or a practical, useful thing. "If there *are* ads, they're for the cool thing, *not* the brand's product," he advises.[1]

One of the early non-ad ads (2001) was the BMW film series, *The Hire,* eight short films directed by major filmmakers and starring Clive Owen as The Driver, a man pushing BMWs to the max. They weren't great ads; they were great short films. And that made all the difference. They knifed through clutter because they weren't ads at all; they solved the fragmentation problem because people were pulling them in, *choosing* to watch them. They generated buzz because people talked about them; they weren't BMW talking to consumers explicitly, just eight short movies with an air of mystery and a lot of adrenaline-soaked BMW action.

Consider branded content

The Hire is an example of *branded content,* another term that defines itself. Something—it can be almost anything—that people find useful or entertaining is brought to them by a brand. Thus "content" is "branded." Many of the non-ad ads that I'll discuss are branded content. The great virtue of all of them is that they circumvent people's unwillingness to sit still for advertising. Marketers hammering away about their wonderful products has become too dreary to be endured. If, however, a brand brings people what they really want, all is forgiven. More than that, the brand becomes associated with the positives of the thing delivered.

Branded content has often been, however, a clunky, obvious, boring thing in its own right, especially *product placement,* wherein the brand just plops itself down in the middle of things. Everyone has seen movies and TV shows with the camera lingering over a succession of brand names (James Bond movies are notorious for this). By show's end, viewers are as worn out as if they'd been marched through a mall.

Do better.

Be entertaining or useful, not pitch-heavy

AEG-Electrolux, European makers of household appliances, sponsored a series of long-form, Web-based videos, each of them about a craft practiced to perfection: "the best butcher in London," "the oldest bakery in Berlin," "the perfect apple strudel," and so on. Nothing is said in the videos about AEG-Electrolux, but, as each artisan demonstrates his craft, the brand becomes associated with excellence and care in how things are prepared. The videos are not quite shows, certainly nowhere near infomercials, with their relentless repetition and hard sell; rather, they're a third thing: compelling, useful nonfiction documentaries demonstrating, in each case, perfect technique. These often surprising stories about excellent craftsmanship serve as metaphors for AEG-Electrolux's own craftsmanship, a sensible claim since AEG has been a pioneer in industrial design (AEG's slogan is "perfekt in form und funktion"). Very watchable, winning work.

11.2. Viewers can move things on the Web. A selling argument that's fun to fiddle with.

Watch the puzzle and slider banner ads in action at fig. W-11.2.

FIT THE MESSAGE TO THE MEDIUM

CP+B "loathes" banner ads on social media like Facebook, says Wiggins. Instead, he and his agency suggest, do something connected with why people are there and how the medium works. Don't just stick an idea on the medium, like a Post-it note. Build it in (fig. 11.2).

CP+B tapped into one perplex of social networking—the disparity between the quantity of one's "friends" and their quality—by creating for client Burger King the Whopper Sacrifice, a Facebook application that allowed users to remove ten friends for a free Whopper hamburger; they even got to "flame broil" the friends in a motion graphic. CP+B used a human truth as a starting place, as their point of tension.

Another truth is that people create personae in social media, representing themselves to others in many, often joking ways. Why not take advantage of that? One such non-ad ad CP+B created, again for client Burger King, was Simpsonize Me. People could Simpsonize their faces, have them transformed into personal versions of the cartoon characters, then use them however they wanted—as their Facebook images, for example. The revenue stream came from things people could buy with their face on them: hats, aprons, T-shirts, etc. CP+B wrote memorable theme lines for Simpsonize Me, too: "Turning the world yellow one Simpson at a time" and "Eat. Drink. Be Yellow." (Here is a link to a Burger King ad promoting Simpsonize Me: http://www.youtube.com/watch?v=w_3RQe_zg1A)

Use the characteristics of the medium to create the "cool thing." Since people create personality profiles on Facebook, MoMA (The Museum of Modern Art) in New York designed a website that worked with them. It analyzed a user's profile, then matched those preferences with exhibits at the museum, thus tailoring a visit to MoMA for just that person. Given the size and scope of art museums, these recommendations helped people make the most of their visits. Facebook users were able to share this information with network friends, save it, and adapt it, too.

Since search engines direct so much Internet activity, what can be done with them? In a creative understanding of how people use search engines, Alec Brownstein, a fellow looking for a job in advertising, set up his own résumé as a top hit for six advertising heavyweights when vanity got the best of them and they Googled themselves. He landed interviews with most of them and was hired at Young & Rubicam. Again, the idea comes from within the medium's characteristics, not from outside them. (See fig. 11.3 for another Web ad that takes advantage of the medium's characteristics.)

All these ideas are fresh and fun. They aren't ads, but they do marinate consumers in the brand, so they're not commercially irrelevant. They fit their messages to the medium. And best of all, they connect consumers to the brand (more precisely, consumers connect themselves) without a heavy hand. With the Whopper Sacrifice, for example, Burger King didn't force-feed consumers some burnt-up advertising line like "Flame Broiling: The Special Way A Whopper Satisfies." They let consumers do the flame broiling themselves.

MAKE THE COOL THING A USEFUL THING

Most people need all the help they can get. How can your client's product or brand help them beyond whatever it's doing already? For example, running shoes help people run. The product is already doing something for people, or it wouldn't exist. But regard that something as insufficient, way insufficient, and you've begun to think outside the running-shoe box.

Nike did so by creating Nike+, a Web-based brand extension that embodies usefulness (nikeplus.com). Runners can get customized training programs, challenge friends to races or invite them along for a run via Facebook, download maps of routes, time and measure their runs, find out about marathons, get advice from specialists, follow Nike Run Reporters around the country, and do a zillion more things besides just taking shoes out of a box. In fact, NIKEiD encourages people to customize those shoes *before* they take them out of the box, and the NIKE+ GPS app helps runners keep track of their workouts. With "PowerSongs" and voice feedback during the run, the app makes sure that no runner is alone.

In short, Nikeplus.com is a community surrounding that shoebox, a network of fellow runners, and a host of branded, buyable, downloadable things (often in concert with Apple gear) wrapping the runner in a world nearly without end. By extending the brand's meaning to consumers, Nike+ puts in play the multiplying power of interactive advertising and social media. Nike is doing what your client's brand should be doing: following the ripples out from the stone.

Here's another instance of moving beyond product. Best Buy discounts electronics. That helps people, certainly, but it's not enough. In the bewildering category of electronics, people need advice as well as discounts. So Best Buy created TwelpForce (the name is a portmanteau pun: "Twitter" plus "help force"), a collection of employees ready to answer consumer questions and deliver technical advice, one tweet at a time, every tweet free of a sales pitch. It's a truly useful non-ad ad: help without a catch.

Best Buy even posted online its instructions to employees who wanted to join TwelpForce so that anyone could read them. Doing this dissolved corporate walls; there was no inside or outside. Consumers couldn't feel tricked by some marketing scheme.

Let's listen to part of Best Buy's instructions to its employees:

Why customers might want to talk to you on Twitter? The promise we're making starting in July is that you'll know all that we know as fast as we know it. That's an enormous promise. That means that customers will be able to ask us about the decisions they're trying to make, the products they're using, and look for the customer support that only we can give. And with Twitter, we can do that fast, with lots of opinions so they can make a decision after

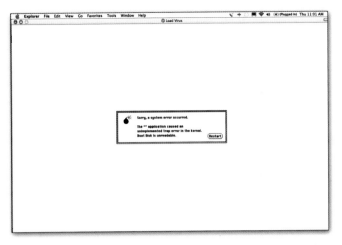

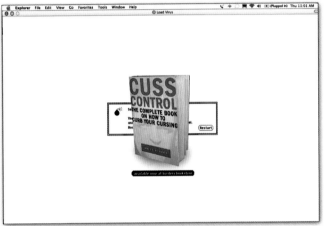

11.3. If you saw the first screen of this Web ad, chances are you uttered a few of the words this book addresses. No matter what the medium, the principles of good advertising always operate: create awareness of a problem, announce a solution, and make getting it easy.

weighing all the input. It also lets others learn from it as they see our conversations unfold.

When you start, remember that the tone is important. Above all, the tone of the conversation has to be authentic and honest. Be conversational. Be yourself. Show respect. Expect respect. The goal is to help. If you don't know the answer tell them you'll find out. Then find out and let them know.

This sounds so consumer-directed that, as a reader, you have to keep reminding yourself that it's the company talking to company employees. Inside voice and outside voice have merged. Alex Bogusky and John Winsor put what's at stake with customer service this way: "Would you rather make how well your company communicates with customers a part of why people trust you, or a part of why they *don't* trust you? That is the only question left."[2] Any company interested in survival now enters into dialogue with consumers. Figure 11.4, for example, shows Comcast's Twitter help center, where Bill Gerth, the company's social media leader, nimbly fields questions, one by one, from consumers.

SYNCH THE COOL THING WITH THE BRAND

Don't do something unrelated to what the brand is about. Use digital advertising and social media to demonstrate that.

Best Buy wants to be seen as the big-box electronics retailer with a genuinely knowledgeable staff, and the free technical advice from Twelpforce helps prove that position.

If your client makes tires, go past them to why people buy tires in the first place. Talk about travel, not tread patterns. BFGoodrich, the tire brand, extended itself in just this way by creating The Nation of Go, a web community for people who love cars and car trips, a site on which to post favorite drives, videos, photos, and such. "It's part social network, part user-generated content and part Web tool, built on the Google Maps platform and integrating data from the EveryTrail powered mobile app," explained Odopod's Matt Jarvis, the agency's chief strategist.[3]

Let extensions like these suggest ones you could undertake for your client. Determine the core expertise of the brand, then think how you might spread that out to other media and venues, how you might express those skills in new ways.

If possible, appeal to consumers, not by making them listen to a message, but by letting them help create it. For Playland amusement park, known for its death-defying rides, advertising agency Rethink created the Scream-O-Meter, which invited people to scream into their computer (to gauge how ready they were to handle the rigors of the rides at Playland). Those who screamed loudest got discounts on Playland tickets. This "cool thing" communicated the brand's core benefit by encouraging consumers to communicate it themselves.

The "cool thing" may well be an app

Since apps can be so specific, they continue to replace big, clunky websites as ways to interact digitally (fig. 11.5). The future is mobile. As a writer, you'll be asked, more and more often, to "language" an app. Writing for mobile apps is an exercise in wayfinding. You're helping people find their way through a place but doing so a few words at a time; you're giving directions, ever so briefly.

Some fundamentals:

1. First things first. Know what you're trying to do: find out who your audience is and what they want. What are the possibilities? What are the sequences? Create a brief for this app just as you would for any advertising problem.

2. Write so tight you squeak. Take to heart every piece of advice in this book about tightening and sharpening your sentences. Your words will have no room to turn around. None. Look again at chapter 10, Words II: Writing Well, and its suggestions: write with nouns and verbs (strip out unnecessary adjectives and adverbs), write straightforward sentences (start with subjects and get right to their verbs), be precise instead of fuzzy, and so on. Brevity demands clarity; when you're writing at your best, they become one.

3. Be a friendly wayfinder. Help your users navi-

11.4. Free technical advice, and who couldn't use some? By being helpful, the communications technology company Comcast creates good advertising for itself with every tweet. (https://twitter.com/comcastcares)

11.5. Try on shoes without leaving the house or opening twenty boxes.

gate the experience without being frustrated by it. People want to feel in charge, so keep things simple, unambiguous, and positive. Being brief doesn't mean being curt. Use contractions and the second person ("you"). Pull your reader/viewer/user close. Command forms of the verb speed users along: "Search flights," "Swipe for more results," "Find gas near me." Remember, the app is an extension of a user's hand and mind; it should feel like it.

4. Speak plainly. Your audience may well be international, so the English you use should be accessible to all. Don't talk down to your audience, though. Assume their intelligence and respect them.

5. Craft it. Once you've got the language tight enough that dimes bounce off it, do the usual: rewrite it, again.

SYNCH THE BRAND WITH PEOPLE'S BEHAVIOR

We're back, as we so often are, to the principle of features and benefits. Don't put a pretty face on what you already make; find out what people want and then make that. Begin from the benefits end. If your client makes pizza, don't start with pizza; start with pizza lovers. What's true about them? For one thing, they can't wait for delivery, and, for another, they'd like to create their own pizza, not just choose it from a list. Domino's wanted to be the brand that solved those

problems. To help consumers gain control and reduce waiting-for-the-pizza anxiety, Domino's (with Crispin Porter + Bogusky) created the Pizza Tracker, a Web-based timeline pinpointing just how far the pizza had journeyed from oven to front door (this descended from an early brand promise to have pizza delivered in half an hour or less). Additionally, Domino's set up a way for consumers to build their own pizza, name it, and save it to their online Domino's shopping cart, ready to re-order anytime they wanted.

So track back from people's needs and wants to things your client's brand might make. What are people looking for that they can't yet find? What habits lie unaddressed? Help your client's brand come to the aid of the people.

MAKE SOCIAL RESPONSIBILITY CENTRAL TO THE BRAND

"What we're starting to see being borne out again and again is that good service, social responsibility and sustainable practices aren't just for Vermont ice cream makers; they are a collective economic imperative for every kind of company."

—Teressa Iezzi, editor,
Advertising Age's Creativity

Ask what capabilities and social concerns ripple out

11.6. Use the brand's past to move it forward.

ⓢ Watch the train run through *Time* in fig. W-11.6.

from your client's brand. What does the brand believe in? What possibilities for social good are implied by the things it sells? Here are some suggestions for expanding a brand's meaning.

Enact the brand's position

It may be in the slogan, and if it is, start there. Pepsi, for example, has consistently positioned itself as the "new" cola (as opposed to their antecedent and main competitor, "old" Coca-Cola), identifying with young people and those who like to think they are. Slogans have included "The choice of a new generation," "Generation Next," "Be Young, Have Fun, Drink Pepsi," and, recently, "Refresh everything."

Taking this idea of renewal out of talk and into action, Pepsi created The Pepsi Refresh Project, a social media extension that embodied the brand's positioning and grew out of the campaign theme line: "Every generation refreshes the world. Now it's your turn." People were invited to propose socially valuable projects (using Facebook, Twitter, and Flickr to help promote their cause); these projects were posted on refresheverything.com, and visitors could vote for the

ones they liked best. Winners received major money (up to $50,000) from Pepsi to go forth and do what they had proposed. "Every Pepsi Refreshes The World" and other such lines transcended adland hoo-ha by actually meaning something.

Coca-Cola has extended its slogan "Open happiness" in a similar way. One project, Expedition 206 (the number of countries in which Coke is sold), canvased the world to document people's differing ideas of happiness and where to find it. Coca-Cola created the theme line "Where will happiness strike next?" and found inventive ways to answer the question. Trucks dispensing free Cokes and other goodies appeared around the world, and, in a socially conscious effort, Coke helped reunite Filipino workers away from their home with their families.

Use the brand's history

The slogan for Evian bottled water is "Live young," and for some time the brand has been doing things with babies like creating hugely popular videos of baby ballet and roller babies and launching a YouTube Evian baby channel people can participate in. All this may seem a long way from bottled water, but actually it's part of the brand's history. In the 1930s, when safe drinking water in France wasn't a sure thing, Evian produced bottled water known as "the water for feeding-bottles" because it was bacteria free and didn't need boiling. Evian was about babies in 1935, and it's about babies today. Part of the brand's history has simply been pulled forward.

Coca-Cola has done this by taking one of its advertising icons, polar bears (they date back to 1922), out of advertising and into the real world—Coke teamed with World Wildlife Fund to help preserve habitat for the now-endangered polar bears in the Arctic. Consumers could help make the idea a reality in several ways: each text message they sent, each Coke product they bought, added money to the cause. The campaign created special packaging and websites with which to carry out the project—all of it a smart example of giving a brand's past new relevance, new meaning. (In fig. 11.6, see how Union Pacific Railroad makes the most of its 150th anniversary.)

Address the brand's biggest weakness

What do people or the culture itself have against your client's brand? Don't try to talk your way out of it; enact your way out. Address the problem in a real-world way. Walmart, for example, has been criticized for destroying communities with its giant-sized commercial footprint and price-driven power. So the brand is working to become the eco-friendly big box. If it succeeds in changing consumer perceptions, it will have mitigated its cultural negative.

Snickers knows what everyone knows: candy bars are not on the short list of health-giving foods. So Snickers has attacked that weakness by getting into the let's-get-healthy business with a website encouraging people, especially young people, to live and eat more responsibly.

You may think these are cynical gestures, and since I can't analyze corporate motives, perhaps they are. But doing good is doing good. Many people came to see Pepsi, to name one brand, as an *idea* as well as a drink: "refresh everything," which could have been puffery, instead became a cause. Similarly, Coca-Cola appears serious about exploring the dimensions of happiness.

IF YOU DO MAKE ADS, MAKE COOL ONES

"On the Internet today, advertisers don't merely compete with other advertisers, they also have to compete with anyone who has a video camera. A traditionally clever TV spot stands no chance against a ten-second video of grandma falling off a stepladder."

—Joe Shepter, *Communication Arts*

The guiding principle of the new advertising is this: Don't interrupt entertainment with your ad; be entertaining yourself. As Yash Egami, editor in chief of *One. A Magazine*, puts it, "The age-old argument has finally been answered with an almost Zen-like proposition: People will pay to see commercials if the commercials are what they are paying to see."[4]

One way to be interesting is to be surprising. This banner ad from BMW (fig. 11.7) breaks the "rule" of brevity, but does so with such wit that people, once they start reading the copy, probably continue. Do they read it all the way to the end? Hard to say. But no

11.7. In a "short-form" digital world, exceptions will always have their place as antidote, which is why this long-form BMW banner ad works so well. It's got so many things to push against. I can show you here only a few hundred of the 5,500 words that unfurl when the banner box is rolled over: the entire text is 20 feet long. But if you have time for a fun read, roll over the ad on the book's website and settle back.

 For the actual, nearly infinite ad, go to fig. W-11.7.

INTRODUCING THE ALL-NEW BMW X3.
ROLL OVER TO SEE HOW ▸

We bet that you hardly ever read ads. Yet for some reason, you're reading this right now. You must have sensed that this banner was something special. And you were right. Not only is this an ad for the all-new history-making BMW X3, but it's also the world's longest web banner, ever. Now you're probably very tempted to just scroll down to the bottom to see how long it is. Resist the urge. We thought this could be a great chance for us to spend some quality time together. Think of this ad as a metaphor for a journey in the all-new BMW X3 – we bet when you clicked on this ad, you didn't realize you were actually clicking on a metaphor. And the best part about a journey is that you never know what will happen next. Watermelon! See? You didn't think we would just suddenly scream out watermelon. Granted, shouting watermelon isn't really much of a surprise. We just thought of it on the spur of the moment. But we can assure you that there are a lot of much better surprises to come below that we put a lot more thought into – and none of them involve us screaming out random words. So sit back and enjoy the ride because this BMW X3 ad can take you anywhere.

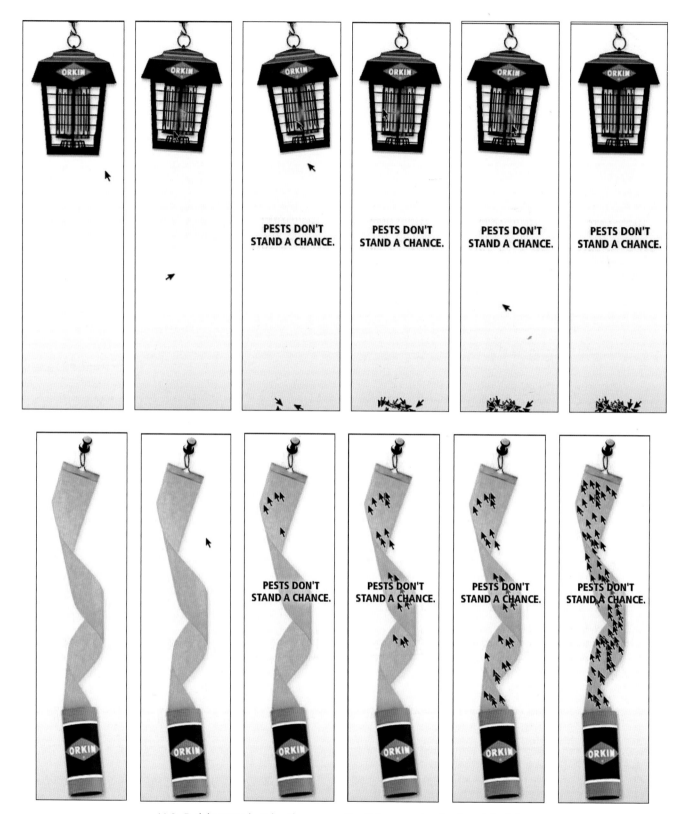

11.8. Each banner ad catches the cursor—the sticky paper stopping it, and the light zapping it. Very clever ways to show through metaphor what these products do.

See the fly paper and zapper in action in fig. W-11.8.

matter how far they get, they'll remember this ad more than all the ones that, by taking no chances, made no impression.

In another surprise, a banner ad created by Vancouver ad agency Rethink releases a monitor that follows a person's cursor as it moves around the screen. If that person clicks on the monitor, he or she is sent to the security company's site. A clever and fun way to link the ad—and the potential consumer—to the brand.

In figure 11.8, two more banner ads from Rethink use the medium's characteristics to enact the brand's promise.

Fun doesn't have to be the only draw. Make your ad helpful and interesting enough that it becomes a go-to resource. As Keith Byrne advised in *Creativity* magazine, "Whenever possible [on the click-through idea] give the opportunity to relate directly to users' lives."[29] For example, web ads for Parentsoup.com invited people to enter their child's name and find out its etymology or enter her age and find out what her college education would cost. Ads for CondéNet's Epicurious.com website invited people to enter their favorite ingredients to receive recipe suggestions.

Even when you're selling, write about the brand's values at least as much as the things for sale. Nikeplus.com sells lots of things, but those things emerge from a worldview that sees running as not just healthy, fun, and social, but also somewhere near the meaning of life. The website seems less like a retail outlet (although it is certainly that) than a great big running club full of true believers. Nike has carried its meaning way beyond the box. No brand should be just an assortment of things, even persuasively described things. Thingness is inert, and brands, like friends and groups of friends, do far more for the people they care about.

The Purina Cat Chow site (fig. 11.9) shows how to rise above product and also how to use interactive, digital space: make it alive with possibilities. Create a series of things that can't just be looked at; make every moment a clickable moment. No matter where on this page a visitor looks, there's something to do.

The designer, Resource Interactive, explains the site: "A social widget gives users on-demand access to the newest Flickr photos, YouTube videos, and Facebook and Twitter posts on every page. The Stories page continues the website's personal feel, highlighting . . . stories and pictures from brand fans."[5] There are videos from experts and a searchable compendium of articles and tips, the "Catipedia," to answer questions about cats. The site has been search-optimized to help it become a go-to source for cat lovers. And all the articles, stories, and videos can be commented on, tweeted, or shared on Facebook and Twitter, so users can network with friends and fellow cat lovers via the site.

In short, Resource Interactive has created a full-service, online cat-lovers community, as well as demonstrated what a website is supposed to do: involve its viewers actively in substantial, useful content. If someone loves cats, this site is determined to hit as many of that person's hot buttons as possible. And hit them in a visually oriented, click-here, watch-this, tell-your-story, send-your-photo, ask-a-question way.

How to write for the Internet

Once you've found a "cool thing" or a strong ad idea and start putting words to it, you'll see that the principles of writing well still apply. But like the leap from college football to the NFL, the game gets faster and more precise. Speed and clarity matter more than ever.

What follow are principles for interactive, digitally based prose. While much of the advice assumes that you're writing a website, these guidelines concern quick, clear functionality, so they apply nearly everywhere in digital space.

BE AN INFORMATION ARCHITECT FIRST, A WRITER SECOND

Reading online still differs from reading offline: people are scanning before reading, if they're reading at all, in the sense of word-for-word. To orient themselves quickly, they look for headlines, subheads, dominant type, dominant images.

If you're writing a brand website, microsite, or app, decide what these big things should be. Let the outlines you created for essays in high school and college be your model, boring though they may seem. Digital architecture, the words part, *is* outlining. Maybe like me, you wrote that outline *after* you wrote the essay. That's okay. Maybe, also like me, you have to write a lot before you can even think to outline. That's okay, too. But eventually you'll need to organize the scrum, so either start by creating a scratch outline or keep sections-to-be in your mind as you write.

Here are questions to help you organize. Notice that they're like those on an advertising creative brief, but with a web sensibility:

1. Who are you targeting? How wide or narrow is the audience for this brand and site? Make that list

11.9. I dare a cat lover to stop here only briefly.

⑤ See fig. W-11.9 for more selected screen shots.

of users and uses and then design the site and its language to fit that list.

2. What are you trying to accomplish? How many needs should this site or app serve? What do you want people to *do* with it? Will they learn about the brand, from mission to history to products to personnel? Buy from it? Find nearby restaurants with it? Define what a successful visit to the site or use of the app would be.

As you're organizing, remember these practical matters:

- **Put the most important stuff in the most important places:** at the top of the page, in headlines, subheads, boldface type, links. Since people are scanning, they'll notice these first. Be search-engine friendly. SEO, search-engine optimization, is a science unto itself, but it entails putting key words in key places, so that search engines using such keywords will return your client's site high on the hit list.
- Provide a slogan, tagline, or theme line on the home page, so that visitors will know immediately what the site, app, Twitter account, or blog is about. Let's say they stumble upon stumbleupon.com. What is that? Its descriptor, right below the logotype, tells them: "Discover cool stuff personalized to you. Explore the best of the web with a single click." And that's accompanied by a simple flow chart that shows how the site works.

  Twitter encourages those who tweet to give themselves a brief bio, right up top, to serve as a tagline, a brand statement for visitors:

  @Etsy says this about itself: "The world's handmade marketplace."

  Susan Orlean's Twitter bio makes its point: "Writer, writer, writer. Oh, I also write."

  Nike gets right to it: "If You Have a Body, You're an Athlete."

  Old Spice puts product line and brand image into less than a sentence: "Drop-kicking dirt and odor, doing a clothesline on them and then slamming them with a folding chair."

- **Make every screen clear about what and where it is on the site.** Since you can't tell where people will first enter a site, repeat header information on every page.

- **Write captions for everything:** pictures, graphs, tables, embedded videos. A visual without a caption is just floating decoration. Label anything that comes from somewhere else (users' comments, external reviews, republished material). Let visitors know who is behind any chunk of text.
- **Invite people to get involved.** You want visitors to *do* something: vote, chat, choose, tell their story, add a comment, play the game, see the floorplan, take a virtual test drive, tweet a link, retweet a comment, jump to the brand's Facebook page or Twitter account. If they're just watching or reading, you're not involving them enough. (The Purina Cat Chow site, opposite, is a model for many of these guidelines.)

3. Find the right voice. People will often say that they're reading Malcolm Gladwell or Sarah Vowell before they'll think to name the book. They read novelists, essayists, and other writers because they like to listen to them. When you're writing for the Web, you want people to like to listen to you—and your brand—too. You just face a less patient reader than do Vowell and Gladwell and other long-form writers.

See fig. W-11.10 for banner ads whose voice—straightforward, encouraging, and funny—makes people want to listen.

So, no matter how briskly you need to say things, speak with a voice worth listening to, and make it congruent with the brand. As online writer Nick Usborne points out, "Not only will a personal voice help your company connect more easily with your customers online and hold their attention and loyalty for longer, but it will also represent your best defense against the competition. Competitors may be able to duplicate your products, services, pricing, and offers, but they won't be able to duplicate your voice."[6] (For more on brand voice and how to create it, see chapter 9.)

4. Make site navigation consistent and intuitive. Plan a strategy to pull people into the site and then through it. Just as you can write copy by asking what would persuade you to buy a product (using yourself as a test consumer), so too can you and your colleagues organize a site by asking what you'd want to know at each point along the way. What questions would you have? What would you like to be able to do or find out next? What leads to what? See figure 11.11 for a website home page whose organization makes giving easy.

11.11. Here's a very stripped down website, clear and quick. The site's organization and visitors' options are apparent at a glance. (This screen grab looks empty, but go to the site—dontalmostgive.org—to see it fill: the home page begins, "Don't almost give," replaced by "Give," as images of need replace one another.)

5. Get people to come back. Devise ways to get people to return, regularly, to your site. Change what's up there, often. Ask viewers to help build the site themselves: to tell their story, rate the products, comment on the blog, and so on. Be useful: provide information, if you can, that people will rely on, day to day, week after week. Be a go-to site, the way news sites are. Make news of your brand; provide services to your visitors.

How to wordsmith in the digital world

After you've organized like a demon, write like an angel. The following truths become even more true in digital space:

1. Write tight. Don't lead to the point; begin with it. Anything tight enough for print must be tighter still online. Many writing coaches suggest using half as many words as you'd use in print.

And print itself seems to use half the words it once did. In explaining why his newspapers were increasingly using graphics and charts to explain complex ideas—and writing less copy—the chairman of Knight-Ridder newspapers, Alvah Chapman, said, "We are not in the business of manufacturing paragraphs. We are in the business of moving ideas into the minds of people."[7]

You're in that business, too.

So keep paragraphs short. Start them with topic sentences. Develop only one idea in each paragraph. And be specific whenever possible. Keep sentences short, putting the subject and its verb up front, so readers will get your point right away. You and I have been told such things by English teachers since grade school. That's fine: some things *need* to be repeated.

Don't think in phrases; think in words. Writing teacher John Trimble says, "Good writing really begins with a profound respect for words—their precise denotations, their connotations, even their weight and music, if you will."[8] Ask of each word whether it's necessary; hold each one up to the light. Also, look more closely at the subject. Clichés often show up because the writer hasn't gotten beneath them. All circumstances have their own particulars, their own specifics, and if you look more closely at whatever you're writing about, you can often see beneath the patina of cliché to more interesting material.

2. Be fun to read without being obscure. Clarity and cleverness don't have to be enemies, but if there's a conflict, clarity must win, especially in headlines, section heads, and other prominent places.

Which is the best headline?

"What's up with hot air balloons?"
 or
"It's all hot air"
 or
"Hot air balloons rise in popularity"

While they all offer little jokes, only the last header says clearly what it means. You'd know why to click through. The first two headlines pun at the expense of meaning. You can't know what they lead to, so you'd click through only if you had nothing else to do. But when is that the case?

With links, make what you want people to do clear and, if possible, irresistible. "Click here" makes people wonder why. "Find out how" or "Start now" or "Download the app" are stronger, yes? And why say, "Click to see my picture" if you can say, "I had hair once. See?"

Even wacky ideas need to be clear and straightforward in their presentation. Jeff Benjamin, interactive creative director at Crispin Porter + Bogusky, said this about writing the Whopper Sacrifice, that idea of trading in one's friends for a hamburger:

We looked at that copy over and over again. People think, oh just make a thing where you delete a friend—but it had to be funny, it couldn't be mean, and it had to be clear what you had to do because Facebook apps were complicated to some people. Those were big challenges for a writer to take on.[9]

If your working model for Web prose (even in a blog) is the essay, you're in trouble. Essays meander; one thought suggests another. That's their beauty. But on the Web, no one is looking for a stroll through whatever beauties come to a writer's mind. Be on point, be pungently interesting.

Read only the headline and subheads of a blog entry and see if you get the point of the piece. If you don't, then the writer (who could be you) is leaving too much slack in the lines, letting the thesis drift.

3. Invert the pyramid. When you write copy, use the journalist's principle of beginning with the conclusion and working backward. This way, you help scanners get the who-what-when-where-why of a story immediately. You also keep everyone else's mind on the central idea, while letting people interested in the full story read down into it. Since most people won't read big chunks of text, nor will they scroll, make it easy for them to ca-chunk their way through material via links.

4. Use lists to deliver information. If sentences get too full or too long, break them out into lists instead. Like outlines, lists:

- Get attention
- Save eyestrain (the joy of white space)
- Reduce copy
- Aid comprehension
    No lengthy sentences
    No buried points
- Show relationships among ideas
    Parallel entries for equal ideas
    Indentation for subordinate ideas
- Enable quick scanning
    Bullets for lists
    Numbers for sequential entries

5. Write long—a little at a time. The Internet has infinite depth—some sites feel as though you could read down into them for miles. So, when you do write long, get in the habit of making depth available rather than compulsory. In other words, don't lay down long skeins of copy. Break it up. Give people a short version, then let them click to get more information, then click again to get yet more information, should they want it. Create links to help people rappel down into the text.

Here's an example of a basic difference between print and web prose:[10]

BEFORE:
[This chunk of text could be from a company's printed brochure]:
Resource Interactive, founded by Nancy Kramer in 1981, was a digital marketing firm before such

a thing existed. From the beginning, the agency thought and worked in digital media. Its first client was Apple, and since then RI has collaborated with many Fortune 500 companies to open their brands and advance their interactive marketing. RI has grown significantly in the past 30 years, but its goal has always been to combine consumer insight, e-commerce innovation, and technological skill to address, even anticipate, the new marketplace and the new consumer. . . .

AFTER:
[How that same information, and a little more, might be handled on the company's website]:

Text:
Since 1981, Resource Interactive has been a pioneer in digital marketing. Its first client was Apple, and RI has collaborated with many Fortune 500 companies since then. Its principles remain constant: develop consumer insights, innovate in e-commerce, and stay on the leading edge of technology.

Links:
- Follow a timeline of RI achievements
- See RI leaders speak
- Explore case studies
- Sample RI's books about the new consumer and e-commerce innovation
- Watch videos of RI-sponsored iCitizen symposiums
- Tour RI offices in Columbus, Cincinnati, Chicago, and San Francisco

In addition to putting links like these below a copy block (or instead of doing so), you can make any word or phrase in the copy a link itself (for example, "consumer insights," "e-commerce," or "Fortune 500 companies"), inviting readers to jump immediately to whatever interests them most.

You can see how, for the Web, the writer took the copy back toward outline form rather continue the essay-like structure. Also, the Web version inverts the pyramid: the copy starts with the biggest idea, then divides the rest into subtopics. Each link lets readers bypass the linear sequence of print copy—a major distinction between the Internet and print, one that determines so much of how to write for it. Another obvious difference, as we've seen, is the Web's ability to weave in other kinds of material (in this case videos and an

RETHINKCHURCH

10THOUSANDDOORS

What if church wasn't just a building, but thousands of doors? Each of them opening up to a different concept or experience of church – and a journey that could change the world. Would you come?

WATCH

What will you see here? People just like you telling their stories and making a difference in the world and their own backyards.

READ Read on and you just might get enlightened...

NOW

Access headlines, people and causes here and abroad, right now.

FIND

Here, you'll find an experience that is everything from practical to spiritual. And always meaningful.

GO/DO

Google Earth locates needs across the globe. Use it to seek out a cause, to learn more about a need and when it moves you - to take action.

TALK

Here's a place to ask those questions. Those questions you need answered. Who knows what you'll discover?

LISTEN New music, relevant dialogue, intriguing commentaries.

US We are The United Methodist Church. We're helpers, healers, listeners...

11.12. This site for the United Methodist Church knows how to keep things simple and how to use the command form of the verb to invite action.

interactive timeline), options unavailable in print. Web prose is more outline- and link-driven, as well as being video- and motion-enabled.

Everyone intuitively accepts these differences between the Web and print, but they're easy to forget when it's time to write a website. Use interactive media the way they want to be used. Take advantage of their possibilities. (See fig. 11.12 for a website's home page, crisp and focused, that helps viewers get where they want to go.)

How to write for social media

"The market started out as a place where people talked about what they cared about, in voices as individual as the craft goods on the table between them."

—Doc Searls and David Weinberger,
The Cluetrain Manifesto

When you work in social media, you're a copywriter, but you're not writing copy; you're having conversations. Whether you're writing for your client's Twitter account or Facebook page, creating and sustaining a blog on its website, or entering social media in some yet-to-be-determined format, your skill as a conversationalist is what's for sale.

HOW HARD CAN TALKING BE?

It sounds easy enough, but real conversation is rare. If I monitor my "conversations" for a day, I see that often I'm doing all the talking or someone else is—and it's unclear whether either of us is really listening. Genuine conversation, in which each person thinks about what the other has said and responds to it, is so rare that many people are surprised when they encounter it. I usually am.

Your goal in social media is to be that surprising. Listen and reply without resorting to scripted shtick: "Thank you for your interest in our products. Your message has been forwarded to the appropriate department." No one is home, and it's audible.

HOW TO TALK BETTER

"A conversation, like dancing, has some rules, although I've never seen them stated anywhere. The objective of conversation is to entertain or inform the other person while not using up all of the talking time. A big part of how you entertain another person is by listening and giving your attention. Ideally, your own enjoyment from conversation comes from the other person doing his or her job of being interesting. If you are entertaining yourself at the other person's expense, you're doing it wrong."

—Scott Adams, creator of the comic strip *Dilbert*

Here are suggestions for improving your conversational chops:

Start by listening

Open yourself to what the other person is saying, a skill few of us can say we've mastered. Work on it. Remember: the best way to get people to listen to you is to listen to them. Which leads to this:

Find out what people want to talk about and talk about that

What kind of dialogue do consumers want to have with your brand? Make a short list of topics that your brand can "own." What's your brand's point of difference, its point of view? What useful knowledge can your brand share with people? Start sharing. You want to get people talking about your blog or tweet or website or Facebook page. If you don't get that bounce, rethink what you're talking about.

Don't be boring, part one

How do you get people to want to talk with you and tell their friends and associates about you? By being interesting. What kind of people are interesting? Friendly ones, smart ones. People who are helpful, funny, surprising. Nicke Bergstrom, a creative director at Mother, New York, encourages writers to imagine that they're dating the customer.[11] Make it a good date.

Bring news, assistance, and insight to the conversation—and mind your manners. Ask real questions rather than fake ones. For example, ask what you're doing badly and how you can do it better; ask what people want from your site or blog or brand; ask them if they think the new app is crummy. Be genuinely curious about things said to you and things you notice. Don't be a huckster (remember, it's a *social* medium first, not a sales medium).

Don't be boring, part two

If you speak or write badly, you're boring. Lots of times people tune out not because the subject bores them but because its treatment does. Say whatever you're saying well: hit the ground running. Be organized. Shape your message for your audience. Tighten and sharpen. Create pictures. Speak truth.

Design your message for your audience

You evoke responses from a set already inside your listener; you don't "inject" him or her with your meaning. As branding consultant Tom Hinkes points out, "Consumers choose brands they agree with. . . . A successful brand's message has to be consistent with and confirm the consumer's map."[12]

So say things in terms your audience already uses; reinforce their point of view (their values, beliefs, ideas, and interests) when you talk with them. Attach your idea *to* something your audience already believes. That's the only way you have a chance of persuading anyone of anything.

In *The Good Listener*, Hugh Mackay provides this example of working with an audience's mindset. Range Rover created an ad campaign whose theme line was "Write your own story." (This now seems like *every* brand's mantra, but the campaign predates the cliché.) Mackay says, "They were not persuading people to change their attitudes: they were persuading people who *already dreamed of escape* to focus those dreams on Range Rover. Their purpose was to change people's behaviour by tapping into an existing attitude."[13]

Interactive copywriter Nick Usborne says it this way: "Don't write about the thing you're selling. Write about the people to whom you're selling it."[14] Cast everything—especially what matters to you—into terms that matter to your listener.

If you say, "Let me explain our wonderful new solar panel," that's you talking to yourself about something you find interesting. Why should anyone else care? Recast it:

"Looking at your heating bills this winter, maybe you've started to think about solar panels. We've been thinking about them, too . . ."

Better, yes?

If you say, "New distribution methods are coming," what's that mean to anyone?

"We've streamlined shipping so you can get faster service."

Better.

How can people *do* something as a consequence of what you're saying?

Doing reinforces any communication, as people realize whenever they're asked to put an idea to use. They can read about how to play baseball, but nothing replaces a sharp grounder hit right at them.

If people don't have to do anything with a message, they might not even listen to it. Create responsibility by encouraging a response. The simplest thing is to use the command form of the verb. "Play the game now." "Choose your favorite color." "See all the podcasts." "Learn more." A command is exactly that.

More than saying things at people, you're encouraging them to have an experience. Think that way.

For example, people like to enter contests, accumulate points, and gain rewards, simple as these things are. If you're Ace Hardware, maybe you can, with your rewards program (points given for purchases), have categories of participation: when a person first joins the program, he or she is a "do-it-yourself-er." After so many points, that person rises to "craftsman" or "craftswoman" (with extra benefits), and so on. Let people in; reward them for participating; encourage them to advance. These are universal human needs.

Make an emotional connection

"Brands are like people. They have to have a heart."
—BOB THACKER, senior vice president of marketing and advertising, OfficeMax

How do you do work on behalf of the brand without turning it into a shameless—and counterproductive—pitch?

"Look for the emotional lever," advises teacher and online writer Larry Asher. "People don't buy beer, elect candidates, or order stock photos for rational reasons. Figure out what emotional fuse your product lights and talk about that—whether the topic is fine French perfume or used dump trucks."[15] This is an honorable way to be authentic while still intersecting the brand. Be yourself, but be the parts of yourself interested in what your client's brand evokes in consumers.

What feelings are connected with your client's brand or products?

Copywriters used to try to *persuade* people (sometimes they still do). But now, especially in interactive media, they try to *engage* people enough that they'll persuade themselves. To do that, make an emotional connection:

At Goodby, I learned how you build brands, how you make people feel something, which is, ironically, maybe the most primal of interactive things. When we say interactive, you think, oh, I got someone to do something, but a more basic part of interactive is to make people feel something.
—JEFF BENJAMIN, interactive executive creative director, Crispin Porter + Bogusky[16]

Take the conversation somewhere

You don't have the same circling conversation with friends every day. If you do, they're not really friends, just people you ride the elevator with or meet at the mailbox. Friends take their relationship out for a walk. A relationship is a journey. A brand's fifth contact with a consumer shouldn't sound like the first one. The relationship will have developed; talk like it has:

One of our philosophies is to think of a campaign as a continuing conversation or correspondence. It should always be bringing you [the consumer] something new, something you didn't know already. Whereas most advertising is like the same Xeroxed letter that gets sent to you over and over again.
—ALEX BOGUSKY, co-founder, Crispin Porter + Bogusky[17]

Create a persona

"Authentic persona" isn't a contradiction. Be yourself or some version of yourself, not just Universal Nicey-Nice Person #38. Create, by how you talk, a character, an individual.

Here's an excellent example, from *Time* columnist James Poniewozik, of how to be someone instead of no one, this time within the confines of Twitter:

Twitter is pure voice, an exercise in implying character through detail and tone. [Comedy writer Justin] Halpern's inaugural @shitmydadsays tweet is so economical that it should be taught in writing workshops: "I didn't live to be 73 years old so I could eat kale. Don't fix me your breakfast and pretend you're fixing mine." Instantly, we know how old Dad is; we know he has a fine-tuned b.s. detector; we know he is fond of pleasure and not of rabbit food; we can infer that his breakfast-fixing adult son has moved in with him. All in fewer than 120 characters, including quotation marks.[18]

Tweets by journalist and food expert Michael Pollan wrap links in Pollan's distinct point of view.

 See tweets by Michael Pollan at fig. W-11.12.

Learn from print

Tweets—to name just one of the tight spaces in which digital copy lives—are studies in being succinct. Twitter's great virtue is its quick, of-the-moment nature, and many tweets are brief utilitarian comments, replies, or links. If you're tweeting for a brand, you may assume that maintaining the customer base—answering questions, routing problems to whoever can solve them, slapping high fives with happy consumers—limits you to quotidian exchanges without stylistic polish. Clarity, yes. Pizzazz, not so much.

But print headlines are studies in brevity, too, and the best headline writers keep their wits about them. So, if you wish, study chapter 16's advice about headlines to see what might make a tweet last longer than an M&M.

Which of these are tweets and which are headlines from the archives of print advertising?

> Ever want to shower but don't feel like getting wet?
>
> Studies find top three most stressful moments in people's lives: death, divorce, and properly pronouncing "Worcestershire sauce."
>
> Napping at work can boost productivity.
>
> Where is it written that rain falls only on men?
>
> If you really want to see great creative [work], let me do your taxes.
>
> Contrary to popular opinion, enough grapefruit *can* make you fat.

Hard to tell which is which, isn't it? For the record, the first three are tweets, the last three are print ad headlines.

Forward into the past: learn from old-fashioned direct mail

Another genre by which to learn how to write compel-

ling lines is direct response advertising. The Internet is direct response, of course, but I'm talking about old-fashioned direct mail, the kind that used to stuff mailboxes before e-mail stuffed inboxes instead. Direct mail practitioners, many dead and gone, often lie outside the awareness of young writers. If you're working on, say, a Twitter headline or a promotional headline at a retail website, you want to pull in traffic. The masters of direct mail had exactly the same problem: write a line that compels action.

So they did. Consider, for example, the following headlines from the now defunct Sharper Image catalog, a compendium of upscale, urbanite accessories. Imagine these lines as Twitter headlines linking to offers or other content. Notice how each headline pinpoints product and benefit:

> For an electronic, pocket-sized Spanish/English translator: "5 lbs. of Spanish on a microchip."
>
> For a teensy, clip-on reading light: "Marriage-saving light for bookworms."
>
> For a 2-in-1 travel product: "Hair dryer elopes with the travel iron."
>
> For a car cover that automatically gathers itself up: "Self-retracting instant garage."
>
> For a talking scale: "Your weight, well spoken."

Each headline is succinct yet intriguing. Go back to the work of the direct mail copywriters; their techniques still apply.

Be specific

Details are another way to say something instead of nothing. Here are two of the abundant Twitter comments when Steve Jobs stepped down at Apple in 2011: "Steve Jobs is the greatest leader our industry has ever known," wrote one Tweeter. "It's the end of an era."

"Funny how much emotion you can feel about a stranger," wrote Susan Orlean, the author. "And yet every phone call I make, every time I'm on a computer, he's part of it."

Susan Orlean's comment lingers, the other one fades. Why? Because she's giving readers moments to visualize, tangible moments, with emotions attached. He's being general and clichéd. They're saying similar things, both things are true, but the key to entering the brain long enough to get remembered or retweeted is being valuable. Specifics have value.

Can there be too much of a good thing?

There's a backlash to all this socializing, of course: too much muchness. How long and how often do people want to talk about laundry detergent or toothpaste or spark plugs? How many times a week do they need updates from their hardware store? People's interruptions are now being interrupted, their digressions digressed upon, every moment up for digital invasion, revision, or augmentation. People are prodded into sharing their every half-thought with the rest of planet earth, invited to comment on each single thing, engage in unending dialogue with all the brands that can get at them. "Tell us! Right now! What you think!" the brands implore.

Enough already.

Word of mouth is the oldest advertising channel on planet earth, and the truest one, too. That's why social media have become so ubiquitous: when real people say what they really think, they don't set off what Hemingway claimed everyone had: a built-in bullshit detector. Social media speak the people's truth, which is a lot more reliable than what passes for truth from many public relations firms, media conglomerates, and advertisers.

But too many words from too many mouths too often is a working definition of cacophony. It gets too noisy to hear anyone.

Even Bob Garfield, former ad critic for *Advertising Age* and an evangelist for new media, especially social media, confessed in a blog post:

> There's no bigger proponent of the Relationship Era than yours truly; I can talk the talk as well as anyone. As you know, in books and lectures and columns and consulting, I make a living at it. But, when push comes to shove, do I really walk the walk?
>
> Oh, sure, I have a Twitter account. But @bobosphere doesn't hit send very often. I follow people who ovulate more than I tweet. I have a Facebook page, though it mostly gathers dust. I haven't looked at my own radio show's Facebook fan page in six months. You can put jumper cables on my privates and I still won't join FourSquare. I don't want you to know where I am ever, and I sure don't care where you're sipping chai, either. Have a scone. Go crazy, but leave me out of it.[19]

Garfield sounds fed up enough to head for the Montana mountains, but I'm betting he's just worn out and cranky. He needs a little silence. As do we all.

12 · Television and Video

The Electronic Weedwhacker Age, when TiVo and Replay walk the earth, is here. . . . [TV ads] will have to be voluntary destinations, as all companies will suddenly be in the entertainment business—embracing the idea that they are not just carmakers or airlines.
—JEFF GOODBY, co-chairman,
Goodby, Silverstein & Partners

You and I know that Goodby is right, and he's been right for years. Viewers watch voluntarily now, or not at all. The control is in their hands, a truth that leads to this one:

The first, last, and only rule: be interesting

Zipping, zapping, muting, avoiding, ignoring, and just generally hating TV commercials constitute a national pastime—unless, of course, viewers happen to love the ads; then they'll watch them over and over, which is where you come in. Make your client's spot so inherently, compulsively, unavoidably watchable that people will sit still for it every time they see it, then find it on YouTube and send it to others.

A lot to ask, I know. But keep viewers' self-interested, pleasure-principle-seeking habits of mind uppermost in yours as you dream up your spot. Otherwise, they will dispatch you and it to Adland Abyss. Make people refuse to zap your spot. How?

Begin at the beginning

Start with your strategy. What are you trying to do? What's the creative brief telling you? What's your objective? TV can handle any of the strategies examined earlier: generic claim, product feature, unique selling proposition, positioning, brand image, lifestyle and attitude. Here, as everywhere, idea is king. It's not technology, it's idea, that will make or break the spot. (See fig. 12.1 for an idea in action.)

Think demonstration, or story, or both at once

TV's dramatic possibilities are nearly limitless, but start by considering the two techniques that TV handles so much better than print: *demonstration*, the testing of the product's selling point, and *narrative*, the telling of a story. Many, if not most, TV spots can be considered some combination of demonstration and story.

DEMONSTRATIONS

Show viewers how your product works; demonstrate its benefits. The key is to twist the format, have fun with it. You can do this in several ways.

Literal demonstration

The ad shown in figure 12.2 couldn't be simpler; the copy makes it memorable. Viewers watch a fellow take out and open a condom package, with this voice-over: "It's easier than changing a diaper."

There are no spoken words in the TV spot in figure 12.3, just rock music and people energetically building something. Viewers can see cement being mixed, wood being sawed, posts being stuck in post holes—all punctuated by title cards: "12 lb. sledgehammer, aisle 9," "8 inch anchor bolts, aisle 7," "4x4 pressure treated posts, aisle 20." The spot closes with this: "Cutesy artichoke-shaped cabinet knobs. Not in stock." . . . "Ever." "McCoy's. Go build something."

Metaphorical demonstration

Dramatize the product's selling argument by comparing it to something else. What might thrill rides at the Playland amusement park be like? How about like a speedboat racing across the water and nearly flipping over into disaster. But just before the boat crashes, the picture stops and then rewinds. Viewers see the boat un-flip, land back down safely, and speed backward across the water. Soundtrack screams at the immi-

12.1. Dramatize the benefit—or in this case the problem to be solved: finding the right printer cartridge at an office supply store. Anyone who's ever searched for one knows the frustration, here dramatized as a painful game of bingo. A simple, smart, and fun idea, don't you agree?

(S) Watch the TV spot at fig. W-12.1.

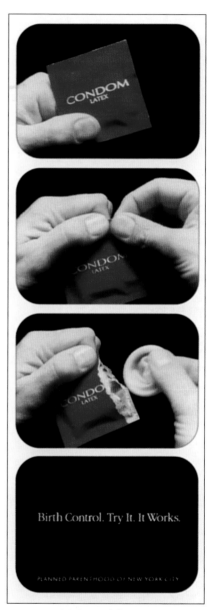

12.2. A straightforward demonstration, whose wit comes from the disarming truth of the voiceover.

(S) See the TV spot itself at fig. W-12.2.

1

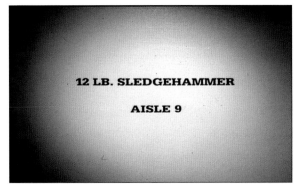

12 LB. SLEDGEHAMMER

AISLE 9

2

3

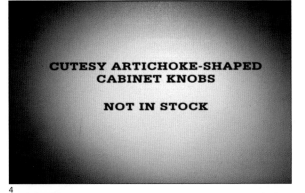

CUTESY ARTICHOKE-SHAPED
CABINET KNOBS

NOT IN STOCK

4

5

EVER.

6

7

12.3. In this spot McCoy's positions itself as the real builders' store, not one of those nicey-nice, everything-for-everybody places. The rock soundtrack and energetic workers make even *me* want to build something, no small feat.

Ⓢ See and hear the TV spot at fig. W-12.3.

12.4. A metaphorical demonstration. This is exactly what a thrill ride at an amusement park should be like, don't you think?

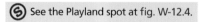
See the Playland spot at fig. W-12.4.

nent disaster are replaced by laughter and the sounds of an amusement park ride. The closing card shows the Playland logo and says, "Actual rides may vary." A terrific idea (fig. 12.4). For another TV spot that uses metaphors of sight and sound to make its selling point, see figure 12.5.

Whimsical demonstration

The VW New Beetle didn't look like other cars, but so what? How to make its shape matter? Why not compare that singular curve with all the square shapes in people's lives? The surprise is in their number and variety (fig. 12.6). Who knew the world was this square?

12.5. Drama in a glass of wine. The hyperbole of the "nuclear holocaust" metaphors raises the stakes of this problem-solution TV spot, helping it appeal to the core audience: tidy people for whom such a spill is a catastrophe.

See the Hoover spot at fig. W-12.5.

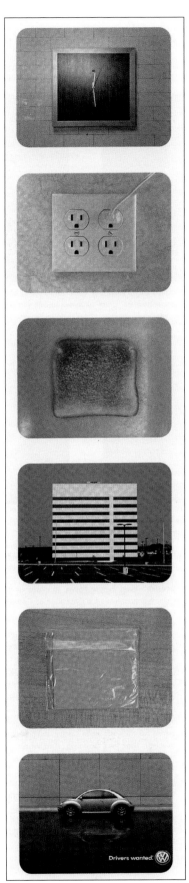

12.6. A whimsical series of comparisons that demonstrates the unique silhouette of the New Beetle.

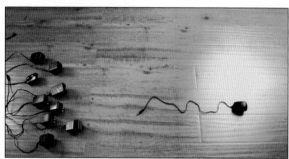

360electrical.
it's revolutionary

Ⓢ Watch this surprising TV spot at fig. W-12.7.

Viewers laugh at the squares' juxtaposition with the car's shape and the relief that curve affords. This spot dramatizes the uniqueness of the New Beetle (and therefore any consumer who owns one), not by comparing it with other cars—too boring—but by comparing it with the unexpected (web link to VW spot: http://www.youtube.com/watch?v=tCXGniT0agw).

Visual advice

As you're developing and visually expressing your ideas, consider the following:

MAKE IT MOVE

Start strong, close strong, don't waste anything. The same obligations of economy and speed that I've discussed with print advertising operate even more so in TV. Whatever your idea, get to it fast. Don't segue toward something interesting. Start with it.

Rely not only on consumers' sophisticated ability to unpack symbols and images in microseconds but also on their demand that you keep those images coming. If your spot doesn't move, forget it—you've probably been zapped. Part of what's exciting about TV advertising is that it moves so much: there is the illusion of great energy, all of which transfers to the product and makes it seem energy-giving. Notice how much movement is a part of TV ads, even the simple ones.

IF IT DOESN'T MOVE, MAKE THINGS ASSOCIATED WITH IT MOVE

One virtue of stories and demonstrations is that, by definition, they move. Even if you're working on an idea that's neither, try to find a way to get movement into the spot. Ask yourself, "What part of my product story moves? What motion is inherent in my client's product?"

If your client's product doesn't move, consider creating movement by changing camera angles or by finding things associated with the product that do move (fig. 12.7).

The writers behind a TV spot for Ricoh copiers realized that copiers don't move but repairmen do. The ad dramatized reliability by emphasizing the omnipresence of the repairman if the company bought the wrong brand. Viewers watched a man's feet moving back and forth through the office, without knowing

12.7. The clever use of metaphor here animates electric cords and plugs, objects otherwise motionless and very short on drama.

until the spot's end who he was. The ad closed, "Because business should depend on a copier that works. Not a repairman. Ricoh Copiers built to work. And work. And work."

Figure 12.8 is another example of creating movement when it seems impossible. Frost Bank is one of what are now only a handful of Texas banks actually based in Texas, and the company wanted to hang an ad on that fact. But how to make a fact move? Show a fellow lowering a Texas state flag to half-mast. That's the whole spot. It's simple, funny, and surprisingly watchable—partly because it's so audible: viewers hear the flag blowing, wind whistling, birds chirping, the rope's metal buckle clanking against the pole. They watch the flag being lowered; read, first, "80% of the biggest banks in Texas are no longer from Texas"; then, "Bummer"; and, finally, "Frost Bank. We're from here." This ad vivifies the fact and does so with a dry wit, equating the loss of banks headquartered in Texas with a cause for statewide mourning.

Sometimes, of course, it's possible to get attention by moving nothing. In a TV world jammed with nonstop visual extravagance, a quiet or motionless or nearly motionless spot can be arresting. Imagine an ad that shows a couple sleeping in. That's it: man and wife asleep, with summer sunlight streaming in the window; viewers hear snoring, birds twittering, clock ticking. Voice-over: "Remember what life was like before you had kids?" Camera card: "YMCA Summer Camp. Minneapolis 822-CAMP. St. Paul 292-4100."

Soundtrack advice
Like words in print ads, the soundtrack in TV spots is half the trick.

BE RELEVANT, BUT NOT REDUNDANT
Be sure that whatever is being said, sung, or sounded relates to what viewers are looking at. Just as in a print ad, however, don't be redundant. If people can see it, don't say it, too. Say something else. If you show a car splashing through the mud, don't say, "Built for the worst weather." Viewers can see that. Instead say how it endures what they're witnessing; talk about features or the emotional benefits to the driver.

BE SURE ON-SCREEN TYPE MATCHES THE VOICE-OVER
The only exception to the previous don't-repeat-yourself advice—and it's an important one—is that when you put type on the screen, either say nothing or have

12.8. In this spot for Frost Bank, a fact—only a few Texas banks are still based in Texas—becomes visible and audible.

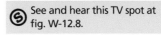
See and hear this TV spot at fig. W-12.8.

the voice-over say exactly those words. You never want to say words and show words that aren't exactly the same. People can't process separate sets of language simultaneously. Remember how irritating Keynote and PowerPoint presentations become when you're trying to read the words on the slide while the presenter insists on saying something else? Your viewers hear better and learn harder when you imprint the message visually as well as aurally.

USE MORE VISUAL THAN AUDIO

Remember the obvious: TV is visual. Don't talk too much and move too little. *Listen* to some TV spots. Notice that in the soundtrack there's less language—and more music and sound effects—than you supposed. (And visually, of course, there is almost always some dramatic movement.) A working rule of thumb is no more than two words per second, so a 30-second spot can manage only 60 spoken words—or fewer. Let your words breathe; give them some air. Air around your words is like white space in print advertising.

DEVELOP TENSION BETWEEN VISUAL AND AUDIO

The tension between headline and visual, so frequently the essence of print advertising, has its counterpart in TV advertising: the tension between what is shown and what is said. Interesting tones are created by running one sort of language on top of another sort of imagery.

Many years ago a great Sony ad showed a monkey standing in water listening to a Walkman. Part of the ad's memorability was that arresting image, but the ad elevated it by running opera music on the soundtrack. The monkey was, apparently, listening to opera and being uplifted by it—viewers could see by his expression, as he stared out to sea, that it enraptured him. Thus they got the idea that music and technology combine to help man evolve. The ad almost planted the idea, whimsically, that Sony had helped make evolution possible—as deft an example as I've ever seen of claiming the highest possible benefit for a product.

Opera music has been run over many different visuals, often ironically: sandwich-making, in one instance, thus elevating the spreading of mayonnaise into an art. Another TV spot ran a soprano's aria over the slow-motion, attempted smashings of locks—sledgehammers banged on them, cars tried to drive through locked fences, and so forth. The ad, for Masterlock,

included the brand mnemonic of a rifle shot failing to crack the lock, but the soundtrack and slow-mo violence themselves created an odd, ironic tone—almost the orchestration of violence—and it was this tone, really, that raised the spot, that announced a new feeling. Viewers got absorbed in the pleasure of destruction, nicely accompanied, and the beauty of the music also suggested that everything was finally secure, thanks to Masterlock.

You don't have to think music, either. The original Levi's "Go Forth" TV ad featured what may be a voice-over by Walt Whitman himself speaking lines from his poem "America" as various assemblies of young people go forth across America (and somehow also back in time).

Years ago, Reebok's controversial "UBU" TV ads also raided American literature but did so more ironically: seemingly ancient, scratched recordings of epigrams about individuality from Ralph Waldo Emerson were run over imagery of weird people doing weird things, creating a nicely unsettling mix. It was as though Emerson's voice itself had been found and resurrected, throwing viewers into the American past as the imagery launched them into an eccentric American future, an outland of oddness. That campaign showed just how rich a mix you can create by placing soundtrack and imagery into creative tension. So think about juxtaposition and irony. Try running something over the images that is neither redundant nor too safe. See what effects you can create (fig. 12.9).

And remember the tremendous power of audio to alter people's response to video. In a simple TV spot, a mud-splattered Range Rover in a studio was washed off with torrents of water. A flat idea, right? But the advertisers replaced the sound of the rushing water with jungle noises—shrieking animals, rhythmic African drums, and so on—adding novelty and excitement to the spot. Now the off-road thrills of driving the vehicle were dramatized through the wild sounds viewers heard as they watched the mud being washed off. From no idea to great idea—by simply altering the soundtrack.

Two Nike TV ads did similar things with sound. One spot showed athletes warming up for competitions while viewers heard a classical orchestra warming up before a concert. In another spot the human sounds of a group of athletes running cross country were replaced by those of galloping horses. Cool synergy. Each half of the ads needed the other to complete it.

Stories

Hook viewers with a story, and do a little selling inside it. After all, you *can* tell a story on TV, something you almost cannot do in a print ad. And you can often demonstrate within that story, wrap a demo up inside the narrative.

What's so special about stories, as opposed to, say, exposition or argumentation? Advertisers Alex Bogusky and John Winsor, who have used narrative in much of their work, make the case:

> Stories work well at connecting people because they are baked into our DNA. Our stories, and the ability to share them, are what make us human. They bring context and meaning to everything we do. Stories carry our hopes, dreams, and values. They arouse our curiosity and invite us to wonder. They resonate deeply in our souls. And, told well, they stick in our minds forever.[1]

Kinka Usher, a TV ad director, emphasizes the critical importance of imbuing an ad with human truth—which he accomplishes by incorporating little stories:

> I don't do ads with voiceovers. Or ads that list product points. I don't think that type of advertising is effective. I tend to want to work on branding and I want to work on original ideas. With image or brand advertising, you're more likely to be able to make a little film, with the product seamlessly woven in—so that people are having an experience based on the film and less on the product. Because you really can't get emotional about a car. No matter how much Ford may think that their car is the most emotional thing they've ever seen, the average person doesn't get emotional about it. Now you can get emotional about the person who's driving the car. You can relate to their human nature. And that's the difference.[2]

HOW TO TELL A STORY

As you remember, the essence of storytelling is *conflict*: someone wants something but someone else stands in the way. A *protagonist* goes up against an *antagonist* (see chapter 7, Telling Stories, for more on plot and story). The story takes shape from the conflict and its resolution.

Once you figure out the story you're telling with

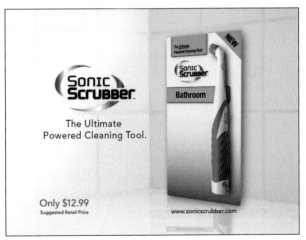

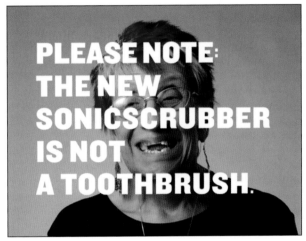

12.9. A tinny recording of a World War I marching song ("Pack Up Your Troubles in Your Old Kit-Bag, and Smile, Smile, Smile") finds new meaning with a new product, creating a light irony that keeps these losers lovable.

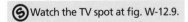

Watch the TV spot at fig. W-12.9.

your client's brand, think of it as a very short play, one with three acts.

Act I. Either open the story on some unbalanced, out-of-kilter situation or quickly knock things out of kilter via your antagonist—introduce a calamity of some sort, whether an event, object (competing brand?), or person. In other words, set conflict in motion: the protagonist tries to restore order; the antagonist does the opposite.

Act II. Escalate the conflict (this is sometimes called *rising action*) and take it to a *climax*—a decisive action, a decisive moment, when someone wins and someone loses.

Act III. End the play with what's called *falling action* (the consequences of the climax) and with a *resolution* (which, in advertising, often contains a joke or at least a smile). If your play is a comedy, balance is restored; if it's a tragedy, it isn't. Most advertising is comedy.

How many parts there are to a dramatic structure depend on who's counting. In the sequence above, drawn from theater, there are three: a beginning in which the problem becomes apparent; the middle, in which conflict occurs as the problem is confronted, and the situation reaches a climax; and an end in which the problem is resolved and the character(s) are changed, at least a little, by what has happened. They are not quite the same as they were at the beginning.

HOW TO GET PAST THE OUTLINE AND DEVELOP A STORY

Screenwriting guru Robert McKee considers what he calls "the gap" key to conflict and storytelling, defining it as the split "between what a human being expects to happen when he takes an action and what really does happen." Audiences side with a character and "[w]hen the gap opens up for character, it opens up for audience. This is the 'Oh, my God!' moment, the 'Oh, no!' or 'Oh, yes!' you've experienced again and again in well-crafted stories." [3]

Here is one of McKee's examples of the gap:

I pick up the phone, call Jack, and say: "Sorry to bother you, but I can't find Dolores's phone number. Could you"—and he shouts: "Dolores? Dolores!

How dare you ask me for her number?" and slams down the phone. Suddenly, life is interesting. [4]

In the little story from Staples (fig. 12.10), office employees come to the supply manager, hoping that what they want they might receive. The gap occurs in that man's sadistic denial of their simple requests. "Oh, no!" the audience says, siding with the supplicants. The conflict (rising action) is the manager's increasing cruelty as he denies each person's request, while their pitiful gifts of donuts accumulate but never suffice. The climax comes via hero Staples and its mobster muscle. The look of shock on the supply manager's face and his ironic "You monster!" close the spot and the gap.

In another TV spot (fig. 12.11), this one for Canada Trust bank, the unsettling incident is the golden retriever's perpetual misbehavior, the littered world of broken things—and expenses—he leaves behind. Rising action is his ascending out-of-control pile of misdeeds. The climax, the decisive moment, comes when the dog's owner, presumably helped by a line of credit at the Trust ("You do the living. We'll do the math"), enrolls Cash in obedience school.

In the Staples spot, the supplicants triumph and the sadist is undone. In the dog spot, the owner finds comfort for his problem, even though the problem sweetly remains. In dramatic storytelling, people are changed, at least a little, by what they go through. They enter the conflict as one person, emerge from it as another—with brand as intercessor. The Staples workers acquire a sense of freedom and self-worth; the dog owner gains at least the illusion of control.

QUIRKIFY THE STORY

That is, add memorable bits to its telling. The Staples story could exist without "gifts" to the office manager, but they add to his sadism, and, especially since they're donuts, they add a quirk to his temperament. He doesn't want money or a corner office or some other substantial thing: this cruel man wants people's small personal pleasures, their donuts. Odd—and funny. So, too, is the mobster hit man who enters late as avatar for the supplicants. He surprises viewers with his presence. A mobster working on behalf of office types? Quirky. The story could even exist without the manager's assistant, but he adds such a funny second beat of doom.

The quirk in the dog story is the owner's torn pants pocket at the end, contrasting with his tone of naive

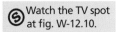

12.10. An old story in a new setting: Davids meet Goliath at the office.

Watch the TV spot at fig. W-12.10.

1

2

6

3

4

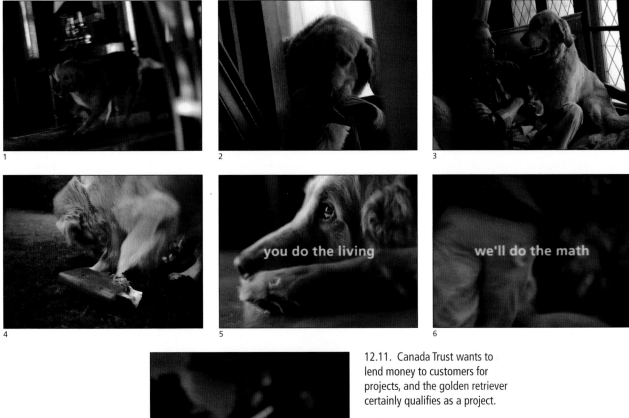

you do the living

we'll do the math

1

2

3

4

5

6

12.11. Canada Trust wants to lend money to customers for projects, and the golden retriever certainly qualifies as a project.

See the TV spot itself at fig. W-12.11.

Canada Trust

7

12.12. A TV ad so simple that it even looks good in print.

optimism. Though he doesn't notice the pocket, his audience does—and realizes that, despite everything the owner may do, the dog will still win. That moment seals the deal: people's sympathy may lie with the owner, but their hearts go with the dog.

Final advice

It's easy to create hyperkinetic complexity with TV and video. Instead, follow the advice of copywriter Bruce Bildsten, who likes simplicity and clarity: "I see a lot of commercials where there is a good idea, but it's buried in production values or too many benefits. The spot can still be beautiful and richly produced, but it's more the simplicity of the idea itself. You have to make it work so that the idea comes through."[5]

All the spots in this chapter share a simplicity of idea. Try to create spots that work as economically, wittily, and powerfully, as these do. Architect Mies van der Rohe's "less is more" dictum can apply just as well to TV advertising as to buildings (fig. 12.12)..

13 · Radio

When I sign off my television newscasts by saying, 'See you on the radio,' it's my way of saying that radio is like television, but with better pictures.
—CHARLES OSGOOD, CBS News

Osgood's insight is essential to understanding radio. He invokes the "theater of the mind" quality that you may have heard your grandparents talk about, from the days when listening to the radio—rather than watching TV, surfing the Internet, or using smartphones—was the national media pastime. The most fundamental distinction between radio and any other medium (except reading) is its demand—an inescapable invitation, really—that you, not the medium, create the pictures in your mind. This unique-to-each-listener imagery, especially its extravagant possibilities, ought to dominate your thinking about how to advertise on the radio.

How to create radio advertising

You create a radio spot by manipulating no more than three things: words, sounds, music. With them, and only them, you create entire worlds, the miniature auditory universes that are radio ads.

> "Radio is really the most intimate medium of all, which is why you have to be so careful in how you create it. It's so intimate because the listener is actually the art director . . . all the listener has is the words and the sound effects, so in effect the listener becomes a collaborator."
>
> —Joy Golden, radio copywriter

THINK WORDS, WORDS, WORDS

Radio is a copywriter's medium, since your words become everything. Almost. The talent cast to deliver those words adds a lot to a spot, of course, as reading the radio typescripts in this chapter will indicate. You realize how much better—richer, more nuanced—the spots become when you hear them, with their great voices and rhythms. But good radio spots are still good—funny, imaginative, persuasive, memorable—simply sitting there in type.

What words to use? The most fundamental and most common radio ad language is simply that of an announcer, someone who gets listeners' attention and then delivers a specific offer, complete with copy points, much like someone reading the headline and body copy from a print ad. Although sometimes effective, especially when read by well-known radio personalities, the genre of announcers-reading-copy often fails to prove distinctive or memorable. "Radio falls apart when people try to make it newspaper advertising on the air," says Bill West, vice president, Radio Works, Houston, by which he means that good radio should construct images in listeners' minds, not just be data read aloud.[1]

INTRODUCE CHARACTERS, SCENES, DIALOGUE

Think, therefore, in terms of characters and scenes. This can be as simple as creating an unusual persona for the announcer. The Motel 6 ads, with which many people are familiar, rely on the charm of Tom Bodett's folksy persona: he embeds the motel's selling points in his whimsical monologue, and by spot's end his character and values have become the motel's. This is really testimonial advertising, in that the *who* of the message becomes part of the *what*. And it makes sense: why should we listen to Mr. or Ms. Straight Announcer when we can listen better and be sold harder by hearing an unexpected character make the announcements? The following two radio spots create drama through the personae of their announcers (it helps that each spot is terrifically well written, too). The first one, for the National Thoroughbred Racing

DEVITO/VERDI

AGENCY: DEVITO/VERDI
CLIENT: NTRA
PRODUCT: RADIO
TITLE: "Walk the Dog"
LENGTH: :40/:20
ISCI CODE: ZFBI-2603
DATE:

ANNCR: And they're off. Out of the gate its GET UP EARLY and WALK THE DOG. Here comes DO THE LAUNDRY and WASH THE DISHES. Out of nowhere comes CALL FROM MOM followed by NAGGING AND GUILT TRIP. It's NAGGING, it's GUILT TRIP. It's GUILT TRIP, it's NAGGING, and NAGGING is relentless. But wait, it looks like WALK THE DOG has a little left in him. Now it's WALK THE DOG followed by WATCH TV. It's WATCH TV all alone. But here comes TAKE A NAP. Wait a minute I don't believe it-its CALL FROM MOM. She just won't go away! And in the end it's ANOTHER BORING SATURDAY.

ANNCR: For a better time go to the track. National Thoroughbred Racing. We bet you love it.

Association (fig. 13.1), mimics an announcer's call of a race to make the selling argument. The second spot, for Denver Water's conservation program, satirizes the voice of the manly-man to ridicule men into doing the right thing (fig. 13.2).

Voice alone can be how you dramatize a benefit. In a famous radio spot for a suntan lotion, as the announcer cites the brand's benefits, his voice slowly changes from that of an Englishman to that of a West Indian, the change in his voice serving as metaphor for a deepening tan.[2] In another example of voice becoming the message, this radio spot uses a woman's changing voice to embody two coffee choices from Second Cup (fig. 13.3).

The next step is to replace the announcer with a character or characters, often by establishing characters-in-dialogue, and to use announcer commentary, usually at the end, to supplement it. The key is making the people real, not shills for the product, and making the dialogue real, not hokey. Bill West and Jim Conlan of Radio Works give crucial dialogue advice:

Break it up. One of the most common mistakes people make when writing radio dialog is to write long copy blocks. First one person says a whole bunch of stuff, then the other person says a whole bunch of stuff. That's not a dialogue. That's dueling monologues. Effective dialogues require short lines with lots of back and forth. Since you have no visuals, the back-and-forth dynamic in a radio dialogue supplies the conversation with its action.[3]

In figure 13.4, for example, the couple's dialogue, bizarre as it is, sounds real. The man and woman are having a very odd conversation, but a real one; they aren't making windy position statements or reciting product benefits from a creative brief. Robert Frost said that "the ear is the only true writer and the only true reader."[4] It's the only true listener, too. Hear how people talk and get that down. If you let the pitch overwhelm the people, your spot is dead.

And as crazy as the conversation in figure 13.4 is, the wild premise doesn't hook listeners at the expense

client	Denver Water	project #	DW-0388
project	Time of the Month	length	:60
date	4/12/2010	spot title	Still A Man
date produced	4/13/10	spot code	DW0388

AS PRODUCED

MANLY MAN VO:

1 You are a man. You can deny it all you want.

2 You can pluck and tweeze. Powder and spray.

3 Preen and strut and worry if these shoes go with that outfit.

4 But deep inside, you still have the blood of Warriors and Gladiators flowing

5 through your veins.

6 You still have the urge to drink milk straight from the carton, leave the toilet seat up and snarl, "Go

7 ahead, make my day."

8 Because like it or not, you are a man, a y chromosomed seething cauldron of testosterone and you

9 have a Man's Time of the Month.

10 And when that time comes, you can walk proudly to your automatic lawn sprinkler box and dial it

11 down from your summer setting...

12 Or you can sit in the dark and watch a chick flick with a box of tissues until it passes.

13 We think you'll know what to do.

14 Because you are not afraid to howl at the moon,

15 I AM A MAN AND I HAVE A MAN'S TIME OF THE MONTH.

16 Because you are a man.

17 A message from Denver Water. Reminding you to adjust your sprinklers.

18 And use only what you need.

13.2. Denver Water has fun with burly bombast to prompt men to think about water conservation.

Listen to the water conservation spot at fig. W-13.2.

Radio Script

CLIENT:	SECOND CUP
PROJECT:	FALL CAMPAIGN
TITLE:	CARAMEL CORRETTO

SFX: To match

MUSIC: Paris café style music - romantic

FEMALE: (French Female VO) (soft sexy voice): Good morning my darling. Let me embrace you in my tender silky arms and teach you what passion is all about. You like passion no? (Change of tone, very cold now) Well what do you take me for? One of your little hussies? Be gone. I turn my back on you. (In a soft sexy voice again) No wait. darling. I was only playing. Come back and let my sweet Caramel lips caress you. (cold tone again) .ahh you're back again I see. You groveling, little so called human being.

ANNCR: The Caramel Corretto Premium European, can be served steaming hot or ice cold. It's just one of the many coffees at Second Cup.

ANNCR: How do you want to wake up? Second Cup, first thing.

13.3. Tone of voice serves as metaphor for styles of coffee—a clever way to audibly express product features.

Listen to this radio spot at fig. W-13.3.

OURHOUSE.COM
Brand Radio
:60 Radio "Finishing" – As Produced
©2000 Black Rocket

ROOM SOUNDS. WE HEAR A DOOR UNLOCKING. WE HEAR A WOMAN WALKING IN.

WOMAN:	Hi honey.
MAN:	Monkey cakes.
WOMAN:	What's that smell?
MAN:	I'm redoinging the floors.
WOMAN:	You're redoing the floors?
MAN:	Yep. With shellac. Shellaca-dack-adoo.
WOMAN:	Oh come on honey. Jeez open a window. Bob, you're drooling.
MAN:	I like it. Drooling.
WOMAN:	Were you shellacking all day?
MAN:	Heeeeeeeee.
WOMAN:	Oh my god.
MAN:	Hooooooo. *("HOOOO" GOES UP AND DOWN LIKE SLIDE WHISTLE.)*
WOMAN:	Bob, sweetie, look at me. I'm right over here.
MAN:	Mommy....mmm
WOMAN:	That's it. I'm calling Dr. Levine.
ANNCR:	Tools. Advice. Housecalls. Sanity. Everything you need to fix up your house, or have it done for you. Ourhouse.com. We're here to help.
ANNCR2:	Partnered with Ace.

13.4. Characters-in-dialogue. People love to be voyeurs—
and with a conversation like this, what pictures they see.

 Hear their conversation at fig. W-13.4.

of the product benefit; rather, it dramatizes it. Our-House.com promises "Tools. Advice. Housecalls. Sanity. Everything you need to fix up your house, or have it done for you." The conversation/story dramatizes the need for exactly that.

Can you think up a scene with characters-in-dialogue that engages our interest *while* dramatizing the product benefit? You can if you try. Figure 13.5 offers another unusual dialogue, one that relies on a funny exaggeration of the automated phone responses everyone has encountered.

USE "EARS ONLY" PROSE
Remember that you're writing for the listeners' ears only. Listeners will not have the chance to go back and look at what you've said, so keep it simple and read-

ily consumable (no more than two words per second). Use a tape recorder to play your work back to yourself. Let your ears tell you what to do, not the look of the words on the page. And don't neglect the "white space" of radio advertising—silence. By rushing to cram lots of copy points into a small space, far too many ads overwhelm listeners with nearly breathless, over-caffeinated announcers. Unless you're satirizing that tradition, avoid it.

DRAMATIZE SOUND AS SIGHTS

Sound effects (SFX) offer unlimited possibilities—libraries of sounds are available, and with minimal equipment you can create your own sound effects. Think how readily and completely sounds evoke whole places and things. They become parts standing for wholes. Rain drumming on a tin roof, the rhythmic slapping of waves—listeners are suddenly somewhere exotic, in the Caribbean or South Seas. A howl

---

b p n

DATE: April 2000   **As Produced**

CLIENT: Columbia Sportswear

TITLE: **"Info Line"** Co-Op Radio

LENGTH: :50/:10

ANNCR: Welcome to the automated information line. Enter a subject code now.

(BEEP BEEP)

ANNCR: Subject 38. Breeding Mice for Profit.

(BEEP)

ANNCR: Subject cancelled. Enter a subject code now.

(BEEP BEEP)

ANNCR: Subject 73. Today's Forecast for Yemen.

(BEEP)

ANNCR: Subject cancelled. Enter a subject code now.

(BEEP BEEP)

ANNCR: Subject 87. Lost In the Woods. Press 1 if you are currently lost.

(BEEP)

ANNCR: Enter the brand of jacket you are wearing. Press 1 for Columbia
              Sportswear. Press—

(BEEP)

ANNCR: You have entered Columbia Sportswear. Designed by Chairman Gert
              Boyle, your Columbia parka will keep you warm and dry until a
              search party locates you. Until then, here's some helpful information:
              Press 1 for Cooking With Bark, press 2 for Toilet Paper Alternatives,
              press 3—

(BEEP)

13.5. A funny take on getting an automated voice when calling a help line.

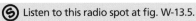 Listen to this radio spot at fig. W-13.5.

DEVITO/VERDI

AGENCY: DeVito/Verdi
CLIENT: For Eyes Opticals
PRODUCT: Radio
TITLE: "Sushi"
LENGTH: :60
ISCI CODE: ZFBI-R154
DATE: 6.21.01

ANNCR: There are some things you shouldn't pay 40 to 60 percent less for. Like Sushi, for example.

SFX: man vomiting violently.

ANNCR: Or say, Parachutes...

SFX: Parachute rustling and a loud thud.

ANNCR: Shotguns...

SFX: Gun going off.

MAN: (screaming) Ahhhh, my face!!!

ANNCR: Pit bulls...

SFX: Dog snarling and barking.

ANNCR: Condoms...

SFX: Baby crying loudly.

ANNCR: Mail-order brides...

SFX: A pig squealing and snorting.

ANNCR: A prosthetic leg...

SFX: Sound like a tree breaking.

ANNCR: A brain surgeon...

DOCTOR: How many fingers am I holding up?

MAN: Thursday!

ANNCR: Aromatherapy.
SFX: Farting sound.

ANNCR: Denture cream.

SFX: A man sneezing hard followed by glass breaking.

ANNCR: Shower radios.

SFX: Sound of shower and radio being tuned, followed by zapping electrical sound and scream.

ANNCR: But when it comes to glasses, you should pay 40 to 60 percent off. Because at For Eyes you get the same designer eyewear you get at other stores, just for less. For Eyes. The store for people who can't see paying a lot for glasses.

111 FIFTH AVENUE, 11TH FLOOR, NEW YORK, NY 10003 TEL (212) 431-4694 FAX (212) 431-4940

13.6. What's a clever way to set up the argument for designer eyewear at discount prices? Get people to imagine all the things they'd regret buying at a bargain price. Wit may be your best friend, but sound effects are a close second.

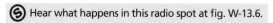

Ⓢ Hear what happens in this radio spot at fig. W-13.6.

of wind, dry crunchings, one after another—listeners could be walking across the Antarctic. An echo to a droning voice—they find themselves in a large hall, listening to a speech. Dogs barking—listeners are in a kennel. Dogs barking with an echo—suddenly the dogs are in the hall, *not* listening to the speech. It's all possible. On the radio.

Not only are sounds rapid transits to almost any scene or situation, however outlandish, but they're emotional triggers, too. Hearing may well be a person's first sense—babies can hear sounds from inside the womb—and the association of feelings with sounds is almost instinctive. Think how readily sounds trigger feelings.

Take, for example, that Caribbean rain. If it's a hard rain, with lightning and thunder, listeners edge toward fear. If it's soft, they feel cocooned, dreamy. As rain slows to a drizzle, they grow restless, expectant of change. Almost all sounds "mean" something to us, so consider using sound not only to establish place and

mood in a spot, but also to forge emotional linkages to products. Figure 13.6 presents a spot for an eyewear retailer that uses a variety of sounds to evoke a lot of pictures in the listener's mind.

See you on the radio

As just this small sample of radio typescripts suggests, radio can be a way to create imaginative, compelling advertising. (Check out the Radio-Mercury Awards—www.radiomercuryawards.com—to hear how good radio ads can be.) Nonetheless, young creatives often dismiss radio in their rush toward more glamorous advertising genres. Let's give the last word about the value of radio to someone who should know, Jeff Goodby, co-founder of Goodby, Silverstein & Partners: "The smart ones love doing [radio]. It teaches you how to think clearly. You can develop a style, learn how to cast and direct properly, and how to work with actors and actresses. Smart writers always welcome radio work."[5]

14 · Other Media and Genres

> To me, all advertising that is truly great reeks of honest humanity. Between every word you can smell the hot breath of the writer. Whether a result of wit, intelligence, insight or artfulness, great advertising invariably transmits itself to the receiver on a fragile human frequency.
> —ED MCCABE, co-founder,
> Scali, McCabe, Sloves

As an advertiser, you will never be asked simply to create visual/verbal relationships in the abstract. You'll always be working on something specific, something with its own demands and opportunities. Here are a few often-encountered advertising genres and media whose characteristics influence how you approach them:

1. **Business-to-business advertising**
2. **Out-of-home advertising**
3. **Guerrilla or nontraditional advertising**
4. **Multicultural and international advertising**

Business-to-business advertising

> "If you work for an institution, whatever your job, whatever your level, be yourself when you write. You will stand out as a real person among the robots."
>
> —WILLIAM ZINSSER, *On Writing Well*

Much advertising writing is not directed to the ultimate consumer at all. It's from one organization to another: an insurance company is talking to a college about handling its faculty's medical coverage; a plastics manufacturer is trying to interest a milk producer in shipping products via its packaging; a magazine is seeking to convince advertisers to use it.

WHY IT'S HARD TO WRITE

Technically one person is not talking to another, and often enough the product also seems vague—some corporation somehow is supposed to help the gears of some other large corporation run better. Business-to-business advertising can seem too amorphous to write well—there's no simple thing or service, no ultimate consumer to put it on her hair, wear it, or drive it to the beach.

THE GOOD NEWS

Your difficulties are mostly an illusion. Everything you've learned about how to write ads to the ultimate consumer will apply here, too. Treat the company as a person, both companies as two people, and you'll be fine. Bad business-to-business advertising wrongly assumes that there is a corporate mentality different from the human one, so it talks stiffly, gets too far into specs and jargon, and engages in corporate metadiscourse (talking about talking about something). Bad idea. Boring headlines, boring copy.

Your readers are still themselves—regular people—when studying business proposals, just more seriously so. They define self-interest in a broader sense—what's good for their company? what's good for them as its employees?—so your advertising's attitude and tone become critical. If you're too flip, hip, and in-their-face, then you might alienate them. They're at work, after all, and in some sense their jobs are on the line. They want to make the right decision, not just an interesting one. Your voice must be serious enough to be trustworthy but singular enough to be human.

Figure 14.1, for example, shows a bank talking to corporations. Sounds sleep inducing, doesn't it? But notice how the ad hooks readers with a human truth and sounds like a real person talking to other real people all the way through. In figure 14.2, another business-to-business ad, Airborne Express invites drug-testing labs to use their services and does so with a smile.

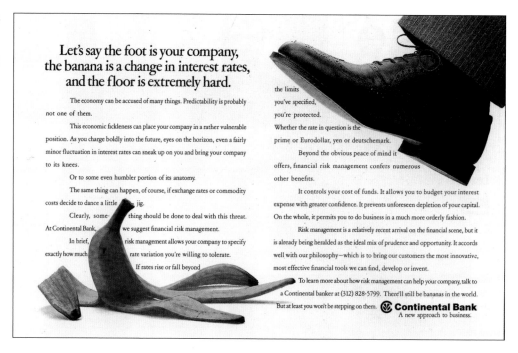

Let's say the foot is your company, the banana is a change in interest rates, and the floor is extremely hard.

The economy can be accused of many things. Predictability is probably not one of them.

This economic fickleness can place your company in a rather vulnerable position. As you charge boldly into the future, eyes on the horizon, even a fairly minor fluctuation in interest rates can sneak up on you and bring your company to its knees.

Or to some even humbler portion of its anatomy.

The same thing can happen, of course, if exchange rates or commodity costs decide to dance a little jig.

Clearly, something should be done to deal with this threat. At Continental Bank, we suggest financial risk management.

In brief, risk management allows your company to specify exactly how much rate variation you're willing to tolerate. If rates rise or fall beyond the limits you've specified, you're protected.

Whether the rate in question is the prime or Eurodollar, yen or deutschemark.

Beyond the obvious peace of mind it offers, financial risk management confers numerous other benefits.

It controls your cost of funds. It allows you to budget your interest expense with greater confidence. It prevents unforeseen depletion of your capital. On the whole, it permits you to do business in a much more orderly fashion.

Risk management is a relatively recent arrival on the financial scene, but it is already being heralded as the ideal mix of prudence and opportunity. It accords well with our philosophy—which is to bring our customers the most innovative, most effective financial tools we can find, develop or invent.

To learn more about how risk management can help your company, talk to a Continental banker at (312) 828-5799. There'll still be bananas in the world. But at least you won't be stepping on them. **Continental Bank** A new approach to business.

DO YOUR HOMEWORK

Business-to-business advertising can often be hard because the writer first has to do the homework required. You've got to understand each business. What does Company A make or do, exactly, and what could Company B possibly get out of it? Who, exactly, will be reading this copy? And who else is a player in this game?

If you're writing an annual report for a lumber company, what are the issues, both in the industry and in the environment? What would shareholders want to know? If you're writing a capabilities brochure for a semiconductor business or a third-party corporate reinsurer, then you've got some studying ahead, right?

Do enough research to wipe away the fog so that you can clearly see the buyer, the seller, the product, and the competition. You need to visualize the commercial situation well enough to write about it. But once you do, you'll realize that the whole large, vague scenario resolves itself into the usual transaction: a product helps someone solve a problem, and your task, as always, is to dramatize the benefit.

FIND THE BALANCE

Too often copy errs on the safe side—it's sober and serious but never speaks with enough verve and authenticity to reach its readers. That's why many people consider business writing interchangeable and unreadable. Put your own life into the corporate voice as you write it. Remember, your readers didn't leave themselves at home when they came to work. They brought along their needs and anxieties, their hopes and plans, so write to them as real people, and your copy will have the life it needs. After all, corporations never look at ads; people do.

Here is the "About us" section on a digital design firm's website. The firm is describing itself in order to sell its services to businesses:

We create best-in-class websites through a multidisciplinary group of user experience directors, brand strategists, information architects, content developers and editors, web designers and multimedia specialists. Each team member brings a different expertise and energy to a project, and we leverage this mix of skills to create interactive marketing solutions that speak to, engage and move the target audience.

It makes sense, but it also makes me drowsy. There's not a single fresh or interesting word here; the prose is full of design-speak and sounds machine generated. If I were a business looking for a design firm, I wouldn't learn who these people really are or what makes them tick, especially what makes them tick differently from every other design firm in the world.

Now look at this from another design studio, Open, in New York:

The first step towards doing good work is finding

good people to do it with. We are designers, photographers, artists and writers. We like to take things apart, see how they work, and put them together again. And we love figuring out solutions that help you understand what the problem really was in the first place.

This self-description covers the same territory, but the prose, by studiously avoiding design buzzwords, sounds like a real person said it. It also sounds "small," which is what the studio is and wants to project.

Reading this, I'd know something instead of nothing. I'd have a sense of Open's size, scope, and personality—and whether the firm might be right for my company's project. Open's prose lives up to its name: it reveals rather than conceals, even in the tight space of that paragraph. The way to sound like yourself as a company is to figure out who you are and write that way.

Out-of-home (OOH) advertising

"[Outdoor is the hardest to do] because it has to fit on a postage stamp. It's not a magazine page a foot in front of your face. You've got to get the logo, get the proposition, get the message and get a laugh— all while you're picking your nose at 35 miles per hour. It's hard to find ideas that stop on a dime."
—Tracy Wong, principal, WongDoody

The major formats are outdoor boards and transit ads, but trucks and delivery vans can be mobile outdoor boards, too—they're one of the original mobile communication devices—and the brand statements on many of them are a delight (see fig. 14.3).

I remember laughing at the side of a big Chipotle semi, which said, "Look, Mom, it's the burrito truck." (The other side said, "No, the driver can't sell you a burrito.") Besides delivering wit, truck signage can pinpoint specific audiences, since, as David Ludington, president of TransMedia Group, points out, "Delivery trucks can reach where buses and taxis can't."[1] They can target particular urban areas, whereas buses just follow linear, main routes, and taxis are unpredictable in their wanderings. I hope you get a chance to put an idea on a truck or van. Write that line, take it to the streets, and watch busy people smile. Advertiser Tom McElligott put its value this way:

In the mundane daily life we all live, when you're in your car and look over at the side of a bus and see a

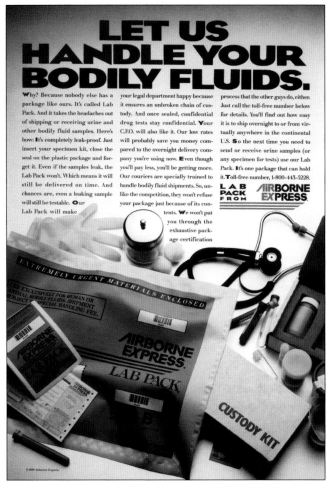

14.2. In business-to-business advertising, be yourself, too, not just your company. Why not make a little joke?

truly wonderful piece of advertising, it's a moment of pleasure. You don't have to know anything about advertising to be delighted by it. And the pleasure of that moment reflects on the product. That's the greatest thing that can happen to the product because it gets the credit for delighting people.[2]

Given today's digital clutter, the value of out-of-home advertising may be increasing. Rob Morris, creative partner at Grounds Morris Campbell, London, explains why:

With digital TV coming along with all these channels, the question becomes, how do you attract and hold the attention of the consumer? With posters, people literally can't turn them off. Also, our cities are becoming more congested. Traffic rates in London were clocked at an average 10.9 mph last year. With people sitting in traffic, some billboards now

14.3. Trucks aren't fun by themselves, but when they talk to people, they can be.

Ⓢ See additional UDF trucks at fig. W-14.3.

represent just about the cheapest 30-second commercial any advertiser can hope for.[3]

Consider the following guidelines when creating out-of-home advertising:

1. Be simple, be fast. If advertising must be simple in order to be quickly comprehended, out-of-home advertising must be instantaneous. After all, people are cruising a highway at 65 mph or dashing down an airport concourse or taking steps two-at-a-time on their way to a meeting. If a public ad is too wordy or too complicated, it's shrugged off as an incomprehensible blur. Posters inside buses and subways, however, are an important exception; seated passengers can study them for a while, so these can say more. (And, as Rob Morris pointed out, if people are stuck in traffic, who knows how long they may stare at your message?) Generally, however, think in terms of one image and a few words. Or perhaps just a few words and the logotype.

2. Think big. Outdoor boards can invoke respect for the monumental. Where else are you given the chance to shout at the world with gigantic words and images? This monumentalizing ability is something Marlboro played like a tune over the years, with its great Montana skies and mountain ranges, massive horses and horsemen, campfires, buckles and boots, the huge Marlboro logo riding over it all. Don't forget that you're using a medium that can inspire awe. Adidas outdoor boards in Tokyo and Osaka, for example, featured a live soccer match (tethered players and a tethered ball). Two fellows playing soccer while hanging sideways above a building can draw a crowd, with the people staring at the spectacle—and the Adidas logo.

3. Take advantage of placement. With out-of-home advertising, you often know, in a way you rarely do in other media, just exactly where you are. You know who your audience is and what's on their minds, too. "158 more oils than this gas station," said an outdoor board, beside a gas station, for a Monet exhibition at the Art Institute of Chicago. A sign in front of a Dairy Queen in a residential district said simply, "Scream until Daddy stops the car." (See figs. 14.4–14.6 for more boards that know where they are.) Regarding figure 14.5, Merkley Newman Harty's Dan Sutton explained the pro bono campaign: "If you need to get your head and spirit together, a chapel is better than a bar or phone booth."[4]

4. Consider manipulations and sequences. Outdoor boards, bus cards, subway cards, airport posters, and the like allow, even invite, successive manipulation over time and/or space. You can say something on a board and then add to it the next week, and add to that a week later. Or you can ask a question on one board and answer it farther down the highway or airport walkway or subway line. Or begin something on one board and complete it on another. Or demonstrate the product's benefit by making changes over time (fig. 14.7).

Nike boards in California showed an Oakland Raider quarterback throwing a pass in one board and a receiver catching it in another farther down the freeway. An outdoor board for a shopping center said, as people drove toward the center, "Wearing that again?" (in smaller type: "South Coast Plaza 17 miles ahead"). As people left the center, a second board said, "You

Right
14.5. A perfect union of idea and place. Another board said, "Just passing through? Aren't we all?"

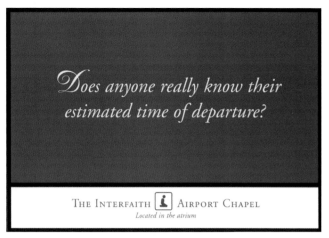

Does anyone really know their estimated time of departure?

THE INTERFAITH ✝ AIRPORT CHAPEL
Located in the atrium

FAME
IS JUST FIFTEEN
MINUTES AWAY.

THE ANDY WARHOL MUSEUM
ONE OF THE MUSEUMS OF THE CARNEGIE

Above
14.6. This outdoor board in Pittsburgh lets you know you're close by playing off Andy Warhol's most famous line, "In the future everyone will be world-famous for fifteen minutes."

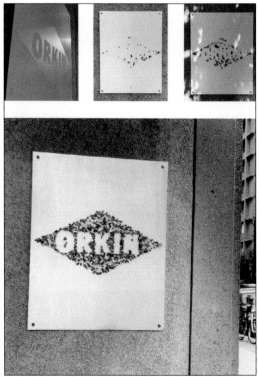

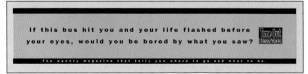

If this bus hit you and your life flashed before your eyes, would you be bored by what you saw?

Above
14.4. Most out-of-home ads pretend not to notice where they are; these ads take advantage of it. (The quotation-marks boards are for The Weather Network.)

Left
14.7. Each day, as bugs accumulated on the sticky surface, Orkin's pest-control argument grew a little stronger.

Other Media and Genres • 171

14.8. This campaign encourages readers to do a double take.

AT **CHIPOTLE**, WE LIKE TO TALK ABOUT WHY MEAT RAISED WITHOUT HORMONES **TASTES** SO **DELICIOUS**, BUT THE AD AGENCY INSISTED WE BE DIRECT.

CHIPOTLE MEXICAN GRILL

WE WANTED TO **HAVE** FARMERS IN OUR ADS, BUT OUR AD AGENCY SAID PEOPLE WANT **BIG BURRITOS**, NOT LESSONS ON SUSTAINABLE FARMING.

CHIPOTLE MEXICAN GRILL

look fabulous" (in smaller type: "South Coast Plaza. Thanks for shopping").

5. Think interactive. What can people do with an outdoor board besides look at it or read it? At the very least, they can read it two ways, not one (fig. 14.8). Increasingly, outdoor boards can respond in other ways to those driving or walking by. QR codes can be embedded in the outdoor board to send viewers to a website or mobile app. Technology allows MINI to salute drivers by name when they go past certain outdoor boards in their MINIs. Lots of transit posters invite people to talk into them, listen to them, spin a dial, pull a lever, add a comment, do something besides just stand there (fig. 14.9).

Guerrilla or nontraditional advertising

"You have to try to sneak under the BS radar. Everyone's so media savvy these days that unless you play it perfectly, you're going to get killed."

—JOHN PEARSON, art director,
Wells Rich Greene BDDP

Ads that don't look like ads—that's a good definition of guerrilla advertising. Use nontraditional media, often in nontraditional ways, to bypass people's filters, get their attention, and do positive work for your client's brand. Spring up in unexpected places and ways. Ambush your target audience. Let's say they're walking through an airport and see a guy all pretzeled up, arm bent above his head, holding a piece of luggage that says, "Give me time to unwind. I didn't fly Sun Air's Exec Economy." They probably won't dismiss him as an "ad" right away; they'll notice him and smile. He's harder to ignore than an airport poster, that's for sure. This contortionist, hired by Sun Air, is guerrilla advertising.

So is a guy dressed up like a rat and "dying" of

14.9. This nontraditional advertising, a kind of outdoor board, invited people to enact its meaning. Passersby could pull off the sticky-notes, each one reminding them to participate in the Alzheimer Society of British Columbia's annual Walk for Memories. This Memory Wall became a double metaphor: it mimicked the need for such notes by people experiencing memory loss, and as the wall itself slowly disappeared, note by note, it represented the increasingly blank memories of those with the disease.

 Watch a video about this unusual poster, its creation, and its effect at fig. W-14.9.

14.10. To discourage people from drinking and driving, a "drunk" valet outside a nightspot was ready, willing, but not exactly able to park patrons' cars. People's reactions showed their worry about what he might do to their car, himself, and other people. Exactly the message the campaign hoped to deliver.

Ⓢ Watch the valet in action and his effect on patrons at fig. W-14.10.

cyanide poison on the streets of Manhattan, as part of **truth**'s anti-smoking campaign—demonstrating that cigarette smoke, just like rat poison, contains cyanide. Yet another example is the airline Virgin Atlantic's practice of slipping trays of unbroken eggs labeled "Handled by Virgin Atlantic" onto the baggage carousels of competing airlines at airports. In each case, passersby are caught unawares by this form of advertising, hence the term "guerrilla." (Because the events often take place outside while people are on the move, guerrilla advertising is sometimes called "ambient advertising," and because the category itself has proliferated, the most inclusive term for it has become "nontraditional advertising.") See figure 14.10 for a surprising stunt that's probably more persuasive than any number of traditional ads.

But street theater is only one of many ways you can bend advertising out of its traditional forms. MINI Cooper has done lots of unusual advertising for its little car: placing it on top of an SUV driving around town ("What are you doing for fun this weekend?"); attaching it to the sides of buildings ("Nothing corners like a MINI"); putting tire marks on airport floors, as though the car had been careering through obstacles; placing a MINI hobbyhorse in front of stores ("Rides $16,850"); and playing tricks with changes in scale (fig. 14.11).

Think of guerrilla or nontraditional advertising as

14.11. Whimsy, MINI style. An ad that doesn't feel like one.

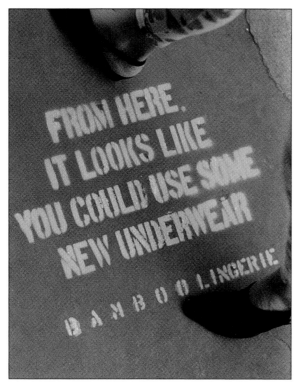

14.12. Sidewalks in front of Bamboo Lingerie retail shops were stenciled with a message both clever and unexpected.

Ⓢ For another kind of street theater see fig. W-14.12.

partly location, partly concept: find a new place—out there or in consumers' heads (figs. 14.12 and 14.13). And don't be limited by preconceptions of what constitutes an ad. Especially when it comes to guerilla advertising, the words of advertising pioneer Charles Austin Bates from more than a century ago still ring true: "More things enter into advertising than are generally supposed. In fact, everything that connects a name and a business in people's minds is advertising."[5] Besides, there are empty spaces to be filled everywhere: car windows, walls, ceilings, the front of shopping carts, the sides of buildings, almost any place people look—even down (figs. 14.14 and 14.15).

WHEN TO DO IT

Guerrilla advertising makes a lot of sense for startups and other small clients with teeny advertising budgets. Like guerrilla warfare, it's asymmetric, making the most of whatever you have, maximizing results while minimizing cost. But it makes sense even for big players because people so distrust and tune out advertising that if you do something that doesn't seem like advertising, something unexpected, you improve your

chances of getting through, and you encourage consumers to feel good by interacting with your client's brand in this new way.

Another benefit of guerrilla advertising is the attendant publicity and press coverage—the bounce or buzz—it creates. That may be even more important, since it can reach more people than did the original guerrilla event or placement. In fact, advertisers often link publicity and guerrilla advertising, the one feeding off the other. Stage the event, then try to get as much coverage as possible (see fig. 14.16).

ADVICE FOR CREATING NONTRADITIONAL ADVERTISING

Stay on strategy

What does your client's brand need to do or say, and can guerrilla advertising be a way to get it done? Remember, you're not just staging a stunt, you're com-

14.13. A South African gun-control group placed these vending machines with apparently real handguns in them on university campuses and in shopping malls. (Putting money in the machines was a way to donate to the cause.) People are so used to seeing innocuous products in vending machines that this substitution shocks them—and dramatizes the argument.

municating a brand truth. As marketer Tom Himpe says, "The golden rule is that good stunts must be a gigantic extrapolation of the core of the brand."[6] That Running Toilet qualifies, don't you agree?

Marry a human truth with a brand truth

One famous stunt for Starbucks involved putting coffee cups on car roofs (held in place by magnets), cups that looked like ones the drivers had set there when getting in the car and forgotten. Then a number of such cars were sent out into several cities over the winter holidays. If someone were kind enough to point out the coffee cup to the driver of such a car, that person received a Starbucks gift card. The stunt itself received a lot of media coverage (the "multiplier effect," a term for the bounce a stunt gets in word of mouth and press coverage). Its human truth makes people smile. Who hasn't put something on the roof while getting in a car, especially a coffee cup, then driven off?

Get to people when and where they're most susceptible

By this I mean, get as close to the moment of purchase as you can. Tennis advertising does better at a tennis tournament than it does in a magazine; TV spots for pizza and hamburgers do better in the evening than in the morning. Guerrilla advertising is no different. Pick a place and time in consumers' lives when they will be open to your idea and able to do something about it. Supermarkets where I live abound in food theater: people are cooking, food on trays is circulating, chefs

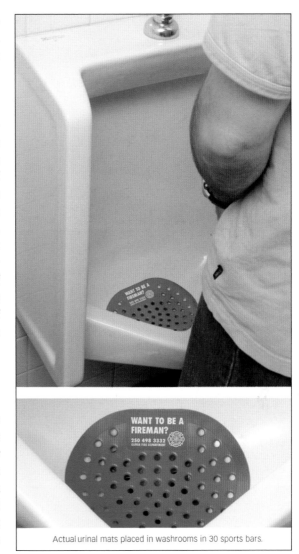

Actual urinal mats placed in washrooms in 30 sports bars.

14.14. Medium and message coincide.

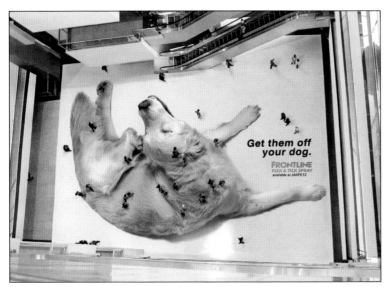

14.15. A trick of the eye makes this ad's argument surprising and memorable.

14.16. This stunt at a college football game (top) was part of the "Use only what you need" conservation campaign from Denver Water. The stunt got a lot of press coverage, so much so that the Toilet became a Denver celebrity and has since appeared all over town. This pun-in-action not only encouraged people to do something about that running toilet at home, but its over-the-top memorability heightened awareness about water conservation generally. Good bounce.

Watch the toilet run at fig. W-14.16.

are conducting classes, department heads are even circling up and doing cheers. I walk in looking for a few items, get caught up in the swirl, and leave, much later, with a dazed expression—and a full cart.

Going to where his audience was, a golf pro placed balls with his name, phone number, and the line "We need to talk" in golf course sand traps, bunkers, rough, and out-of-bounds areas—exactly where bad golfers would find them. Everyone who picked up a ball probably needed lessons. (See fig. 14.17 for another unusual example of fitting an idea with its placement.)

Handicapped parking spaces at high schools in Seattle were painted with the following sign right before graduation in June: "Every 48 seconds, a drunk driver makes another person eligible to park here." Powerful placement, timing, and message.

Take advantage of your surroundings

Use them, interact with them. Make your idea fit this place and this medium. For example, in twenty low-income, high-rise apartment buildings in Beijing, IKEA transformed the interiors of the elevators to show residents what could be done, cheaply, with small spaces, implying that residents might change their apartments for the better on a budget, too. In Berlin, IKEA redid the lighting, walls, and color palette in a train station to show what a difference a few good choices could make. "We use nontraditional media so that we can be

14.17. Direct-response vehicle and alternative medium: the stick. The Sydney Dog Home takes care of abandoned, abused, lost, and hurt dogs; nurses them back to health; and puts them up for adoption. But the home needed money to stay open and had nothing to spend on a campaign. So M&C Saatchi threw sticks with messages tied to them into public parks. When somebody fetched one out of curiosity, the copy explained the Sydney Dog Home's mission and encouraged donations, while the headline pointed out the obvious: "All you need now is a dog."

a big presence. It's a strategic decision to go where the competition isn't," says Bill Agee, external marketing communications manager for IKEA[7] (figs. 14.18 and 14.19).

In fact, if you can "own" the whole space, so much the better. Clutter makes everything equally unimportant and unnoticed. To clear a space for itself, Target stores, for example, bought all the advertising in the August 22, 2005, issue of the *New Yorker* magazine. Then, rather than running ads, Target commissioned

Left

14.18. Opportunities for nontraditional advertising abound: the world is all around you. The "do" campaign from Blue Cross and Blue Shield of Minnesota renames (and sometimes reconfigures) utilitarian public spaces, inviting people to see them, not as their mundane selves, but as fun opportunities for exercise. (Another elevator sign says, "Don't let the machines win. Take the stairs.")

Ⓢ See more images from this campaign at fig. W-14.18.

Below

14.19. A shoe retailer placed these ads in the bottoms of airport bins, the ones people put their shoes and other items in when going through security. Hard to get closer to shoe consciousness than that.

artists to illustrate, in their own idiosyncratic styles, New York scenes, incorporating Target's bulls-eye logo and other red brand identifiers into the images (fig. 14.20). These non-ad ads were fun and striking—the illustrations created a kind of art gallery inside the magazine—and they pitched nothing, except that Target had the wit and style to fit right into New York. A good selling argument, accomplished without saying a word.

If you do use a traditional medium, use it untraditionally

As did Target. Tourism advertising invariably shows big, colorful beauty shots—a pristine beach or dramatic waterfall or snowy mountain, which are sensory appeals but also clichés. Why not go the other way? Reduce the ad's size, withhold the image. North Caro-

14.20. More than two dozen illustrators contributed to a special Target-ads-only issue of the *New Yorker*. The only constraints were that they had to include the Target bull's-eye and be New York City–based.

Ⓢ See more examples at fig. W-14.20.

lina Tourism (visitnc.com) put small-space, all-type ads in the backs of travel magazines. Here are four of these copy-only ads:

> If you're reading tiny ads in the back of magazines, it might be time for a vacation.

> Most readers will overlook this ad. Which just leaves more room for you on the beach.

> Consumer testing shows ads this small to be ineffective in drawing large crowds to North Carolina. Perfect.

> See. You're always attracted to open spaces. [the ad was all white space, except for this line at the bottom]

Rules are there to break. An award-winning direct-mail letter for *The Economist* magazine contained just that, a letter, but it came shredded. You had to put it back together—how's that for an involvement device?—and when you did, you were congratulated for your curiosity and energy, your can-do spirit, exactly what *The Economist* is all about, and you were encouraged to subscribe to reward those virtues.

Be surprising

Surprise is essential to nontraditional advertising. As Zak Mroueh, executive creative director at advertising agency TAXI, says, "You have to keep innovating because nontraditional advertising has a way of very quickly becoming traditional. For example, ads in public bathrooms once seemed so different and clever—but now they're a cliché."[8] Even so, you can still create clever restroom ideas, as Mroueh's own agency demonstrated. To encourage people to get a colon cancer screening, TAXI wrote on toilet paper in public restrooms, "Is this the only time you think about your bottom?" (See fig. 14.21 for another ad that surprises.)

Be fan friendly

You risk offending people by "wilding," that is, sticking your message in their eye and ear without permission. You're also intruding on the landscape—often an open, public, supposedly advertising-free zone. Such an intrusion can irritate people mightily. Therefore be funny, be temporary, don't mess with people unduly. See things from their point of view, not just yours. As advertising writer and editor War-

14.21. With nontraditional advertising, one tip is to look for something in the environment that's doing what your branded thing does and make a connection. The supermarket conveyor belt becomes a metaphor: keep things moving. (Denver Water is encouraging people to use only the water they need, so that rivers "keep flowing.")

ren Berger asks, "How would you feel if this particular sidewalk ad were stamped on the walk in front of your own house—would you still find it amusing? What if it showed up in the halls of your kid's school?"[9]

For example, a guerrilla campaign against SUVs in the San Francisco Bay Area surreptitiously tagged SUV bumpers with this sticker: "I'm changing the climate! Ask me how!" It's funny if someone is against SUVs, but it's not funny to the SUVs' owners. The campaign definitely raises awareness but probably inflames opinions rather than changes minds.[10]

14.22. The argument is made, but not in the usual, finger-wagging way. "Tell it slant," Emily Dickinson advised.

Tread lightly on the sales pitch

You also risk alienating people if your pitch becomes blatant. When people sense an ad coming their way, their eyes glaze, disbelief descends like a curtain, and they look for an exit. So don't make this a commercial. If you've got enough nerve, don't even brand it.

> "Images in public that aren't advertising make people curious."
> —Shepard Fairey, graphic designer/street artist

Burger King's celebrated subservientchicken.com is a case in point. A man dressed in a chicken outfit in what appears to be a sleazy motel room does whatever people ask (within reason; he wags his finger at naughty requests). The idea is to express literally Burger King's have-it-your-way claim: "Get chicken just the way you like it. Type in your command here." The selling argument is so bizarrely presented, the branding so minimal, that the whole thing slides into people's heads almost without their noticing, and the idea is nutty and fun enough to generate a lot of buzz. The site scored twenty million hits in its first ten days and quickly spawned 700 Google links to sites discussing Subservient Chicken.[11]

See figure 14.22 for another selling argument delivered with a light touch.

> "There's a huge lure to obscurity. That's one of the keys—giving people something to discover—which is the antithesis of the way most advertising works."
> —David Art Wales, founder, consulting firm Ministry of Culture

Can it be interactive?

That is, can those people who experience it do more than just watch? Marketer Tom Himpe distinguishes between participating and co-creating. Participating is when people involve themselves with a script and scenario already worked out by the company, as they do, for example, at amusement parks. Co-creating is when people complete something that's incomplete without them. Himpe prefers that people complete the thing (as they do, for example, with the Chicken): "Unless consumers have a final say in the content of an experiential platform, they continue to think in terms of 'them' versus 'us', no matter how fun, inclusive or memorable the experience is."[12] Figure 14.23 shows an ad campaign that would be nothing without participants.

Be disarming

There may be greater creative pressure on you in the guerrilla arena than elsewhere, since nothing is as irritating or fails as loudly as a big gesture gone wrong. So make your guerrilla advertising friendly and fun. People will resent a same-as-usual sales pitch. Make them smile, don't overstay your welcome, hope for good press, and move on. And keep moving the idea forward, too, if it's a good one. Don't become static or predictable.

Viral marketing

"Viral is impossible to guarantee. You're competing with sex, drugs, rock 'n' roll and cobras swallowing hippopotamuses. How can you rise above that?"
—Ian Grais, partner, Rethink Advertising

As Grais points out, you cannot plan on something going viral; you can only hope that it will. *Viral marketing* is advertising that people participate in by passing it on, and whether they do that is, of course, up to them. If they send it to other people, the ad or event will have gotten into their bloodstream, so to speak—because it's funny or interesting—and they pass it on like a virus to others. Viral marketing can use any medium; the key idea is that consumers enlist themselves to spread the ad around.

Advertiser Jonathan Bond points out the value of getting consumers to spread a message: "People don't trust advertising; they trust other people. No one ad is as credible or effective as the recommendation of a friend. But good advertising can program people to say what you want about a brand, to forge the kind

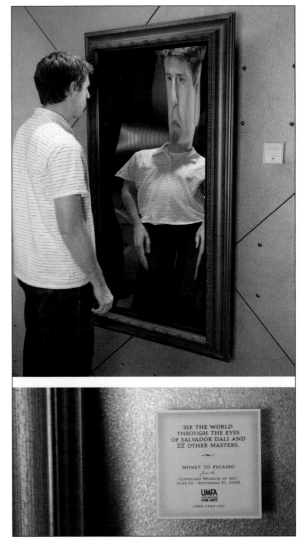

14.23. Here people are invited to do more than contemplate a museum show. These nontraditional ads let them experience the points of view of the artists themselves.

of connection consumers make with Volvo and safety. That's the word-of-mouth channel, and you can't buy time on it. You earn it with a message that has actual news value and gets people talking."[13]

So how do you get people talking? Create something that satisfies these criteria:

1. Would anyone *not* interested in this product still be interested in the idea? Ed Robinson, co-founder of The Viral Factory, says, "This is key for us—does the idea hold a human truth which goes beyond us (an advertising agency getting paid to flog some stuff) and the client (who thinks only of their product). If it doesn't then it has no viral potential."[14]

2. Does it work the way a Hallmark card works? That is, does it say for people what they can't say for themselves? Ed Robinson again: "This is the hardest facet of viral to articulate. . . . But if we make a work which one person can send to another and it helps them articulate love, loss, fear, hope, etc. then we have something which has viral potential."[15]

3. Don't forget this corollary: "Viral means people send stuff to their friends, and no one wants to send a salesman over to a friend's house," says Crispin Porter + Bogusky co-founder Chuck Porter, so your YouTube video or microsite or event or ad had better be soft sell, if it sells at all.[16]

4. Is it new? People pass surprises along to their friends, not un-surprises. If you're reiterating or just refining what's already out there, you won't draw flies, or, to vary the cliché, hardly a dog will bark. Give it a hook. Make it wiggle.

Multicultural and international advertising

"It took millions of years for man's instincts to develop. It will take millions more for them to even vary. It is fashionable to talk about changing man. A communicator must be concerned with unchanging man, with his obsessive drive to survive, to be admired, to succeed, to love, to take care of his own."

—William Bernbach, founding partner,
Doyle Dane Bernbach

"I'm of the opinion that there is no such thing as a global advertising campaign. To try and market one product in different cities and cultures is just about impossible."

—Steffan Postaer, creative director, Leo Burnett

Part of why advertising is so difficult is that both men are right. People are and aren't the same. The trick is knowing how so and how not.

HOW TO DEAL WITH PEOPLE'S DIFFERENCES
If you want to cross international borders with the greatest of ease, follow the two universal guidelines discussed in this section.

First, don't use words. Use pictures. (If you're a copywriter, life just got easier.) Ideas in one language won't always cross over into another. For instance, "curiously strong," the key phrase for Altoids mints, doesn't translate well, if at all, into other languages, thus limiting the campaign to speakers of English. Similarly, a Saab campaign whose headlines pivoted on "versus" (for example, "Saab vs. Oxygen Bars" or "Saab vs. Parenthood") didn't work in Japan because Japanese has no ready equivalent for "vs."[17] To give you an idea of how big a problem language can be, I'll just mention that Singapore alone has four national languages, and if you're aiming a campaign at all of Asia, you'll encounter hundreds of languages.[18]

Even if the language will translate, assumptions may not. Avis's celebrated 1960s car rental campaign, whose theme line was "We're no. 2. We try harder," wouldn't have worked in Asia. Ian Batey, former CEO of Time, Inc., and author of *Asian Branding*, explains why: "Self-deprecation is not an Asian trait. Asians want to save face, not lose it. If you surround your brand with negative irony, they will walk away in droves."[19] This is good to know, especially since so much American advertising—from DDB's original campaigns for Avis and VW to work created last week—delights in making fun of itself.

But ads that don't trip on translation and idiom difficulties, ads that present the human condition rather than a cultural condition, ads that are entirely or primarily visual, such ads have their visa papers ready (figs. 14.24 and 14.25).

Second, when you do use words, be prepared to translate ideas, too. The witty "Got milk?" campaign, for example, wasn't going to work, straight up, for the Spanish-speaking Hispanic market, and research showed why.[20] For one thing, "Got milk?" translated into something like "Are you lactating?" For another, milk is central to a loving Hispanic mother's duties in caring for her family. To joke about its absence, the milk deprivation strategy, calls her competence into question. Also, peanut butter and jelly sandwiches and chocolate chip cookies, central to the campaign, didn't resonate. Finally, milk in Hispanic homes is used more

14.24. This ad will cross any border known to man. It's not just funny to one culture, it's funny to humans. Words would only get in the way.

14.25. Although this ad has been used only in the U.S., it's ready to travel. With no headline to create language problems and a visual message that's universally understandable—both as a metaphor (the beer that stands out in a crowd) and as a symbol (the brand-differentiating Corona parrot)—this ad could go anywhere.

to cook with than to drink. For all these reasons the campaign had to undergo significant alteration—the joke and tone had to be jettisoned—to work. The theme line that replaced "Got milk?" in Spanish-language advertising to Hispanics, translated, was "And you, have you given them enough milk today?" The selling argument is still there, but it's had surgery.

HOW TO TAKE ADVANTAGE OF PEOPLE'S SIMILARITIES

It can be easy to overemphasize the differences across cultures and countries and make one of two mistakes: (1) appeal too narrowly to a regional difference or cultural predilection, or (2) make no impression at all by pulling your punches, thinking you'd better not speak specifically or engage in humor or take one single chance. These problems are twin horns of the same dilemma: be too general and go blah; be too specific and narrowcast yourself into insignificance. Or, worse, watch your selling idea backfire as your audience feels patronized, as though they couldn't handle a mainstream argument.

José Mollá, co-founder of la comunidad, Miami, makes a good suggestion: "To me, the best thing to do is have one strategy—and then to do the fine-tuning at the executional level, so that you can deepen the connection with each culture. Often, there is a small twist you can add to the concept that will make it resonate more with the Hispanic market. But the multicultural aspect of a campaign shouldn't come from just the media buy, or the casting—it should come from the content of the message. And the way to do that is to connect with human truths."[21]

Citibank's advertising has encouraged people to be responsible with their money. How to take that idea into the Spanish-speaking Hispanic market? To advertise Access Account, a starter checking account that facilitates money transfers, Citibank created ads spotlighting problems Hispanics encounter every day, often small things like ordering coffee or speaking with a pharmacist. Contrasting those experiences was the tagline: "There are better reasons why you chose to live in the United States. Citibank Access Account. Access to what you came here for." In other words, access to economic advancement: making money and improving their families' lives (Hispanics send home millions of U.S. dollars to their families in Latin America).[22]

The ads, created by Mollá's agency, put into play his advice to start with a central strategy, then adapt it to connect with a particular culture. Outdoor boards in south Florida said in Spanish, "The red should come from too much sun, not too much spending." In this case the Citibank selling argument—we'll help you use your money wisely—is translated into terms that work for the audience and location. Other outdoor boards, translated, said, "We speak to you in the language you dream in."

In brief, all multicultural and international advertising will benefit from these five guidelines:

1. Appeal to human truths, universal truths.
2. Don't base the ads on culture- or language-bound idiom.
3. Be visual whenever possible. Images trump words.
4. Establish a brand identity or selling argument, then tweak that theme to fit the audience.
5. Don't shoot lower than you should. Respect your audience's intelligence.

And remember, too, that people of all countries increasingly are consuming American popular culture, advertising, and imagery (Elvis and Marilyn will never die). The Americanization of the world is binding people together with shared cultural themes and capitalist assumptions. Advertising from international corporations like Audi, Honda, Sony, Coca-Cola, and many others has a universal sensibility, so much so that you can't tell where the advertising originated. Ads created in the U.K., Europe, or the Pacific Rim rather than in the U.S. have often become a distinction without a difference.

In short, if you're creating advertising for international audiences, be aware of the issues discussed in this section, but don't let them undo your instincts. Start with basic human truths, and you'll be fine. After all, that's where humans start.

PART THREE
THE TOOLBOX

"Things come toward you when you walk."

—WILLIAM STAFFORD, *poet*

What follow are techniques to help you have ideas. Think of them as tools. We accept the need for tools in other areas—no one thinks about working on wood without hammers and saws, or gardening without spade and shears, or playing baseball without bat, ball, and glove—but we'll try to think without anything at all. The techniques in the following chapters are tools for thinking creatively about advertising. They lie like objects on a workbench. Pick up the ones that seem right for the task. Let them give shape to your ideas.

15 · How to Be Creative

Imagination cannot be taught. . . . But until craft is mastered, imagination is a useless, largely inapplicable abstraction. Mastering craft gives the writer access to the fullness of his or her imagination, because it gives the writer the ability to deploy and apply it. Everyone can imagine a house. Only a carpenter can build one.

—Tom Grimes, *The Workshop: Seven Decades of the Iowa Writers' Workshop*

Inspiration is highly overrated. If you sit around and wait for the clouds to part, it's not liable to ever happen. More often than not, work is salvation.

—Chuck Close, painter

Creative skills, like any others, improve with practice, and creativity follows, however idiosyncratically, a method. You get better at being creative by exercising these inventive skills, and you improve your invention by going at it step by step. How to do so?

Create a routine

"I need a fence before I'm motivated to climb out. So clarity and order are important. Establish a discipline up front, and then I feel free to explore."

—Harry Jacobs, chairman, The Martin Agency

Whenever you're solving any advertising problem, don't neglect practical matters. Establish working routines that follow your mental instincts. For example, I start early work on a clipboard, making lists of phrases, words, and strategy-like statements, all done as a gathering process. I'm pulling words together that seem to belong to the problem. Soon I take this list-making into the computer; but for early efforts, there's still nothing as comforting to me as a sharp pencil and a clipboard full of paper. Art directors often think best with markers and a sketchpad in front of them. Find your own comfort zone and enter it. Advertiser John Vitro talks about his process:

As I'm coming up with ideas, I'm usually scribbling on a little pad. Somebody once told me, "It's not a good idea unless it's a good idea on a plain white piece of paper." [My partner and I] get together once or twice a day and pass paper back and forth between us. Usually, at this stage, we're trying to come up with an idea in the form of a line—often a headline—that gets to the heart of what we're trying to say.[1]

Let the assignment set some boundaries

"Small rooms discipline the mind; large rooms distract it."

—Leonardo da Vinci

The specifics of your advertising problem will help center your thinking. Are you writing copy for a corporate website? If so, you'll be thinking about how to organize the information and sequence it and what will unify the site, screen to screen (an issue you'll develop with the designer sharing the project). Maybe instead you're writing a series of newspaper ads for a local dry cleaner, so you realize that these will have to be quick and simple, probably price or service oriented, with strong headlines. Perhaps you're writing a self-promotion piece for a photographer. Using photos as samples is expected in such self-promotions, but what would you say about them? A more original advertising strategy might be to mail out only copy, no photos, in order to get attention (fig. 15.1). Or perhaps you're creating an integrated media campaign for a packaged good for your portfolio, in which case the only limits are those of your own devising.

In short, *how* you think through an advertising problem comes from the nature of the project. It will lead you in certain directions—and give you ideas. The cool thing about working on something is that you don't have to be a genius. Just start trying to solve the problem, and ideas will arrive. Teacher and ceramics designer Eva Zeisel explained it this way:

> I came to the conclusion that what we call limits—yes, industrial design is very limiting—was just the opposite; it was very unlimiting. I set my students this project. I said, "Please sit down and do the most beautiful thing you can imagine. You must have been thinking a lot about it." And they were sitting around totally frustrated, without the slightest idea of how to fulfill their dream. Then I gave them limitations—"Make something this high, with this function"—and suddenly they were all sitting there working like beavers.[2]

Start with basic thinking techniques

> "I always write a thing first and think about it afterwards, which is not a bad procedure, because the easiest way to have consecutive thoughts is to start putting them down."
>
> —E. B. WHITE, essayist

If you've taken a creative writing or thinking course, you've probably used free association, brainstorming, and list making. They are ways to provide structure to the notion of having ideas. They're the first techniques, really, the first how-tos.

Free association is the process of letting one idea suggest another, one word imply the next, one image beget two. (*Brainstorming* is this process performed by a group, in which the members become one speaking, collective mind.) Free association of either sort should be fast and loose—a rapid-fire, automatic-thinking kind of thing. No one can really prescribe anyone else's free association because the connections in people's brains are so individualized. But I can offer suggestions.

Give yourself a working topic, a focus for the free association. (Let's assume that you've already done research on the product and the target audience, so you have a store of information.) Write down rapidly whatever comes to mind as it comes to mind. Don't stop. Writing teacher Peter Elbow calls such a thing

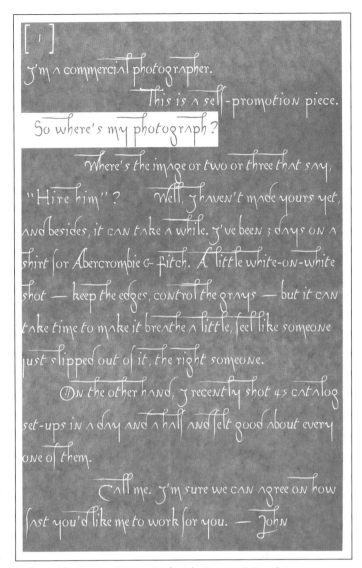

15.1. In this direct-mail campaign for John Strange & Associates, commercial photographers, Crit Warren and I created a series of poster-sized "letters" from John to prospective clients. I wrote them in a straightforward voice to represent John's, and Crit designed them to be striking but also suggestive of handwriting. This is the first of thirteen such letters, each explaining why John wasn't sending out photos.

freewriting, and suggests that you write for ten minutes without stopping.[3] The only way to do a freewriting "wrong" is to go slowly and edit your thoughts as you have them, deciding which are worth saying and which not, what's grammatical and what's not, and so on. Such interference defeats the purpose of scanning your brain and letting it, at speed, show you connections. If you slow down, your associations become less free, more arranged. You can't surprise yourself if you peek around every corner first.

One way to freewrite/free associate is to imagine that the product itself is a friend, and you're explaining the relationship to the reader. Imagine that you're the target market, and try to say what you get out of using the product. Write it like a letter to someone about the relationship; confess: "The thing I really like about Wheaties is their athletic associations and their goofy orange box. I feel more masculine when I eat them. They're American, they're traditional, they taste good, no frills, not a complicated food. Somehow they center me for the day. They also go great with strawberries and blueberries in the summer since they're flakes and they . . . " (This can work as a strategy creator, too, since you can investigate such confessionals for *strategic* ideas.)

Lists are a favorite of mine; maybe you use them, too. They're like the first outlines, helping me get my head on straight, start seeing the issues and possibilities. Make different kinds of lists: lists of benefits delivered, problems solved, items associated with your client's product, objections to the product, human truths that surround the brand or product, and so on. If I can list it, I can see it, and often I can get something started.

The value of lists is that they give you things to think with; they help give expression to your selling ideas. A common error with early work is to rush past items, closing each up and going on, rather than letting them linger open. When you've made lists, you can suspend yourself in each word or phrase, let yourself nurture it for a while. What does it suggest? What images do you see? How might it lead to an idea?

Suspend judgment

"Be fearless around bad ideas. There is no such thing as a bad idea when concepting. Often the worst ideas are your tour guide to the best ones. It wouldn't be a cliché if it weren't so damned true. My ratio of bad to good is probably 50 to 1. I fill pages with bad. I build a monument to good on a trash heap of crap."

—David Baldwin, executive creative director, McKinney & Silver

Get those half-ideas, bad ideas, and nonsense ideas out of your system and onto the page. All of them either imply transformations or let other, related ideas slip out that would have stayed hidden otherwise. The next time you're brainstorming in a group or simply working inside your own mind, notice how pervasive is your self-critical editor, the "Oh-never-mind-it-was-a-stupid-idea" self who kills thoughts before they even hit the floor. Suspend judgments. Be a critic later, not now. As Edward de Bono says in *Lateral Thinking*, a very good book about creativity:

The purpose of thinking is not to be right but to be effective. Being effective does eventually involve being right but there is a very important difference between the two. Being right means being right all the time. Being effective means being right only at the end. . . . The need to be right all the time is the biggest bar there is to new ideas. It is better to have enough ideas for some of them to be wrong than to be always right by having no ideas at all.[4]

Use both lateral and vertical thinking

"I think brainstorming and coming up with concepts is like a muscle, and the more you work it, the better. We push our people to try to think of a lot of different ideas . . . so they don't feel that if something gets killed, they can't start again. You don't want people to think, Okay, this is it, this is the idea—and stop there."

—Tracy Wong, principal, WongDoody

Creating ads is an alternating process of expansion and contraction. That is, you must be abundant and uncritical—generating a variety of approaches, a number of different starts and little thumbnails and half-ideas (de Bono calls this *lateral thinking*)—but then you must take the few that seem strong, the hot spots, and worry them into shape. You must exercise analytical skills—see what's wrong with a headline and fix it, prune extraneous images to their essentials, take that half-idea and think it through, and so on (de Bono calls this logical, analytical process *vertical thinking*).

Accustom yourself to shifting between these two kinds of thought. Each needs the other: you must find ideas outside the boundaries of the obvious, but then you must make them work. As you think up your ideas and then sweat them through, notice how you alternate modes—dreaming and judging, inventing and refining, thinking loose and thinking tight, being generous and being cold-blooded.

Throughout exploratory thinking, you will continually wander as well as leap away from your strategy.

This is inevitable. The trick is to keep your strategy/objective in your mind like a porch light while you wander around in the dark. When you feel too out-there-in-nowhere, come back to that light: *what, exactly, are you trying to communicate and to whom?* Always use the strategy as your centering device. Come back to it after exploring in the dark for that Big Idea.

Imitate

"Only those with no memory insist on their originality."

— COCO CHANEL

Writers internalize the people they read. Then they imitate them, if only indirectly. I remember reading Alexander Pope in college and writing balanced sentences, heavy on parallelism, for a long while afterward. How could I help myself, with all those heroic couplets seesawing in my head?

Hunter S. Thompson copied out in long hand the whole of *The Great Gatsby*, to try to get into his own system Fitzgerald's beautiful prose style.

Elmore Leonard looked to Hemingway: "Reading Hemingway inspired me to think about my own sound on the page. I would copy down a paragraph from *For Whom the Bell Tolls*, and, without looking at the book, I'd try to continue writing in that voice. It was an exercise I'd do to try and find my own sound."[5]

It's the same way with advertising. All ads have antecedents. No ad comes from nowhere. Be careful about "imitating," though, because you never want to steal. If you lift an ad from an annual, shame on you. Instead, learn from the great work in the annuals. Study the way it thinks; don't just repeat surface features. Here's Ernie Schenck on this point:

> The idea [of studying awards annuals] isn't to imitate. It's to assimilate. It's to try and figure out the common elements uniformly inherent to all great work and to bring these elements to bear on our own efforts. And believe me, there are common elements. If you don't see them, then you aren't looking hard enough.[6]

One saving grace is that even if you try to copy, you probably can't. That other person's idea will come out your way. Gerry Graf, copywriter and executive creative director, TBWA\Chiat\Day, explains: "First you copy, then if you have any talent, what's inside you

starts coming out in a nice mixture of what you admired and whatever talent you bring to it."[7]

"STEAL" BETWEEN CONTEXTS

Innovation is often defined as applying an idea to a new context, or bringing two old ideas together to make a new one. "Steal," but only from another genre, category, or kind of thing. Apply something to something else. Metaphor does this. When he visited CCAD and critiqued student advertising portfolios, Mark Fenske suggested talking like a bank to sell a Porsche and vice versa. In other words, put one language system into another context. You avoid clichés of the category and you give yourself fresh ways to regard the thing you're selling. See chapter 23, Verbal Metaphor, for more on this technique.

Have I thoroughly muddied the waters of what's original and what's plagiarism? I hope not. You know when you're too close to a source of inspiration. You really do. Let that instinct be your rudder.

Find more than one solution

"You cannot dig a hole in a different place by digging the same hole deeper."

—EDWARD DE BONO, *Lateral Thinking*

Most people get a pretty good dose of analytical (vertical) thinking in their educations. They are taught to take things apart, label constituent parts, a-n-a-l-y-z-e (literally, "loosen throughout"). But one of the skills you'll need most in advertising is the opposite habit of mind: lateral thinking. Given an advertising problem, how many *different* solutions can you find—and how quickly? Are you able to see a problem from multiple points of view? How dissimilar are your ideas from each other? Can you leap around, or is each idea just a logical half-step away from the last?

Sometimes the best solution isn't arrived at logically. How, for example, might you sell a magic store? You could do something sensible like focus on the things in it or maybe on famous magicians of the past, but what about seeing magic from the other end—the person on whom it is practiced? Take a look at figure 15.2. Copywriter Mike Roe, who created these transit posters with art director Jason Wood, explains their development: "I usually try to create advertising that builds on a human truth. Something that most of us believe in. However, when we tried to find a logical connection on why adults should practice magic, we

BEING A GOAT FOR THREE DAYS
HAS TAUGHT ME A LOT ABOUT MYSELF

SPECIFICALLY, I'VE LEARNED THAT I'M ARROGANT, CONDESCENDING, AND INSENSITIVE TOWARD THE PEOPLE AROUND ME. AND TO ROB, I WANTED TO SAY THAT I AM VERY SORRY FOR HAVING EVER CALLED YOUR MAGIC TRICKS "GOOFY" AND TELLING YOU WHERE TO STICK THAT MAGIC WAND OF YOURS. IT WAS WRONG AND I APOLOGIZE. NOW PLEASE, FOR THE LOVE OF CHRIST, CHANGE ME BACK!! I PROMISE TO BE A BETTER SUPERVISOR FROM HERE ON OUT.
SEATTLE MAGIC · 106 1ST AVENUE SOUTH, PIONEER SQUARE · YOU WILL BELIEVE

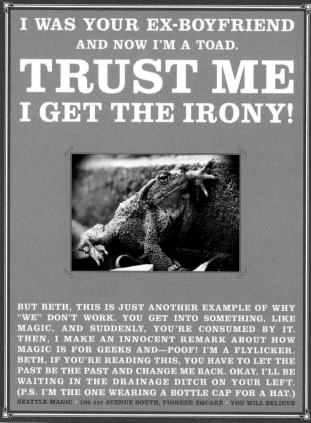

I WAS YOUR EX-BOYFRIEND
AND NOW I'M A TOAD.
TRUST ME
I GET THE IRONY!

BUT BETH, THIS IS JUST ANOTHER EXAMPLE OF WHY "WE" DON'T WORK. YOU GET INTO SOMETHING, LIKE MAGIC, AND SUDDENLY, YOU'RE CONSUMED BY IT. THEN, I MAKE AN INNOCENT REMARK ABOUT HOW MAGIC IS FOR GEEKS AND—POOF! I'M A FLYLICKER. BETH, IF YOU'RE READING THIS, YOU HAVE TO LET THE PAST BE THE PAST AND CHANGE ME BACK. OKAY, I'LL BE WAITING IN THE DRAINAGE DITCH ON YOUR LEFT. (P.S. I'M THE ONE WEARING A BOTTLE CAP FOR A HAT.)
SEATTLE MAGIC · 106 1ST AVENUE SOUTH, PIONEER SQUARE · YOU WILL BELIEVE

couldn't find any. Okay, we found some connections, but they were horribly boring. So, we threw out all the logical reasons and just had fun. And boom! We had a campaign of non-believers who were now pleading for their life back. The moral of the story is stay loose and stay open. You never know."[8]

CONSIDER MULTIPLE POINTS OF VIEW

Illustrator and designer Timothy Goodman, asked if he had a personal philosophy, said, "I've been mentoring this wonderful young boy for about 2½ years. The other day I told him it was raining in San Francisco, and he said, 'That sucks for you, but it's fun for the trees!' I like his outlook."[9]

One way people get stuck when creating ads is by continuing to consider only one point of view—usually that of the consumer, the target audience for the product. But every scenario has lots of players, so take a little time and list them. If you're selling shoes, don't limit yourself to the wearer. Consider, for example, feet themselves. A copywriter for Rockport created a clever campaign underneath the theme "Your feet have feelings, too." All the ads whimsically made consumers consider those poor guys below their ankles, and if you read enough of those ads, you almost began to feel that someone was living down there who deserved better treatment—not only a clever campaign but an effective one for shoes like Rockports. Other possible players? The surface you walk or run on: "Soften the sidewalks" was a campaign theme for another shoe company. How about the dog who jogs with you? Ever see that great Nike TV spot narrated from the visual and verbal point of view of the dog accompanying his owner on a jog? Here's the copy, written by Mark Fenske. The dog is talking:

> I used to like it when she ran. She really didn't go much faster than now when she's walking, but she'd tire out quicker. And then we'd go home and she'd fall asleep in front of the TV. I used to like that. I'd go sit on the chairs I'm not supposed to and she couldn't do nothing about it. Now, we go 3 miles a day, 10 miles on weekends. You know dogs were meant to sit in the sun and sleep. They ought to engrave that on the president of Nike's forehead.

15.2. Here a magic store is sold, not by considering magicians, magic tools, or the history of magic, but by thinking about the person on whom magic is practiced. What if it worked?

Every advertising situation has more *points of view* than you are currently considering. What you're selling becomes a different thing, depending on who's looking and where from. A celebrated campaign for a sleeping medication didn't show the restless non-sleeper in bed, the cliché of the genre, but instead looked at things from the point of view of the characters in the non-sleeper's dreams (Abe Lincoln, a beaver, an underwater diver), characters who felt left out. "Your dreams miss you," the ads said. "When you can't sleep, you can't dream" was the line that gave birth to the campaign's unusual point of view.

Can you make an ad from a less-than-obvious participant, from an unusual point of view? Yes, you can (see figs. 15.3–15.5).

RESTATE THE PROBLEM

Another way copywriters get hung up is by resaying the problem without re-imagining it. They keep pounding on that same nail, that same strategic thought or problem-to-be-solved, and getting nowhere. Force yourself to say the problem another way; make yourself restate it in other terms. Often this will free you from the hole you're in. Goodby's famous "Got milk?" campaign happened only when its creators stopped thinking about

milk as something unto itself and started thinking of it as half of a duo: it was always milk *and* something.

BE NAÏVE

"I want to approach each picture like a beginner. A beginner has many possibilities. An expert, few."
—YURI DOJC, photographer

Most people surround problems with invisible boxes, parameters they don't even notice that tell them which solutions lie inside and which lie outside the fence, how they should attack this problem and how they shouldn't. The more experience people have solving problems, the more firmly in place their boxes are likely to be.

Paula Scher, a partner in Pentagram, spurs invention this way: "In my work, I always try to adopt the perspective of a first-time user. If I'm designing a package, a book, or a magazine, I approach it as if I've never heard of it before. If it's signage or an identity project, I approach it as if I were a foreigner and didn't speak the language."[10] When Scher was branding a hotel in New York City, among the signage she changed was the door tag that always says, "Do not disturb" (which is strictly hotel language). She changed it to

15.3. The argument isn't unusual—that this place sells great clothes—but the presentation is. Seeing clothes from the moth's point of view makes them all the more valuable.

15.4. We may think readily enough of the consumer who buys Zoop, the animals who make it, the flowers that benefit from it, but have we ever thought of the guy who collects it? We have now. And this point of view puts the product's unique difference even more vividly in mind, don't you agree?

"Go away," which is everyday people's language (at least in no-nonsense New York). This small but important gesture is an example of Scher seeing the situation freshly, noticing that the corporate voice had usurped our own.

BE FRUITFUL AND MULTIPLY

A decent solution can make you quit looking for something better. It seems to solve the problem well enough. De Bono calls this being "blocked by openness." Don't be.

Put yourself into the writing

Dig into your own self. Get some personal connection, some personal truth, out and onto the page or screen. Bleed a little. The best work always costs you something, and you'll *feel* that. If it doesn't and you don't, chances are you haven't dug deep enough. Dan Wieden explains:

> The most powerful things you do are trying to get at the truth of something. I think most good work is personal. It's hard. If you can't find something interesting to you, you have to start there. You have to have a personal relationship with that challenge you are faced with, and the truth you are dealing with is not some sort of universal truth, but it is the truth to you in that subject. The best work has that sensibility about it.[11]

Here's a way to measure if you've broken into personal truth, advice from poet Stephen Dunn:

> One of the things I hear myself saying over and again to my poetry-writing students is "Your poem effectively begins at the first moment you've surprised or startled yourself. Throw away everything that preceded that moment, and begin with that moment."[12]

Hang tough

> "A good ad is a tricky, slippery, evasive beast that doesn't like to be caught, won't stand still, won't come out when called. A good ad is a greased pig when it comes time to put your hands on one. Masters of disguise, good ads sneak out of you in bars, the shower, dreams, even in advertising meetings, and run away to lost pages in your workbook or torn up sheets in office wastebaskets."
>
> —MARK FENSKE, advertiser and professor,
> VCU Brandcenter

Creativity doesn't arrive; it's earned. Don't get frustrated because a great idea simply will not come when called. Its elusiveness does not mean that you're "uncreative"; it means that good ideas require work and that problem solving resists shortcuts. Cultivate open-mindedness and relaxation when facing the "I-don't-have-an-idea-yet" state. Too many people feel anxious over this uncertainty and rush to end it with the relief of an idea, any idea. Learn to suspend yourself in a problem without being panicked by the sense of weightlessness that comes with no-idea-yet. It's not an easy skill to acquire, but as you solve advertising problems, going from nothing to something, you'll get accustomed to both the free-fall and the saving parachute of a good idea.

Bill Westbrook, then creative head at Earle Palmer Brown, commented on the difficulties, even at a major shop, of finding a good idea:

> There's basically a time line when the writer and art director sit down to do an ad. The first things they think of are all the puns and clichés and the really stupid answers that their psyche knows from somewhere else. Then they go through a period where they think they're hacks, they don't have a clue and they think they're worthless: "How did I get into this business?" And then they come out of that into getting very smart and focused on what they have to do. And they get a good idea. [If you rush yourself,] your answers can't be as smart or as sophisticated as they should be because you haven't had time to be stupid yet. You still have to go through that time line to get the really good work.[13]

Lower your standards

When I was in college, getting good grades was what I took to be my mission, and I turned it into a stress-filled ordeal. Maybe you did, too. Years later, the idea of being graded still floats in my head, but I try to make it work for, rather than against, me. When I feel blocked, I realize that I'm often trying too hard to get that invisible A. So I reduce my expectations. Aim for a C, aspire to mediocrity, I tell myself. (I've even markered a big C on a 3x5 card and taped it to the wall in front of me.) Lowering my expectations can relax me into finding a good idea and the right words. Aim lower to reach higher. It's a paradox, but it works. Try it next time you're squeezing too hard.

Let the client solve the problem

This sounds flippant, but I mean it: listen closely when talking with your clients. They know their business better than you do, and often when they're talking, a phrase or idea will slip out that, if you can hear it, will be what you should say. Or it will help you see what you should say. Ad writers try so hard to be clever that they often fail to hear the simple truth when it's spoken. Paula Scher comments again:

> Creativity requires a certain optimistic naïveté. You have to develop simple solutions to complex problems and ask, "Why not?" My best ideas are usually sparked by some innocent observation or comment the client made in the initial meeting. I've found that if I don't get an idea immediately thereafter it's because I have too much information or I've done similar projects too many times before—and I have become jaded.[14]

Read, stay curious, try to know at least a little about a lot

"Every really good creative person in advertising whom I have ever known has always had two noticeable characteristics. First, there was no subject under the sun in which he could not easily get

15.5. How to sell car wax? See things from the car lover's point of view: warblers aren't beautiful to everyone.

15.6. "What if writers didn't push themselves?" the copy line asks. This call for entries to the magazine's annual Student Fiction Contest has fun butchering Dickens's classic opening of *A Tale of Two Cities.* But you can't have fun with Dickens unless you've read him.

interested—from, say, Egyptian burial customs to Modern Art. Every facet of life had fascination for him. Second, he was an extensive browser in all sorts of fields of information. For it is with the advertising man as with the cow: no browsing, no milk."

—JAMES WEBB YOUNG,
A Technique for Producing Ideas

It's hard to be creative without raw material. The more you've got, the better. Keep filling up with ideas and images from history, art, movies, music, travel, psychology, literature, fashion, photography, children's books, walks in the park, flea markets—you name it. The more

strings you've got, the easier it is to pull on one. And the more things you know, the better your chances of getting two old things to combine in some new way—a common definition of creativity (fig. 15.6).

And when you're tempted to settle for having created a so-so ad, one that could be better if you dug deeper, think about the following comment from Jay Chiat, co-founder of Chiat/Day. Perhaps you'd even like to put it up where you work as challenge and inspiration: "A lot is said in this business about excellence and order, but not enough about mediocrity and chaos. Too many ads don't intrigue, don't work. They are worse than forgotten—they are never even noticed. Forgettable is unforgivable."[15]

16 • How to Write a Headline

Headlines are everything in my book. They serve as a direct window into how a copywriter thinks about a marketing problem. They tell me everything about their personality. If they have a sense of humor. If they're stealing lines from *CA* or *The One Show*, or worse yet, the Columbus ADDYs. If you can write good headlines, you'll always have a job in this business.

—MARK HILLMAN, creative director,
Resource Interactive, Columbus, Ohio

It usually takes a hundred headlines to come up with one great one.

—SALLY HOGSHEAD, copywriter,
co-founder, Robaire & Hogshead

Remember rule number one in writing a great headline: stay on strategy. Nothing works if you're saying the wrong thing. Once you know what to say, the problem becomes *how* to say it. Which is where rule number two comes in: pull up a chair and plan to stay a while. Sally's right: it'll take a lot of saying it wrong to say it right.

You're looking to generate energy among the words: create collisions, make sparks, get some drama going. You may think such energy is a mysterious affair, but there actually are ways to be clever, techniques writers have used for centuries to make language interesting all by itself—ways to write a line that, if it won't exactly hum down the corridors of time, will at least bounce around inside your readers' skulls for a day or two.

When you're sitting there writing those hundred headlines, you're running techniques through your head like beads on the rosary, whether you know it or not. You're turning phrases around, searching for synonyms, trying to say something paradoxically or in a hipper tone of voice, trying—one way or another—to get words to bump into each other and release some energy.

When you've written a bunch of headlines but haven't yet found magic, try the techniques in this chapter. I'm grateful for knowing them. You will be, too. The more tricks you know, the more beads you've got.

Wrap it in a smile

"He didn't like his facts bare and stark; he wanted them accompanied by comedy—you unwrapped the laugh and there was the fact, or maybe vice versa."

—JAMES THURBER, explaining *New Yorker* editor Harold Ross's approach to the magazine's personality

Thurber's sense of how to write a *New Yorker* piece can work for ads just as easily as magazine articles. I'll show you what I mean. A coffeehouse in my neighborhood has a policy it wants me to know about, one I read as I walk through its door: "No pets allowed in the store, unless you bring a walrus, then who are we to say no?" It tells me something I can't do and gets me to smile about it, in the process communicating the vibe of the place: friendly. "No pets" would have just growled at me.

As Victor Borge, pianist and comedian, pointed out, "A joke is the shortest distance between two people."[1] So wrap your idea in a smile, and watch it work better. Figure 16.1 is a great example of a headline

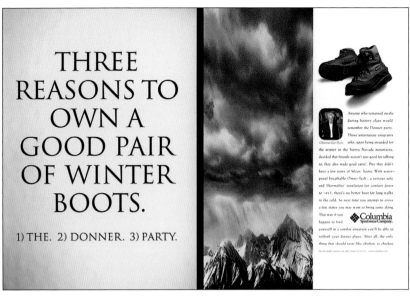

16.1. "Keeps you warm in cold weather" wouldn't have been nearly as good a headline, would it?

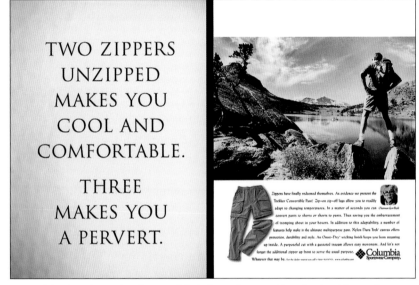

16.2. Here the product feature sinks in better because it's going in with a smile.

putting a light human touch on a product benefit.

The next time you're selling a product fact or feature, make a little joke about it. This VOX vodka headline knows how to deliver a fact:

Most people can't tell the difference the fifth distillation makes. Let them drink their dirty little vodka.

See figure 16.2 for yet another example of a feature being sold with a smile.

Reward your reader

You don't have to write jokes to write good headlines. But you should reward your reader for his or her time. Sometimes a laugh or smile can be that reward. "Effective surprise" is a phrase sometimes used to say what a great ad should be, and it's what a great joke is, too.[2] Can you teach yourself to be funny? Let's put it this way: you can teach yourself to be funnier. Comedy uses patterns. Learn the patterns and you've got a chance.

Lee Clow, global director of media arts, TBWA\ Worldwide, says this about rewarding your reader or viewer: "The essential rule is to always understand that your job is to create a bridge between the brand or the company you're talking about and the people you're trying to talk to. And that bridge better be rewarding. It better be likable, engaging, entertaining, charming, interesting, funny, fun. . . . You've got to create a bridge that, one, doesn't allow them to ignore it and, two, makes them feel good for the 30 or 60 seconds they've spent with that company or brand."[3]

The sections that follow discuss other techniques that help you create that bridge, deliver that effective surprise. Let's see what the possibilities are.

Parallelism

One of the workhorses of headlines (as well as slogans and body copy) is parallelism. The best way to define it is to show it.[4] Here are two sentences:

> George liked Jean and often walked beside her on the way to school.
>
> Jean was also accompanied sometimes to school by Ronald, who also liked her, but who often could be seen walking behind her.

Made shorter:

> George liked Jean and often walked beside her on the way to school.
>
> Jean was also accompanied by Ronald, who walked behind her.

Made *parallel*:

> George liked Jean and walked beside her to school. Ronald liked Jean and walked behind her to school.

Now you can *see* the meaning, can't you? Now you know who will win the girl, and who will worship from a distance. *Parallelism* is the notion that sentence elements identical in thought should be made identical in grammatical form, that form and function should coincide.

Parallelism involves repetition—often of words, but more important, of structure—and you can choose to repeat long structures or short ones. The point is to say similar things similarly. To do this, determine which of your ideas are equivalent in meaning, then express them in equivalent structures: a word for a word, a phrase for a phrase, a clause for a clause. Parallelism is to language what twins dressed alike are to child-

hood. Find your twins (or triplets or quads) and then put them in the same clothes.

For example, one of the most famous phrases in history is Julius Caesar's "I came, I saw, I conquered" (*Veni, vidi, vici*), and parallelism is what makes it so memorable. Had Caesar said, "I came, things were seen by me, and victory ensued," I wouldn't be quoting him now.

Parallelism throws a sharp light on your ideas, clarifying your distinctions. It also makes an ordinary idea *sound* better, if only because it now has new clothes. It looks dressed up, cleaned up, sharp:

> How to keep food you can't finish from becoming food you can't identify. (Sterilite food containers)
>
> If an air freight company can't fly on the ground, it doesn't matter how fast it flies in the air. (Emery Air Freight)
>
> Life is too short to get there too fast. (Cunard Lines)

In persuading people they would win big at Mystic Lake Casino, this headline uses parallelism to joke about how money changes people:

> Walk in a Democrat. Walk out a Republican.

Rockport justifies the price of its hiking boots:

> We could make them less expensive. God could make rain less wet.

Notice that in addition to being parallel, the last two examples are *balanced*: the second parallel clause is about as long as the first one. This technique allows you to raise an issue on the one hand and complete it nicely on the other. You appear both reasonable and complete—what more need be said? Balance parallel structures when you want to add resonance and authority to the expression.

Parallelism is so powerful that even its absence is audible. Consider figure 16.3, an ad for United Hospital that encourages parents to talk to their teenagers and conveys the need to do so right in the headline. The poignancy comes from readers' desire to hear that missing ending; its absence pulls them into the ad.

GO IN ONE WAY, COME OUT THE OTHER
Try reversing the elements of succeeding parallel constructions—go in one way and come out the other. A

Three years old.

What a great age.

Ten years old.

What a great age.

Fourteen years old.

This community service message is sponsored by The Grand Forks Public Schools and United Hospital.

16.3. Parallelism creates such strong expectations that readers hear it even when it's not there, and that's the strength of this headline.

famous example is JFK's "Ask not what your country can do for you, ask what you can do for your country." People hear how it goes out in one order and comes back in another—reversed, a mirror image—and they like it for having done so. Mae West, the sexy 1930s movie star, used the structure to comic effect: "It's not the men in my life, it's the life in my men."

Here are more examples:

Should your back fit the chair, or should the chair fit your back? (Steelcase/Coach office chair)

When you get into a Volkswagen, it gets into you.

A TV spot:

Voice-over: The only time he removes his car from the road is when he removes the road from his car.

Visual: A dusty BMW is washed, then immediately driven back out onto the road.

HOW TO THINK ABOUT PARALLELISM

Start by having something to say. You can't stick mumbo-jumbo into parallel structures and expect an advertising miracle. Create a real distinction, benefit, or promise.

How? Go to your list of benefits for the client's product and start looking for "two-fers," language that separates out into "this versus that," or "this plus that," or "this but not that," "either this or that," "not only this but also that," and so on. You're trying to take the benefits and deliver them in a one-two punch. And you're usually looking for some kind of opposition, a contrast to throw into relief.

Look at all the so-so headlines you've written. Can any of them be made parallel? Often it's not what you're saying that's wrong, it's how you're saying it. Throw ideas into parallel structures and see if they get better:

No: What's best about Holiday Inn is how there's never a bad surprise.
Yes: The best surprise is no surprise. (Holiday Inn)

No: A young person shouldn't get pregnant unless she's prepared to be a mother.
Yes: Because she's old enough to have a baby, doesn't mean she's old enough to be a mother. (visual of 14-year-old pregnant girl)
Tagline: Planned Parenthood. Abortion is something personal. Not political.

No: We developed our soft luggage to handle the difficulties of travel.
Yes: We didn't forget the hard side of travel when we developed our soft luggage.
Tagline: Beautiful on the outside. American Tourister on the inside.

Parallelism frequently relies on punning repetition, where the meaning of a repeated word or phrase changes:

If it weren't so tough out there, we wouldn't make it so tough in here. (Pace University—A Real Education for the Real World)

Don't squander your disposable income on a disposable car. (BMW)

Stop handguns before they stop you. (Handgun Control)

See figure 16.4 for another example of punning repetition.

As a writer, you'll find parallelism handy, if not indispensable. Besides shaping headlines, it can add clarity and punch to otherwise meandering or mushy sentences in copy. For more examples and discussion, turn to any grammar handbook and you'll find plenty of both.

Introduce misdirection: the kicker

"The basic two-step in humor is (1) to state some commonly acceptable problem, frequently with a cliché, and (2) in the last word or two change the expected ending to a surprise."
—Melvin Helitzer, *Comedy Writing Secrets*

A lot of great headlines are essentially jokes: they have a surprising twist at the end, a stinger in their tail. This last word, phrase, or sentence—the punchline or *kicker*—surprises by subverting expectations. You get a sequence or line of thought going and then pull the rug out from under it. This is an ancient and honorable comedy trick. It's a verbal bait-and-switch technique based on misdirection. People are led down one path, only to be surprised by a sudden switch in point of view or by an unexpected drop-off point. Here it is from a comedian (Woody Allen):

It's not that I'm afraid to die, I just don't want to be there when it happens.[5]

From a journalist (Hunter S. Thompson):

The music business is a cruel and shallow money trench, a long plastic hallway where thieves and pimps run free, and good men die like dogs. There's also a negative side.[6]

From ad guys:

The wind is screaming in your ears. Or are those pedestrians? (Roces in-line skates)

It's like Mom used to make. Just before she was arrested. (Cider Jack Hard Cider)

$4 haircuts. Because you're worth it. (Moler Barber College)

Add a little something to your coffee. Breakfast. (Starbucks)

You know all those smug, wing-tipped, perfectly coiffed, $2000 suit–wearing, perfect-smile guys you see flying charter? Be one. (Corporate Express)

See figure 16.5 for examples of misdirection. And consider the following headline, which accompanied a visual of a woman lifting weights in a health club:

Because power comes from within. Because strength gives me freedom. Because a cute guy just joined the gym and I don't think he's gay. (Marika)

The headline begins with a litany of accepted truths (clichés, used intentionally) of women's empowerment language as applied to so many products; then the last of the three is the kicker, the comic surprise that saves and makes the ad.

16.4. The surprising switch in the meaning of "freeze" creates the joke that powers the headline.

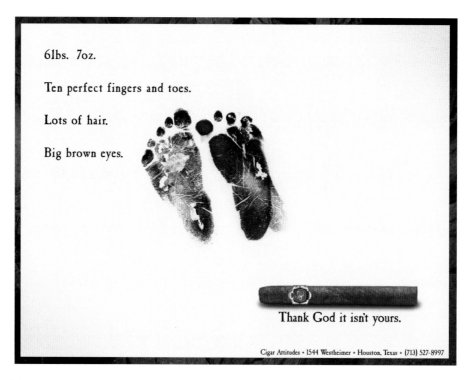

16.5. In the Checkered Past Records ad (above), the kicker makes readers laugh and positions the company. In the Cigar Attitudes ad (top), the opening language, baby footprints, and congratulatory cigars argue for one interpretation; the kicker provides another.

16.6. The parallel items couldn't be more brief; nice surprise at the end.

Misdirection often uses parallelism to deliver the setup and punch line, to establish the pattern that the last item breaks—to the reader's surprise (see fig. 16.6). The Marika line above uses parallelism to encase the joke. So does a print ad in a *Sports Illustrated* campaign selling the magazine to potential advertisers (theme line: "You may not get it. But our 21 million readers do"). The campaign presented various core moments in sports, one ad showing a Cleveland Browns football fan at a game with this headline:

> He knows the alma mater for all 72 players.
> He knows the exact day Kosar threw for 489 yards.
> He knows what Jamir Miller eats before a game.
> He thinks his wife's birthday is sometime in May.

The following headline for fishing reels surprises with its last item. The argument is traditional ("good but cheap"), yet it's expressed freshly enough to stick:

> Overthought. Overdesigned. Overbuilt. Underpriced.

You might think that to write kickers you have to be funny, and not everyone is. But part of being funny, or at least clever, is knowing *how* to do that, the forms that witticisms take. Just as you can ask yourself to express a thought in parallel form, you can ask yourself to try the repeat-and-vary principle of comic misdirection. Set up expectations and break them. Besides,

where is the ad as funny as Chris Rock or Jon Stewart? You need only to rise above common thought commonly expressed. You don't need to be a professional comedian. Just get your readers going one way, then surprise them—drop them off elsewhere.

Kickers don't have to be funny at all. They can be quiet and serious. Just punch your readers at the end, as Ambrose Bierce does in *The Devil's Dictionary* with this definition: "Edible, adj.: Good to eat, and wholesome to digest, as a worm to a toad, a toad to a snake, a snake to a pig, a pig to a man, and a man to a worm."[7] Another example, considerably less dark, is a headline for Aveda's all-natural, no-preservative line of skin-care products:

> The ingredients in our products aren't purchased, procured or acquired. They're borrowed. From the earth.

A poster for the Violence Against Women Coalition had this headline:

> By age six, many little boys have already learned to tie their shoes, ride a bike and abuse their wives.

The following cover headline, the most famous in *Rolling Stone*'s history, accompanied a photo of the Doors' Jim Morrison:

> He's hot. He's sexy. He's dead.

Here's another kicker, also from journalism, and also using parallelism to deliver the surprise:

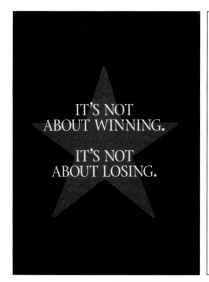

IT'S NOT
ABOUT WINNING.

IT'S NOT
ABOUT LOSING.

OH WAIT,
IT IS ABOUT WINNING.

THE 1999 COLUMBUS AMERICAN ADVERTISING AWARDS PREVIEW PARTY

DATE: Thursday, January 28, 1999 • TIME: 6:00 p.m.-9:00 p.m. • PLACE: MEKKA, 382 Dublin Ave. *(Call for directions, 621-2582)* • ADMISSION: $7 *(At the door)*

16.7. This invitation to an advertising awards show (*left*, exterior; *right*, interior) uses misdirection the way funny greeting cards do: it sets readers up on the outside in order to surprise them inside.

"Hey, there's a black one."

Drivers wanted. VW

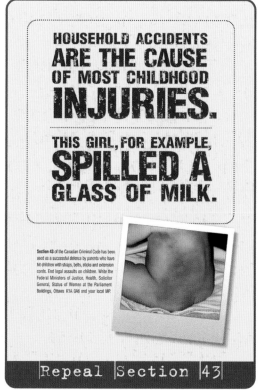

HOUSEHOLD ACCIDENTS **ARE THE CAUSE** OF MOST CHILDHOOD **INJURIES.**

THIS GIRL, FOR EXAMPLE, **SPILLED A GLASS OF MILK.**

Section 43 of the Canadian Criminal Code has been used as a successful defence by parents who have hit children with straps, belts, sticks and extension cords. End legal assaults on children. Write the Federal Ministers of Justice, Health, Solicitor General, Status of Women at the Parliament Buildings, Ottawa K1A 0A6 and your local MP.

Repeal Section 43

16.8. One of these ads is funny and the other deeply disturbing, but both use the interplay between headline and visual to generate misdirection. The kicker in the Repeal 43 ad, the visual, is set up by the headline. The kicker in the VW ad, the headline ("Hey, there's a black one"), is set up by the visual.

Bin Laden's death is the bookend to an extraordinary decade that began with the 9/11 attacks. He lived in our imagination, in our fears, and, as it turns out, in a quiet suburb of Islamabad.[8]

Periodic sentences (sometimes known as suspended sentences) can be used to deliver a kicker. A *periodic sentence* withholds an important part of its meaning until the end, piling up phrases and clauses while delaying readers' ability to understand the whole thought. It makes them wait, and they will, as you build toward completing your meaning, as you build toward your climax. You can slide the kicker in right at the end, as does this ad's headline for L.A. Gear Jeanswear:

Before he loves you for ever and ever 'til death do you part and brags to his friends about how smart you are and becomes the father of your children, he has to call back.

Kickers also work well for cards and brochures. Set the kicker up on the front panel, pay it off inside. Greeting cards do this for a living (fig. 16.7).

You can use visuals to help create kickers. Write a headline that demands one visual, then surprise with another. Or show something that demands one headline, then give another (fig. 16.8). You can even use the kicker idea in an entirely visual way, as do these TV spots (see figs. 16.9 and 16.10).

Emphasize repetition

People like to hear things repeated, as any good songwriter, speechwriter, or poet knows. Sometimes simply repeating a word or phrase works all by itself. Repetition keys Gertrude Stein's memorable quip about why she left Oakland: "There is no there there." It powers film critic Pauline Kael's dismissal of a John Cassavetes film, which she said had "the kind of seriousness that a serious artist couldn't take seriously."[9] Repetition adds an intriguing paradox to Malcolm Gladwell's book title *Blink: The Power of Thinking Without Thinking.*

In the examples below, I write a blah version of a headline, then follow it with the real headline, so you can see how a repeated word or phrase gives it energy. Read my bad, fake headline and then the good, real one. Hear the difference?

Bad headline for Caribou Coffee:
A day when you don't have coffee is pretty blah.

Good one:
A day without coffee is like a day without coffee. (Caribou Coffee)

Bad headline for PMS Escape:
From now on, he won't seem so irritating.

Good one:
From now on, if he's irritating you, it's because he's irritating.

Here are other headlines whose "pop" relies on repetition:

Make an original, original. (VW showroom poster inviting people to modify the Beetle to their own specifications)

There's no road rage because there's no road. (Amtrak)

In every city there is one restaurant like Murray's. In Minneapolis it's Murray's.

The man your man could smell like. (This Old Spice campaign theme line *depends* on repetition. Replace the second "man" with "husband" or "guy" and see.)

Many repetitions of word or phrase rely on punning (even the ones above rely on slightly different meanings in the second use of the word, so they're puns, though quiet ones). You're changing the meaning of the word:

Women run companies. Women run households. Women run nations. Women run. [Visual of woman jogging] (Insport apparel for women)

The recipe for a great dish starts, surprisingly, with a great dish. (CorningWare)

A Lava soap print campaign showed dirty hands becoming clean hands, with this theme line: "Leave work at work." Again, Lava is punning on "work," meaning the grime the first time and the job the second. (See figs.16.11 and 16.12 for two more examples of the power of repetition.)

A celebrated 1960s TV spot showed a county workman driving his VW Beetle through heavy snow to

1   2   WE'RE FROM HERE.

3   4   AND FROM HERE.

5   COUNT YOUR BLESSINGS.   6   Frost Bank   WE'RE FROM HERE   frostbank.com

16.9. As the camera pulls back, one idea becomes another.

Watch the spot at fig. W-16.9.

reach the garage and the snowplow. The voice-over: "Have you ever wondered how the man who drives the snowplow, drives to the snowplow?"

During World War II many Brits were angry at the special treatment and status of the Yanks who came to England. They said the Yanks were "overpaid, over-sexed, and over here." It was said that the problem with the Brits was they were "underpaid, undersexed, and under Eisenhower." Both statements surprise by switching the meaning of the last word in the sequence.

Use opposition

"In a sense the whole point of language is to give separate units that can be moved around and put together in different ways."

—EDWARD DE BONO, *Lateral Thinking*

Copywriters sit down, after filling up on product in-formation, and play around with words, trying to get them to interact, trying to spark something, create collisions. As a writer you are constantly moving words around to get them to release their power.

Look at language you find interesting and notice how often oppositions are doing the work. The following title of a chapter about grammar in a how-to-write book actually sounds interesting because of opposition: "False Rules and What Is True about Them." The title of a book about memoir, *Inventing the Truth*, catches the reader's attention with an apparent conflict between making things up and remembering them. The slogan for Perdue chicken hooks the reader with opposition: "It takes a tough man to make a tender chicken." So, too, does this line from comedian/actor Dan Aykroyd about his friend John Belushi, whose self-destructive excesses eventually killed him: "He was a good man, but a bad boy."

GET WORDS TO COLLIDE

Play around with all sorts of collisions between words: head-on, at an angle, tail-light to front bumper—you name it. Make some noise.

Circuit City (an electronics retailer) could have sold big-screen TVs with this lame headline:

16.10. This man is in for a surprise, as are the viewers.

Watch the spot at fig. W-16.10.

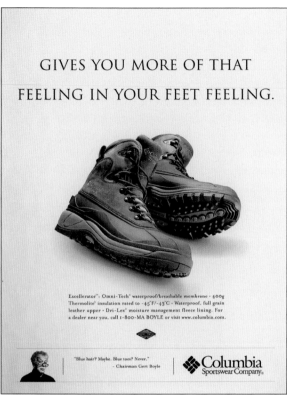

16.11. It's amazing what repetition can accomplish. In the Green Genius trash bag ad, it helps fuse two arguments into one. In the Columbia boot ad, it transcends this piece of nothing: "Gives you more feeling in your feet."

16.12. In this ad announcing the breast cancer awareness Race for the Cure, repetition provides both truth and inspiration.

TURN YOUR AB NEGATIVE INTO SOMETHING POSITIVE.

THE **BLOOD CENTER**

PULL ← PULL ← PUL

16.13. Often, copywriters don't find opposition; they create it by how they say things.

The bigger the TV, the better.

But it had the wit to write this instead:

There are no TVs too big. Only rooms too small.

A trade ad for Cigna corporate insurance showing an employee's face in pain could have said:

Is ensuring against employee disability a problem for your corporation?

But the copywriter did better:

Why should his backache be your biggest headache?

This headline uses opposition to create surprise:

Before it leaves the factory, it gets the once over. Twice. (Honda Accord)

A healthcare ad encourages awareness of genetic risks by posing a surprising opposition:

You may not choose the same path as your father. But your body might.

This ad's headline puts numbers in opposition:

In a world that can't wait 24 hours for a package, there's a place that still waits 18 years for a whisky. (Glenlivet)

See figure 16.13 for another headline whose surprise relies on an unexpected opposition.

GET PAST THE OBVIOUS
Can you be too predictable and adland-y with opposi-tions? Sure. Headlines like "Big savings on small appliances" or "Tomorrow's solutions today" are junk. But this headline for Asics running shoes isn't: "Completely gassed and completely stoked are the same thing." Neither is this headline for BMW: "Foot goes down. Pulse goes up."

SAY WHAT CANNOT BE
A related kind of opposition is *paradox*. For our purposes, let's define a paradox as a proposition that doesn't seem sensible or possible but proves true nonetheless. Paradoxes are compressed insights, juxtapositions of contrarieties that pique interest. *Time* magazine's obituary for Cy Twombly, the abstract artist, says of his paintings, "To call them scribbles is both inappropriate and perfect," a paradox that invites readers to resolve it by reading further.[10] Also in *Time*, veteran astronaut Story Musgrave creates an oxymoronic image, itself a kind of paradox, when he says of the space shuttle, "It's very unsafe, very fragile. A butterfly bolted to a bullet, you know."[11]

Paradoxes have stopping power, making readers do a double take at the apparent contradiction. Oscar Wilde loved them: "Charity creates a multitude of sins." "Life is much too important a thing ever to talk seriously about it." Mahatma Gandhi made people think with this paradox: "If you don't find God in the next person you meet, it is a waste of time looking for him further."

Have you discovered something in your product's story that just doesn't seem possible, something that hooked you with its incongruity or unlikelihood and might hook your target audience, too?

Beat your wife and your son will most likely go to prison. (Milwaukee Women's Center)

That's a powerful headline because it expresses, as a paradox, the truth that children often learn violence at their father's knee.

FORTY-TWO PERCENT OF ALL MURDERED WOMEN
ARE KILLED BY THE SAME MAN.

Each day women are beaten to death by their husbands or boyfriends. Just as frightening, each day neighbors just like us make excuses for not getting involved. For information about how you can help stop domestic violence, call 1-800-END-ABUSE.

THERE'S **NO** EXCUSE
for Domestic Violence.

Ad Council

Family Violence
Prevention Fund

The following headline, also for the Milwaukee Women's Center, is an example of paradox using the kicker format. The ending surprises because of preceding misdirection:

He threatened her. He beat her. He raped her. But first he married her.

Can you express your selling argument as a paradox? Often you don't find a paradox as much as you create one:

Is it possible to specialize in things that haven't happened yet? (Credit Suisse First Boston, financial services)

You can't see nematodes, but you can make them disappear. (Counter, an agricultural pesticide)

Heroin can end your life. Even while you're still in it. (Partnership for a Drug-Free America)

Figure 16.14 offers two more examples of paradox created by copywriters.

Above and below
16.14. Paradox drives both headlines.

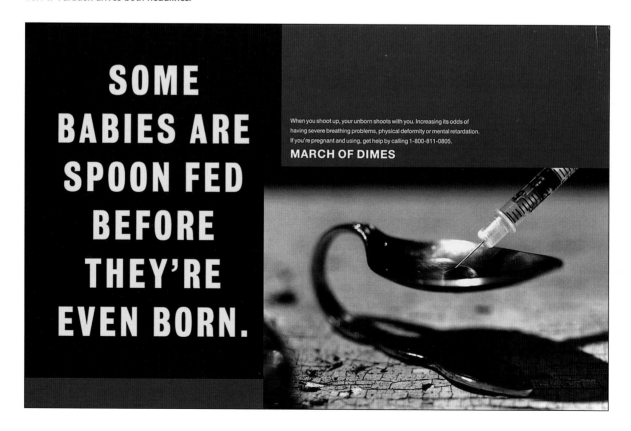

SOME BABIES ARE SPOON FED BEFORE THEY'RE EVEN BORN.

When you shoot up, your unborn shoots with you. Increasing its odds of having severe breathing problems, physical deformity or mental retardation. If you're pregnant and using, get help by calling 1-800-811-0805.

MARCH OF DIMES

Highlight omission

"I always listen for what I can leave out."

—MILES DAVIS

Advertisers like visual cropping: show just part of the image—the hand rather than the whole arm, the eyes rather than the whole face, a slice of the product or scene rather than all of it. The ad gains power through its immediacy and simplicity. And, most important, it gets people involved. They have to do some work themselves: they have to complete the image.

Do the same thing with headlines: cut them down, shave them off, start them in the middle, stop them before the end—one way or another, crop their completeness.

"The secret of being a bore is to tell everything."

—VOLTAIRE

ANSWER QUESTIONS THAT HAVEN'T BEEN ASKED

Recently I saw a person working out at a health club and wearing a college T-shirt that said on the front "Duke Crew" and on the back "I can't. I have crew." That line is something crew members must say all the time because they're dedicated to the team and its arduous training. It's also the answer to a question people haven't asked. They have to back up and supply the question themselves ("Want to go shopping? To a club? To a movie?"), and in doing so they feel the team's commitment and drive. A cool T-shirt. Omitting the questions, the way this T-shirt does, pulls people in more quickly; they're involved before they know it.

One ad in a Winston cigarette campaign presents a hip young gal looking right at the reader and saying, "Yeah, I have a tattoo. And no, you can't see it." (Winston's slogan: "Leave the bull behind.") Again, readers are pulled in more quickly with her answer—to a question they haven't asked—already in their face.

An outdoor board for Crystal Springs bottled water shows a picture of the Loch Ness monster with this headline: "Because you wouldn't believe what's in other waters." The headline jump-starts readers' involvement by assuming they've already asked, "Why drink Crystal Springs bottled water?" It also surprises them by switching the meaning of "waters." Figure 16.15 is another example of an ad kick-starting itself by answering an unasked question.

16.15. When a headline starts with the answer ("No wonder people . . ."), as this one does, readers involve themselves in the ad to find out the question.

IMITATE SPEECH RATHER THAN WRITING

People speak in fragments. So make your ads sound the way people talk. For example, an ad announcing a Marilyn Monroe U.S. postage stamp could have said this beside the stamp's image of the gorgeous star: "She's so beautiful that you almost want to lick the front of the stamp rather than the back." But the copywriter jumped in more quickly: "The back. You're supposed to lick the back." Another example is the title of a *Texas Monthly* profile of actor Bill Paxton, on the verge of making it big: "Bill, due." Here the omissions reinforce the pun.

MAKE THE CONSUMER DO SOME OF THE WORK

Don't discuss the product; discuss what happens after the consumer uses it or what precedes or necessitates it (see fig. 16.16).

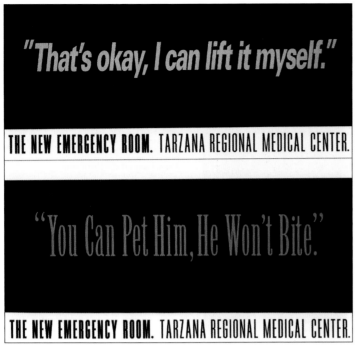

START IN THE MIDDLE

Don't start at the beginning of the brand conversation; intersect it deeper in. A clever campaign to encourage supposedly indifferent young people to vote showed moments in their lives when they *had* made choices easily enough—one ad showed an empty pizza box, with the olives in a little pile. Another showed a young person on his way to a football game with a giant foam fan finger on his hand. The headline on all the ads: "See, you do have an opinion." Notice how the headline jumped ahead, as though a conversation had already been started (see also fig. 16.17).

Be specific: Find the corner of 4th and Pulaski

> "I've never been much for the vague, planetary, philosophic school of songwriting. I'm from the start-with-the-detail school."
>
> —WARREN ZEVON, musician

16.16. Since the best pictures are often in people's heads, let your headline create them. I'd rather imagine the calamities surrounding these headlines than read them or see them, wouldn't you?

Elsewhere I've argued that if you've got an interesting fact about your client's product, use it. Nothing cuts through the crap and clutter of advertising better than

16.17. The headline already knows what travelers have been up to: "borrowing" hotel towels is a minor American industry. This ad was part of a Holiday Inn marketing campaign, Towel Amnesty Day, in which the hotel chain gave away guilt-free, iconic Holiday Inn towels at beach parties and at the hotels and invited people to tell their towel stories online, with Holiday Inn donating to charity for every story posted.

a real, true fact about the product. Nothing is more persuasive. But even if you're being general, try making up facts to express that general point. Replace generality with specifics.

Let's say that you're encouraging people to license their pet. You could show a picture of a bewildered cat against a white background and say, "License your pet because it might get lost and not be able to find its way home." But imagine describing that scenario specifically (fig. 16.18). Even though your readers were probably never lost in quite that spot, the specifics perform their miracle: they stand in for, even help readers see, their own lost places. Plus the headline pulls their pet more closely to them, relating its problem to one of theirs when they were young.

In figure 16.18 the copy flows directly from the headline, continuing the specific recollection of being lost as a child (notice the tight tie-in of the first line):

> Or was it the vast expanse of the Small Electrics department? After that experience, they pinned a name and address on you. Remember? . . . For your free pet licensing kit, call the Wisconsin Humane Society . . .

Look at figure 16.19, another ad from the campaign. Its headline uses the kicker: it gets a sequence going and then alters it, to readers' surprise. What's important in both figures, though, is that the headlines are specific. That's what makes them memorable.

Almost any advertising problem can be solved with specifics if you think into it enough. This headline isn't

16.18. The miracle of specifics: they put the reader right there.

16.19. Would "She can sit. She can speak. What she can't do is find her way home" be as good?

16.20. Inventing numbers gives this argument punch. Putting them into opposition helps, too.

> *Fish are cold blooded. You can be too.*
>
> The Sigma 2200 reel: anodized aluminum, machine tooled brass and stainless steel. Take no prisoners. *Shakespeare*

16.21. The switch in the meaning of "cold blooded"—for fish a metabolic state, for people a killer instinct—is the surprise that makes the ad.

memorable: "Are you spending more on your kid's shoes than on her helmet?" But this one is (see fig. 16.20).

The following example is one more instance of being specific even if you're making it up. In a Dewar's Scotch whisky ad, a beautiful young woman looks right at the reader, beside this headline:

> Trust us, she does not want to hear the story about you and your friend Danny doing watermelon shooters in Daytona.

The general argument is, "Grow up. Get the attention of adult women. Drink Dewar's." But generalities conjure up nothing. It's the headline's specifics that create the image of two immature kids.

Dare to pun

Common advice about writing headlines is never to use puns. A *pun*, of course, is a figure of speech in which a word means more than one thing; people hear and respond to the double meaning. If someone said, "I'm dying for a cigarette," people might say, "Yes, you are," responding to the unfortunate double meaning in "dying." John Deere's slogan, "Nothing runs like a Deere," is a double pun. People hear the two meanings of both "run" and "Deere"—"run" like an animal and "run" like a machine; "deer" as in animal and "Deere" as in brand of machine. Kind of complicated for a simple phrase, but it works.

The criticism against puns in headlines is that, first, they're dopey (puns are often called the lowest form of wit); second, they celebrate themselves more than sell

16.22. One meaning of "given birth" is probably sitting in the back seat right now.

OF ALL THE REASONS TO BUY A VOLVO, YOU'VE PROBABLY GIVEN BIRTH TO A FEW YOURSELF.

16.23. It's hard to argue with this pun on "cover."

It also covers your ass.

TROJANS

MISTER HARD HEAD
OVER 100 VARIETIES OF CONDOMS. 420 EAST WELLS

the product; and, third, they're lazy. Puns are among the first things copywriters think up when trying to solve an advertising problem, the argument goes, so they should be bypassed for something earned with more sweat. Puns replace further thought; they're something catchy that will do in the absence of a better idea.

Ironically, the people who tell copywriters to lay off puns are often the same people who judge advertising for competitions, and if you open up an annual of the year's best ads, you'll find that puns abound. The judges are smart people who know a good ad when they see one. It's just that they're moving down those tables fast as judges, the same way most people are moving across ads fast as consumers. Puns work fast; they quickly do a lot of what ads must do (capture attention, lodge in the brain, communicate some fairly simple product virtue).

Puns aren't bad. Bad puns are bad ("A science fiction offer that's out of this world!"). I think what the critics really mean is: don't use bad puns; use good ones. Don't make readers groan; make them smile. And connect your pun to the selling argument.

How to pun

1. Use one word, but surprise readers with its double meaning. Let it straddle two meanings or contexts or uses. Consider the following headline from Jewelry Depot: "A diamond is formed by thousands of tons of pressure. And if you've ever bought one, you know what that feels like." The surprise comes in using "tons of pressure" with two different meanings, one literal, one metaphorical.

Two Volvo slogans, "Drive safely" and "For life," make the brand's safety argument with puns. "Drive safely" means "drive carefully" and also "drive a car that will help you avoid injury." "For life" implies both long-term loyalty and the avoidance of injury or death. A satellite TV service argues for itself by punning on its name: "Don't just watch TV. DIRECTV." Tabu Lingerie tells readers, "It's better than nothing." The double meaning? It's better than

16.24. A German restaurant makes fun of itself by punning on well-known phrases. The second ad puns on the double meaning of "it's not even funny": the cliché itself and the German cultural stereotype.

Ⓢ See more from this campaign at fig. W-16.24.

not buying anything; it's more exciting than simple nudity. See figures 16.21–16.24 for other good examples of headlines that know how to pun.

Double meanings often work most powerfully when you jump categories. In other words, get way off the usual meaning of the word. The ad shown in

The cartilage in your nose never stops growing.

A BRUTALLY HONEST BEER.

16.25. "Honest" has been given another meaning, a literal one. Other "brutally honest" headlines in the campaign: "Nearly 80% of your brain is water" and "General Douglas MacArthur's mother dressed him in skirts."

and Juliet walked into the tomb to find Romeo, lying cold and still on the stone. "What's here?" she asked, knowing all too well the answer. Carefully, she bent and kissed her lover, then picked up his dagger and prepared to plunge it into her own heart. And at that moment Romeo awoke, looked at Juliet and said, "Oh this darn narcolepsy. I fell asleep again, didn't I?" And Juliet put down the dagger and they ran out to discover that their families had reconciled and were playing volleyball and lawn darts together and had bought the happy couple a brand new utility vehicle.

The End

EVERYTHING TURNS OUT BETTER ON DOMTAR PAPER.

16.26. *Romeo and Juliet* turns out a lot better than you remember.

figure 16.25 puns on the advertising buzz-word "honest." People are always being told about an "honest" this, an "honest" that: an honest scale, an honest beer. Hey, okay, an honest beer. What would "a brutally honest beer" say? You'd be surprised.

A paper campaign punned on the paper's printing-capability claim that "Everything turns out better on Domtar paper" by rewriting famous novels and plays so they did indeed "turn out better" (fig. 16.26). Funny and memorable.

2. Repeat a word, but change its meaning.

We raise questions that raise eyebrows. (*Harper's* magazine)

The shortest distance between two points isn't the point. (New Balance running shoes)

A novel concept in a New York hotel room: room. (The Waldorf Towers)

3. Substitute a word that sounds like the expected word. Major League Baseball's Colorado Rockies use the slogan "Baseball with an Altitude," in which readers hear both "attitude" and its clever substitution. Bridgewaters restaurant, which caters large

events, announces, "Eat. Drink. Be married." See figure 16.27, as well as the headlines below, for more examples of effective word substituting.

Didn't sleep last flight? (British Airways)

Think someone under the table. (*The Economist* magazine)

4. Pun later off a word used earlier; that is, pun off a meaning inside an earlier word.

The new Chrysler New Yorker has a huge trunk. But it doesn't come with a lot of Detroit baggage. ["Baggage" is a pun made possible by the preceding "trunk."]

You can't run away from your problems. But you can wade. [Both the extension of a cliché and a pun.] (Stoddard's fishing store)

Want to rekindle an old flame? Try a blowtorch. [Visual of red lingerie in white space] (Tabu Lingerie)

5. Let the picture be half of the pun. Pun off the visual. Figures 16.28 and 16.29 illustrate the double-whammy that a good ad can achieve when the visual is an essential part of the pun.

6. Let the picture be the whole pun (fig. 16.30).

As a writer, you're trying to generate energy. That's why (good) puns are good. They're energetic by definition: you've said two or more things in one spot; the language has an extra jolt right there. The poet Ezra Pound said, "Great literature is simply language charged with meaning to the utmost possible de-

16.27. Makes me smile. Makes sense, too.

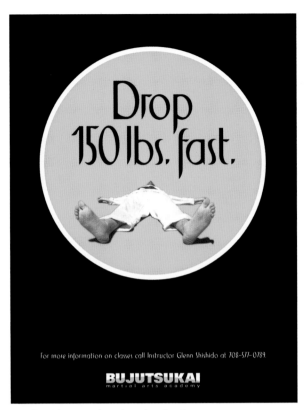

16.28. Write a pun based on the visual.

16.29. The can opener is a double pun: Warhol is famous for painting soup cans, and the museum is "opening."

gree,"[12] and although one pun is a long way from great literature, it does charge the language with (double) meaning, making it richer and denser, giving it more stopping power. Shakespeare loved a good pun. So did James Joyce. So should you.

Twist or extend a cliché

"If you can't say something good about someone, sit here by me."

—ALICE ROOSEVELT

Clichés, which are overused ideas and expressions, are bad and should be avoided like the . . . well, you know the next word, don't you? And that's the problem. Everyone knows the next word in a cliché, so your chance for "effective surprise" is zero, unless the next word isn't what people expect. Then you may have something. So clichés *can* work in advertising, drawing people in with their familiarity but surprising them with your witty alterations of the expected language. Take that cliché and change it, ex-

16.30. With this visual pun, enough's been said already.

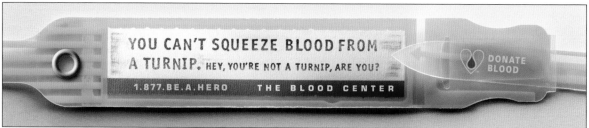

16.31. Everyone has heard these sayings, so keep going. Extend them.

tending the line or replacing something in there with something else, something surprising but appropriate, just as Alice Roosevelt, gossip-loving Washington socialite, did by altering her cliché's expected ending (". . . then don't say anything at all"). Drop your readers in a new place, rather than the old one. Surprise them.

Harvest clichés that might work with your client's product. Where to find them? There are books of clichés and websites that list them. Find ones particular to your client's product, brand, category, or commercial circumstance. Or think more broadly. What part of your scenario or your audience's mindset could you use? What clichés best express the benefit?

How to tweak a cliché

1. Take the cliché literally. Often clichés contain a dead metaphor, "dead" because people no longer hear it. Surprise your audience by taking the metaphor seriously. Bring it back to life. Help your audience hear it again:

> Opportunity is knocking. Or is that just your knees? (*Investor's Business Daily*) [Slogan: Don't read it. Use it.]
> Opportunity no longer knocks. These days, it darts past the door before you can even react. (SAS e-Intelligence, a data access service)

See figures 16.31 and 16.32 for more examples of clichés that have been tweaked, either by extension or by an unexpected context.

2. Substitute a new word or phrase for something in the cliché. Follow Alice Roosevelt's example: change the ending, change a word or phrase, change something. Get your audience's attention again:

> Time waits for no mom. (Schwan's Home Service)

> See how the other two-thirds lives. (Seattle Aquarium)

See figure 16.33 for another example of substitution.

Draw a distinction between words

> "I can't say as ever I was lost, but I was bewildered once for three days."
>
> —DANIEL BOONE

Daniel Boone makes a sly case for himself as an unflappable explorer with a joke whose charm derives from an unexpected distinction between near synonyms. Repositioning products in consumers' minds means getting consumers to substitute one thought or impression about the product with another. Lots of headlines say, in effect: the product isn't this; it's that. And "that" will be a near synonym elevating the product. Such headlines exploit connotations on the product's behalf. Try it. Let Daniel Boone lead the way.

Jackson Hole Mountain Resort extols its pleasures with this distinction: "Just because you were born doesn't mean you've lived."

An ad campaign's theme line for Major League Baseball's Chicago White Sox made this distinction: "There are traditions, and there are White Sox traditions." One ad showed a veteran fan sitting in the stands multitasking and used this headline: "Watching the game while listening to the game while recording the game at home. A tradition since 1982." By showing loyalists taking baseball's traditions to extremes, the campaign differentiated the White Sox from other teams and made its fans feel special in their specialness.

An ad campaign for Brut deodorant targeting young men used the contrast between near synonyms in its tagline: "Inside every man is a guy." Headlines tried to prove it, too: "Smell better than guys twice as smart" and "Makes armpit farts smell great."

16.32. Clichés can be visual, too. This worn-out image is being taken literally, and that has made it powerful again.

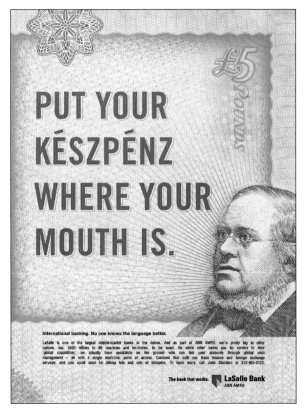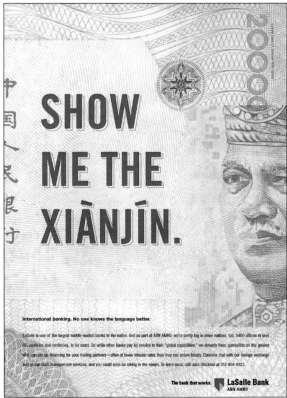

16.33. A bank announces its international services by taking money clichés and tweaking them into other currencies. Cheeky. These ads don't talk like banks talk, and that can be good.

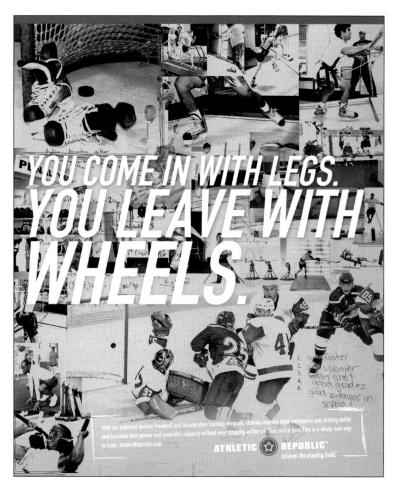

16.34. Athletic Republic, which trains athletes for performance, tells them what they want to hear.

The long-running theme line for an anti-drunk-driving campaign, "Buzzed driving is drunk driving," makes its salient point by equating what too many people hoped was a difference.

In a *New Yorker* cartoon, a woman chastises her errant husband by drawing this subtle, but true, distinction: "I don't want your apology. I want you to be sorry."

See figure 16.34 for a brand dramatizing its benefit by drawing a distinction.

But exercise caution. Adland hooey is one over-promise away. Avoid puffery like "You're not buying a car, you're finding your soul." People hear that and know you're lying. Surprise your audience with an unlikely pairing; don't dispirit them with unearned hyperbole.

Apply as needed

All these headline techniques have power, but I encourage you to start writing headlines any which way (aim for Sally Hogshead's 100), drawing on whatever ideas and techniques come your way. When you've run dry or haven't found what you're looking for, then put these techniques into play. They will give you ways to think and ways to structure your thoughts. Konstantin Stanislavsky, the great acting teacher, said this about his craft, but it applies to any of the creative arts: "The purpose of technique is to free the talent."[13]

17 • How to Create Slogans, Theme Lines, and Names

If you would be pungent, be brief; for it is with words as with sunbeams—the more they are condensed, the deeper they burn.

—ROBERT SOUTHEY

Everything should be made as simple as possible, but not simpler.

—ALBERT EINSTEIN

Lots of brands use *slogans* (sometimes called *tag lines* or *theme lines*). These usually run alongside the logotypes (as well as on website home pages and in voice-overs or supers in TV, video, and radio). They state the essence of the brand—memorably, their creators hope. Slogans stand by themselves as language, as selling argument. They're purely verbal in this way, not requiring a visual.

Slogans are portable pieces of persuasion, little chunks of language people carry around in their heads (Nike's "Just do it," Apple's "Think different"). They're durable—often meant to last for years, if not decades. Motel 6's "We'll leave the light on for you" has identified the chain since 1986. "Nothing runs like a Deere," the slogan for John Deere, a farm and lawn equipment company, has been running since the mid-1970s. De-Beers' "A diamond is forever" was first used in 1948. Wheaties has called itself the "Breakfast of Champions" since 1935. "I ♥ New York" and "Virginia is for lovers" have been ubiquitous tourism slogans for over thirty years.

Many ad writers recommend distilling a product's selling idea into a slogan or theme line to focus your thinking, whether you end up using the line or not. Writing slogans also teaches you, in a compressed form, many copywriting lessons that longer exercises can obscure. As a copywriter, you'll often be asked to give short but interesting names to all sorts of things: presentations, exhibitions, collections of items, events, and so on. Copywriters are phrasemakers. For all these reasons, writing slogans is good practice.

It's worth noting, however, that a number of advertising people think slogans aren't worth the trouble. They argue that it's impossible to say anything in a few words, and that so many slogans sound so much alike that they become interchangeable claptrap. And since marketing circumstances change more and more rapidly, trying to write a line that will last for decades is a fool's errand. These are sensible arguments. But I like slogans—good ones, that is. If you have a chance to do some work for your client's product, why not take it?

Make them smart, not just pretty

Slogans are often clever—rhyming, punning, or in some way using wit to create a rhetorical flair that makes them memorable. Slogans are the art of the well-made phrase. But their real job is to be an ad in miniature: make the case for the product, position it relative to its competition, justify it. More than being clever, slogans need to be smart.

For example, one of the great slogans was Campbell's "Soup is good food." But at first it didn't seem so great—it wasn't witty, it was all monosyllables, and its promise seemed banal. What it really was, however,

17.1. Ben Franklin created this in 1754 as a rallying cry for the colonies in the French and Indian War. It's proved to be a remarkably durable slogan/symbol, used later in the Revolutionary War, the Civil War, and beyond. If you look at it as a print ad, it's a classic example of the form: the headline and visual complement each other, neither making complete sense alone. Ben Franklin, the original Mad Man?

was durable and right on a smart selling strategy. The monosyllables helped emphasize soup's simplicity—its basicness—and the message positioned soup (in case people might think otherwise) as real food itself, not just an accessory to a meal. Smart. But not glittery. The Campbell's slogan illustrates the difficulty in distinguishing a good line from a merely glittery one. So be thorough and thoughtful when creating and critiquing slogans. Hold them up to the light. Turn them this way, then that.

The Campbell's line redefined soup in a positive way, and the strategy is fundamental. Often consumers need to be shown that products aren't just regular, boring, ordinary things, but are instead much more. Use slogans to elevate products in consumers' minds, to make them see these products and brands in the best possible terms. Bally's health spa slogan, "You don't just shape your body, you shape your life," is a classic example of this principle.

It's no surprise that good slogans incorporate many of the techniques good headlines do. In fact, if you're writing a bunch of headlines, chances are you've written some slogans, too. Headlines and slogans aren't always interchangeable—slogans need to be short, must stand alone, and should be memorable and durable—but they do share techniques.

One way to get the knack of writing slogans is to run a number of them through your head. You'll see how similar their purpose often is and how variously it can be expressed. Do this enough, and you'll notice patterns.

How to think up slogans

There is no *one* way. Here are several ways:

RALLY THE TROOPS

Advertiser John Emmerling says to think of a slogan as a battle cry, not a mission statement. It should be short and focused, turned outward to consumers rather than inward toward corporate goals. He once asked Bill Gates to say, in ten words or fewer, how he got Microsoft code writers to develop software that people would want. Gates immediately answered: "Information at your fingertips." Says Emmerling, "Four powerful words—a battle cry—that gave staffers marching orders for creating revolutionary software. Those four words also told customers what to expect in Microsoft's shrink-wrapped boxes."[1]

Think of battle cries that echo through history: "Remember the Alamo." "No taxation without representation." "Every man a king." "Damn the torpedoes." "Make love, not war." Their succinct conviction is why people remember them (fig. 17.1).

Given your client's product, brand, and core consumers, what cause or idea might they rally around? What unites them as true believers?

- Pedigree: "Dogs rule." It's what every dog lover believes. A perfect bonding statement. Say it and own the feeling.
- Continental Airlines: "Work Hard. Fly Right."
- *Survivor* TV show: "Outwit. Outplay. Outlast."
- McCoy's: "Go build something."
- Cloud Star pet products: "Wag more. Bark less." A rallying cry for dogs *and* people.

BE AUTHENTIC

Speak in a true voice. Whatever your selling argument, say it, not as a corporation or ad agency would, but as a human being would. Be real. Be honest. Be colloquial, funny, irreverent—whatever you need to be to deliver that thought. If your slogan doesn't sound spoken, if it doesn't sound like a real person said it and meant it, then it's dead. It joins all the other forgotten lines adrift in the land of unbelief, all the empty phrases buried in unmarked graves.

- Nissan Sentra: "Because rich guys shouldn't have all the fun." See how this sounds spoken? It rallies the troops, too. Talking about the line, Lee Clow of Chiat said, "I think it's a really cool way of saying, 'Affordable sports sedan,' which we all balked at."[2]
- Iomega data storage: "Because it's your stuff."
- "Got milk?" Real people say this. And, as Goodby, Silverstein & Partners point out, "How many other campaigns have been able to compress headline, tagline, product name, and brand positioning into two words?"[3]

ELEVATE THE PRODUCT

It's not just one more damned thing. Look for the highest possible benefit. Climb that ladder. Keep in mind what Andrew Keller, co-chief creative officer of Crispin Porter + Bogusky, said of MINI's "Let's Motor": "I think all great tag lines are a call to action; they're a call to something bigger. It's not just 'hey, buy this product,' but a call to something more transcendent or philosophical."[4]

- Federal Express: "It's Not Just a Package. It's Your Business." See how FedEx raises the stakes? This slogan typifies the fundamental strategy, not only of slogans, but of advertising itself: claim the highest possible meaning for the product, assert its importance to life well lived.
- Verizon Wireless: "Rule the Air." No small promise.
- People aren't wasting their time watching the TV game show *Jeopardy*. They're having "The most fun you can have with your brain."
- Amtrak: "Advancing Civilization Daily." The brand truth, based on interviews with train lovers, was that traveling by train was "the nicer way to get there." Amtrak then turned that truth over to the creatives, who said it better.
- BMW: "The Ultimate Driving Machine." You can't climb higher than this.

DIFFERENTIATE IT FROM THE COMPETITION

A generic claim might work, but since most brands face lots of competitors, make the case for *your* client.

- New Balance: "Shoes that fit better perform better." New Balance sells itself as the only ath-

letic shoe that comes in widths. Its slogan *is* its position. Tight parallelism, too.
- "Beef—Real Food for Real People." An attempt to downplay the health negatives of beef by insulting the bean-sprout eaters and flattering the beef eaters.
- MasterCard: "It's more than a credit card. It's smart money."
- Altoids: "The curiously strong mints." Made me curious. You too?

DON'T SELL FEATURES; SELL BENEFITS

After all, they're what people want.

- Old Spice: "Smell better than yourself."
- Black & Decker: "How Things Get Done."
- Marshalls, a discount retailer of brand-name clothing, realizes that bargain shoppers are really on a treasure hunt: "What will you find this time?"
- TIAA-CREF, the financial services and retirement provider for academics, knows how to flatter its clients: "Managing money for people with other things to think about."
- Braun shavers also want to free up people's brains: "We thought about shaving so you could think about something else."
- For another slogan that looks beyond mere things to what they might become, see figure 17.2.

FIND THE HUMAN TRUTH

Say what people are thinking but may never have said. Point out what's hidden in plain sight.

17.2. Slogans that promise (in this case, demand) a benefit help people see the big picture.

17.3. Power Trip sells morotcycle gear. How to say "we're tough" without saying it.

- Harvey Hardware: "Sometimes it is the tools." Usually the *homeowner* is the problem with home repairs. But not always.
- Rogaine: "Stronger than heredity." For men worried about losing their hair, that is the hope, isn't it?
- Contemporary American Theatre Company's slogan makes fun of most people's reluctance: "Live theatre. It won't kill you."

DON'T JUST CLAIM IT, PROVE IT

Merely asserting something often makes people doubt the claim. (The surest way to show you're not cool is to claim you are.) Nike didn't say, "The most authentic sports brand, ever." It *proved* its core position as sports authority and tough-love coach by speaking in that voice: "Just do it." So don't claim something. Body it forth.

- Bruegger's Bagels: "Totally completely obsessed with freshness." Sure, there's a claim here, but with its over-the-top repetition and breathless lack of commas, the voice proves the claim. These people *sound* obsessed.
- Blue Cosmos Design wanted to say that its designers were smart professionals, but also fun people to work with. Instead of announcing it, copywriters tried to prove it: "Serious strategic design. Say *that* fast 3 times."
- See figure 17.3 for another example of a slogan embodying a claim rather than just asserting it.

FORGET CLEVER, BE CLEAR

- Alibris: "Books you thought you'd never find."
- Call of Duty video game: "There's a soldier in every one of us."

- The Home Depot: "You can do it. We can help." I feel better about that proposed deck already.

ABOVE ALL, SOLVE THE PROBLEM

Slogans solve advertising problems. Say what is most needed.

- "Amway. We're Your Neighbors." Since Amway isn't well understood, this slogan goes to work on that problem, reducing any stigma and making Amway seem as inevitable as the people next door. This slogan may do as much as any three words can.
- Many people have heard of this university but can't quite place it. They can now: "Seton Hall. The Catholic University in New Jersey."

MODIFY AS NECESSARY

Be prepared to change your slogan. Durable doesn't mean permanent.

- "Do you Yahoo?" worked when search engines were new. But increased competition and expanded capabilities made the question no longer relevant. Yahoo needed to promise more, so it did: "Life engine."
- Federal Express's original slogan was, "When it absolutely, positively has to be there overnight." But as business changed, so did the slogan. "The World On Time" succinctly expands FedEx's mission beyond mere overnight delivery, claiming the high ground of the product category—and doing it all without even using a verb.
- Saturn's "A Different Kind of Company. A Different Kind of Car" used parallelism to make the case that an American automaker had restructured itself enough to build an internationally competitive car. Written in 1990, the slogan lasted until 2002, when it was shortened to "It's different in a Saturn." In 2004 Saturn decided to say what it meant, changing its slogan to "People first," a line it had used internally for years. In 2009 Saturn quit altogether, but it would be hard to blame bankruptcy on bad sloganeering.

The following suggestions aren't strategic so much as rhetorical. They're for making a good idea better by *how* you say it.

TRY PARALLELISM

- Round-Up weed killer: "No mercy. No pity. No weeds." Misdirection: the last item surprises and makes the point.
- NicoDerm CQ stop-smoking aid: "The power to calm. The power to comfort. The power to help you quit."
- Moen (well-designed faucets, sinks, etc.): "Buy it for looks. Buy it for life."
- Radio Shack: "You've got questions. We've got answers." This line stakes out a position in a crowded field—Radio Shack as demystifier of technology, a place with not just hardware but help.
- Figure 17.4 shows how parallelism is often waiting to be invoked; here it helps you take advantage of a brand's name.

TRY OPPOSITION

- Audio Books: "It's a great way to read. Just listen." Not only true, but it makes reading sound easier. Good benefit.
- Crunch fitness clothing: "Outerwear for your inner self."
- MasterCard: "There are some things money can't buy. For everything else, there's Master-Card."
- Air France: "Making the sky the best place on earth."
- Sharp 70-inch LCD TVs: "Big is too small a word."
- Chrysler: "Imported from Detroit."

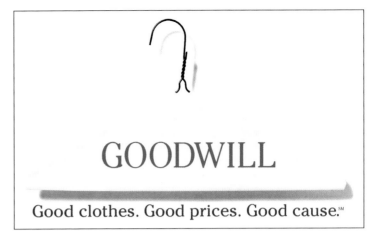

17.4. Truth in parallel form.

TRY PARALLELISM AND OPPOSITION

- Sony PlayStation: "Live in your world. Play in ours."
- MassMutual Financial Group (investment and insurance): "You can't predict. You can prepare."
- Yamaha watercraft: "Solid thinking for a liquid world."
- Bigg's superstores: "Where men who hate to shop love to shop."
- Nynex yellow pages: "If it's out there it's in here."
- Figure 17.5 demonstrates how parallelism can throw a spotlight on the problem-solution scenario.

17.5. If you want to stress an opposition, nothing does it better than parallelism.

USE METAPHOR

Bring in language from other contexts and change the way consumers see your client's product.

- The American Floral Marketing Association updated the original FTD slogan "Say it with flowers" by extending the metaphor: "Increase your vocabulary. Say it with flowers."
- MET-Rx (high-performance food supplements) has used "Food has evolved" and "Engineered nutrition." Both metaphors (one organic, one technical) elevate the product by making it more than, better than, food.
- Bell helmets: "Courage for your head."
- Corona beer: "Find your beach." In the ads, people sit on a beach and stare out to sea. Making the literal metaphorical, Corona invites consumers to discover for themselves where their beach lies.
- Ice Mt. bottled water: "Born better."
- Kashi: "7 Whole Grains on a Mission." Food develops a mind of its own.

TWEAK, TWIST, OR ADD TO A CLICHÉ

- Caribou Coffee: "Life is short. Stay awake for it." Caribou Coffee invigorates the cliché by adding a joke.
- Fatbrain.com (books and software for Web-heads): "Because great minds think a lot." Here the line twisted is "Great minds think alike."
- *Village Voice*: "Not America's Favorite Paper." Reversing the adland cliché that this, that, or the other thing is "America's favorite."
- See figure 17.6 for the reinvigoration of another cliché.

LEAN IT UP AGAINST SOMETHING ELSE

If your client's product or brand is not well known, relate it to something that is.

- Downtown Cincinnati is on the Ohio River. How can businesses across the bridge cash in? Here's how: "Northern Kentucky: The Southern Side of Cincinnati."
- A poster advertising Harold Pinter's obscure play *The Birthday Party* clarifies things: "Part Hitchcock, part 'I Love Lucy,' part film noir, part vaudeville."
- The National Pork Board, realizing that people weren't eating pork, allied itself with ever-popular chicken: "Pork: the other white meat."
- Oreo: "Milk's favorite cookie." Oreos are well known, of course, but this connection adds its own truth.

REPEAT A WORD OR PHRASE

- Jeep: "The things we make, make us."
- Las Vegas: "What happens here, stays here." Would "What happens here won't be brought up later" work? The succinct power of repetition and parallelism wins out.
- Monster.com: "Your calling is calling."
- Dogfish Head Craft Brewed Ales: "Off-centered ales for off-centered people."

INVOKE THE RULE OF THREES

I can't explain why, but a whole lot of things come in threes—from the Holy Trinity to Larry, Curly, and Moe—and are better for it.

- Mack trucks: "Heart. Steel. Promise."
- Starbucks, introducing pre-packaged coffee: "At grocery. At home. At last."
- Sony PlayStation PS one: "wherever. whenever. forever."
- KAOS, an ad agency: "[outwit] [outwork] [outwonder]."
- Campiello Ristorante: "Eat Well. Laugh Often. Live Long."

17.6. A slogan whose witty reversal of a cliché encourages people to smile about sad music.

- Tagline for the movie *The Promotion*, a comedy about two people competing for exactly that: "Two guys. One job. No rules."

PLAY TRICKS WITH TYPE AND PUNCTUATION

- Baker's Bourbon: "Best. Sipped. Just. Like. This."
- Wrangler: "Real. Comfortable. Jeans."
- Friends In Deed (the name of a helping community for victims of AIDS and other serious illnesses)
- SONY: "make.believe" Type creates a pun. The double meaning: "make believe" as one phrase, and "make. believe" as two actions.
- "Cop. An attitude." A similar typographical pun, this tagline is for the TV drama *Prime Suspect*, about a female homicide detective having to insert and assert herself in a male-dominated world.
- See figure 17.7 for another typographical pun.

DON'T SHUN PUNS

I recommend being smart before being glittery, and many writers recommend avoiding puns altogether. But a quiet, well-chosen pun still works for me.

- Tecnica in-line skates: "Advanced thinking on your feet." The pun, of course, is the two senses of "thinking on your feet."
- American Express Gold Card: "Worth Its Wait." A high-quality pun that not only asserts the achievement of getting the card, but also deftly invites the reader to complete the meaning: "(worth its weight) . . . in gold."
- Mitsubishi: "Technically, Anything Is Possible." Adverb as pun, and a good one, too, considering the wide range of Mitsubishi hi-tech products, from TVs to cars.
- "Live without a plan." Virgin Mobile targeted young people with a no-contract, pay-as-you-go offer that endorsed spontaneity.
- "What's holding you back?" Slogan for various organizations encouraging people to buckle up before driving.
- Nike's slogan for the U.S. Women's National Team (soccer): "Pressure Makes Us." The pun refers to two kinds of pressure: psychological (competing against the success of their predecessors) and physical (being molded; pressure *makes* things). And that's Nike's core argument: *make* yourself into something.

17.7. Syllables create the word that creates the pun. And a true one. Founder Jeni Britton Bauer brings her art background to Jeni's handcrafted ice creams.

OH, OKAY, RHYME

- Ocean Spray: "Crave the wave" (copy line in TV spots: "Tartly refreshing. Refreshingly tart.")
- Oil of Olay: "Love the skin you're in."
- Mars candy: "Pleasure you can't measure."
- Half Price Books: "Waste Not. Read A Lot."
- "To help stay well, Purell." (hand cleaner/ sanitizer)
- Smart Water bottle copy: "Electrolyte enhanced for a kick in the pants."

USE EUPHONY

Make your slogan memorable by maximizing the way the words sound together.

- "Intel inside"
- "OnStar On Board"
- "Win from within" (Gatorade combines euphony with a pun, the two meanings of "within": the drink and one's willpower.)
- "Power to the pedal" (Shimano)
- "The softer side of Sears"
- "The incredible edible egg" (American Egg Board)
- "You'll never roam alone" (Travelocity delivers a near-rhyme and a strong benefit, too.)
- Threadless Tees: "Nude No More." Whimsy meets euphony.

RELEASE THE FIGURE FROM THE STONE

When slogans are too long, they fall out of the reader's head—or never get in there. So cut yours down; circle hot spots and see if they work all by themselves. Frequently two or three words in a seven- or eight-word slogan are the heart of the matter. Look for the quick, punchy, tight version of your thought.

- Slogans often slim down over the years. Ace Hardware's original slogan was "Ace is the place with the helpful hardware man." Now it's "The helpful place." Wordiness, rhyme, and sexism are gone.
- Starbucks' holiday theme line turned adjective into verb: "Let's merry."
- Sometimes a slogan can incorporate the logo, not just stand beside it: "The best jazz is sung with Verve."
- Adidas: "Feet You Wear." A line so compressed and oxymoronic that it becomes almost a poetic image. Anything longer would be weaker.

STOP MAKING SENSE

Be evocative instead. Tell it slant. I admire this slogan for Walking Man, a brand of urban clothing: "Challenge. Fury. Neatness." (fig. 17.8.) Quirky and original, it suggests more than it states, expressing the principles of the clothes (or, more important, the clothes wearer). This line's a long way from something crummy like "Quality clothing that works as hard as you do." It invokes the Rule of Threes, too.

17.8. What's the line mean? Michael Cronan and Karin Hibma, founders of Walking Man clothing, wanted to make a wry comment on the human condition: life may be a challenge but attack your goals with fury and, hey, while you're at it, wear neat clothes.

To see other manifestations of the Walking Man symbol, go to fig. W-17.8.

Combine unexpected *kinds* of words. David Letterman calls his production company "Worldwide Pants," two words you'd never heard together before. A Columbus rock band, Movieola (the name itself an unexpected combination), calls its music company "No Heroics Music" after a member saw the category "no heroics" (that is, use no extraordinary measures to save a life) in a nursing home file. The band's lyrics use the phrase "durable dream," another unexpected pairing. Copywriters need to pay attention to the energy such wordplay offers. It's often what they're hired to deliver.

But ad writers are so accustomed to making sense that unusual combinations can be hard to create. When you can't get fresh phrases, try "cut ups," the term for cutting your prose apart and sticking it back together in odd combinations. Or splice your words with words from other places—magazines, Web pages, flyers, street signs, pop music titles, slang, posters in windows, your mail, a supermarket's bulletin board, police talk, diaries, famous novels, anything—to create new combinations. As novelist William S. Burroughs, himself a cut-and-paste man, said, "You cannot *will* spontaneity. But you can introduce the spontaneous factor with a pair of scissors."[5]

KEEP THREE THINGS IN MIND WHEN CREATING SLOGANS

First, the difference between a not-so-great slogan and a great one can be just a word or two, so examine carefully what you've written. You're trying to do a lot in a few words; any change will have a big effect. See what a different word or word order does.

Second, it's hard at a glance to tell what a good slogan is. I'd have nixed Campbell's "Soup is good food" and held out for something more glitzy. But it proved an extraordinary slogan, wearing well over the years and selling a lot of soup. So turn slogans around and look at them from all angles. See what you've got.

Third, as Dan Wieden of Wieden + Kennedy points out, it can take a while for a slogan to become good, to grow into the culture: "By itself, especially in the early days, [a slogan] feels shallow, but as time goes by and as more ads are put inside of that basket, the more weight and imagery it carries. When we first presented 'Just Do It,' there was a resounding silence, and we just went on. That's just the way a really strong theme line works."[6]

How to name things

BEYOND SLOGANS

Lots of times you'll be asked not to write a slogan, exactly, but to do something similar: name a conference, campaign, exhibition, event, website, app, blog, sale, presentation, promotion, seminar—anything that needs a handle. If that's the case, then be vigorous and specific. Give people a peg to hang this thing on. For example, when a Minneapolis typographer and copywriter were speaking to the ad club I belong to about that city's advertising, the club could have called the presentation "How Concept and Typography Make Great Advertising," but since type-dominant layouts were what Minneapolis advertising was all about then, the club called it simply "Big Words." More enigmatic and interesting, don't you think? If you've got the room and the inclination, you can have it both ways—at least with the titles of some things—via the colon. Start with the punchy title, then explain it after the colon: "Big Words: How Concept and Type Make Great Advertising." (For another example of a theme line, see fig. 17.9.)

NAMING DIFFICULTIES

Whatever you're asked to name, you want the name to express the gist of the thing and do so memorably, to sink a hook into it. Accomplishing this task is harder than it looks. Sensible can often be too sensible, and unusual can simply be odd. English has only so many words, and a lot of them are already taken. Naming gets tougher when you add marketplace crunch—20,000 new products every year, accelerating global competition, the hyperspeed of digital and Internet innovation. More people are creating and selling more things more often in more media than ever before. And most of these things need a name. Keep lawyers and naming consultancies handy for the big stuff.

But let's put off the lawyers and consultants for now. As simply a language issue, how do you name something?

AS ALWAYS, DO YOUR HOMEWORK

Start by researching your client's product, audience, and competition. Ask and answer these questions:

1. What are you trying to accomplish? What problem are you trying to solve?

2. What do you want to emphasize about the

17.9. This was the theme line and central visual of a capital campaign for the Ontario College of Art & Design. It shows how word and image, when they're working well, interrelate; each relies for part of its power on the other.

product? What's its key idea? What should its name describe?

3. How does your client's brand distinguish itself from the competition? What's its position? What positions are competitors claiming? What names are they using?

4. At whom are you aiming this name? How should those people be addressed? What are they expecting? How might you surprise them?

5. Do you have any constraints? Are you adding a name to a group of names already in place? Are you extending a brand? Constraints reduce your wiggle room, but they also provide direction.

After you've got answers, you're ready to tackle the naming game. Read on.

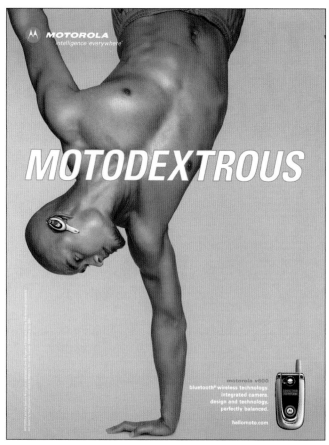

17.10. "Motorola" is itself a portmanteau word—"motor" + "ola" (sound)—so named because one of the company's earliest inventions was the car radio. This campaign for Motorola's cell phones took that "moto" root and combined it with different beginnings and endings to express phone options. Other headlines were "Primamoto," "Gossipmoto," and "Motorazr."

HOW TO CHOOSE A GOOD NAME

1. Take words right out of the dictionary. These can be good because people already know what they mean and can apply them to whatever you're naming. Ask what words gather around this thing—its appearance, definition, function, meaning. Look for something appropriate, but unusual, a word that fits but isn't brutally obvious. *Dwell* and *Metropolis* are magazines whose names tell us what's inside but do so more interestingly than would *House* and *City*, yes? A startup ad agency called itself Anomaly because the principals thought their approach to business was just that. Zip was a good name for Iomega's digital storage disks. A quick verb, it suggested a fast zipper for storing and protecting data. You can also use metonyms, in which a part stands in for the whole, as when business executives are called "suits": Chevrolet Volt (electric car), Urbanspoon (restaurant-finding app).

2. What are metaphors for what it is or does? Sprint, Mustang, Dove, Ocean Spray, DustBuster, Dirt Devil, Twitter, Android, Leaf (Nissan's electric car). Vivid and specific, they *show* what the product does. Find the essence of your thing-to-be-named, then express that metaphorically. National Public Radio's interview show *Fresh Air*, with Terry Gross, uses two metaphors: "air" for radio, and "fresh air" for new ideas, as in "[a breath of] fresh air." Iron Mountain is a good name for a data protection and storage company, don't you think? Sounds impregnable.

3. Make words up. You can make them out of whole cloth (Oreo, Zune, Kodak, OXO, Dasani) or partly so (the portmanteau words I talk about below). The downside of completely made-up words is that it costs a lot of money to teach them to your audience (they're not in consumers' heads already), but once you get them in there, people won't mistake you for someone else. Connotations, as always, count plenty. Swiffer isn't a word but suggests "sweep," "wipe," "swift." It sounds like what it does, and it sure beats Mop-Pro, yes? Febreze is another made-up word that suggests the right things ("fabric," "breeze").

4. Invent portmanteau words. Two words, or parts of them, fused to create a new word, are easier to grasp since they contain identifiable parts. Portmanteaus come in all flavors. Sometimes they're a true fusion of part of this word with part of that one to create a word people have never seen before. Other times they're two words, more or less unaltered, simply pushed together to create a "new" one (PlayStation, WordPerfect, ChemLawn, PowerPoint, FireWire, Facebook, StumbleUpon, social media agency BoldMouth).

How to create portmanteaus? Cut and paste prefixes, suffixes, and word roots. Stick half of this word onto half of that word; stick all of that word onto the front or back end or middle of another, get some Latin and Greek into the mix. Lewis Carroll coined the term *portmanteau* because such combined words reminded him of the way different things could be crammed into a suitcase, or portmanteau, and they're widely used. Such words can be good: KinderCare, Groupon, Instagram, Pinterest, DieHard, Volunteen (for teenage volunteer programs), Synchilla (Patagonia's synthetic chinchilla), Sneakerina (a Puma shoe for women that combines "sneaker" and "ballerina"), the recipe website Epicurious.com ("epicure" and "curious"). But such words can be stinky when they're too obvious or too dumb. I called an early version of this book *AdThink*, and reviewers rightly rejected it as too glib, too mechanical, an invitation to make ads by the numbers. Connotations again.

Why create portmanteaus? Because you get three words for the price of two: the two original words plus the energy of the new, invented word. Allegra, an allergy relief medicine that doesn't cause drowsiness, is a brand name that's also a new thought. Consumers can hear "allergy" in there, and also "allegro" (brisk tempo) and "allegra" (cheerful), implying that the pills work fast and won't knock people out. Good name. Consumers don't consciously hear the portmanteau, but they subconsciously do, don't you think? The word sounds fast, and it sounds new (fig. 17.10). Gowalla, a location-based social network, is "go" plus "wallaby," a small kangarooish animal that hops from place to place. It's a name both odd *and* appropriate, a perfect combination to shoot for.

5. Use acronyms and letter clusters. Acronyms you can pronounce (IKEA, TED, GEICO, MADD, Sunoco); letter clusters you can't (IBM, BP, ESPN, VW). Combine the initial letters or parts of words (Sun Oil Company became Sunoco) into a new "word." English lexicographer H. W. Fowler called all these truncated coinages "curtailed words," and they include, if you think about it, words people use every day: ad(vertisement), (in)flu(enza), photo(graph), sit(uation) com(edy), cab(riolet), and a host of others. Everyone loves shorthand, reducing something windy to something quick.

Can you be too quick? Some people think that when Kentucky Fried Chicken reduced its name to KFC, the company lost a lot. Now people couldn't tell whether they should eat there, let KFC insure them, or hope the company got to the bargaining tables with NATO and OPEC. That confusion may be why the Colonel's face still accompanies the logotype. You gain speed with acronyms, but you lose clarity. Also, the initials should have some kind of cohesion—either say something when pronounced, as do acronyms (FUBU, NASCAR), or sound good together as letter clusters (NPR glides smoothly off the lips; ABC, NBC, BBC, and CBS all have nice consonant- and vowel-sound sequences).

6. Play word tricks. Flickr, Rdio, and Tumblr are missing letters, which makes them seem faster and hipper than if spelled correctly. (Since these are Web-based services, the misspellings may also have helped the companies find available domain names.) Digg and Dribbble add a letter. Klout, IgoUgo.com, and

Nike Shox misspell themselves. Urshuz (your shoes) does everything wrong. Häagen-Dazs (two made-up words) and Löwenbräu (a real one) employ diacritical marks to add "authenticity," whether imagined or real. All such tricks draw attention to the names and add piquancy, which is the point. (See fig. 17.11 for a triple pun as brand name.)

7. Use place names. The unique specificity of a place transfers to the thing named: Columbia, The North Face, and Patagonia sportswear; Southwest and Northwest airlines; outdoor retailer Gander Mountain. Where was this thing invented, or where is it from? Grab a name from its geography. A brewery's location is often the beer's name: Shiner Beers, Iron City Beer, Great Lakes Brewing Company—what better way to say local, fresh, and one of you?

17.11. Type helps create a triple pun: "evolution" and "revolution"—and, with the registered trademark symbol, both words become a third, the brandmark itself.

8. Find words unique to the corporation, maybe the founder's name (perhaps the most common naming technique) or names inside the company. Wendy's, for example, is named after one of founder Dave Thomas's daughters. Kinko was the college nickname of that company's founder. Get up to speed on the company and its story. Maybe the owner's dog or cat or summer retreat has a quirky name. Maybe her father's middle name was unusual. Maybe not. But check to see what's inside the company's storage box. Lift the lid.

9. Make puns. People see plenty of them, that's for sure: Primal Knead (a bakery), Blood Vessel (a bloodmobile), VanGo (an art outreach program using vans), WillPower (H&R Block's will-preparation kit), No Puffery (a gel to soothe skin around the eyes), Souplements (soup for dogs), a portmanteau pun: "soup" + "supplements." A series of books on female graphic designers was titled "Hall of Femmes." I like all these, but every copywriter has to decide for himself or herself when a pun works and when it's too corny or won't wear well.

10. Jump out of category. Look at what everyone else is doing, then do the opposite, or at least slant away from the trends. The surest way to get lost in the mix is to sound like the competition. If you're naming an e-business, don't start with "e-"; everyone does that. Start with something else. Danny Altman, co-founder of the naming company A Hundred Monkeys (from the old joke that if you put 100 monkeys in a room with 100 typewriters, eventually you'll get Shakespeare), says, "If you went to a company trying to name their airline and gave them a choice between Trans-AtlanticAir and Virgin, they'd take Trans-AtlanticAir, because it sounds like something people would take seriously. The problem is, with that name they become one of the trees in the forest."[7]

The same problem confronts anyone who wants to begin a brand name with a lowercase "i"; Apple pretty much owns that opener: iCloud, iPhone, iPad, iTunes, etc. Apple's online tool for resetting your password when you can't remember it? iForgot (http://iforgot .apple.com).

11. Ask yourself what the heart of something is, then express that in terms a little off center. Get people interested. What's a good name for an educational cable network for kids? How about Noggin? A word that says kids, a word everyone has fond associations with, and a word they remember from the phrase "That's using your noggin." When Volkswagen and Apple devised a promotion in which anyone who bought a VW New Beetle received an iPod, the question was what to call the promotion, how to theme the ads? "Pods Unite!" became the call-to-arms for two products sharing pod-dom.

Burger King's website for the man in a chicken suit who'll do whatever people request isn't called "chicken that will do goofy stuff" or "chicken that does tricks" or even "obedient chicken" or "agreeable chicken." The site is called Subservient Chicken, an unusual, multisyllabic adjective, one you don't hear often, right? Memorable once you do hear it, though. Combining sense and surprise, Subservient Chicken is the embodiment of a good name.

12. Bring in language from elsewhere. Repurpose words or phrases from pop culture, street signs, literature (Starbucks), TV, mythology (Pandora radio), music—you name it. For example, A Hundred Monkeys renamed Career Central (a career placement service) Cruel World (a cliché repurposed). As Altman explains, "If you're first in a field, it works to have a name that is somewhat descriptive. But once you're facing lots of competition, a descriptive name is no longer very useful. You end up with Career Central, Career Link, Careers-R-Us. The whole point of a name is to stand out. Look at what others in your category are doing, then do the opposite."[8] The Monkeys have named an advertising agency Left Field, a unified platform for IT management Jamcracker, a personal medical database 98point6, a venture capital fund Ironweed, and mail-order windowsill gardens Farm-in-a-Box.

But the words you find "over there" have to resonate. Not just anything will do. Try to make intellectual or emotional sense. However odd the name, it should strike something in the target audience and "work," as do the ones above. With the ad agency name Left Field, for example, people hear "out of left field" and know that original ideas come from there.

13. Say the obvious. With everyone being oh-so-clever, the obvious is often ignored. A board game for dogs is called, obviously enough, "Hey, my dog can do that." A shampoo was named "Gee, your hair smells terrific." A moving company calls itself "Two Men and a Truck." NPR titled its CD collections of favorite stories "Driveway Moments" because those were the ones that kept people listening in their cars, even after arriving home. If your client's focus is narrow enough, put it in the name: Budget Blinds, Lean

Cuisine, Healthy Choice, Fast Company. Norton by Symantec, which sells security systems for PCs, invites people to visit ProtectYourStuff.com. Houghton Mifflin's microsite for *The American Heritage Dictionary* is youareyourwords.com, a truth that's also the highest possible benefit. A fellow in my neighborhood calls his business Joe Cuts Grass. These names are zigging when everyone else is zagging—one way to get noticed. They're also examples of "raising the obvious to the conscious," something always to consider. After I got *AdThink* out of my system, I named this book by simply saying what was in it: *Advertising: Concept and Copy.* Clever? Nope. Clear? Let's hope so.

14. Say the unobvious, by which I mean, pick a specific thing, a very specific thing, and let it stand—in mystery, if it must—for the whole brand or one of its products. E. B. White wrote a story called "The Second Tree from the Corner" about a man's puzzlement with life. Why a tree, especially why the *second* tree? He never said. That's part of the mystery of life.

A landscaping company in Columbus calls itself 9 Trees. Founder Matt Forchione didn't want to use his last name (no one could spell or pronounce it) or call his company, too obviously, Matt's Landscaping. His lucky number had always been nine, Matt explained, "so 9 Trees it was. I thought it rolled off the tongue and was easy to say. Consequently and fortunately, I have found that we come up first in listings and all alphabetical areas such as the phone book, vendors lists, etc., due to the numeral 9."[9] A lucky number for sure.

Jane Matthews, director of business development at the ad agency 22squared, explains their unusual name:

> We wanted to re-brand our agency about 6 years ago (we've been around since 1922 . . . first as Tucker Wayne, then WestWayne), and struggled for many months trying to find the perfect name. We even hired a naming consultant. One day over lunch someone referenced a piece of research that said throughout a typical person's life, one makes 484 friends on average. 22 is the square root of 484.
>
> We're an agency focused on creating work that is talk-worthy, so that the value of your advertising dollar continues on through the power of word of mouth advertising long after the TV spot has aired, etc. So we like to say that 22squared represents the exponential power of brand advocacy.

It also helped that the name was available.[10]

Charles C. Mann wrote a book about the Americas right before Columbus landed and called it *1491*, a precise way of collapsing a lot of information into one word, and a catchy way, too, since 1492 is embedded in every American schoolchild's head. Mann's follow-up book on the consequences of Columbus? *1493*.

Although my examples suggest otherwise, numbers don't have to be what make a name idiosyncratic: BlackBerry pretty much came out of the blue; StrawberryFrog, too.

15. Vet the name. Sooner or later you do get to the lawyers and the painful questions. Is the name in use already? Has someone trademarked it? Since globalism requires universality, will the name translate? Does it work in other cultures? Chances are you'll also want the corporate or, perhaps, product name to function as an Internet domain name, so it has to be a name that's free and clear.

Vetting the name involves performing trademark screening, doing linguistic analysis, determining cultural fit—all that. You don't want to enter the marketing texts alongside this blunder: Chevy tried to sell its Nova in Mexico, among other Spanish-speaking countries, without realizing that "No va" means "It doesn't go." Ouch. When VW was creating advertising for the Spanish-speaking Hispanic market, it discovered that its slogan, "Drivers wanted," if translated straight up into Spanish, implied that VW needed chauffeurs. After considering 100 variations, VW finally chose "Agarra calle," slang for "Let's hit the road." Close enough.

WHICH NAME SHOULD YOU CHOOSE?

Made-up words, all connotation and no denotation, are omnipresent, especially for corporate and brand names (Acura, Accenture, Verizon, and so on). Many of these are portmanteaus in that it's easy to hear part of one word being added to part of another to make something that could be a word, if it weren't. Some people find such creations empty, interchangeable, and way overused; others think they sound like the future. You decide. Companies specializing in naming and branding make a lot of money coming up with these things. I tend to like funky, real words more than made-up, vague ones, but I just celebrated Allegra above, so go figure. Hey, Go Figure, an accounting firm. Get it? Oh, never mind.

18 · The Power of Fact

I would want to tell my students of a point strongly pressed, if memory serves, by [George Bernard] Shaw. He once said that as he grew older, he became less and less interested in theory, more and more interested in information. The temptation in writing is just reversed. Nothing is so hard to come by as a new and interesting fact. Nothing so easy on the feet as a generalization.
—JOHN KENNETH GALBRAITH, economist

The more particular, the more specific you are, the more universal you are.
—NANCY HALE, novelist

Facts beat generalities every time

In this book I argue that you cannot know too much about your product, and that digging out facts is an important part of your research. Not only can facts inform an advertisement, they can control it. Find a strong enough one and let it run the concept. If people distrust generalities (and they do) and if they distrust advertising (and they do), then present facts with which they cannot argue.

Recently I saw an outdoor board in Columbus that relied on fact for its effect. It said simply, "Roaches carry six known diseases," under which was the Orkin logo. Amazing—and, I assume, true. I didn't like cockroaches before seeing that ad, but I liked them even less afterward. If I were bedeviled by them, I'd call Orkin, a pest-control company, and quickly.

Here's another example of the power of fact in an advertising world riddled with the overly general and the overenthusiastic. I was driving behind a large, slow, diesel-powered city bus, never a pleasant experience. Since traffic was congested, I had plenty of time to read the signs on its rear end, one of which was: "Fully loaded, this bus replaces 40 automobiles." Suddenly, I felt better about its presence. Another of its signs read, "This bus in service since 1982." Since it was then more than a decade later, I wondered why tell me this? Then I realized it was to let me know, with a dramatic fact, just how careful the bus company had been with taxpayers' money. I felt better yet.

Both dramatic facts cut into my consciousness in ways generalities like "City buses are working for you" or "Buses—the economical way to travel" simply would not. Those phrases don't have enough rhetorical flair, of course, but even if a copywriter made them rhyme or pun, I doubt that they could be as memorable or convincing as those two specific facts.

Read this headline: "Imagine. More than 26 bones, 56 ligaments, 38 muscles, and several yards of tendons packed into the space of one foot. Yours." If people took their feet for granted before that Birkenstock brochure headline, they'd be less likely to do so afterward. E. B. White has spoken of "the eloquence of facts," and facts really do have power to persuade, a power all the more potent in an adland full of puffery, hoo-ha, and propaganda (fig. 18.1). "News" is the term some advertisers use for facts. If telling people the news about your client's product helps you dig for facts, then tell the news. Apple does that every time it invents something.

Let's assume, then, that you've found potentially interesting facts about your product. But how will you express them? A large part of their power comes from *how* you think about and write them. As powerful as facts can be, the cliché "cold, hard facts" exists for a reason. There's often no human softness about

Its razor-sharp teeth can bite

through a **two-by-four.**

Do we really need to explain
why he's behind four inches

of glass?

SHEDD AQUARIUM | Rediscover Shedd. Come see splashing seals, cuddly otters and a fish with a rather unusual little appetite. Don't miss the red-bellied piranhas and other amazing animals.

Open weekdays, 9-5. Weekends, 9-6. Visit www.sheddaquarium.org.

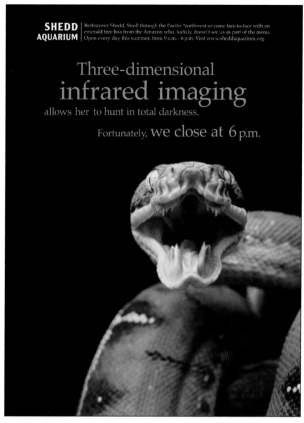

SHEDD AQUARIUM | Rediscover Shedd. Stroll through the Pacific Northwest or come face-to-face with an emerald tree boa from the Amazon who, luckily, doesn't see us as part of the menu. Open every day this summer, from 9 a.m. - 6 p.m. Visit www.sheddaquarium.org.

Three-dimensional
infrared imaging
allows her to hunt in total darkness.

Fortunately, we close at 6 p.m.

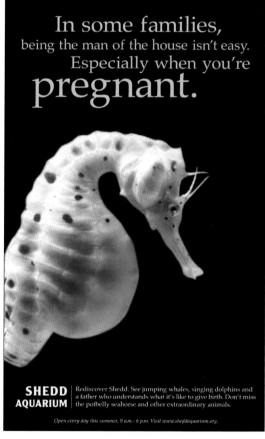

In some families,
being the man of the house isn't easy.
Especially when you're

pregnant.

SHEDD AQUARIUM | Rediscover Shedd. See jumping whales, singing dolphins and a father who understands what it's like to give birth. Don't miss the potbelly seahorse and other extraordinary animals.

Open every day this summer, 9 a.m. - 6 p.m. Visit www.sheddaquarium.org.

18.1. The challenge was to get people interested in the lesser-known fish and reptiles at the Shedd Aquarium in Chicago—not big stars like beluga whales and dolphins but the little guys. Facts have a way of doing that, don't they?

18.2. A funny way of putting it, but no exaggeration: Seattle's Pike Place Market really does cover nine historic acres.

them, no emotional content. They're just solid, stand-alone factoids with a big "so what?" problem. You really need to do two things: find a good fact, then say it well. Here are some ways to say it well, to make it matter.

Give your facts a human voice

It's usually not enough to just "say" the fact. Get in the habit of presenting it wrapped in a funny, warm, wry, or ironic voice. Spin it. "Voice" the fact. Sometimes advertisers say, "Wrap the fact in a smile." (See chapter 16, How to Write a Headline, for more on this.)

An outdoor board for Boston's Franklin Park Zoo wanted to let people know it had birds, too, lots of them. Here's how they informed the public, with facts and a smile:

7 acres. 300 birds. Wear a hat.

See figure 18.2 for another example of a fact that speaks to the human condition in a human voice.

Give your facts as sharp an edge as possible

Don't be "fact lite." State the fact specifically enough that it feels like one. For example, it may be a "fact" that women are often paid less than men for equal work. But that statement is vague, almost uninteresting. Look at the ads in figure 18.3. The facts have now been made precise, and their specificity gets readers' attention.

Likewise, it may be a "fact" that England's Canterbury Cathedral is historically important, so it should be preserved. But say that specifically enough to get people's attention, as the following restoration fund headline does (also note the well-used parallelism):

St. Augustine founded it. Becket died for it. Chaucer wrote about it. Cromwell shot at it. Hitler bombed it. Time is destroying it. Will you save it?

Consider unusual quantifications

Can you quantify or measure your client's product in a new and unusual way? DDB's classic VW campaign did this repeatedly. One ad showed the Beetle with this headline: "$1.02 a pound." Another showed two VWs, with this headline: "There are a lot of good cars you can get for $3400. This is two of them." The cologne Bleu Marine for Men placed one drop from the bottle on the page, under the headline "There are only 624 drops to a bottle. Plan each one carefully." Any such unusual measurement of your client's product catches the mind with its unexpectedness (see fig. 18.4).

Lean your facts up against something

One problem with facts is that too often they're inert, just a big number, a small number, or some statistic that alone means nothing. Facts often mean more when placed in human contexts, especially ironic ones (see fig. 18.5). If you just tell people that "Henry Weinhard beer has been brewed in Oregon since 1856," they're likely to say, "Yeah, so?" The fact alone seems unimpressive, a number without a meaning. But if you say, "Oregon had a beer before it had a capitol," as an ad for Henry Weinhard once did, suddenly the fact becomes interesting, doesn't it? Likewise, you could say of Old Grand-Dad whiskey, "First introduced in 1796," but a copywriter did better: "Introduced fifty years before ice cubes."

Look for a contrast you can exploit

A lot of factual ideas strike the mind because they present themselves as an opposition: this fact versus that one. The tension of facts-in-opposition powers the headline. For example, what if you discovered that New Balance athletic shoes were partly created by scientists at MIT? You could just say, "The shoe that MIT created," or you could write a headline that gives that fact some contrast:

Is this ad worth 28% less because it was written by a woman?

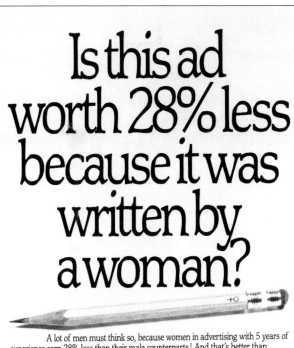

A lot of men must think so, because women in advertising with 5 years of experience earn 28% less than their male counterparts.[1] And that's <u>better</u> than average for working women — who make about 60¢ for every dollar a man earns.[2]

That's not exactly liberty and justice for all.

Find out more about the status of Minnesota's working women and about their pay, power and poverty. Watch WCCO TV's five part "Cover Story." And if you are a woman, get your boss to watch.

Maybe you'll get a raise. [1]ADWEEK, Salary Survey, June 1984 [2]U.S. Department of Labor, April 1983

"Working Women" tonight through Thursday night on WCCO TV's 10 PM REPORT.

WCCO-TV ◢

We're thinking news. We're thinking of you.

© 1984 WCCO TV

THE HUMBOLDT PENGUIN

1,478 *left on earth*

ℐN THE AGE BEFORE MAN,

THE EARTH LOST ONE SPECIES EVERY THOUSAND YEARS. TODAY, WE LOSE ONE EVERY TWENTY MINUTES. THE WORLD WILDLIFE FUND VANISHING SPECIES CAMPAIGN NEEDS YOUR HELP. 1-800-CALL-WWF.

18.3. Since generalities often seem too blurry to get attention or stir emotion, replace them with specifics.

4 minutes a day. 28 minutes a week.
2 hours a month. 1,344 hours in a lifetime.
Make the best of it.

Most people see shaving as something that you do for a few minutes a day. But at Braun, we see shaving as something you do for a lifetime.
Which is why we've designed our shaver's thin profile to fit the contours of your face as comfortably as your hand. And why the rubber knobs on our grip actually quiet motor noise, as well as provide a firm hold. Our rechargeable shavers charge in an hour instead of the usual twenty-four; and perform equally well with or without a cord. Even our foil is ultra-thin and platinum coated to help provide a closer, smoother shave.
This comprehensive approach to shaving has made Braun the best-selling foil shaver in the rest of the world. Now it's finally available in America. And not a moment too soon.

BRAUN
Designed to perform better.

Left

18.4. An unusual quantification engages the mind more strongly than would something like "people spend a lot of time shaving, so they should choose a good shaver."

Right and below

18.5. Lean it up against something.

Each year, a woman spends as
much as $600 on her hair.
(Unfortunately, she only spends
$26 a year on her shampoo.)

KMS

18.6. How to sell an expensive salon shampoo? Invite readers to contemplate this contradiction.

Over the years, MIT professors have been responsible for 150 computers, 47 rockets, 6 satellites and one shoe.

An ad promoting prunes showed one, beside this headline:

> There are five types of fiber your body uses. Here are four of them.

This following copy line from a World Wildlife Fund ad similarly juxtaposes facts so that readers better understand the issue:

> In the age before man, the earth lost one species every thousand years. Today, we lose one every twenty minutes.

See figures 18.6–18.8 for more examples of effective contrasts.

Remember that facts about your client's product imply facts about the competition's

For every fact you discover about your client's product, there is a corresponding fact about the competition (see fig. 18.9). Your ad might be more impressive if it used *their* facts in addition to or in place of yours.

Make your facts visual

Don't lock into thinking that facts must be statis-

tics, quantifiable, verbal. And that the only way to express them is through headlines. Many facts are visual—or can be visually energized (see figs. 18.10 and 18.11).

Demonstrate your facts

Don't claim them, prove them (see figs. 18.12 and 18.13). Nothing's stronger than a demonstration.

A Shar-pei pup is worth a thousand dollars.
Hanna Mayer sold hers for $13.95.

When Hanna went to sell her Shar-pei pup, she looked to the one source that could fetch her the best price. A three day, three line Sun Classified. After one quick phone call, her ad was delivered to hundreds of thousands of people all across Maryland. And all it cost was $13.95. That's the dog's truth. Sun Classifieds. Buy it. Sell it. Find it. **Sun Classifieds**

3 days, 3 lines, only $13.95. Call 539-7700

18.7. A clever contrast between numbers drives readers into the ad and delivers the selling point.

18.8. This specific contrast dramatizes the problem better than would "it's easy to spill things."

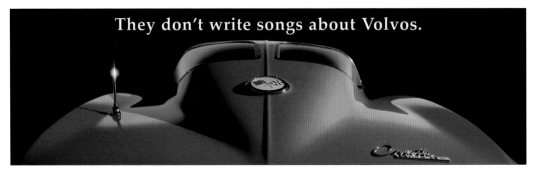

18.9. Who can argue with this?

18.10. The small-print headline, "More than 3 million readers every week," is complemented by the visual, suggesting one issue being read that many times. Funny and simple, this visual idea gives the fact stopping power.

18.11. The copy says, "More battery. More talk. LG GX200 with 13.5 hours of talk time and 1700 hours of standby battery life." This mobile phone's dominant selling feature has been made visual and funny. A strong example of using facts (features) without inducing sleep.

Bernice is not a honey baked ham. Must sing? No can do. Watch the fish swim. They are Ethel Merman.

See. People will read anything on a subway poster.

TRANSAD

Your product *goes* here.

18.12. How do you demonstrate the power of transit advertising? This ad just did.

DOG WALKER
Call Zoe   555-999-3927

We care about small business.   **1STBANK**

efirstbank.com   Member FDIC

PIANO LESSONS
Mrs. Bennett   555-999-3925   Beginners welcome.

We care about small business.   **1STBANK**

efirstbank.com   Member FDIC

BABYSITTER
$12/hour   Call Abbey   555-999-3928

We care about small business.   **1STBANK**

efirstbank.com   Member FDIC

18.13. FirstBank says, "We care about small business," but rather than content themselves with that unprovable piece of self-congratulation, they demonstrate its validity by placing these outdoor boards around Denver. The people—and small businesses—are FirstBank customers.

19 · Testimonials: The Power of Personality

Personalities appeal, while soulless corporations do not.
Make a man famous and you make his creation famous.
—CLAUDE HOPKINS, *My Life in Advertising*

One of the most durable of advertising techniques is the *testimonial*: someone speaks *for* the product. Testimonials may seem dopey and obvious—"Hi, I'm Joe Famous. I use Blotto, and you should, too"—but they don't have to be.

Testimonials are a very old technique, related to word of mouth (the first cave man said to the second cave man, "Here, use this pointy thing, not that pointy thing," and the testimonial was born). When people want to buy something, they often ask a friend with knowledge of the brand what he or she thinks of it as a way of testing its worth. With testimonials, people's interest or belief in the spokesperson rubs off on the product.

No matter what you're selling, someone can testify for it. And since people find other people more fascinating than they do anything else, why not use them?

Keep two things in mind:

1. Finding a likely candidate is only half the job. Once you drag someone on stage, use your wits. Tie that character to the product, cleverly. Your idea and words will make or break the testimonial more than will your choice of spokesperson.

2. Decide whether you'll press the truth button or the whimsy button. You can ask your audience to believe that this is a real person who really uses the product, or you can just have fun with the character or person without requesting anyone's belief. Either approach can work, though I prefer real people with a real connection to the product. There's more substance in that argument, more pull power.

It's not just a joke, even though joking testimonials can be mighty good. So before you take the joke route, look through your research for people who can help you sell the product. They're not just arresting; they're the truth.

Figure 19.1 shows how to use real people (rather than celebrities with no connection to the brand) in testimonials and make them interesting. This approach is funny, requires just a little work from the viewer (those make for the best ads), and proves that real people with real connections to the product work terrifically well—provided the creative people give them just the right twist, which is where you come in.

Whom might you pull onstage?

1. Extreme user. Find the heavy user or the over-the-top user and let that person demonstrate, often with hyperbole, how great the product is.

2. Expert. Find somebody who stands outside the brand and has the expertise to evaluate it. If you're selling food, find a chef. If you're selling cars, find a mechanic. If you're selling a prison, find some criminals (see fig.19.2).

3. President/CEO, founding mother or father, employee. Give the brand a human face. Take the monolith out of it. Find someone to personify the corporation, one that people might otherwise think too big, too corrupt, too remote, or too something (see fig. 19.3). If, for example, banks are seen as cold institutions long on financial analysts but short on real

MIKE KOPP
political reporter

KXMB
NEWS 12®

"Your Local News Source"

CBS Station Of The Year

19.1. Do your homework, learn about companies, and recognize that within any brand's story are people who can help tell it.

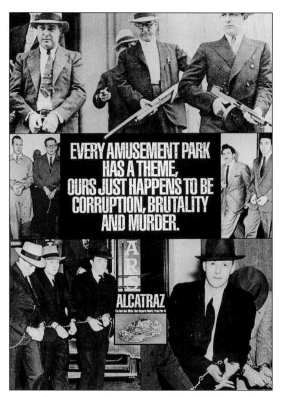

19.2. Why go to see Alcatraz? Just think of all the people who've already been there.

19.3. I wasn't interested in DuPont—until I read this ad (headline: "With a single idea she can stop trains"). It's amazing what Stephanie Kwolek, Kevlar®, and DuPont can do, isn't it? Delve into your client's product. Tell the stories. Show the heroes.

19.4. Frost Bank in Texas uses its employees to help consumers see past the corporate logo. Their various opinions about barbeque embody the bank's differential: Texans first, bankers second.

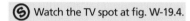 Watch the TV spot at fig. W-19.4.

people, have employees talk about something besides banking (fig. 19.4).

4. Celebrities. There are a million of them. The key is to give your treatment of that famous person some snap (see figs. 19.5 and 19.6). The campaign for Bell BMX helmets used celebrity endorsers (famous BMX pros) but treated them unusually. Writer Dave Schiff, of Crispin Porter + Bogusky, explains: "BMX is probably the harshest, most cynical target audience on earth. Concepts are mocked, high production values are dismissed and authenticity—athlete-driven advertisements—is the only accepted form of communication."[1] So he and his colleagues used images of BMX pro athletes, but placed the helmets on top of demon masks. The ads were painted on urban surfaces by Miami sign painters using Haitian voodoo-style graphics, then photographed for the print ads. The mask and copy become a kind of incantation, a prayer to ward off evil spirits—fear and self-doubt—while doing bike tricks.

The copy reads, "May the helmet which surrounds the head of Steve McCann also surround the head of me. May it protect me from unseen forces that make the sure foot stumble and the strong mind weak. Oh helmet of Steve McCann, help me to ride like Steve McCann, and bring doom to those who oppose me." Schiff got the broken English this way: "In order to get the tone right, we used one of those free online translators and wrote all the copy in Spanish, then converted it to English."[2]

5. Not the person, but something associated with the person. You may want to bypass the person altogether and just use something associated with that person, as a Spiegel catalog campaign once did with celebrities, showing the silk gown Bianca Jagger bought or the shoes Priscilla Presley bought from the catalog. There was an extra poignancy to this use of a metonym—a part standing for the whole—in place of the celebrity (see fig. 19.7).

6. The wrong person. The quintessential example may have been Fallon McElligott's 1980s print campaign for a Minneapolis hair salon that used famous people with bad haircuts (see fig. 19.8). The centerpiece of that campaign was an image of Albert Einstein with his famously messed-up hair and this headline: "A bad haircut can make anyone look dumb." What a smart idea. Similarly, Del Monte introduced shelf-stable, microwave vegetables by using horrified kids as spokespeople. Their unified fear: if vegetables are this easy to prepare, now we'll have them *all* the time. Yikes!

Often consumers are persuaded to buy things because of a negative endorsement. If a teenager's parents don't like a product, that could be all the reason

19.5. If you use a celebrity, get the most out of him: make sure the ad resonates with your audience. The Bell ad starts with Steve McCann, but it doesn't stop there. Boys & Girls Club of America surprises readers by adding a twist to the traditional celebrity endorsement.

19.6. These posters promoting a new baseball season used celebrities (Chicago Cubs baseball stars), but the ads were made memorable by the headlines as much as by the athletes. Don't just show the famous athlete; give him a spin.

19.7. Instead of succumbing to cliché by showing a shiny, happy client, this investment bank reduced him to a phone and phone number, then invited readers to call him—or any other client—and ask how well the bank performed.

19.8. By its witty use of the "wrong person," this campaign avoids ad clichés overused for hair salons (fashion-ad approaches, beauty shots of hair), thus creating a distinctive image for its client. Partly *because* this is so unlike a hair salon ad, people figure that this place knows its business.

necessary for wanting it. Spend some time thinking about who can't use or doesn't use or doesn't like your client's product. Can you twist that negative into a positive? Could the product be sold by someone unlikely? Very likely.

7. Ironic testimonials. You may want to go further and devalue the seller, make jokes on the idea of credible spokespeople. Given people's cynical attitude toward advertising and endorsements, such ironic testimonials gain absurdist power. Some years ago, the car company Isuzu played off the cliché of the dishonest car salesman by inventing one, the smarmy Joe Isuzu, whose hilariously overstated promises the spots ridiculed. E. & J. Gallo Winery created two hayseeds, one garrulous, the other silent, Bartles and Jaymes, who apparently sold the wine they made from their front porch. Viewers were invited to laugh at their cardboard nostalgia—two guys too dumb to know they needed an ad agency. More recently, Altoids has used geeky spokespeople in their ads, oddballs who humorously embody various benefits of the brand's position: mints and gum that are "curiously strong." Burger King sent its namesake, the King (in this case a fellow in costume, wearing a great big, plastic Burger King head) to visit backyards and even bedrooms—his looming, silent, smiling face becoming both hilarious and disturbing.

Many ads play ironic jokes on their own clichés, sharing a wink with viewers at the testimonial genre. So think about subverting, subordinating, or in some way altering the usual position of the spokesperson as authority speaking for the product. (See also chapter 24, Postmodern Advertising.)

8. Historical figures, unreal people. The per-

Everyone's taking Presidents' Day off, except us.

19.9. Famous figures can gain attention while delivering the selling idea.

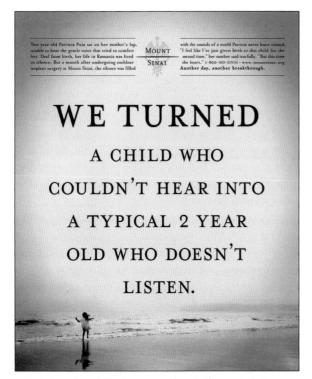

WE TURNED

A CHILD WHO

COULDN'T HEAR INTO

A TYPICAL 2 YEAR

OLD WHO DOESN'T

LISTEN.

19.10. Even though the testimonial here is the most obvious one possible—someone helped by the hospital—this little girl's story is told so well that it's inspiring. As always, good ads aren't the result of lucky choices. They're the result of thought and labor: you make them good, or you make them bad.

Ⓢ For more from this campaign, see fig. W-19.10.

son in the testimonial needn't be alive or even real. Characters from history, legend, literature, movies, and cartoons can be used for their attention-getting quality as well as their unusual "relationship" to the product (fig. 19.9).

Apple's "Think different" campaign, for example, used a variety of famous innovators, most of whom had no relationship with computers, Apple or otherwise. Amelia Earhart, Pablo Picasso, Muhammad Ali, Mahatma Gandhi, Buckminster Fuller, and all the rest served as symbols of creative thinkers, risk takers, people who challenged assumptions, who dared to be great. That was their "relationship" to Apple, and, tangential though it was, it worked. Apple became the computer expression of the rebel in everyone, a way for people to celebrate and encourage their own potential.

Thus, you needn't limit yourself to living people, nor do you need to be reasonable. I've seen images of Laurel and Hardy used to sell windshield wipers, Franz Kafka to sell beer, James Dean for tennis shoes. Rummage through history or Hollywood, myth or literature. See who turns up.

9. Just plain folks. Given all the celebrity testimonials, can "normal people" with an obvious relationship to the product be effective? Absolutely. Figure 19.10 is another example of perhaps the best sort of testimonial: a real person who was really helped by the product, in this case a hospital. A great headline introduces a little girl whose congenital deafness has been overcome by surgery at Mount Sinai. Terrific work. For me at least, the truth trumps everything else.

And the truth about brands and products can be found in abundance online. Testimonials from real people, unbought and unscripted, have become part of all brands that choose to involve their customers, and what smart brand doesn't? Blogs, discussion groups, unedited consumer reviews on the brand's website and elsewhere, people telling and posting their stories of life with the brand—all of these testimonials make clear, transparently clear, just how well the company's products perform and how well the company's customer service does, too. People trust other people more than they do corporations. What people say is real, what corporations say is propaganda. Real testimonials from just plain folks have become more important than ever.

20 • Two-fers: Comparisons, Before and After, and Other Dualities

I once was lost, but now am found,
Was blind, but now I see.
—John Newton,
from "Amazing Grace"

A fundamental way to get attention, organize information, and be persuasive is to use paired imagery, what we might call *two-fers*: comparison-and-contrast, before-and-after, and other side-by-side set-ups. Such ads float through people's memory like old reruns. On the left she is fat; on the right she is fit. Once he was bald; now he has hair. This shirt had chocolate stains, but now it's lily white. On and on, ad nauseam.

Although my examples are clichés, two-fers don't have to be. Lots of great ads exploit this structure because it's fast, simple, clear, and often startling. Usually you consider this format only when comparing your client's brand with brand X or in a before-and-after scenario—and two-fers work well to express such intentions. The TV and video Apple ads in which the Mac fellow makes fun of the bumbling PC fellow are studies in comparison-and-contrast, this versus that (see also figs. 20.1 and 20.2). But you don't need to restrict yourself to those categories, nor must you be so literal minded in using this format.

Stay on strategy

Try to express your strategy, whatever it is, as a two-fer. Does your client's product have an old image but now

a new reality? An old use but now a new one, too? Is the product good not only for one kind of person but for another as well? Are there two versions of it people should know about? Two benefits? Can you show the product one way and then add to that in the other image? Can you take two benefits and fuse them into one image? Consider the following possibilities:

1. Show two different versions, benefits, purposes, or kinds of consumer of a single product (see fig. 20.3).

2. Compare the product with something dissimilar, something that looks the same or works the same, to dramatize the benefit. Often the more unusual and unexpected the comparison, the better (see figs. 20.4–20.7).

3. Try using two-fers for any strategy that addresses consumer ignorance (see figs. 20.8 and 20.9), corrects a misperception (see fig. 20.10), or talks about problems and solutions.

As so often applies in advertising, it's less what you show and more how you think and talk about what you show that makes the difference (see figs. 20.11–20.13).

Happy Holidays from all of us at Dahl Chiropractic.

20.1. The before-and-after ad is a hardy perennial, but there's nothing old about it here, is there? Other before-and-after comparisons that dramatized this chiropractor's get-the-kinks-out services were the St. Louis Arch vs. the Washington Monument, a camel vs. a horse, and a French horn vs. a clarinet.

20.2. Comparison with the competition doesn't have to be boring either. The Episcopal Church's aggressive tone gets right to the point.

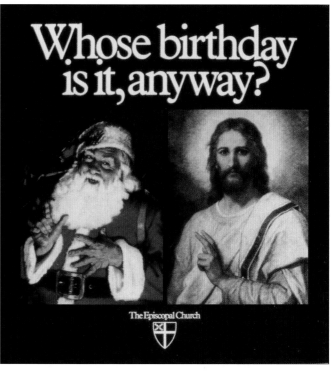

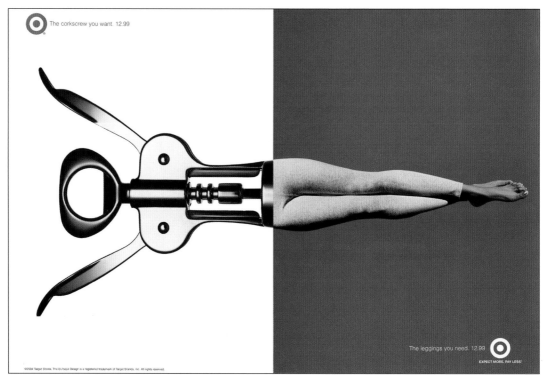

20.3. Why not compare a brand with itself—even if only in terms of shape? Target shows its range of products by fusing "what you need" with "what you want."

20.4. This ad in a beautiful campaign for San Francisco makes a surprising connection between two apparently dissimilar things, though the visual parallelism links them, as does the conceptual one: they're both iconic aspects of life in SF.

Below

20.5. This video for the World Wildlife Fund compares animal and human life, the natural world and the man-made, to reveal startling similarities, ones that make the interconnected-ness of all life inescapable.

Watch the stunning WWF video at fig. W-20.5.

20.6. Other ads in this campaign paired the inverted body of a Les Paul guitar with a nuclear mushroom cloud and the pointed shape of a Gibson SG body with a devil's trident.

20.7. Unexpected metaphorical comparison. Another ad compared a yellow and black MINI with the business end of a bumble bee.

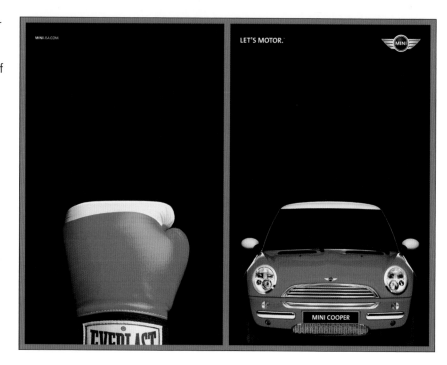

20.8. Can a two-fer be a three-fer? Why not? The copy line reads, "No race, creed or religion should endure the ridicule faced by Native Americans today. Please help us put an end to this mockery and racism . . ."

20.9. Another three-fer. Denver Water's conservation program encourages people to water their lawns less because, as they can see, grass is too dumb to notice.

20.10. Ohio State has a huge athletic program, but men's football and basketball had so dominated that plenty of high-energy, well-played sports were neglected by the fans. Partly because of the program's size, there also was no perceived continuity among the teams. The goal of this campaign was to unify the brand (the athletic program), raise interest in smaller, less well-known sports, and increase ticket sales. By using an unusual—but appropriate—dissimilarity to complete each athlete's shape, these metaphorical two-fers surprise viewers, dramatize the energy of the sports, and pull the program together into a distinct brand.

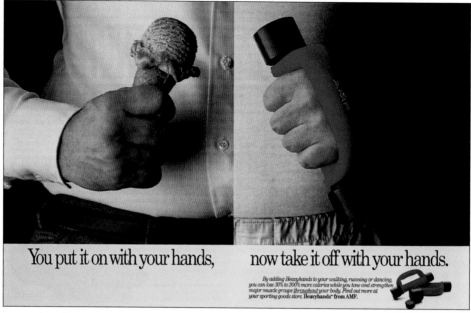

20.11. This ad seems to make more sense than it really does, thanks in part to tight visual and verbal parallelism. Eating with one's hands doesn't lead to any necessary wisdom in exercising with them, but it seems to, doesn't it? The two-fer format lends its rhetorical weight to the argument.

20.12. You can use two-fers to solve just about any problem. As this example shows, they're as creative as you are and work when you make them work.

reasonpartners.org

20.13. This dramatic, but puzzling, two-fer would drive me right to the website. You too?

Create sequential ads

Budget willing, you can create sequential ads: a series of two or more ads that occupy, usually, the same space on succeeding pages in a newspaper or magazine. Readers see an incomplete message and then turn the page(s) for the rest. These ads gain cumulative power: if readers page past the first ad, the repetition, with variation, of succeeding installments eventually registers. It's one way to beat clutter: repeat yourself until people notice.

You can use outdoor boards in sequence, too, setting something up in the first board, then paying it off farther down the highway with the second board. Or have a single board evolve, by adding information to an incomplete message over time.

Many Internet banner ads are two-fers and sequential ads: images and language succeed one another, or the ads invite readers to click on or roll over them to reveal the next part of the message.

Regardless of medium, all two-fers show the swift transit from one state of affairs to another. Think of the power in that. People usually look at a world so muddled, slow moving, and indeterminate that sudden change becomes a welcome surprise. When you present two realities at once—presto!—you perform magic: a trick of the eye, a sleight of hand and mind. You cast ideas into binary relief, create strong contrasts, and make the truth seem as inevitable as this versus that.

The best two-fers are fast, clear, simple, and surprising—four words that also define the best advertising.

21 · Reversal

How well you can write has little to do with your success as a copywriter. Clients don't care what the words mean. No great campaign was ever bought because the client loved the sentences. Great campaigns happen when a creative sees the product differently than it has been perceived before.
—Mark Fenske, creative director and associate professor, VCU Brandcenter

Discovery consists of looking at the same thing as everyone else and thinking something different.
—Albert Szent-Gyorgyi, Nobel Prize–winning biochemist

As a copywriter, you're in the business of being interesting. Whether you're writing a three-word slogan or thousands of words for a corporate website, one way to be interesting is to think in reverse.

All great communication employs *reversal*: something significant has been put in, left out, inverted, visualized oddly, colored wrong, talked about differently, or in some way had violence done to its ordinariness. Otherwise, if your readers' or viewers' preconceptions have been fulfilled instead of violated, they'll be looking at clichés. They won't even blink because nothing has moved out of its same-as-usual spot.

If you want people to look or to read, you've got to make them, and that's where reversal comes in.[1] For example, a quintessential VW ad (fig. 21.1) took the American maxim "Think big" and reversed it to "Think small." It also ignored an advertising maxim—use the whole page to display the product—and instead filled the page with emptiness, sticking an itty-bitty image of the VW Beetle up in the corner. The ad reversed viewers' expectations twice: once as users of clichés, and once as viewers of ads.

How to think in reverse
The best way to think backwards is to practice techniques that by definition *are* backwards.

WHEN EVERYONE IS GOING ONE WAY, GO ANOTHER
"[D]o the opposite of what everybody else is doing —that will almost always get you halfway to success. Then all you need is to figure out why you're doing the opposite."

—Alex Bogusky, co-founder, Crispin Porter + Bogusky

First, determine the usual direction taken by ads in your product's category. How is the product sold? What expectations do people have when they encounter, say, a beer ad or a car ad? Violate those expectations. If you're selling a car, people expect to see it on a mountain road after a rain—so show it still on the boat from Korea; possible headline: "Every Hyundai comes with 6,000 miles on it." Or people expect to see it sitting on a page surrounded by lots of type—so show just part of the car, as VW once did, displaying only the engine underneath the headline "Introducing the 1981 Rabbit"; the point was that nothing else had changed.

How do most ads in your product's category talk? Talk some other way. For example, ads warning people not to drink alcohol excessively usually cite the dangers and are somber, serious, even scary. But the

Think small.

Our little car isn't so much of a novelty any more.

A couple of dozen college kids don't try to squeeze inside it.

The guy at the gas station doesn't ask where the gas goes.

Nobody even stares at our shape.

In fact, some people who drive our little flivver don't even think 32 miles to the gallon is going any great guns.

Or using five pints of oil instead of five quarts.

Or never needing anti-freeze.

Or racking up 40,000 miles on a set of tires.

That's because once you get used to some of our economies, you don't even think about them any more.

Except when you squeeze into a small parking spot. Or renew your small insurance. Or pay a small repair bill. Or trade in your old VW for a new one.

Think it over.

21.1. This classic VW ad from 1960 may have created a longer ripple effect than any other single ad in the twentieth century. Its approach remains influential, both graphically and conceptually, even today.

"Know when to draw the line" campaign created for Labatt by Axmith McIntyre Wicht, Toronto, headed in the opposite direction (see fig. 21.2). The glow-in-the-dark bull's-eye pillow says, "Hopefully you won't need this tonight." The poster's optically undulating visual is headlined "Feel familiar?" And this TV spot in the campaign is a funny take on a girl who wakes up married to an Elvis impersonator after a night of heavy drinking. Says writer Brian Howlett, "As far as we know, it's the first advertising that attempts to deliver this serious message in a light-hearted manner. The kids in research kept telling us they didn't want to see another 'drink responsibly' spot that had body bags or car crashes in it. Response has been fantastic."[2]

EXPLORE NEGATIVE SPACE

"Often the most interesting angle in any problem is the negative. This area often seems more human; it has possibilities for entertainment and humor. You demonstrate how good you are by showing what you're not. The trick is to do it in such a way that the positive ultimately comes through."

—SUE CROLICK,
Sue Crolick Advertising & Design

Artists talk about the *negative space* of an object: not the tree but the broken-up sky that interpenetrates it; not the model's fingers but the space that wraps itself around them. Artists learn to draw not just the contour of the object, but also the contour of the

21.2. The light-hearted tone of this drink-responsibly campaign is 180 degrees from the voice of doom people expect in this genre.

Ⓢ Watch the Labatt TV spot at fig. W-21.2.

space around it. They learn a different way of seeing.

Similarly, you can think about the negative space of a product, the "un-things" around it: the non-uses and wrong places and wrong times and wrong people for the product. Ask yourself:

- Who doesn't use the product?
- When isn't it used?
- What's an unusual use for it?
- Where don't you find it?
- When is the one time it *won't* come in handy?
- Can it be broken, used up, disassembled, or defaced?
- If it has lots of features, what *doesn't* it have?

- If it solves lots of problems, what problem *won't* it solve?
- How can it be placed out of context?
- What's an odd point of view, visually or psychologically, from which to see it?
- What's the worst thing that can happen if you use it?

In other words, explore the empty, absurd areas around a product (see figs. 21.3 and 21.4).

SAY IT "WRONG"

"Advertising should stun momentarily. It should seem to be outrageous. In that swift interval be-

21.3. Exploring negative space. The Harley-Davidson ad (left) uses the "wrong person," someone who doesn't (yet) use the product. What better way to indicate the long-standing loyalty that Harley-Davidson engenders than with a pre-rider? The Volvo airport sign (below) points out something Volvo doesn't do in order to emphasize how well it does something else.

21.4. Don't interview consumers happy with a product; interview unhappy ones. Much more entertaining.

Ⓢ Watch—and almost hear—the TV spot at fig. W-21.4.

21.5. A perfect example of advertiser George Lois's dictum: stun momentarily.

21.6. By inverting the word order of a cliché ("how much you love her"), the diamond ad (below left) reveals a deeper truth. With the anti-smoking ad (below right), readers so hope to see a sentence that ends ". . . cures cancer" that the reversal stops them in their tracks, then makes its point.

Tear this out and use it for toilet paper.

50¢ off bathroom tissue

This coupon is valid for 50¢ off the regular price of any four pack of in-stock bathroom tissue. Limit one coupon per purchase per customer. Offer expires 10/31/91. Redeemable only at Eden Prairie Grocery, 7447 County Road No. 4, Eden Prairie, Minnesota 55344, 937-8892.

"Lil-Red" Eden Prairie Grocery
7447 County Road No. 4, 937-8892

11 GOLD

EVERY ONCE IN A WHILE
IT'S NICE TO
REMIND HER
HOW MUCH
SHE LOVES YOU

A DIAMOND IS FOREVER

CANCER CURES SMOKING.

CANCER PATIENTS AID ASSOCIATION

tween the initial shock and the realization that what you are showing is not as outrageous as it seems, you capture the audience."

—GEORGE LOIS, founder, Lois/USA

Instead of taking a reasonable idea and reversing it into unreason, do something less extreme. Take that reasonable idea and simply reverse the way you say it. Invert the normal expression of a benefit (fig. 21.5). If your client's airline serves lots of cities, then there are some that it doesn't. One of Pan Am's benefits was that it flew more places than other airlines. But saying "more places than," "greater than," "the most number of," and the like is a cliché (as is drawing a bunch of arrows on a globe). So, in a moment of genius, the advertisers showed a photo of a cluster of penguins strolling past an ice floe in the Antarctic and said, "It's easier to remember where we don't go." Similarly, Volvo wrote the headline "It does 60 to 0 in 4 seconds flat," a nicely inverted way to express brak-

ing capability. An outdoor board for VW's New Beetle surprised viewers by saying, "0–60? Yes." A headline for Mercedes-Benz said, "Does your airbag come with a car?" (The reversals in fig. 21.6 make readers do a double take.)

Remember, when you gain one thing, you lose something else. If you get richer in some ways, you become poorer in others. If you gain freedom, you lose security. If you gain stature, you lose anonymity. The same reversals apply to products. Say the benefit backwards. Examine your list of straightforward benefits, asking how each could be said by emphasizing its opposite. *The Economist* magazine has expressed its contribution to subscribers' corporate success this way: "Lose the ability to slip out of meetings unnoticed." A loss that emphasizes the gain. Another *Economist* headline: "It's lonely at the top, but at least there's something to read." See figure 21.7 for an example of reversal that injects humor into the liability of gaining a benefit.

21.7. Is it possible to have *too much* of a good thing? If you're channeling your inner Keith Moon, yes it is.

Ⓢ See the TV spot at fig. W-21.7.

BITCH AND COMPLAIN SOONER.

The Weather Network

21.8. Cast the benefit in terms of its opposite; find the downside of the upside. In this case, if people know the forecast sooner, they can be upset about it longer.

TURN DEFICITS INTO ASSETS

"Every artist knows that sunlight can only be pictured with shadows. And every good biographer shows us, as Boswell did, that only the faults of a great man make him real to us. But in advertising we are afraid of this principle, hence less convincing than we might be."

—JAMES WEBB YOUNG, *Diary of an Ad Man*

TOO WEIRD.
TOO NOISY.
TOO DIFFERENT.

AZUR

RESTAURANT · BALLROOM
GAVIIDAE COMMON

21.9. Makes you want to go, doesn't it?

Every product has liabilities, but most advertising ignores the deficits and concentrates instead on making good seem better. Great campaigns, however, have been built on turning deficits into assets.

"If you have a big wart on your face, you'd better make that your thing. Make people love that wart. Convince everyone it's a beauty mark. But don't waste a second trying to hide it."

—ANDREW KELLER, executive creative director,
Crispin Porter + Bogusky

Make a list of all the reasons your client's target audience would *not* want to buy the product. What's wrong with it? Costs too much? Too little? Doesn't last long enough? Lasts too long? What? Then examine these perceived liabilities to see if you can flip one around—turn a deficit into an asset (figs. 21.8–21.10).

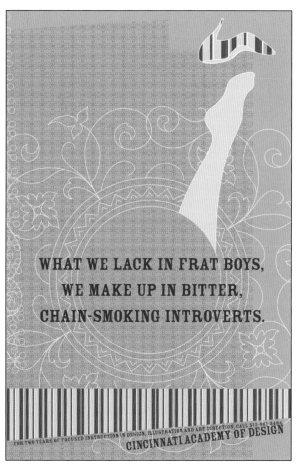

WHAT WE LACK IN FRAT BOYS, WE MAKE UP IN BITTER, CHAIN-SMOKING INTROVERTS.

FOR TWO YEARS OF FOCUSED INSTRUCTION IN DESIGN, ILLUSTRATION AND ART DIRECTION, CALL 513-961-2484
CINCINNATI ACADEMY OF DESIGN

21.10. Artists and designers often see themselves as a hardy little band of like-minded people in a world of "others." This campaign knows just what to say: emphasize art school negatives until they sound positively irresistible. Other headlines: "Math. Our best recruiter" and "Economics 101. We don't have it. And based on junior designer salaries, you don't need it."

One problem with D'Amico Cucina, a restaurant in Minneapolis, is that it's open only in the evening. How to turn no lunch into a virtue? "We don't serve lunch. It takes us all day to prepare dinner."

Bazooka chewing gum built a campaign around a liability. If you've ever had Bazooka, you know that it's hard to chew at first—more like hard candy than gum. Most advertisers wouldn't even address that problem. Not Chiat/Day, whose campaign theme was "Bazooka chewing gum. If you're tough enough to chew the hard stuff." One TV spot had a close-up of a man starting to chew a piece to the soundtrack of a car trying to start and then stalling out. The voice-over: "It's harder to get started, but once it gets going, it never stops." Clever and memorable. And the campaign successfully differentiated the brand—no small feat in a category chock full of look-alike, taste-alike competitors about which it's hard to find much to say.

TURN THEIR ASSETS INTO DEFICITS

"The best and simplest way of selling a product is to say: 'It is better than what you are about to buy.'"
—Dave Trott, copywriter, BMP

Instead of taking a product's deficits and showing how they're really assets, take the competition's assets and show how they're really deficits. That is, push your product up by pushing the competition down, by arguing that competitors' apparent strengths are really weaknesses. Reposition the competition (see figs. 21.11 and 21.12).

Make a list of what's wrong with your product's

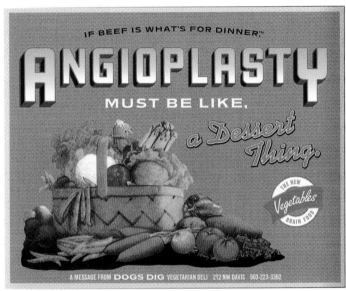

21.11. By mocking the cattle industry's own slogan ("Beef. It's what's for dinner"), these ads for a vegetarian deli go right after the competition's soft underbelly.

21.12. You can't drink and drive. Or can you?

competitors; better yet, find in that list weaknesses they think are strengths. Find a deficit in what is otherwise the strong position of the market leader. Point out Mr. Big's liabilities. For "offensive warfare" that repositions the leader, marketing experts Al Ries and Jack Trout give this advice: "Find a weakness [inherent] in the leader's strength and attack at that point."[3] For

example, Coca-Cola for many years had virtually no significant competition, and its distinctive 6½-ounce bottle shape was its symbol. So in the late 1930s, when Pepsi went after Coke, it attacked the bottle. Its key selling concept was a 12-ounce bottle for the same nickel, and the strategy worked.[4]

Royal's golf ball isn't exactly number one with Tiger

21.13. Literally upside down becomes conceptually right side up. Nice visual pun, too, between the zoo's symbol, the hand/animal, and "learn firsthand."

Woods, Phil Mickelson, and other touring pros; they play Nike, Titleist, and other brands. So Royal simply took a close-up picture of a Royal golf ball resting on the grass and put on it the headline "Play the ball the pros ignore." Although Royal also wrote a lot of copy to explain why, the nervy headline alone challenges and intrigues, don't you think? (The slogan: "The perfect golf ball for the imperfect golfer.") This approach re-positioned the Big Boys; playing the ball the pros play now looked like a bad idea. And the ball-from-nowhere, the also-ran Royal, suddenly seemed more special, its humility entirely appropriate to all those imperfect golfers.

Final advice

"A safe ad is a bad ad. In fact, it's not an ad at all. If you're not prepared to get attention, you're not prepared to advertise."

—Marsha Lindsay, president/CEO, Lindsay, Stone & Briggs

"There are so many ads that are okay and nice and it's hard to find something wrong to say about them, but the ads that are exceptional are usually a little irreverent, foolish, or dangerous. Some even cross the line and get the creative in trouble with a client. Exceptional advertising is like walking a very delicate tightrope, but if you don't have the courage to take a chance, you'll be doing mundane work forever."

—Roy Grace, executive creative director, Doyle Dane Bernbach

Working with reversals helps you take chances, but it's a difficult way to think. It runs counter to the copywriter's usual desire to make sense, plus it deliberately puts the client's product in jeopardy, creating a non sequitur from which you must then make sense follow. But remember the great ads and campaigns you've admired. Not one was a straightforward presentation of the traditional way of seeing a product, with the usual arguments for buying it. Each one jolted you by reversing some expectation. As a creative person, you are dedicating yourself to transcending clichés. Try the techniques I've suggested. After all, in the great work, upside down is indeed right side up (fig. 21.13).

22 · Visual Metaphor

But the greatest thing by far is to be a master of metaphor. It is the one thing that cannot be learnt from others; and it is also a sign of genius, since a good metaphor implies an intuitive perception of the similarity in dissimilars.

—ARISTOTLE, *Poetics*

Consumers like to think they choose among products on the basis of what they can see, hear, feel, taste, and touch about those products. In other words, they make their judgments via *tangible* distinctions. Is this a good hamburger? Let's taste it. Is this a good car? Let's drive it. Does this shampoo get my hair soft? Let's wash with it and find out.

But what happens when consumers can't literally apprehend the product? Services are not concrete the way goods are, so often the product is itself *intangible*—people cannot see insurance or feel banking or test the plumpness of a college education with their finger—but they certainly demand a strong sense of a service's effectiveness before they buy it. Just as often an otherwise tangible good—that car, for example—offers *intangible* benefits that need expression, such as feelings of power or freedom or security. These don't literally adhere to the hardware, yet they're part of why consumers buy cars and ought to be part of how you sell them. Some goods, like computers, are too complicated to apprehend with the senses, while others—most packaged goods, for example—are shielded away from the immediate senses by tin, plastic, or cardboard. All these instances invite the advertising use of metaphor—talking about one thing in terms of something else—because the product's "one thing" is intangible, allowing the metaphor's "something else" to vivify it.

In short, when consumers can't apprehend the product's benefits with their senses—either before trial or ever—then they rely on substitutes, images that stand for those things. As Theodore Levitt notes, "Metaphors and similes become surrogates for the

tangibility that cannot be provided or experienced in advance."[1] And while you'll primarily think of using metaphors in specific ads, consider the general point—it explains why IBM insists on a rigorous dress code for its employees; why Apple goes to such lengths with the package, product, and graphic design for its computers; why you'll spend hour upon hour designing your website, portfolio, and résumé. Again, Levitt notes, "The less tangible the generic product, the more powerfully and persistently the judgment about it is shaped by the 'packaging'—how it's presented, who presents it, what's implied by metaphor, simile, symbol, and other surrogates for reality."[2]

How metaphors work

Think of all the insurance companies that use a metaphor or symbol to stand for the security they offer: Prudential's Rock of Gibraltar, the Travelers' umbrella, Hartford's elk, the "good hands" of Allstate, and so on. Since insurance is less a thing than a feeling or a state of mind, these metaphors help define the feeling, give consumers something to grasp in the absence of anything tangible. Metaphors don't always need to be visual images, either. They can be stated in the copy line or slogan—or, in the case of State Farm insurance, sung: "and like a good neighbor, State Farm is there."

A *metaphor*, of course, is a figure of speech in which one thing is talked about in terms of something else; a comparison is made between dissimilar things. If you compare Ohio State and Penn State or compare the Cleveland Browns and the Chicago Bears, you aren't making metaphors; you're making literal comparisons between similar things. But if you say, as Ralph Waldo

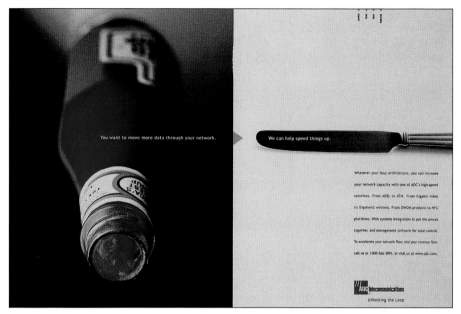

22.1. How do you *show* slow communication systems and the solution to that problem? With a ketchup bottle, a knife, and a headline that links the tangible (the visual) with the intangible (the problem and its solution): "You want to move data through your network. We can help speed things up."

Emerson once did, that "an institution is the lengthened shadow of one man"[3] or that a football team is like a harnessed set of horses, then you are making metaphors. (Remember that a *simile*, which uses "like" or "as," is a kind of metaphor.)

> "A metaphor forces everyone to look at your product in the simplest term. We get so caught up in the bells and whistles that we forget the basic function. The idea of any decent ad is to help us digest the information easily. Metaphor is a way of doing that."
>
> —JENNIFER SOLOW, art director, Ammirati & Puris

Two ways to be metaphorical

When you're creating metaphors for ads, think of them as being of two kinds.

USE PURE METAPHOR

Sometimes you can just show something that isn't your client's product at all and say that it is. In this case, you're using a *pure metaphor*: something that stands in for the product (or its benefit or the feeling people get from it) and helps clarify and persuade. This is a good technique when the product is intangible but also when it's boring to look at or complicated or obscure or unknown. Or when everyone else in that product category does one thing (show the car, for example), and you want to do something different.

I once saw a poster in a public library featuring a big photo of a hiker with backpack pausing in a glorious solo trek through the Grand Canyon, the awesome spectacle looming over his shoulder. The poster could have been advertising Timberland gear or Arizona, but when I read the small headline, "Knowledge is free. Visit your library," I saw how well the visual worked. Going to the library *is* like an odyssey through immense, spectacular country; just think of what's there. The pure metaphor required me to leap to libraries and books from the Grand Canyon, but I could, and I felt invigorated by doing so.

Ad agency Martin|Williams used pure metaphor when it printed a Boy Scouts annual report using no ink, just raised letters, to enact the Scouts' "Leave No Trace" motto. (See figs. 22.1–22.3 for other examples of pure metaphor.)

CREATE A FUSED METAPHOR

Pure metaphors are rare. Why? Probably because it's easier to create *fused metaphors*, in which you take the product (or something associated with the product, the way a toothbrush is associated with toothpaste, a comb with hair care products, or the highway with cars) and fuse it with something else.

Unlike pure metaphor, fused images help contextualize the selling argument; viewers don't have to leap quite as far when part of what they're looking at is what's for sale. You catch their attention and demonstrate your selling argument by metamorphosing the product into something new that expresses your selling idea (see fig. 22.4).

22.2. This dust jacket image for Stephen King's *On Writing* seems, at first glance, to have nothing to do with the subject. But the bay window and the cellar door are apt metaphors for writing itself, which, at its best, combines opposites: the rational with the irrational, the conscious with the unconscious, light with dark. Making the door and window part of a home also suggests that the best writing is personal: it comes from inside the self.

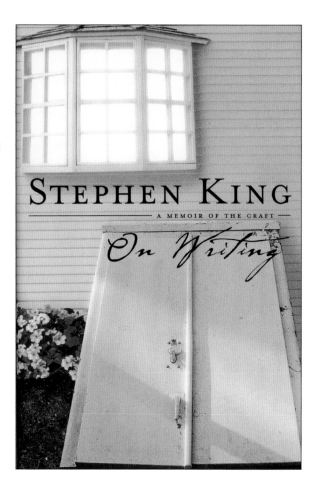

Left

22.3. Traveling toward a destination via GPS serves as a metaphor for something else navigating its way through too many people's lives.

Ⓢ Watch the TV spot itself at fig. W-22.3.

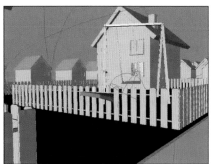

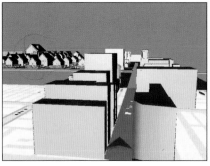

22.4. Many brand identities fuse two aspects of the selling situation. Dogpeople, a maker of food supplements for dogs, brings its principals together; the Mexican restaurant Prickly Pear creates a cactus from a splash of guacamole.

22.5. The fusion of city sign and religious symbol. If too many churches are too remote from urban problems, this one sure isn't. Strong visual positioning.

CHURCH ᴵᴺ ᴛʜᴇ CITY
Contemporary worship Sundays 10 a.m.
2648 North Hackett Avenue.

How to fuse? Get in the habit of looking for latent pairs in whatever advertising problem you're working on; push two things together into one image. For example, if you're selling a home security system for Warner Amex, you could use a house and then metaphorically do something to it. Or you could begin with a lock or barbed wire or an armed guard and then "house-ify" that. A lot of arresting images are really a combination of the product and a metaphor, or of two aspects of the problem (fig. 22.5).

Objects that are "wrong," that have been assaulted or transformed in some way, are attractive to viewers, more so than unmodified ones. Unmodified images are often just clichés. For example, one of David Ogilvy's famous ideas was The Man in the Hathaway Shirt, who wore an eye patch and was thereby more interesting than a man who didn't. He wasn't just the cliché of hunk #73; he was a wounded, brave, singular fellow with a story to tell. Absolut Vodka metamorphosed its bottle in various amusing ways for years: turning it into a swimming pool for "Absolut L.A.," fogging it in for "Absolut San Francisco," blowing off its letters for "Absolut Chicago," and so on. Many other ads gain visual strength from a "what's wrong here?" approach.

Photographer and art director Henry Wolf, famous for his conceptual work for *Esquire, Harper's Bazaar, Show,* and other magazines, worked frequently with metaphors and explained how he thought them through: "The working method that accomplishes these results [shock and surprise] is not easy to quantify. There are two major categories: addition—in which one or more elements are added to an image; and substitution—in which part of an image is replaced by another that does not normally belong with it."[4]

The power of graphic fusion comes from combining two clichés, symbols, or aspects of a situation into one new image. When you're working visually, think in terms of either *addition* (see figs. 22.6–22.11), adding something to an image, or *substitution*, replacing part of an image with something else (figs. 22.12–22.19).

Also when dealing with images, don't be too literal. Try to find metaphors that capture the psychological essence of a problem more than simply its external reality. Let's say that you're developing a poster to announce a seminar in business fundamentals for graphic designers, one called "The Business Primordial." You may start thinking of cavemen and clubs—clubs as felt-tip markers, business cards made out of stone, cavemen dressed in business suits, and so on. In other words, you try to fuse some image of business or graphic arts with some "primordial" image. But you don't have to. A visual of two dogs in a tug of war (a pure metaphor) can also express the psychological essence of basic business difficulties, but less obviously. It's a metaphor off to the side; the dogs symbolize not the thing, but the emotional center of the thing. They're unexpected but appropriate. (See fig. 22.20 for a similarly unusual metaphor.)

WHEN IT'S BUDGET CUTTING TIME, THEY ALWAYS START WITH THE EASIEST TARGETS.

Children can't stand up for themselves. Which makes them an easy mark for politicians when they're cutting back. Give children a voice. Yours. Kids can't vote, but you can. **THE CHILDREN'S DEFENSE FUND**

22.6. The bull's-eye is a simple, clear example of addition. The headline complements, rather than repeats, the visual, and the copy is well written, too. Read it; you'll be moved.

22.7. One little addition visually expresses this beer's name.

22.8. Another example of addition. How do you visually say "a very Italian Italian restaurant"? Why not add a distinctive tilt to the waiter?

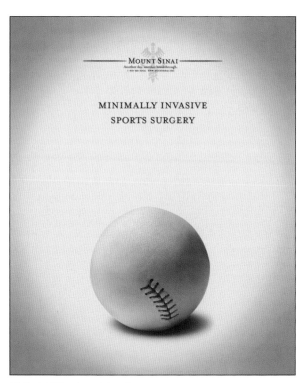

22.9. Addition by subtraction.

22.10. To create interest in Turner Classic Movies, famous film stills were metamorphosed into fuzzy images to suggest film buffs' fuzzy memories of the movies themselves. As the headline put it, "You might need to see it again."

Headline advice for metaphors

Remember, if your visual is loud, then you can speak quietly, as the Grand Canyon library poster did. It didn't scream, "Whole Worlds of Awesome Ideas!" It said simply, "Knowledge is free. Visit your library." So if you shout with the picture, whisper or make a little joke with the words, and vice versa. Don't shout twice.

And, of course, never resay in words what you show in pictures. Marry the headline and the visual. In the Warner Amex home security problem, if you show a house all wrapped up in barbed wire or a great big padlock on the roof, don't shout, "Lock Up Your World With Great Protection!" Readers can see and hear your image. Perhaps show that visual and then say, "Or call Warner Amex." See?

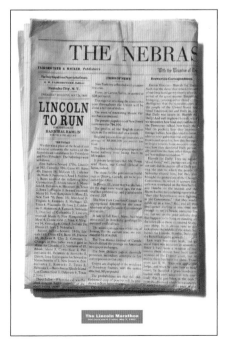

22.11. Every year ad agency Bailey Lauerman creates a poster to announce the Lincoln, Nebraska, marathon, and every year the agency metamorphoses something associated with Lincoln to suggest that Abe himself will be struggling through his namesake race.

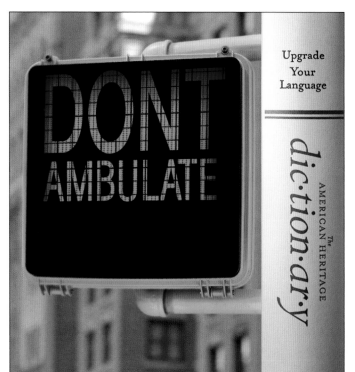 

22.12. Since language surrounds people in both consumer culture and public space, think about substituting new words for the expected ones.

22.13. A terrific visual fusion for a motorcycle café and lounge, don't you think?

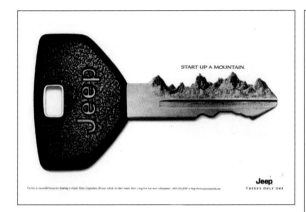

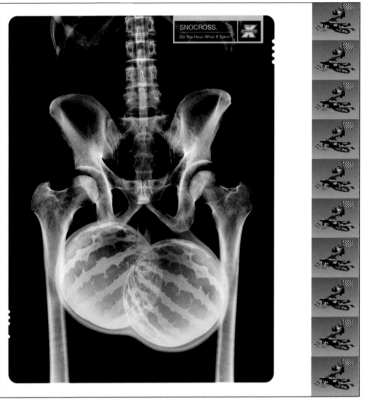

Above and right
22.14. Metaphor as hyperbole.

22.15. This impossible—but delightful—image uses a metaphorical substitution (package replaced by popsicle) and the playful truth of hyperbole to say "fast." (The headline reads, "No one is more express than us," but besides the brand name, who needs words?)

22.16. With the logic of metaphor, ads for Denver Water's conservation program practice what they preach, encouraging people to save water the way the words save letters and the bus bench saves space.

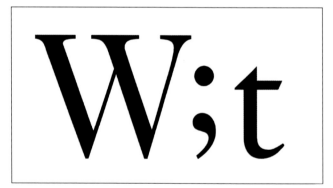

22.17. Logo/title of Margaret Edson's Pulitzer Prize-winning play about a witty English professor (a scholar of John Donne's witty poetry) dying of cancer. The professor takes punctuation seriously as an aspect of literary criticism, and since semicolons are end stops, the mark suggests both her passion and her predicament. Very clever, tight visual idea.

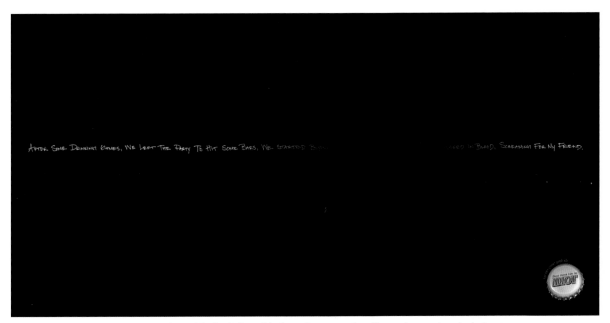

After some drinking games, we left the party to hit some bars, we started b... ...ked in blood, screaming for my friend.

22.18. Type as metaphor, with the fade-to-black analogous to the effects of excessive alcohol consumption. The way the language changes—going into the fade and coming out—is the shocker. The perils of too much drinking haven't been preached against; they've been demonstrated. Other headlines: "It was ladies' night. Everybody was there. We left the bar about 3 in the morning . . . how I got this unicorn tattoo on my butt" and "I met this really cute guy. He was so sweet. We danced and he bought me drinks and . . . with my panties around my ankles." In all the ads, the beer cap says, "Don't drink like an idiot."

22.19. A stunner of an ad, seeing the problem in a new way, both visually and verbally. It's a disturbing image, and that's the point.

22.20. A funny, unexpected way to show how dizzying the fun might be (the amusement park is known for its wild rides). Translating this moment from people to a stuffed toy lightens the circumstance and makes the joke.

23 · Verbal Metaphor

Ideas do not need to be esoteric to be original and exciting. . . . What Cezanne did with apples, Picasso with guitars, Leger with machines, Schwitters with rubbish, and Duchamp with urinals makes it clear that revelation does not depend upon grandiose concepts. The problem of the artist is to defamiliarize the ordinary.

—PAUL RAND, *A Designer's Art*

Ads that people ignore are ones in which nothing seems amiss: expected imagery is accompanied by expected language; nothing is out of place. So consider another way to "defamiliarize the ordinary," to move things out of their clichéd resting places: *verbal metaphor*. Think of verbal metaphor as the opposite side of the metaphor coin. Rather than changing the product visually, change it verbally, by putting it in another language system. Instead of making it "wrong" visually, call it by the "wrong" name.

How the wrong name can be the right one

"Marketing isn't an expense; it's an investment in how the world sees a company."

—LEE CLOW, global director of media arts, TBWA\Worldwide

Clow has just made marketing seem indispensable by renaming it. Not only does verbal metaphor like this gain attention by assigning something the wrong name, it also helps sell a product by elevating it. As an advertiser, you want to reposition products in consumers' minds, make people reimagine those goods and services as more than they might otherwise seem. With verbal metaphor, you can help people see products—and their benefits—at the highest level of possibility, just as Clow did with marketing.

For example, Club Med has called itself "the antidote to civilization." This is metaphor, a comparison between dissimilar things. Literally, Club Med is a vacation service; only metaphorically is it a medicine to counteract poison. But the line works by making a vacation seem like much more than just time off. Similarly, Royal Viking cruise lines has headlined ads, "The 7 day refresher course for those who have forgotten how to live." This is metaphor, too; after all, a cruise vacation is not literally a life-skills course. But both services have given themselves metaphorically appropriate names. They have talked about themselves using language associated with something else or language literally meaning something else. Thus they catch readers' attention, and with the logic of metaphor, they elevate their services in the process. This idea of inviting consumers to reimagine a product is so fundamental to advertising that once you begin to look for verbal metaphor, you will see it everywhere (fig. 23.1).

Metaphor and simile

Even though your high school English teacher may have made these seem like two different things, they're just one: metaphor. Metaphor—talking about one thing in terms of something else—is the main idea; similes are simply a subset, the kinds of metaphor that use "like" or "as." Don't sweat the distinction. Compare your client's product to something dissimilar, and you're making metaphor (see fig. 23.2).

Consider using the following structures to help create verbal metaphor. Then either keep these structures

Clothes are just accessories.
DSW
DESIGNER SHOE WAREHOUSE®

Hot, live gardening action
24 hours a day.

garden.com

SOME SCENES MAY BE
DISTURBING TO VIEWERS.

The Weather Network

23.1. Verbal metaphor is widely used because of its obvious virtues: it's startling, often funny, and quickly and memorably communicates a product benefit. It works well in outdoor advertising because you can say a lot without using many words.

in your headlines, or drop them off, if your meaning is clear without them:

Think of it as _____.
It's like a ____.
It's like a ____ for your ____.
If it were a ____, it would be a ____.

USE PERSONIFICATION

Personification, the giving of animate qualities to inanimate things, is a kind of metaphor: you're talking about one thing in terms of something else. Since people have relationships with products (they actually *love* many of their things), those products are alive, and people might as well admit it. So animate your client's product. Talk about it, or something associated with it, as though it were alive; or let it talk itself or behave as though it were alive:

Safety marries performance. They elope. (Saab)

The following headlines in Crate & Barrel furniture

ads, each showing an elegant piece of furniture, personify elements associated with each item:

Loose change never had it so good. (comfy couch)

Your remote just may decide to stay lost forever. (leather armchair)

Just think of the positive effect it could have on a crumb's self-image. (dining table)

Arouses feelings of intense jealousy among dust bunnies. (French sofa)

See figure 23.3 for another example of personifying an inanimate object.

How to think about verbal metaphor

Shop around in your mind. If you had to call the product something else, what would it be? If you had to compare it to something else, what would it be? An ad for Washington state apples had this headline: "A snack so good, people even eat the wrapper" and this slogan: "The original health food." An outdoor board selling outdoor boards said simply, "Use your outside voice," an unexpected but true connection between people and out-of-home advertising.

How does this thing you're selling work? What does it do? Headline on an ad showing a speeding Porsche: "Kills bugs fast." How does it differ from the competition (fig. 23.4)? What's its highest possible benefit? What does it give people more of—time, power, love, money? (See fig. 23.5 for two more ads whose metaphors make the most of the products.)

Always ask yourself, "What *is* this product?" For example, what *is* a car? Is it an investment? Durability on wheels? A reward for hard work? A mobile home?

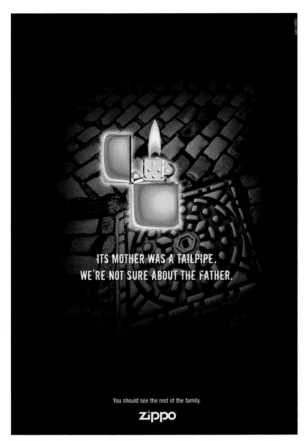

ITS MOTHER WAS A TAILPIPE.
WE'RE NOT SURE ABOUT THE FATHER.

You should see the rest of the family.

zippo

23.3. The headline perfectly captures the rebelliousness of the brand, and since lighters are such a personal item, people can think of them as almost alive.

MADE FRESH DAILY.

FERTILIZER
FROM EXOTIC PLACES.

LET'S JUST KEEP IT AT THAT.

23.4. Funny headlines differentiate Zoop from all those other fertilizers out there.

SINCE THE BEGINNING OF TIME MAN HAS USED TWO STONES TO START A FIRE

DE BEERS
A DIAMOND IS FOREVER

Unclogs major arteries.

Porsche 911 Carrera

(Dealer Name)

Left and above
23.5. Metaphor helps you raise the stakes.

A comment on its owner? An exercise in rationality and sensible spending? (Hyundai outdoor board: "Use your mind more than your money.") Similarly, what's an iPod? A portable concert? A hearing aid? A privacy rite? The rhythm of life? "1,000 songs in your pocket"? Ask yourself, "What is this product doing here? What's its real purpose? What do people go to it for?" (fig. 23.6.)

EXPLOIT LANGUAGE SYSTEMS AND CLICHÉS

Consider whether there are clichés associated with the brand, category, target market, or benefit that you might exploit. What language does the target audience use? For example, Honda has placed "Multiple Choice," "Student Aid," and "Roads Scholar" headlines above its cars in ads aimed at students because a college audience speaks that language. Can you apply a language familiar to the target audience to your client's product (figs. 23.7 and 23.8)?

One quick way to investigate other language systems is to go to websites about whatever system you're considering. If you want to use psychological language, go to mental health or clinical psychology sites, or go to amazon.com and peer inside psychology books. If you want judicial language, go to sites about the law. The Web is the new *Roget's*.

MOVE AROUND

Start with visuals, not words. Imagine the product in various settings and from various angles—from behind, from above, in use, emptied, upside-down, in the driveway, in the showroom, and so on. Often a specific placement, view, or movement of the product will generate a new way to regard it (see figs. 23.9 and 23.10).

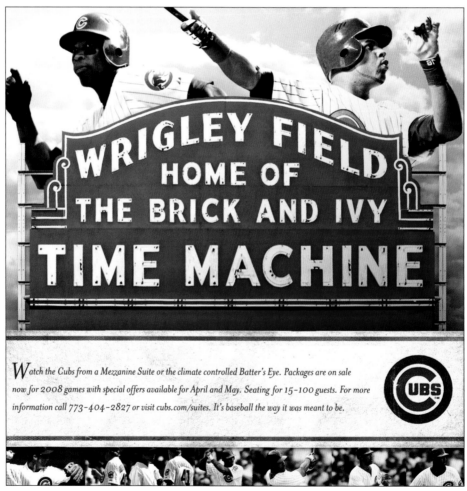

23.6. Chicago's Wrigley Field is an old-fashioned park, and baseball is an old-fashioned game. Watching the Cubs play at Wrigley really is a trip back in time.

23.7. The language of home construction aptly fits the product: customers decide what they want in it, then they get the custom-made product.

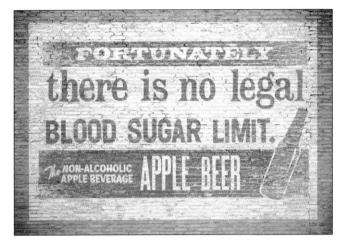

23.8. Apple Beer is discussed in terms associated with alcoholic beer, and that's the fun of it.

23.9. An important part of President Kennedy's administration was the space program and its culmination in a moon landing. A terrific way of re-seeing an image associated with JFK.

23.10. You could say "all natural" or "raised without growth hormones," but starting with this visual is more dramatic and leaves the idea just a little unfinished, giving readers the pleasure of completing the thought.

A COMPLETE LIST OF INGREDIENTS IN AUSTRALIAN RANGE LAMB.

Rename, not the product, but something associated with it (figs. 23.11 and 23.12). As these examples demonstrate, it helps to see through the eyes of the true believer, the core audience, the extreme user. What does he or she think of the product, the competition, or things associated with the product?

As always, consider the opposite of what most ads in the category are doing. If they're zigging, zag (fig. 23.13).

TRY SAYING MORE RATHER THAN LESS

A phrase can sometimes just sit there, inert, little more than a label. So once you rename the product, think about extending the phrase. For example, if you put "dental policy" beside a tube of toothpaste, readers might say, "Yes? So? What about it?" Write sentences, commands, questions. Maybe you'll want to give the new name more context and meaning by making it part of something larger. Consider the implications and circumstances that surround the phrase. The ads

in figure 23.14 all extend the verbal metaphors with which they begin. A car really is a kind of "life insurance," but even more, it delivers a benefit missing from the kind on paper. Similarly, while it's smart to see a YMCA pool as a "fountain of youth," the observation gets smarter if you admit that some work is required. And if a fishing reel is "a metal utensil," so what? Keep going.

REMEMBER THAT THE LONGER THE LEAP, THE STRONGER THE METAPHOR

The farther away the language is from what people expect, the more surprising it is. So if you can pull words in from a long way off, you'll hook your audience harder. The title of Don Henley's greatest hits CD, *Actual Miles*, for example, has been brought in from pretty far away. It's another way of talking about logging lots of tunes and stopping at some point to take stock of them. "Taking Stock" would convey the same idea but wouldn't be as fresh because it's not as much

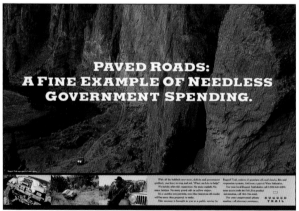

23.11. How to make mundane objects like shock absorbers and weed trimmers interesting? Don't get stuck looking only at the product. Move around. What else is involved? Who are the other players in the drama? What's their point of view?

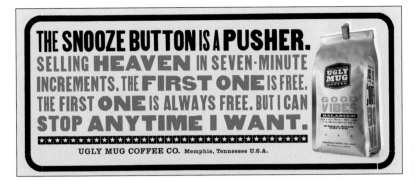

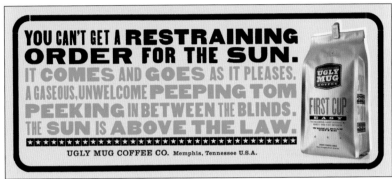

23.12. For people who need coffee to get going in the morning, these aptly describe two of the enemies.

1

2

3

4

23.13. Brilliantly simple TV advertising: don't repeat the cliché of a hot car streaking through city streets; park it and give it a new name. If the voice-over sounds familiar, it's by actor Michael C. Hall (*Dexter*).

Ⓢ See—and more importantly, hear—the TV spot at fig. W-23.13.

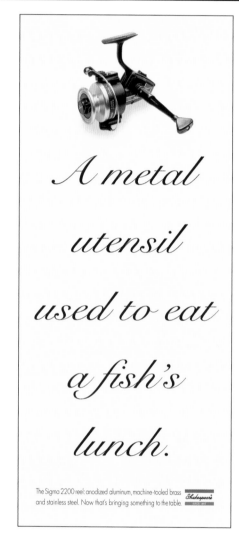

A metal utensil used to eat a fish's lunch.

The Sigma 2200 reel: anodized aluminum, machine-tooled brass and stainless steel. Now that's bringing something to the table.

There is a fountain of youth. You just have to swim laps in it.

Top, left, and above
23.14. Many great headlines do more than rename. Although it's smart to call a Volvo "life insurance," the idea gets even better if you say more. So, too, do the renamings of the swimming pool and the fishing reel.

of a metaphorical leap. "Inventory Clearance" would be negative. There's something, in this culture, almost heroic about lots of highway miles, yet who already thinks of miles as songs? Nice surprise, good title.

The ads in figures 23.15–23.18 gain power and surprise because the copywriters make unusual connec-tions—seeing similarity in very dissimilar things. The surprise of each ad comes from the unexpectedness of the comparison, the audacity of the leap, if you will. Yet once readers think about the connection, they see its appropriateness and feel the selling power of the metaphor.

23.15. A controversial poster whose surprise and shock may just come from its honesty. Where did people think vintage clothing came from?

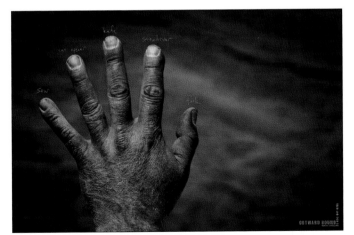

23.16. Outward Bound programs use wilderness survival to teach life lessons. What better way to show ingenuity and self-reliance, the conquering of a new terrain, than by taking that wilderness experience and renaming it?

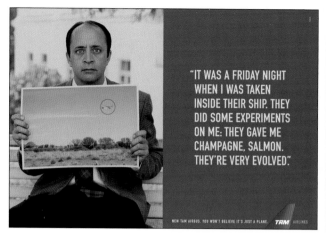
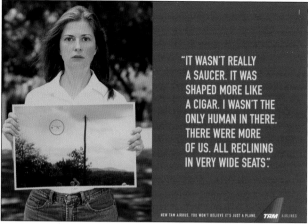

23.17. Once you see something from a new point of view, everything changes. These ads use the tabloid conventions of UFO abduction stories to express the benefits of the new Tam Airbus: "You won't believe it's just a plane." Hilarious and wonderful work.

The lion ![] is the king of beasts, because there are usually more lions than any of the others. He is a light tan color and always faces left. He is sweet and crispy and his rounded shape doesn't hurt your mouth when you eat him. The sheep ![] tastes just like the lion, but he is somewhat taller. Unfortunately, it is hard to find a whole sheep because his thin front legs often break off in transport. Bears ![] are best dipped in milk. You can't soak them in the milk too long, however, as they will get soggy and fall apart. Hippos ![] are usually at the bottom of the box with the sheep's front legs and other assorted crumbs. Hippos just look like blobs from the back; you must see them from the front to even know they're hippos. Zebras ![] too, are light tan like all the others. Their heads are kind of sharp though, which maybe makes them good ones to share with your friends.

It's hard to know what all God's creatures are really like if you can't see them first hand. Wouldn't a zoo in Broward County be great for you and your family? Contribute something, anything, to your educational future. Send your tax deductable contributions to Markham Park Zoo, Box 8844, Oakland Park, Florida 33310. For more information call 472-1976.

Markham
Park Zoo
Broward County Zoological Society

23.18. To encourage the creation of a zoo, the copy explains animals in the endearing, odd, insufficient ways a child would whose only knowledge of them came from animal crackers. As sweet an idea as I've ever seen.

24 · Postmodern Advertising

Any understanding of advertising in American culture must come to grips with the ironic game it plays with us and we play with it. If there are signs that Americans bow to the gods of advertising, there are equally indications that people find the gods ridiculous.

—MICHAEL SCHUDSON,
Advertising, The Uneasy Persuasion

"One peculiar characteristic of advertising is that it creates its own antibodies. One quickly learns, in reading the advertisements of one's own time, to build up automatically an immunity against their persuasions."

—FRANK ROWSOME, JR.,
They Laughed When I Sat Down

What is postmodern advertising?

A lot of the ads in this book might be considered postmodern, and what they're doing—pushing against modernism—you'll often want to do, too. Modernism is, among other things, a belief in rationalism, a demand that form and function coincide. Implicit in modernism is a belief in progress, in creating new and better things.

Postmodernism is what comes after that, and simply within advertising it's a lot of things: an irreverent, I-know-this-is-an-ad attitude; an awareness that people have become increasingly cynical about advertising; an acknowledgement of advertising's past excesses; a critique of consumerism; a return to earlier advertising forms but now with an ironic attitude. Postmodernism is to advertising what David Letterman was to the late night talk show: a subversion of the genre. Dave made fun of being the only thing on NBC (later CBS); stuck his fingers on the camera lens; threw stuff off roofs; baited guests; talked, not to his audience, but to the stage hands; wandered off the set and into the city; in short did any number of things that called at-tention to the artifice and highly mannered thing that was a talk show (much of it a rebellion against the genre's strictures). He not only demanded that viewers pay attention to the man behind the curtain, but he pulled the curtain away himself to reveal that, often enough, no one was there at all. He got past talk show-ness. And all such shows since then have lived on that post-modern circuit. They've had to.

In many ways, advertisers have gotten to the same point with ads. Ads are also highly mannered, artificial things with unspoken assumptions, rules, and various built-in fakenesses. It's become okay—if not ex-pected—that advertisers subvert those rules, get past them. Great ads can, of course, still play it straight, be good modernist stuff. But a lot of great ads bend some-thing, do violence to the expectations inherent in the genre. They start with the assumption that advertis-ing's language and forms have been used up, then go from there.

How to bend an ad

1. Ridicule the product. Traditional advertising thinks its job is to endorse the product. But consum-ers' immunity is such that it may be more effective to call the product's value into question, as do the "slider bar" ads shown in figure 24.1. Alan Russell, chief creative officer, DDB Canada, explains the idea: "TV12 has programming that pretty much appeals to the average couch potato. All the shows are light, fun and entertaining, and we felt that the brand personal-

24.1. Ads can ridicule TV reruns even as they invite viewers to watch them.

ity should reflect that sentiment. We decided 'Truth in Advertising' was the way to go by poking fun at our own product. After all, when was the last time anyone watched Pamela Anderson for the riveting dialogue and profound subtext?"[1]

2. Make fun of the audience. Usually ads tell consumers they're smart for choosing a certain brand, but maybe they've heard that too much (fig. 24.2).

3. Subvert the advertising category or format. If advertising's forms are used up—before and after, comparison and contrast, testimonial, product feature, and so on—then use them ironically (fig. 24.3). Or appropriate the forms of one kind of advertising and apply them to yours. What's an ad for your client's product supposed to look like? Can you use the look of another product's advertising instead (see fig. 24.4)?

4. Speak with tongue in cheek. Since the language of advertising is so worn out it's exhausted, why not joke about it (see figs. 24.5–24.8)?

5. Make old ads new. Find an old form and breathe a new sensibility into it. Remember the ads from your childhood for this thing you're selling? What were their conventions, what was their look? Can you use any of that ironically, spin it, update it? Look at ads from decades past. Go back far enough to be inside another aesthetic or series of assumptions (see fig. 24.9). Can you do anything with what you're seeing?

6. Import material from outside the genre; bring in stuff that's not supposed to be in an ad. Nike did this years ago with Beatle and John Lennon songs, and a seminal Honda scooter TV spot used Lou Reed's "Walk on the Wild Side," both brands creating a new feel and a lot of media buzz. Bass ale has used Franz Kafka and Friedrich Nietzsche as spokespeople. Ads have parodied and manipulated great artwork (Rodin's *The Thinker,* Grant Wood's *American Gothic,* da Vinci's *Mona Lisa,* Michelangelo's Sistine Chapel ceiling), most of these so many times you'd think they'd be worn out, and maybe they are. But lots of things aren't. Get busy. Inspiration can come from anywhere (see fig. 24.10).

7. Call attention to the ad's artifice. Make people notice that it's an ad. Share an understanding with your audience that, yep, they're looking at an ad. Maybe get them to smile about it (see figs. 24.11 and 24.12).

8. Do the opposite: don't look anything like an ad. Despite their best intentions, traditional ads fairly scream, "I'm an ad!" All right, make something

24.2. Ads for an amusement park belittle the consumer (crying and vomiting in search of a good time) while also ironically mimicking the "Having a wonderful time. Wish you were here" postcard tradition that consumers associate with exotic vacation destinations.

24.3. A testimonial that violates expectations. This isn't happy talk from a happy person, testifying to the wonderful things his company can do for the consumer.

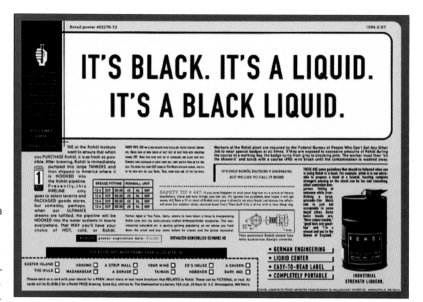

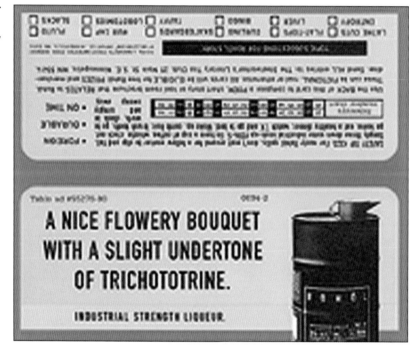

24.4. At first glance, these liquor ads—a poster and a table tent—look like items in an industrial products catalog. The copy, from the "scientists" at the "Rohol Institute," is designed and written to satirize the kinds of injunctions, pronouncements, product specs, and ancillary information that such advertising indulges in. *Rohol* means "crude oil" in German and is a liqueur, meant to be drunk as a shot, so the industrial metaphors and mind-numbed and epicure-mocking headlines make more sense than they appear to at first.

else instead. Since people often hate ads and distrust them, they'll be grateful (see fig. 24.13).

9. Avoid direct, straight-ahead selling, no matter how winsome. Make no sales pitch whatsoever. Since ads are constantly hyping, be mute. Or make an anti-argument for the product (see those Playland ads in fig. 24.2). Or look instead for the odd, perhaps dark, places in people's psyche. Get underneath the pitch to some shared collective space. Help your audience realize that everyone spends time there. Advertising writer Warren Berger and others have

called such ads-beyond-ads "oddvertising."

10. Be deliberately primitive. Since ads have become too "slick," be so dumb it's scary. David Letterman, ambling through what he took to be the shambles of his show, would say, almost amazed, "You know, we're the only thing on NBC right now." He'd perfected the throw-it-all-away attitude that permeated so much of what he did. Okay, throw it all away.

Perhaps the best embodiment of throwing it all away I've ever seen was an E*Trade ad created by Goodby, Silverstein & Partners for the 2000 Super

24.5. Making fun of advertising's "money back guarantee" works well for a parachute center. Flippancy bonds the center with daredevils, exactly the people most likely to exit a plane at altitude. Great first line of copy, too: "We're kidding of course. You would have to pay."

Below center, left and right
24.6. One ad's headline satirizes the ubiquitous advertising claim "New!" while telling the literal truth. The other offers up a common advertising disclaimer, this time with tongue in cheek.

Left
24.7. Adland clichés of overpromise are parodied but in a voice just dumb enough to be a true beer drinker's. This ad gets readers coming and going.

24.8. Chipotle plays with the pop culture myth of "subliminal advertising" in which powerful, persuasive messages were supposedly hidden inside ads.

24.9. These ads invoke the language and style of the old-fashioned banners at fairs. They make readers smile while piquing their interest in the genuine oddity of these creatures from beneath the sea.

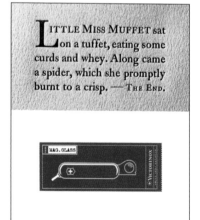

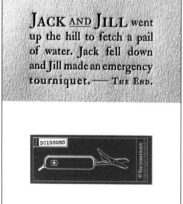

24.10. Nursery rhymes are an unlikely source for Swiss Army Knife ads, but not if you rewrite them. Here the old-time letterpress/literary look is undercut by the rewrite. The ads look one way, talk another. The format says old, sweet, harmless, cute; but the voice is tougher, hipper, more of a wise guy. Nice contrast.

Bowl. Into the middle of all those expensively produced, extravagant TV ads came a spot showing two guys in a garage clapping for a chimp dancing to boom box music. That was it. Thirty seconds of a chimp dancing and guys clapping. It closed with, "Well, we just wasted two million dollars. What are you doing with your money?" It was a wonderfully, awesomely crude ad, especially given its Super Bowl context. And one that couldn't have made more sense: yes, they *did* just waste two million dollars, and, come to think of it, what *was* I doing with my money?

Does postmodern advertising work?

A lot of people argue that the techniques described in this chapter are quickly seen by consumers as just another pitch—this time, the clever anti-pitch pitch. So rather than forming new relationships among consumers, their choices, and the ways they understand those choices, these ads just work the old routes, albeit more cleverly. Many people also wonder how far off a sales pitch an advertiser can drift and still be selling anything. People may be amused and di-

verted, but if they're not also buying, then these techniques aren't working. As ad critic James B. Twitchell says, "What happens to advertising when it loses its grip on the product and becomes just another form of entertainment event is that it ceases to sell."[2]

But from another point of view, ads use these techniques because they have to. Postmodern attitudes and assumptions have become part of consumers' cultural mindset. They form the world consumers live in now. Wieden + Kennedy's Dan Wieden explains:

Consumers today not only know they're being marketed to—they're actually judging how well it's being done. It's like when Toto pulls the curtain back: everybody knows the wizard is just that little guy back there with the machine. So it requires a freshness for the work to be effective now. It's not as simple as focus groups and philosophical formulas anymore. At the end of the day there has to be some fresh look . . . or something that jars your perspective and lets you see things from a different angle.[3]

24.11. The small-space ad sections in the back of magazines provide the perfect place for a small-car ad, especially if it's hip enough to have fun with where it finds itself.

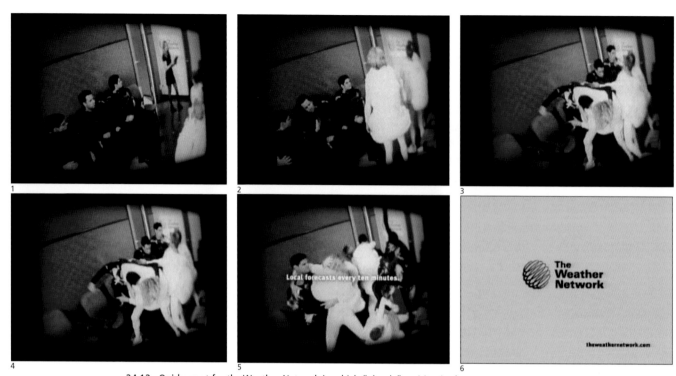

1 2 3

4 5 6

24.12. Quirky spot for the Weather Network in which "clouds" waiting in the green room to go on TV end up in a shoving match—the dark, stormy clouds picking a fight with those gentle cumulus people. The casting director at first says, "Call for Cumulus Clouds. White Cumulus Clouds." But as they get up, she quickly reverses herself: "Sorry. Make that Dark Rain Clouds. Call for Dark Rain Clouds." While the two sets of clouds jostle, a super reads, "Local forecasts every 10 minutes."

This campaign sees its product as a TV station whose performing personalities are the weather itself. As in much postmodern advertising, viewers are being taken backstage; they share in watching the spots create themselves. Characters in other spots include Heavy Snow, three fat guys in white suits who like to fall on top of one another in a big pile, and Freezing Rain, a fellow in a slicker who slips and slides so much he can't stay on camera.

To see all four TV spots, go to fig. W-24.12.

24.13. This magazine-insert ad is a flattened "milk carton," and consumers are invited to pop it open, shake it for their spouse to show that it's empty, and hop in the MINI for a trip to the grocery—a good excuse for some motoring. It's fun to contemplate this idea, and I don't feel pitched to. I smile when I think of the MINI now. Not bad advertising, after all.

25 · Human Truth

You can teach a monkey to write the body copy for an ad. But I can't teach anybody to think. Writing has to be in touch with humanity. There has to be a humanness to it, something that reaches people.
—ED McCABE, co-founder,
Scali, McCabe, Sloves

Advertising is not about being clever; it's about finding a truth that connects the product to the user.
—WAYNE BEST, creative director,
Kirshenbaum Bond + Partners

Any great ad has a simplicity about it, a sense of inevitability, of an idea found very nearby ("Why didn't I think of this?") that makes it great. If you pick the ad up and shake it, it doesn't rattle. There's nothing complicated, extraneous, or superfluous about it. No extra moving parts. It's simple, often funny, true—and it works. It feels found as much as invented. Get in the habit, especially when your thinking has led you (as it so often leads all copywriters) into increasingly obscure and complicated solutions, solutions that still feel wrong and make no sense when you show them to other people—get in the habit of backing out and starting over. Be simple. Find the basic human truth.

"Raise the obvious to the conscious"

This is Wieden + Kennedy art director Todd Waterbury's advice.[1] Locate the obvious things consumers think and say and know about the product, product category, brand, even their habits with it, and write them down. Chances are that one of these things is, or with slight modification could become, your solution. That's what Waterbury means by "raise the obvious to the conscious," and it's excellent advice.

"Got milk?" is probably as pure an example of his advice as you can find. It's something people ask without even thinking, but it says everything: people don't miss milk until they don't have any, and they need it for lots of things—cookies, cereal, sandwiches, the kids,

the cat, and so on (see fig. 25.1). Jeff Goodby explains how his agency arrived at this idea:

If we had started with the idea of milk as a glass of milk you drink alone, we would have ended up addressing the health benefits or the nostalgia of milk. Exactly as had been done in previous campaigns. Exactly wrong. We looked for the truth about milk. We asked people to go without milk for 2 weeks. "Sure, no problem," they said. They came back and told us how hard it was. What else goes with cereal? What are you going to do with a fresh-baked chocolate chip cookie? We arrived at the truth: Milk is never just milk. It is always _____ and milk. Milk as accompaniment. After that, everything fell into place.[2]

QUESTIONS TO HELP YOU FIND HUMAN TRUTHS

"We try to find that long-neglected truth in a product and give it a hug."
—ALEX BOGUSKY, co-founder,
Crispin Porter + Bogusky

1. What do people say to themselves and each other about your client's product category or brand? What do people all notice but never remark on? What has your own inner speech been saying to you? (See figs. 25.2 and 25.3.)

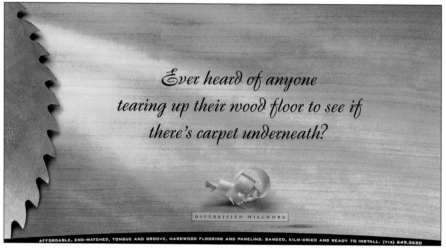

Top to bottom

25.1. When you need it, you really need it.

25.2. This is another truth that lies right below conscious thought, a truth that when spoken, makes people smile in recognition—and value wood floors even more.

25.3. Comedian Steven Wright has built his career on noticing absurdist truths like this.

25.4. A clever way to tie a low fare airline to a truth everyone has either experienced or wished for.

WE'D TELL YOU TO CALL ABOUT THE JOB, BUT NO ONE WOULD ANSWER.

Downtown ad agency needs a receptionist. Bad. Call Shay at 436-9400 to apply.

SEE DISTANT RELATIVES.
SAVE ENOUGH TO STAY IN A HOTEL.

Sun Country Airlines®

A celebrated example from advertising history comes from Doyle Dane Bernbach's work for Chivas Regal Scotch whisky. When the company changed the traditional bottle from dark green to clear and simplified the antique label, an exasperated copywriter said, "What idiot changed the Chivas Regal bottle?" and William Bernbach said, "*That's* the headline!"[3]

When Nike was about to introduce Shox running shoes, whose heels had visible springs, someone at Nike's ad agency, Wieden + Kennedy, looked at the shoe prototype and said, "Oh, boing!" Thus was born the onomatopoetic "Boing" campaign, with that sound serving as the theme line as well as the entire soundtrack of one memorable TV spot in which a stampede of runners "boing" across the screen.[4]

2. Are there any myths or urban legends or other pop culture assumptions surrounding your

```
If other banks
are all about trust,

why are their pens
attached to chains?
```

For banking built on relationships, 952-431-4700.

MIDWAY BANK

Member FDIC

25.5. Ever think of this? Why not? It's been right in front of you for years.

COMFORTABLE SEATS, FRIENDLY ATTENDANTS, CHOCOLATE CHIP COOKIES. WHAT IS THIS, **AN AIRLINE AD?** THE **BLOOD CENTER**

25.6. This ad finds a joke right there for the taking.

Day three: omelets and chocolate sauce.

Oregon. Things look different here.

25.7. When people go camping, sooner or later they're eating what's left—and enjoying it. Raising the obvious to the conscious, sharing human truths, is a powerful way to connect your client's brand with its audience.

They'll match everything in your ROOMMATE'S closet.

Wrangler
k h a k i s

Real. Comfortable. Pants.

Finals start next week.

Time to buy your books.

2338 Guadalupe
2410-B E.Riverside Dr.

Above, left and right

25.8. I don't know about your college roommates, but one of mine had great ties. I might still have a couple.

25.9. How do students really approach college courses? This ad knows.

25.10. Getting people interested in science may be as simple as pointing out its ubiquity and their ignorance.

CONNECT CULTURE

IS THIS THE ONLY TIME YOU THINK ABOUT SCIENCE?

ARTS & SCIENCE COUNCIL

Connect with culture. When you donate to ASC, you allow everyone to be exposed to arts, science and history in ways they never were before. Imaginations run wild. Creativity blossoms. New ideas abound. You'll find science on your mind. And not only at times like this.   www.artsandscience.org

client's product? Any unspoken negatives? (See figs. 25.4 and 25.5.)

3. What's always part of the situation? What are the at-hand visuals and language that stick like Post-it notes to the product category, the product's competitors, or the brand? (See figs. 25.6 and 25.7.)

4. How do people really use the product? What habits are associated with using the product? An AirTran print ad invited people to fly to South Carolina for a golf vacation with this human truth:

"Lose golf balls in unfamiliar trees." (See also figs. 25.8–25.10.)

An ad campaign for Kleenex tissues, "Let It Out and Feel Better For It," came from an obvious but unspoken truth: tissues aren't just for colds and sneezes. People have emotions; they cry, wipe away tears, and just generally feel things, enough so that they often reach for a tissue. So tissues aren't about control; they're about release. For a guerrilla element in the campaign, Kleenex placed interviewers, with sofas and chairs, out on city streets where the interviewers invited passersby to sit down and chat about their lives. These interviews were filmed and turned into TV spots, and in them viewers could see people crying, laughing, hugging—and reaching for a Kleenex. They were letting out their emotions and feeling better for doing so. It was an unusual campaign but an obvious human truth—and it was astute of Kleenex to claim it. Don't use tissues to tidy up or stifle your feelings; use them to let those feelings out. You'll *feel* better. Good benefit, smart campaign.

As you're searching for insights like that one, write down all the truths about your client's product or brand that you can—not adland too-good-to-be-true stuff, but real things that surround what you're selling. Develop a long, honest list of stuff about the product, the brand, the situation, the consumers. Now, which items suggest directions for an ad campaign? Are there headlines lurking? Find the strongest, most resonant human truths and make them visible. Watch people smile with recognition (fig. 25.11).

Aim for the heart

> "There is a road from the eye to the heart that does not go through the intellect."
>
> —G.K. CHESTERTON, essayist and novelist

Lots of ads are clever, witty, funny, spun out of a brainy place. And they work, they're good. But think of all the people in your target audience—they don't just appreciate brainy; they've got hearts, too. If you can hang your product on the line between all those people and their feelings, between the members of that target audience and those they love, if you can find the center of a relationship and suspend your product from the invisible wires between, say, a grandfather and a grandson, between best friends, between people and their pets, between people and whatever feelings are associated with your product, then you have found your audience's heart. You've placed your product right on what matters in their lives, and by extension you've made the product matter because you've gotten it all tangled up in how they feel. It's part of what brings them their emotional daily bread.

> "I begin from the heart, not the mind. The heart is much easier to talk to."
>
> —P. J. PEREIRA, founder and creative director, AgenciaClick, Sao Paulo

25.11. A truth everyone has experienced, Cubs game or not: mixing business with pleasure is an unnatural act.

The following copy, from the De Beers "A diamond is forever" campaign, illustrates my point:

> Because she believes
>   dogs have souls
>   and angels have wings.
> Because she gave
>   nine months of her life
>   to watching someone grow.
> Because she named him
>   after me.
>
> Diamonds.
> Just because you love her.

You're working on a little lump in your throat, and you know it. That's good. See figure 25.12 for another ad that knows where your heart is.

Need another example? Let's consider Father's Day and the ever-popular but oh-so-boring gift: the watch. Father's Day obviously has emotional content, but watches don't. However, when you read the following copy, you'll see that an ad for a watch can really be all about how much you love that guy who is Dad. Somehow a watch becomes part of your love:

25.12. As strong as a logical appeal might be ("quit because smoking will kill you"), it would feel weak beside this one.

Ⓢ For another ad in this campaign, go to fig. W-25.12.

Headline:

Didn't ground you for shaving the dog's butt.

Visual:

Dad carrying son on his shoulders.

Copy:

Made you nutritious fish sticks and ice cream dinners. Let you sit on his lap and drive. Gave you CliffsNotes version of "Birds & Bees" speech. Snuck you first sip of brewski. Participated in the Great Cherry Bomb Mailbox Cover Up. Rode in death seat after you got your learner's permit, on third go round.

Dad. After all he's done for you. Getting him something great for Father's Day is the least you could do. At Watch Station you'll find over a thousand of the latest styles from names like Skagen. Call 1-888-22WATCH for a location near you. And while you're at it, it wouldn't kill you to pick up the telephone and call home once in a while.

Every detail about Dad as co-conspirator is specific and singular; none sounds off-the-rack. Although my father didn't have to cover up a cherry bomb prank, he covered up enough other stupid stuff I did. So, I'm betting, did yours. The copy's particulars speak to universals and show the power of drawing truths from one's own life. The copywriter was thinking of times that Dad's love really came through, and no doubt some of these details are taken from his own life.

Use *your* real life. It works. As Mark Fenske puts it, "Your fear of exposing what seems embarrassingly ordinary about your life denies your audience the only real story it wants. If two files were laid on your desk, one marked 'confidential' and the other one 'unconfidential,' which would you read?"[5]

26 • Grace Notes

Wit is a delight. Be delightful when you can.
—Peggy Noonan, *On Speaking Well*

One beauty of being a copywriter is that you have all kinds of chances to improve the life around you. You've got big projects whose truths you can make interesting. But you've got countless small moments that you can bring wit and distinction to, and I hope you will.

Here is one such tiny moment. It's the top category of giving on a donation card for a nonprofit organization, in this case Thurber House. There are such traditional, expected terms for these categories ("Benefactor," "Sustainer") that it may never occur to a copywriter to surprise and please potential donors here, but Thurber House did so by calling its highest level of giver "Godsend." Sweet, funny, and true. It's just one little word on a card, but it helps people feel the spirit behind the organization and invites them to share in it.

Here's another small moment that could have been perfunctory and boring—a "website under construction" page (see fig. 26.1). The agency could have said exactly that and shown a crane, yellow tape, or orange barrels. Everyone has seen such pages. To everyone's delight, this agency does better.

There are many places in people's lives where they expect to see the same tired thing and too often find it. As a writer, you can do something about that. An open/closed sign on an art museum's front door doesn't have to be boring (see fig. 26.2). Business cards are often handsomely designed but rarely say more than the name and title of the person, contact information, and maybe the company's slogan. Why can't the words on these cards be more arresting? The advertising agency Crispin Porter + Bogusky took that question to heart,

not only on its business cards but also on its letterhead and envelopes (see fig. 26.3).

Sometimes hardware stores give out yardsticks with their name and phone number. In figure 26.4, a hardware store invokes that tradition but takes the opportunity to do something more interesting, and more brand differentiating.

As you and I know, surfing the Web can occupy huge chunks of time. Just roaming around an interesting site can consume hours. MINI Cooper comes to the rescue. After a visitor has been on its site for a while, an alert box pops up:

> Sorry to interrupt, but haven't you been in front of this computer long enough? We here at MINI are worried you're not getting enough exposure to the sun and stars. Don't worry, we'll be here all week. So, get going. Save your retinas for the road.

Charming and unexpected. I like MINIs more than I did before reading it.

Whenever you write something for a client, ask yourself if you can make it more interesting, more fun, more quirky than it has to be. "Plus it," as an advertising friend of mine says, inventing a verb. Go beyond the expected.

It's possible to make anything good, even everyday exchanges between company and consumer. J. Peterman, the purveyor of exotic goods from distant lands, had a blow-in card in one of its catalogs inviting readers to send the catalog to their friends. Peterman was trolling for new business, new names for the mailing-

26.2. The meaning of "open" changes, and readers are surprised into a smile. A pun that meets the definition of good advertising: effective surprise.

26.1. A Web page that's better than most pages *not* under construction. It also says a lot about who works there, how they think, and, by implication, what they might be able to do for me if I were a client.

26.3. Copywriters bring whimsy to this ad agency's materials and keep it fresh by creating many variants: One of the business cards explains how the rounded edge is "25% safer," while the other says what people really do with such cards. This letterhead invites users to remember the "mighty tree" from which it came and the "little woodland creatures" it shaded, and another letterhead admits that while the page is "too compact for novellas, diatribes and manifestos, . . . we shall continue working on it." This envelope's copy discusses the art of flap licking and how to improve it; another envelope likens itself to "the ancient art of origami" and the "pouch of a kangaroo."

This business card is designed to distribute information of a professional nature. But we know that it will be used from time to time to distribute more personal information. Like a phone number written in lipstick. Or a hotel room number slipped into the hand. Hopefully, some of you will use it for something a bit more wholesome like a bookmark or to make your bike sound like a motorcycle. That would be a dream come true. As a matter of fact, if anybody ever uses our cards and some clothes pins to make their bicycle sound like a motorcycle please write us and let us know at:

Steve Sapka
Manager, Agency Communications
3390 Mary Street, Office 300
Miami, FL 33133
T: 305.646.7363 F: 305.854.3419
ssapka@cpbgroup.com

For reasons known only to the designer, this business card has one rounded corner. As a result, it stands to reason that it is 25% safer than most other business cards. We must admit that we know of no conclusive study into business-card-related injuries. But we imagine if such a study were to be done, the results would convince a lot more companies to take the time to round the corners of their business cards. Until then we can only caution you against taking any business card from any organization that doesn't have the common decency to take the necessary precautions to protect you.

Barbara Alonso
Agency Communications Coordinator
3390 Mary St., Office 300
Miami, Fl 33133
T: 305.646.7379 F: 305.854.3419
balonso@cpbgroup.com

This is official Crispin Porter + Bogusky letterhead. At one time this piece of paper was part of a mighty tree, providing shade for friendly woodland creatures. In an effort to remember our fallen friend, why not take a moment and use this sheet to block the harsh fluorescent rays that fill your office. And while you're at it, would making a few happy chipmunk sounds kill you? Remember, it's for the tree.
3390 Mary St., Office 300, Miami, FL 33133 Tel: 305.859.2070 Fax: 305.854.3419 cpbgroup.com

Most envelope flaps are in the shape of a triangle. And as anybody who has licked an envelope can tell you, trying to make that corner with your tongue can be tricky. Lots of folks don't even try anymore. This means a time-wasting "double lick." The envelope companies told us that it had always been this way. But that wasn't good enough for our scrappy team of designers. Their refusal to accept the status quo led to the development of the revolutionary square flap. And a competitive advantage many organizations can only dream about. How much time and money could this possibly save, you ask? Who knows. But rest assured we'll pass the savings on to you.
Crispin Porter + Bogusky 3390 Mary St., Office 300, Miami, FL 33133

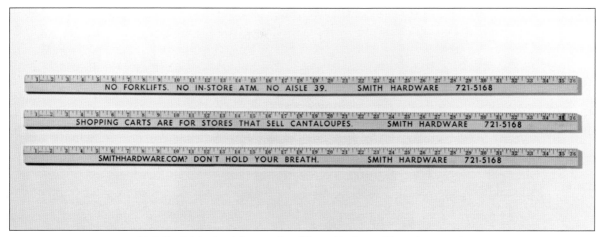

26.4. Yardsticks that bring a smile while positioning Smith Hardware as the antidote to big box madness. They're hip and nostalgic at the same time.

list database. If you were writing this card, you could have said, "Would your friends like our catalog?" But Peterman showed a picture—exotic, tinted—of two turbaned people, sitting side by side, from who knows when or where, and said, "There's nobody else like you in the world. Or is there?" (fig. 26.5). Very winning little moment that played off the brand image (exotica from elsewhere), flattered readers, and invited them in that very moment to name their best friends. I'm more inclined to pause over that than over a straightforward card. You too?

Even something as simple as a sign in a store can avoid the perfunctory. Instead of saying the usual, "Please don't leave your child unattended," a coffee shop spiked the message: "Unattended children will be given an espresso and a free puppy."

A press release isn't a little thing, but because a press release has an accepted format, you might think there's nothing to do except follow it—to say who, what, where, when, and maybe why and let it go at that. But good writers improve the form. Doug Dolan of the Toronto design firm Viva Dolan wrote a press

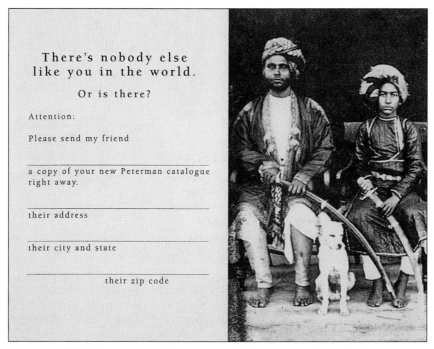

26.5. You can always do more than what's expected, and you should.

release announcing a new destination among a client's travel packages, a trip to Cuba (fig. 26.6). He ultimately covered the who, what, where, and whens, but watch how he started out. He wanted to make sure his readers stuck around for the details.

Getting beyond ads

Work you do for a client that consumers see is a form of advertising, and these "touch points" are everywhere.

So your opportunities to do good work for your clients while providing consumers with grace, wit, even beauty, are everywhere, too.

For a succinct expression of this larger idea of advertising, consider the following copy. I found it on the website for Crispin Porter + Bogusky. It's part of the agency's employee handbook. CP+B is talking to its own people, but all copywriters should take what it says to heart:

Butterfield & Robinson

CONTACT
Press Relations
1-800-678-1147 or (416) 864-1354
www.butterfield.com

GETTING INTO CUBA

B&R's new biking trip winds from Old Havana, through sugar plantations and colonial towns, to beaches on the Caribbean

Toronto, Canada — How do you find out what Cuba is really like? You could buy tapes of Fidel's five-hour speeches and play them in the car. Or mix a pitcher of daiquiris and watch Robert Redford in *Havana.* Or put on a Buena Vista Social Club CD and light up a Cohiba (that's sounding better).

Or you could do something truly radical and join the hundreds of thousands of North Americans who visit Cuba each year. But to immerse yourself fully in this warm, vibrant, hospitable, sometimes controversial island, you can't stay in one of the resort compounds along the coast. You have to explore cobbled streets, colonial plantations and untouched beaches on your own terms — on the new Cuba Biking Expedition from Butterfield & Robinson, the leader in luxury active travel around the globe.

70 Bond Street
Toronto, Ontario
Canada M5B 1X3
1-800-678-1147
www.butterfield.com

26.6. The world is littered with press releases. To get people to read yours, you've got to hook them, then reel them in. The first two paragraphs of this press release show how wit, detail, and an unexpected opening can do just that.

WHY THE WORD ADVERTISING DOES NOT APPEAR ON YOUR BUSINESS CARD

Every person here and every client we have needs to be aware that while the ad that runs Monday is important and will get done, what's arguably more important is the stuff that orbits around the advertising. Like the message on the company voice mail. The line we spray paint on the sidewalk outside the industry convention. The T-shirt we mail to every employee. The wacked idea for a great new product. The bumper sticker every customer gets handed to them on a certain day. The cool new website home page. The letter to every member of Congress petitioning for a new national holiday. This is how brands are built now.[1]

As your work stretches beyond ad copy, as almost everything really does become an ad, it will bring with it an even greater responsibility to both client and consumer. For the client, you're entrusted with interpreting its brand in new ways. You're there to help deliver meaning across an array of media, developing and deepening relationships with consumers. And those relationships are a lot like marriage: both partners better be happy, or someone will be moving on.

To an audience already weighted down with sponsored messages—every American is exposed to 3,500 ads per day, according to one recent estimate[2]—you're about to make the load 3,501 and counting. You're taking up time, or asking for it, from people already bearing up under too much visual and verbal noise, too many choices, too much muchness. What's more, you'll be invading their lives in ways traditional ads haven't.

Respecting your audience has always been an advertising principle. As David Ogilvy said so long ago, "The consumer isn't a moron; she is your wife."[3] As Rich Silverstein of Goodby, Silverstein & Partners said not so long ago, "We once had a debate—should we put 'advertising' on our business cards? No, because we don't want to be doing advertising. I'd never hire a person who 'does advertising.' We do communications. It's a way to move people. Make them think, laugh, cry. We like to treat the public with respect. We try to make advertising smart, intellectual."[4]

Now, in moving beyond advertising, you need not only to understand your client better than before but also to value your audience more—appreciate people's hectic lives, their constraints of time and interest, their desire for authentic, useful relationships. To add more crap to a system already waist deep in it becomes unconscionable.

Grace is in order.

ENDNOTES

CHAPTER 2: Researching Your Client's Product

1. William Bernbach, quoted in Marya Dalrymple, ed., *Is the Bug Dead? The Great Beetle Ad Campaign* (New York: Stewart, Tabori & Chang, 1983), 8–9.

2. Thomas Hine, *The Total Package* (Boston: Little, Brown, 1995), 269.

3. Gerry Graf, discussing the campaign in Teressa Iezzi, *The Idea Writers* (New York: Palgrave Macmillan, 2010), 88–89.

4. Mig Reyes, "Get Miggy With It" (presentation), Columbus Society of Communicating Arts, Columbus, Ohio, June 16, 2011.

5. Alex Bogusky and John Winsor, *Baked In: Creating Products and Businesses That Market Themselves* (Chicago: Agate, 2009), 54.

6. Theodore Levitt, *The Marketing Imagination*, expanded ed. (New York: Free Press, 1986), 81–84.

7. Ibid., 159.

8. Claude Hopkins, *My Life in Advertising & Scientific Advertising* (Lincolnwood, IL: NTC Business Books, 1991), 79.

9. Ernie Schenck, "The Story According to Schenck," *One. A Magazine*, Spring 1998, 8.

CHAPTER 3: Understanding Consumer Behavior

1. Theodore Levitt, *The Marketing Imagination*, expanded ed. (New York: Free Press, 1986), 76.

2. Based on Hierarchy of Needs from "A Theory of Human Motivation" in Abraham H. Maslow, *Motivation and Personality*, 3rd ed., revised by Robert Frager, James Fadiman, Cynthia McReynolds, and Ruth Cox. © 1954, 1987 by Harper & Row, Publishers, Inc. © 1970 by Abraham H. Maslow. Reprinted by permission of HarperCollins, Publishers, Inc.

3. Laura Fegley, "Finding Meaning Beyond Funny," *One. A Magazine*, Summer 2010, 15.

4. Robert B. Settle and Pamela L. Alreck, *Why They Buy: American Consumers Inside and Out* (New York: Wiley, 1986), 24–27.

5. Casey Priest, quoted in Peg Tyre, "Clean Freaks," *Newsweek*, June 7, 2004, 43.

CHAPTER 4: Analyzing the Marketplace

1. The following discussion of segmentation categories is drawn from Art Weinstein, *Market Segmentation* (Chicago: Probus, 1987), 44–47 and 108–27.

2. See Joel R. Evans and Barry Berman, *Principles of Marketing*, 2nd ed. (New York: Macmillan, 1988), 72–79.

3. Robert B. Settle and Pamela L. Alreck, *Why They Buy: American Consumers Inside and Out* (New York: Wiley, 1986), 292.

4. Fred Pfaff, "Levi's Dockers Weigh into Casuals," *Adweek's Marketing Week*, September 24, 1990, 26–27.

5. The following discussion is drawn from Gary Armstrong and Philip Kotler, *Marketing: An Introduction*, 5th ed. (Upper Saddle River, NJ: Prentice Hall, 2000), 191–94.

6. "The Hearts of New-Car Buyers," *American Demographics*, August 1991, 14–15.

7. Theodore Levitt, *The Marketing Imagination*, expanded ed. (New York: Free Press, 1986), 129.

CHAPTER 5: Defining Strategic Approaches

1. Jack Trout and Al Ries, *Marketing Warfare* (New York: NAL, 1986), 66.

2. Gary Knutson, quoted in Jim Johnston, "Howard, Merrell & Partners," *Communication Arts*, May/June 1993, 69.

3. John Hegarty, quoted in Warren Berger, *Advertising Today* (New York: Phaidon, 2001), 197.

4. Jack Trout and Al Ries published a three-part series on positioning in Advertising Age (April 24, May 1, and May 8, 1972), and put it all in a book, *Positioning: The Battle for Your Mind* (New York: McGraw-Hill, 1981).

5. Henry Louis Gates, Jr., "Annals of Marketing: Net Worth," *New Yorker*, June 1, 1998, 48.

6. Alex Bogusky and John Winsor, *Baked In: Creating Products and Businesses That Market Themselves* (Chicago: Agate, 2009), 130–31.

7. Trout and Ries, *Marketing Warfare*, 68–69.

8. Bogusky and Winsor, *Baked In*, 140.

9. David Ogilvy, *Ogilvy on Advertising* (New York: Random House, 1985), 14.

10. Lee Clow, quoted in Eleftheria Parpis, "Creative," *Adweek*, March 10, 1997, 28.

11. Dan Wieden, quoted in Joan Voight and Eleftheria Parpis, "Where Did the Magic Go?," *Adweek*, June 22, 1998, 30.

12. Eric Spiegler, quoted in "Our People," O'Leary and Partners, Advertising and Public Relations, http://www.adagency.com/index.html (accessed October 26, 2011).

13. George W. S. Trow, *Within the Context of No Context* (Boston: Little, Brown, 1981), 8.

14. Jeff DeJoseph, quoted in Barbara Lippert, "Attitude Unbecoming," *Brandweek*, October 7, 1996, 38.

15. Rosser Reeves, *Reality in Advertising* (New York: Knopf, 1961), 82–83.

CHAPTER 6: Developing the Creative Brief

1. Norman Berry, "Norman Conquest" (interview), in *Creative Leaders Advertising Program* (New York: Wall Street Journal, 1991), 7.

2. Bill Westbrook, quoted in Mill Roseman, "Bill Westbrook," *Communication Arts*, March/April 1991, 51.

3. Tom Kelley (presentation), Columbus College of Art & Design, Columbus, Ohio, October 27, 2009.

4. See Lisa Hickey, *Design Secrets: Advertising: 50 Real-Life Projects Uncovered* (Gloucester, MA: Rockport, 2002), 30–33.

5. Mike Howard, "Mike Howard/Creative," http://www.mikehowardcreative.com/?p=243 (accessed July 8, 2012).

6. See Warren Berger, "Creative Campaigns of the Year," *Graphis Advertising 98* (New York: Graphis, 1997), 12–13.

7. Graceann Bennett (presentation), Retail Advertising & Marketing Association's Action Taker Series, "Make Your Mark," Columbus College of Art & Design, Columbus, Ohio, October 17, 2007.

8. Evan Fry, quoted in Teressa Iezzi, *The Idea Writers* (New York: Palgrave Macmillan, 2010), 88.

9. Roseman, "Bill Westbrook," 51.

10. Christopher Cole, e-mail to author, October 18, 2004.

11. Creative brief for Diamonds Direct courtesy of Christopher Cole. Written by Christopher Cole and Kim Portrate. The campaign was created at Chuck Ruhr Advertising by Christopher Cole, art director, and Mark Wegwerth, copywriter.

12. David Fowler, *The Creative Companion* (New York: Ogilvy & Mather, 2003), 6.

13. Creative brief formats from Goodby, Silverstein & Partners and The Richards Group courtesy of Steve Stone, founding partner, Black Rocket (now Heat). For more about Goodby's approach, see Jon Steel, *Truth, Lies & Advertising* (New York: Wiley, 1998), 152–88.

CHAPTER 7: Telling Stories

1. E. M. Forster, *Aspects of the Novel* (New York: Harcourt Brace & Company, 1927), 86.

2. Joseph M. Campbell, *The Hero with a Thousand Faces* (Princeton, NJ: Princeton University Press, 1968), 30.

3. Robert McKee, *Story* (New York: HarperCollins, 1997), 196–97.

4. Ronald Hambleton, *The Branding of America* (Dublin, NH: Yankee, 1987), 61–63.

5. David Fowler, *The Creative Companion* (New York: Ogilvy & Mather, 2003), 22.

6. Tom Himpe, *Advertising Is Dead: Long Live Advertising!* (London: Thames & Hudson, 2008), 170.

7. "Point of view" can also be used loosely as a synonym for theme: "The movie's point of view was that Kodak had failed to embrace technological change." Point of view in this sense is implied or expressed in a brand's mission statement (see chapter 9). What is the brand concerned about? What's its "point of view"?

8. James Patterson, quoted in Jackie Merri Meyer, ed., *Mad Ave: Award-Winning Advertising of the 20th Century* (New York: The Art Directors Club Inc., 2000), 27.

9. Natalia Ilyin, "Pushing Heaven," *Communication Arts Advertising Annual*, December 2007, 183.

10. Bill Moyers, quoted in Mary Pipher, *Writing to Change the World* (New York: Riverhead Books, 2006), 10.

CHAPTER 8: Thinking in Words and Pictures

1. See A. Jerome Jewler, *Creative Strategy in Advertising*, 3rd ed. (Belmont, CA: Wadsworth, 1989), 95–96; and Philip B. Meggs, *Type & Image* (New York: Van Nostrand Reinhold, 1989), 64–65, 67.

2. Donald Hall (interview by George Myers, Jr.), "For Man of Letters, Contradiction Is an Eternal Delight," *The Columbus Dispatch*, September 23, 1990, G8.

3. Chip Heath and Dan Heath, *Made to Stick* (New York: Random House, 2007), 50.

4. "Pong! Why Ping Pong Is Our Official Sport," Rethink Advertising website, http://www.rethinkadvertising.com (accessed August 20, 2004).

5. Steve Hayden, quoted in Lawrence Minsky and Emily Thornton Calvo, *How to Succeed in Advertising When All You Have Is Talent* (Lincolnwood, IL: NTC Business Books, 1994), 112.

6. David Ogilvy, *Confessions of an Advertising Man* (1963; New York: Ballantine, 1971), 92.

CHAPTER 9: Words I: Establishing Voice

1. M. H. Abrams, *A Glossary of Literary Terms*, 3rd ed. (New York: Holt, Rinehart and Winston, 1971), 123.

2. In this light all the Leo Burnett "critters," the Jolly Green Giant, the Keebler elves, Tony the Tiger, and others, reveal their value. By taking these fellows home, consumers add to otherwise mundane products an imagined but nevertheless sustaining emotional and psychological content. When I buy Green Giant peas, I feel that I've put more in my cart than simply frozen peas; I've added the mythic presence of that character.

3. Alan Pafenbach, quoted in Bob Garfield, "VW: Best of All Media," *Advertising Age*, May 31, 1999, S22.

4. David Martin, *Romancing the Brand* (New York: AMACOM, 1989), 89, 96.

5. Chris Adams, quoted in Eleftheria Parpis, "Must Love Dogs," *Adweek*, February 18, 2008, http://www.adweek.com/news/advertising-branding/must-love-dogs-94960 (accessed March 1, 2010).

6. Kelly Mooney, quoted in a meeting, Resource Interactive, Columbus, Ohio, March 13, 2007.

7. Nancy Bernard, "Insight: Lies and Personalities," *Step Inside Design*, September/October 2003, 28.

8. William Bernbach's name for body copy, which he disliked writing. He'd write, edit, or approve a headline, then hand the copy assignment off to someone else. See "Ad Age Advertising Century: Top 100 People: William Bernbach," *Advertising Age Special Report*, March 29, 1999, http://adage.com/article/special-report-the-advertising-century/william-bernbach/140180/ (accessed July 1, 2012).

9. Bryan Judkins, e-mail interview with author, November 15, 2011.

10. Elmore Leonard, "Easy on the Hooptedoodle," *New York Times*, July 16, 2001, E1.

11. Steve Hayden, quoted in Lawrence Minsky and Emily Thornton Calvo, *How to Succeed in Advertising When All You Have Is Talent* (Lincolnwood, IL: NTC Business Books, 1994), 115.

12. *Walden and Other Writings of Henry David Thoreau*, ed. Brooks Atkinson, Modern Library ed. (New York: Random House, 1992), 3.

13. Jack Supple, "Pro File" (interview), *CMYK*, Fall 1996, 49.

14. Tracy Kidder, "Making the Truth Believable," in *Professional and Public Writing*, eds. Linda S. Coleman and Robert Funk (Upper Saddle River, NJ: Pearson/Prentice Hall, 2005), 18.

15. Mark Fenske, "Snake Venom & How Good Advertising Works—Part1," Mark Fenske Blog, January 23, 2007, http://markfeske.com/2007_01_01_archive.html (accessed April 19, 2009).

16. Stephen King, *On Writing* (New York: Scribner, 2000), 147.

17. Keith Richards, quoted in Jay McInerney, "The Rebel Yells," *GQ*, April 2003, 156. Richards had just finished a history of the Krupps arms-manufacturing empire and was reading the multivolume memoirs of Baron Fain, Napoleon's cabinet secretary. Truly.

18. Bob Greene, "Nature Boy Goes the Final Round," *Chicago Tribune*, July 6, 1992, C1.

19. E. M. Forster, quoted in Lynn Z. Bloom, *Fact and Artifact: Writing Nonfiction*, 2nd ed. (Englewood Cliffs, NJ: Prentice Hall, 1994), 65. This line is so good that it has been attributed to a number of writers, among them W. H. Auden, Jerome Bruner, and Isak Dinesen, although it is most often associated with Forster.

CHAPTER 10: Words II: Writing Well

1. Claude Hopkins, *My Life in Advertising & Scientific Advertising* (1966; Lincolnwood, IL: NTC Business Books, 1991), 250.

2. William Strunk Jr. and E. B. White, *The Elements of Style*, 3rd ed. (New York: Macmillan, 1979), 23.

3. Annie Dillard, "Living Like Weasels," *Teaching a Stone to Talk* (New York: Harper & Row, 1982), 11.

4. Raymond Chandler, from *Farewell, My Lovely*, quoted in "How to Think Like a Man," *Esquire*, November 2005, 56.

5. I don't mean to celebrate only prose as spare as this Chandler passage. If you use more modifiers, that's fine. Many writers do. Just make every word earn its place.

6. James Webb Young, *Diary of an Ad Man* (Chicago: Advertising Publications, 1944), 214.

7. Joseph M. Williams, *Style*, 2nd ed. (Glenview, IL: Scott Foresman, 1985), 8.

8. E. B. White, "Will Strunk," *Essays of E. B. White* (New York: Harper & Row, 1977), 258.

9. Chip Brown, "Ken Kesey Kisses No Ass," *Esquire*, September 1992, 160.

10. Alastair Crompton, *The Craft of Copywriting* (Englewood Cliffs, NJ: Prentice Hall, 1979), 152.

11. Gary Provost, *100 Ways to Improve Your Writing* (New York: NAL, 1985), 60–61. See also www.garyprovost.com.

12. Elizabeth Hardwick, quoted in George Plimpton, ed., *The Writer's Chapbook* (New York: Viking, 1989), 111.

13. Barney Kilgore, quoted in Robert J. Samuelson, "How the WSJ Is Like Jell-O," *Newsweek*, April 22, 2002, 45.

CHAPTER 11: Interactive Advertising and Social Media

1. Chris Wiggins (presentation), Columbus Society of Communicating Arts, Columbus, Ohio, September 17, 2009.

2. Alex Bogusky and John Winsor, *Baked In: Creating Products and Businesses That Market Themselves* (Chicago: Agate, 2009), 128.

3. Matt Jarvis, quoted in Sam McMillan, "Odopod: Inside the Pod," *Communication Arts Photography Annual 51*, July/August 2010, 51.

4. Yash Egami, "Editor's Note," *One. A Magazine*, Fall 2008, 5.

5. Resource Interactive, "Purina Cat Chow Case Study," http://www.resource.com/project/purina-cat-chow (accessed October 15, 2011).

6. Nick Usborne, *Net Words: Creating High-Impact Online Copy* (New York: McGraw-Hill, 2002), 235.

7. Michael Harris, "The Man Behind Knight-Ridder's Success," *San Francisco Chronicle*, April 22, 1986, quoted in Richard Saul Wurman, *Information Anxiety* (New York: Doubleday, 1989), 228.

8. John Trimble, *Writing with Style* (Englewood Cliffs, NJ: Prentice-Hall, 1975), 59.

9. Jeff Benjamin, quoted in Teressa Iezzi, *The Idea Writers* (New York: Palgrave Macmillan, 2010), 74.

10. Example drawn from Chris Barr et al., *The Yahoo! Style Guide* (New York: St. Martin's Griffin, 2010), 6.

11. Nicke Bergstrom, quoted in Iezzi, *The Idea Writers*, 70.

12. Tom Hinkes, "Why Marketers Need to Quit Acting Like Real People," *Advertising Age*, November 11, 2010, http://adage.com/cmostrategy/article?article_id=147024.

13. Hugh Mackay, *The Good Listener* (Sydney, Australia: Macmillan, 1998), 236.

14. Nick Usborne, quoted in Kathy Henning, "The Seven Qualities of Highly Successful Web Writing," ClickZ, December 12, 2000, http://www.clickz.com/clickz/column/1702196/the-seven-qualities-highly-successful-web-writing (accessed November 9, 2011).

15. Larry Asher, quoted in Kathy Henning, "The Seven Qualities of Highly Successful Web Writing," *ClickZ*, December 12, 2000, http://www.clickz.com/clickz/column/1702196/the-seven-qualities-highly-successful-web-writing (accessed November 9, 2011).

16. Jeff Benjamin, quoted in Iezzi, *The Idea Writers*, 72.

17. Alex Bogusky, quoted in Crispin Porter + Bogusky and Warren Berger, *Hoopla* (Brooklyn, NY: Powerhouse, 2006), 115.

18. James Poniewozik, "Tuned In: The Soul of Twit," *Time*, June 14, 2010.

19. Bob Garfield, "A Social-Media Evangelist Dons a Hair Shirt: Can You Help This Man Reform His Ways?," *Advertising Age*, September 2, 2011, http://adage.com/article/bob-garfield/a-social-media-evangelist-dons-a-hair-shirt/229612 (accessed September 4, 2011).

CHAPTER 12: Television and Video

1. Alex Bogusky and John Winsor, *Baked In: Creating Products and Businesses That Market Themselves* (Chicago: Agate, 2009), 112.

2. Kinka Usher, quoted in "Understanding Usher," *One. A Magazine*, Spring 1998, 12.

3. Robert McKee, *Story* (New York: HarperCollins, 1997), 179.

4. Ibid., 145.

5. Bruce Bildsten, quoted in *Adweek*, February 4, 1999, C.R. 14.

CHAPTER 13: Radio

1. Bill West, "We're Not As Big As P&G: Case Study: John Moore Plumbing" (address), *Advertising Age* Creative Workshop, Chicago, August 10, 1990.

2. Cited in Paul Arden, *It's Not How Good You Are, It's How Good You Want to Be* (New York: Phaidon Press, 2003), 34.

3. Bill West and Jim Conlan, "Funny, You Should Say That: Five Rules For Writing Radio Dialogue," *Advertising Age's Creativity*, September 1999, 33.

4. Robert Frost, quoted by Amy Clampitt in Robert E. Hosman Jr., "Amy Clampitt, The Art of Poetry XLV" (interview), *The Paris Review* 126 (Spring 1993), 92.

5. Jeff Goodby, quoted in Dyann Espinosa, "Radio Pays," *Advertising Age's Creativity*, September 1999, 26.

CHAPTER 14: Other Media and Genres

1. David Ludington, quoted in Cara Beardi, "Driven to Attraction," *Advertising Age*, July 23, 2001, 4.

2. Tom McElligott, quoted in Lawrence Minsky and Emily Thornton Calvo, *How to Succeed in Advertising When All You Have Is Talent* (Lincolnwood, IL: NTC Business Books, 1994), 240.

3. Rob Morris, quoted by Rogier Van Bakel, "Outdoor Advertising: Primer Alfresco," *Advertising Age's Creativity*, March 1998, 34, 36.

4. Dan Sutton, quoted in *Advertising Age's Creativity*, May 1999, 10.

5. Charles Austin Bates, *Short Talks on Advertising* (New York: Charles Austin Bates, 1898), 1.

6. Tom Himpe, *Advertising Is Dead: Long Live Advertising!* (London: Thames & Hudson, 2006), 190.

7. See Emma Hall and Normandy Madden, "Ikea Courts Buyers with Offbeat Ideas," *Advertising Age*, April 12, 2004, 10.

8. Zak Mroueh, quoted in Warren Berger, "Unconventional Advertising," *Communication Arts*, March/April 2007, 70.

9. Warren Berger, in *One. A Magazine*, Winter 2003, 3.

10. See Karen Gaudette, AP article reprinted as "Bumpers Are Pair's Billboards," *The Columbus Dispatch*, January 6, 2001, 1F.

11. See Catherine P. Taylor, "Playing Chicken," *Adweek*, April 19, 2004, 19.

12. Himpe, *Advertising Is Dead*, 186.

13. Jonathan Bond, quoted in Bernice Kanner, "On Madison Avenue: Brats No More," *New York*, July 20, 1992, 12.

14. Ed Robinson, quoted in Teressa Iezzi, *The Idea Writers* (New York: Palgrave Macmillan, 2010), 86.

15. Ibid., 87.

16. Chuck Porter, quoted in Warren Berger and Crispin Porter + Bogusky, *Hoopla* (Brooklyn, NY: Powerhouse, 2006), 281.

17. Lisa Hickey, *Design Secrets: Advertising: 50 Real Life Projects Uncovered* (Gloucester, MA: Rockport, 2002), 169.

18. See "Singapore Sensibilty," interview with Chris Lee, managing partner, Fallon/Duffy Asian offices, *One. A Magazine*, Summer 2002, 15.

19. Ian Batey, quoted in *One. A Magazine*, Summer 2002, 15.

20. See "When Leche Is Love," interview with Anita Santiago, president of Anita Santiago Advertising, whose agency worked with Goodby to develop milk advertising for the Spanish-speaking Hispanic market, *One. A Magazine*, Fall 2003, 12–13.

21. José Mollá "Adding Loco Humor to Hispanic Advertising" (interview), *One. A Magazine*, Fall 2003, 4–5.

22. See Laurel Wentz, "Banks Tailor Efforts to Homesick Hispanics," *Advertising Age*, April 5, 2004, 30.

CHAPTER 15: How to Be Creative

1. John Vitro, "Vitro Talks," *One. A Magazine*, Winter 1998, 8.

2. Eva Zeisel, quoted in Richard Rhodes, *How To Write* (New York: Morrow, 1995), 56.

3. Peter Elbow, *Writing without Teachers*, 25th annv. ed. (New York: Oxford University Press, 1998), 3–11.

4. Edward de Bono, *Lateral Thinking* (New York: Harper & Row, 1973), 107, 108.

5. Elmore Leonard, as told to Larry Platt, "When I Knew," *Men's Journal*, February 2011, 64.

6. Ernie Schenck, "The Crying Game," *Communication Arts*, January/February 1997, 30.

7. Gerry Graf, quoted in Eleftheria Parpis, "Made in Manhattan," *Adweek*, January 5, 2004, 21.

8. Mike Roe, e-mail to author, November 8, 2004.

9. Timothy Goodman (interview), *Communication Arts Insights*, October 4, 2011, http://www.commarts.com/insights/long-airplane-flights.html.

10. Paula Scher, quoted in Anna Muoio, "They Have a Better Idea . . . Do You?," *Fast Company*, August/September 1997, 73, http://www.fastcompany.com/magazine/10/one.html (accessed November 11, 1997).

11. Dan Wieden, quoted in Ralf Langwost, *How to Catch the Big Idea: The Strategies of the Top-Creatives*, trans. Kim Butcher and Denis Buckley (Erlangen, Germany: Publicis Corporate Publishing, 2004), 95.

12. Stephen Dunn, *Walking Light* (New York: Norton, 1993), 157.

13. Bill Westbrook, quoted in *Communication Arts* March/April 1991, 46.

14. Scher, quoted in Anna Muoio, "They Have a Better Idea . . . Do You?," 1997.

15. Jay Chiat, quoted in Marilynn Milmoe, "Aspen," *Communication Arts*, September/October 1987, 91.

CHAPTER 16: How to Write a Headline

1. Victor Borge, quoted in Dick Wasserman, *That's Our New Ad Campaign . . . ?* (Lexington, MA: D. C. Heath, 1988), 66.

2. To my knowledge, psychologist Jerome Bruner coined the phrase "effective surprise" as a two-word definition of creativity. See "The Conditions of Creativity" in *On Knowing*, expanded ed. (Cambridge, MA: Harvard University Press, 1979), 18.

3. Lee Clow, quoted in Lynda Twardowski, "On the Inside: TBWA\Chiat\Day: Behold The Second Coming," *CMYK*, Winter 1998, 55.

4. Ken Macrorie, *Telling Writing*, 3rd ed. (Rochelle Park, NJ: Hayden, 1980), 136–37.

5. Woody Allen, "Death (A Play)," *Without Feathers* (New York: Random House, 1975), 99.

6. The source of this quote is uncertain. Thompson wrote a similar line in *Generation of Swine: Tales of Shame and Degradation* (New York: Summit, 1988), 43, but the thought itself has become an urban legend, spreading widely in various forms, none of them quite the Thompson original. Its omnipresence is testimony not only to Thompson's hot-rocks style but, with its laugh-out-loud last sentence, to the power of misdirection.

7. Ambrose Bierce, *The Devil's Dictionary* (New York: Oxford University Press, 1999), 44.

8. Richard Stengel, "Editor's Desk: The Story of X," *Time*, May 20, 2011, 4.

9. Pauline Kael, quoted in Nathan Heller, "What She Said," *New Yorker*, October 24, 2011, 79.

10. Elizabeth Dias, "Milestones: Died: Cy Twombly," *Time*, July 18, 2011, 20.

11. Story Musgrave, quoted in Belinda Luscombe, "10 Questions [for Story Musgrave]," *Time*, July 18, 2011, 64.

12. Ezra Pound, *ABC of Reading* (Norfolk, CT: New Directions, n.d.), 28.

13. Konstantin Stanislavsky, quoted by James Lipton, *Countdown with Keith Olberman*, MSNBC, July 2, 2004.

CHAPTER 17: How to Write Slogans, Theme Lines, and Names

1. John Emmerling, "Battle Cry Equals Brand Success," *Advertising Age*, November 17, 2003, 22.

2. Lee Clow, quoted in Karen Stabiner, *Inventing Desire* (New York: Simon & Schuster, 1993), 160.

3. Goodby, Silverstein & Partners quoted in Andrea Birnbaum, ed., *Top Ten in Advertising* (New York: Graphis, 2001), 74.

4. Andrew Keller, quoted in Teressa Iezzi, *The Idea Writers* (New York: Palgrave Macmillan, 2010), 166.

5. William S. Burroughs, from RE/SEARCH #4/5, 1982, http://www.lazarus corporation.co.uk/explanations/explanations 2.htm (accessed July 11, 2003).

6. Dan Wieden, quoted in Steve Woodward, "MIND-SET/slogans," *The Oregonian*, December 14, 2003, adslogans.com/media desk/pdf/AdSlogans_Oregonian.pdf (accessed July 5, 2004).

7. Danny Altman, quoted in Josh Rottenberg, "How to Invent a Brand Name," *New York Times Magazine*, April 8, 2001, http://www.ahundredmonkeys.com/nytimes_ article2.html (accessed June 5, 2001).

8. Danny Altman, quoted in Cheryl Dahle, "How to Make a Name for Yourself," *Fast Company*, September 2000, http://www.fast company.com/online/38/100monkeys.html (accessed June 5, 2001). For a good discussion of naming techniques, also see Beth Brosseau, "How to Win the Naming Game," *Critique*, Spring 1997, 57–63.

9. Matt Forchione, e-mail to author, August 31, 2011.

10. Jane Matthews, e-mail to author, November 11, 2011.

CHAPTER 19: Testimonials: The Power of Personality

1. Dave Schiff, quoted in "PrintCritic E-mail," *Creativity's AdCritic.com*, http://ad critic.com/printercritic/email (accessed July 28, 2004).

2. Ibid.

CHAPTER 21: Reversal

1. I owe the title of this chapter and some of my thinking to Edward de Bono's *Lateral Thinking* (New York: Harper & Row, 1990).

2. Brian Howlett, quoted in "Exhibit," *Communication Arts*, January/February 1997, 125.

3. Al Ries and Jack Trout, *Marketing Warfare* (New York: McGraw-Hill, 1986), 70. As its title indicates, this book likens marketing to the battlefield and explains fundamental strategies in its terms.

4. Ries and Trout, *Marketing Warfare*, 117–36.

CHAPTER 22: Visual Metaphor

1. Theodore Levitt, "Marketing Intangible Products and Product Intangibles," *The Marketing Imagination*, expanded ed. (New York: Free Press, 1986), 97.

2. Ibid., 98.

3. Ralph Waldo Emerson, "Self-Reliance," *Selected Essays*, ed. Larzar Ziff (New York: Penguin Books, 1982), 185.

4. Henry Wolf, *Visual Thinking: Methods for Making Images Memorable* (New York: American Showcase, 1988), 14.

CHAPTER 24: Postmodern Advertising

1. Alan Russell, e-mail to author, July 21, 2004, quoting his comments in *The One Show*, v. 21, 1999.

2. James B. Twitchell, *Twenty Ads That Shook the World* (New York: Crown, 2000), 192.

3. Dan Wieden, "On Global Ambitions, Turning 17, and Memories of 'Revolution': Dan Wieden Reflects" (interview*)*, *One. A Magazine*, Winter 1998, 6.

CHAPTER 25: Human Truth

1. Todd Waterbury (address), Columbus Society of Communicating Arts, Columbus, Ohio, October 16, 1997.

2. Jeff Goodby, quoted in *Advertising Age* "The Age of Ideas" advertising campaign, "This is not milk," print ad, in *Ad Age's Creativity*, Dec. 2000–Jan. 2001, 30–31.

3. Doris Willens, *Nobody's Perfect: Bill Bernbach and the Golden Age of Advertising* (Seattle: CreateSpace, 2009), 51.

4. Jayanta Jenkins, creative director, TBWA\Chiat\Day, visiting artist, Columbus College of Art & Design, Columbus, Ohio, November 17, 2008.

5. Mark Fenske, "My Art Center Class in 800 Words or Less," *CMYK*, Fall/Winter 1998, 64.

CHAPTER 26: Grace Notes

1. Excerpt from *New Employee Handbook*, "Employment" section, Crispin Porter + Bogusky web site, http://www.cpbmiami.com/ (accessed December 29, 2003).

2. Lisa Sanders, "Fight for the Streets," *Advertising Age*, May 31, 2004, 58.

3. David Ogilvy, *Confessions of an Advertising Man* (1963; New York: Ballantine Books, 1971), 84.

4. Rich Silverstein, quoted in Chris Barnett, "Cruising a Steady Course: Goodby, Berlin & Silverstein," *Graphis*, 46, no. 265 (January/February 1990), 50.

RECOMMENDED READING

CREATIVE THINKING

Adams, James L. *Conceptual Blockbusting: A Guide to Better Ideas.* 4th ed. Cambridge, MA: Basic Books, 2001. A book that takes its title seriously: breaking the blocks that inhibit our creativity.

De Bono, Edward. *Lateral Thinking.* New York: Harper & Row, 1973. This is his best-known book about creativity, but he has written a number of others.

Fletcher, Alan. *The Art of Looking Sideways.* New York: Phaidon Press, 2001. A renowned designer's cabinet of wonders: oddments, curiosities, and profundities gathered for your consideration. If this book doesn't give you ideas, nothing will.

Von Oech, Roger. *A Whack on the Side of the Head: How You Can Be More Creative.* 25th anniv. rev. ed. New York: Business Plus, 2008. *A Kick in the Seat of the Pants.* New York: Harper & Row, 1986. Both books seem almost too simple: easy to read, easy on the eyes, funny. But both are head stretchers.

VISUAL THINKING

Heller, Steven, and Gail Anderson. *Graphic Wit: The Art of Humor in Design.* New York: Watson-Guptill, 1991. This really powers up your visual acuity. There's a revised version: Heller, Steven. *Design Humor: The Art of Graphic Wit.* New York: Allworth, 2002.

McAlhone, Beryl, and David Stuart. *A Smile in the Mind: Witty Thinking in Graphic Design.* Rev. ed. Boston: Phaidon Press, 1998. A feast of graphic wit, categorized and analyzed.

Pricken, Mario. *Creative Advertising: Ideas and Techniques from the World's Best Campaigns.* 2nd ed. New York: Thames & Hudson, 2008. One way after another to dramatize a strategy. Lots of cool ads—and lessons in visual thinking.

WRITING

Barr, Chris, et al. *The Yahoo! Style Guide: The Ultimate Sourcebook for Writing, Editing, and Creating Content for the Digital World.* New York: St. Martin's Griffin, 2010. Crisply presented guidelines and examples of what to do and what to avoid when writing for digital media. A handy reference.

Hale, Constance. *Sin and Syntax: How to Craft Wickedly Effective Prose.* New York: Broadway Books, 2001. Hale organizes her advice by the parts of speech and draws examples from fresh, unusual sources.

Marius, Richard. *A Writer's Companion.* 4th ed. Boston: McGraw-Hill College, 1999. Marius is talking to college students about how to write essays, but we can easily slip into the room. Our copy will thank us.

Provost, Gary. *100 Ways to Improve Your Writing: Proven Professional Techniques for Writing with Style and Power.* New York: New American Library, 1985. Practicality itself. All of Provost's books about writing demonstrate how well he understood the craft.

Strunk, William, Jr., and E. B. White. *The Elements of Style.* 4th ed. Boston: Allyn and Bacon, 2000. This classic little book combines Strunk's gruffness with White's grace. If you haven't read it, you should.

Trimble, John R. *Writing with Style: Conversations on the Art of Writing.* 3rd ed. Upper Saddle River, NJ: Prentice Hall, 2011. This is another classic, though less well known than *The Elements of Style.* Trimble, like Marius, is a professor talking to college students about how to write essays. Excellent advice, pungently expressed. Proof that the best profs are always worth listening to.

Tufte, Virginia. *Artful Sentences: Syntax as Style.* Cheshire, CT: Graphics Press, 2006. Read it slowly.

Williams, Joseph M., and Gregory G. Colomb. *Style: Lessons in Clarity and Grace.* 10th ed. New York: Longman, 2010. If you really want to study the engine of style, this book (along with Tufte's) opens the hood. Williams and Colomb have also written a cut-to-the-chase version: *Style: The Basics of Clarity and Grace.* 4th ed. New York: Longman, 2010.

Zinsser, William. *On Writing Well: The Classic Guide to Writing Nonfiction.* 30th anniv. ed. New York: HarperCollins, 2006. A much-admired book, full of sound advice. I think it's the single best book on how to write.

COPYWRITING

Aitchison, Jim. *Cutting Edge Advertising II: How to Create the World's Best Print for Brands in the 21st Century.* 2nd ed. Singapore: Prentice Hall, 2003. I don't know another book in which the thoughts of advertising creatives have been as usefully organized. Rather than presenting his subjects one by one, he integrates their comments into chapters that track how you'd work on a problem, from beginning to end.

Bendinger, Bruce. *The Copy Workshop Workbook.* 4th ed. Chicago: Copy Workshop, 2009. An energetic potpourri of advice and resources. You'll want to make ads after reading it.

Bly, Robert W. *The Copywriter's Handbook: A Step-by-Step Guide to Writing Copy That Sells.* 3rd ed. New York: Holt, 2006. Conservative, no-nonsense features-and-benefits approach to advertising. A kind of ground zero. Read this when you're starting out, then consider breaking its rules as your talent and experience tell you to.

The Copy Book: How 32 of the World's Best Advertising Writers Write Their Copy. Crans-près-Céligny, Switzerland: Designers and Art Directors Association of the United Kingdom and RotoVision, 1995. Great copywriters show their work and talk about how they did it. Most are British; much of the work you may not have seen. (A paperback edition is entitled *The Copywriter's Bible.*)

Iezzi, Teressa. *The Idea Writers: Copywriting in a New Media and Marketing Era.* New York: Palgrave Macmillan, 2010. What copywriters do and how they do it has changed mightily in the digital, interactive world. Iezzi and the professionals she interviews explain.

Sullivan, Luke, with Sam Bennett. *Hey, Whipple, Squeeze This: The Classic Guide to Creating Great Ads.* 4th ed. Hoboken, NJ: Wiley, 2012. It's hard to be either funny or wise. Sullivan is effortlessly both. A great book. If you read only one on how to make ads, this is it.

ADVERTISING

Himpe, Tom. *Advertising is Dead: Long Live Advertising!* New York: Thames & Hudson, 2006. Nontraditional advertising, well organized, explained, and illustrated.

Minsky, Laurence. *How to Succeed in Advertising When All You Have Is Talent.* 2nd ed. Chicago: Copy Workshop, 2007. Substantial interviews with people like Steve Hayden, Lee Clow, Susan Hoffman, Rich Silverstein, and Alex Bogusky. Lots of advice about how to think, how to solve advertising problems, and how to grow in the profession.

Paetro, Maxine. *How to Put Your Book Together and Get a Job in Advertising.* Newly rev. ed. New York: W. W. Norton, 2010. This book's title fits it like a lid fits a jar: Q&As with Paetro, an ad agency headhunter, and lots of advice from industry professionals. If you're just leaving college with advertising as a career goal, buy this book immediately.

Steel, Jon. *Truth, Lies & Advertising: The Art of Account Planning.* New York: Wiley, 1998. How they think things through at Goodby, Silverstein & Partners from someone who should know. Steel starts from the consumer's point of view, which is where ads themselves should start but too often don't. He helps you see into the psychology that underlies great advertising.

Vonk, Nancy, and Janet Kestin. *Pick Me: Breaking into Advertising and Staying There.* Hoboken, NJ: Wiley, 2005. Organized around key questions and fun to read, with plenty of advice from professionals.

HISTORY OF ADVERTISING

Berger, Warren. *Advertising Today.* New York: Phaidon Press, 2001. A great big dreamboat of a book. (Takes two hands and a strong lap.) Lots of handsomely reproduced ads (from the 1960s on—many you've seen, many you haven't), interviews with major players, and, not least, a fine writer on the bridge. Ask for it for your birthday. Or give it to yourself.

Goodrum, Charles, and Helen Dalrymple. *Advertising in America: The First 200 Years.* New York: Abrams, 1990. Beautifully illustrated, well researched, clearly written. Organized chronologically within categories: cosmetics, automobiles, travel, causes, etc. Out of print but easy to find via websites like alibris.com, amazon.com, bookfinder.com, and my favorite, abebooks.com.

Twitchell, James B. *Twenty Ads That Shook the World.* New York: Crown, 2000. Smart, wide-ranging analyses of seminal ads. History in bite sizes.

ILLUSTRATION CREDITS

Chapter 1

1.1. Courtesy of Reader's Digest Foundation and Ruhr/Paragon.

1.2. Courtesy of Reader's Digest Foundation and The Martin Agency.

1.3. Courtesy of Jac Coverdale, Vice President/Executive Creative Director, Clarity Coverdale Fury (Minneapolis), on behalf of the Minnesota chapter of Mothers Against Drunk Driving.

1.4. Bar tab ad courtesy of Ogilvy Brasil and Bar Aurora. Man under glass ad courtesy of Leo Burnett, London, on behalf of the Department for Transport's THINK! campaign.

Chapter 2

2.1. Courtesy of Volkswagen of America, Inc.

2.2. Reprint courtesy of International Business Machines Corporation, © 2011 International Business Machines Corporation.

2.3. Courtesy of Metro Transit and Periscope.

2.4. Courtesy of BVK.

2.5. Used with permission from GNP Company.

2.6. Courtesy of Fallon.

2.7. Courtesy of L.L.Bean and Martin|Williams. Creative director, Jim Henderson; art director, Tim Tone; copywriter, Jan Pettit.

2.8. Courtesy of True Fitness Public Relations, ORCA Partnership.

2.9. Courtesy of Howard, Merrell & Partners.

2.10. Courtesy of Chopin Vodka and Clarity Coverdale Fury. Creative director, Jac Coverdale; art director, Glenn Gray; copywriter, Kelly Trewartha.

2.11. Courtesy of Scott Maney, Founder/ECD, Jones.

Chapter 3

3.1. Courtesy of Starkey Labs.

3.2. Courtesy of Kohnke Hanneken Advertising, Inc.

3.3. Courtesy of BBDO Canada.

3.4. Courtesy of Tracker Network (Pty) Ltd, Johannesburg.

3.5. Courtesy of Sawyer Riley Compton. Creative director/art director, Bart Cleveland; copywriter, Al Jackson; photographer, Jim Erickson.

3.6. Courtesy of the Animal Humane Society and Sally J. Wagner Inc.

3.7. Courtesy of Rethink.

3.8. Courtesy of Holmes & Lee.

3.9. Courtesy of Sawyer Riley Compton. Creative director/art director, Bart Cleveland; copywriter, Al Jackson; photographer, Jim Erickson.

3.10. Courtesy of the Agency for Healthcare Research and Quality (AHRQ).

3.11. Courtesy of Peter Judd, Director of Design, Hub Strategy, and the University of San Francisco. Paul Kagiwada, lead designer; Leona Frye/Jason Siciliano, writers; Peter Judd (design)/DJ O'Neil (copy), creative directors; Jason Rothman, photographer; Mike Ornellas, mechanical artist; Michael Blair, producer.

3.12. Courtesy of Martin|Williams.

3.13. Courtesy of Gibson Guitar Corp., Carmichael Lynch, and Shawn Michienzi, photographer.

Chapter 4

4.1. Courtesy of Black Rocket.

4.2. Courtesy of Winnebago Industries, Inc.

4.3. Courtesy of Paul Carek. Terry Rietta, art director.

4.4 Courtesy of L.L.Bean and Martin|Williams.

4.5. Courtesy of Harley-Davidson, Carmichael Lynch, and Chris Wimpey, photographer.

4.6. Courtesy of Sawyer Riley Compton. Creative director, Bart Cleveland; art director, Kevin Thoem; copywriter, Kevin Thoem/Ari Weiss.

4.7. Courtesy of White Wave.

4.8. Published with the consent of the De Beers group of Companies.

4.9. Porsche ad courtesy of client, Porsche Cars North America; agency, Carmichael Lynch; and photographer, Georg Fischer. PORSCHE, BOXSTER, CARRERA, and the Porsche Crest are registered trademarks and the distinctive shape of PORSCHE automobiles are trade dress of Dr. Ing. h.c. F. Porsche AG. Used with permission of Porsche Cars North America, Inc. Copyrighted by Porsche Cars North America, Inc. Volvo ad courtesy of Volvo. Used by permission.

4.10. Courtesy of Viking & Indianhead Councils, BSA; and Carmichael Lynch.

4.11. Courtesy of Kohnke Hanneken Advertising, Inc.

4.12. Courtesy of Church Ad Project.

4.13. Courtesy of Tom Bedecarré, AKQA.

4.14. Courtesy of Legacy.

4.15. Courtesy of Scott Maney, Founder/ECD, Jones.

4.16. Courtesy of Rethink.

Chapter 5

5.1. Honda ad courtesy of American Honda Motor Co., Inc. For Eyes ad courtesy of DeVito/Verdi, New York.

5.2. "The Day The Earth Stood Still" courtesy of Cellular One®—Washington/Baltimore. "200 minutes" courtesy of Jim Schmidt, McConnaughy Stein Schmidt and Brown.

5.3. Courtesy of Howard, Merrell & Partners.

5.4. Courtesy of BVK.

5.5. MINI and MINI Cooper are registered trademarks of BMW NA, LLC. All rights reserved. Ad used by permission.

5.6. Courtesy of DeVito/Verdi, New York.

5.7. Courtesy of BVK.

5.8. Courtesy of BVK.

5.9. Courtesy of Big Bang Idea Engineering, San Diego, CA. Creative director, Wade Koniakowsky.

5.10. Courtesy of Volkswagen of America, Inc., and Arnold Worldwide. Photography © Smari. Used by permission.

5.11. Courtesy of Butch Blum, Inc.

5.12. Courtesy of O'Brien International.

5.13. Courtesy of Ace Asphalt.

5.14. Courtesy of Gabriel deGrood Bendt.

Chapter 6

6.1. © Schwinn Bicycles. Reprinted with permission of Pacific Cycle.

6.2. Courtesy of L.L.Bean and Martin|Williams.

6.3. Courtesy of Legacy, Arnold Worldwide, and Crispin Porter + Bogusky. Chief creative officer, Ron Lawner; group creative directors, Pete Favat and Alex Bogusky; creative directors, Roger Baldacci and Tom Adams; art directors, Rob Baird and Lee Einhorn; copywriters, Roger Baldacci, John Kearse, and Mike Howard; production manager, Linda Donlon; art producer, Kathy McMann; photographer, Garry Simpson.

6.4. Courtesy of Legacy.

6.5. Courtesy of American Standard, Carmichael Lynch, and Shawn Michienzi, photographer.

6.6. Courtesy of Christopher Cole. Art director, Christopher Cole; copywriter, Mark Wegwerth.

Chapter 7

7.1. Courtesy of DeVito/Verdi, New York.

7.2. Courtesy of McGarrah Jessee.

7.3. Courtesy of Winchester/Olin Corporation.

7.4. Courtesy of Reason Partners Inc.

7.5. Courtesy of Paul Russell and of Zync Communications Inc., Toronto, Canada. Creative director, Marko Zonta; designer, Michael Kasperski; writer, Michael Kasperski; client, Bretenic Limited. Photograph courtesy of Rockport Publishers. Used by permission.

7.6. Courtesy of BVK.

7.7. Courtesy of Denver Water, March 4, 2012.

7.8. Courtesy of Jeni Britton Bauer, Jeni's Splendid Ice Creams.

7.9. Courtesy of Bailey Lauerman.

7.10. Courtesy of Evian/Great Brands of Europe and Polan+Waski Branding and Design.

7.11. Courtesy of Peter Judd, Director of Design, Hub Strategy, and the University of San Francisco. Paul Kagiwada, lead designer; Leona Frye/Jason Siciliano, writers; Peter Judd (design)/DJ O'Neil (copy), creative directors; Jason Rothman, photographer; Mike Ornellas, mechanical artist; Michael Blair, producer.

7.12. Courtesy of McGarrah Jessee.

7.13. Courtesy of Blue Cross and Blue Shield of Minnesota and Hunt Adkins.

7.14. Courtesy of Gary Smith, CEO, Big Red, Inc.

7.15. Courtesy of Martin|Williams.

Chapter 8

8.1. VW ad courtesy of Volkswagen of America, Inc. "Don't Vote" courtesy of Borders Perrin Norrander.

8.2. © Amtrak. Reprinted with permission.

8.3. Excedrin ad © Bristol-Myers Squibb Company. "Elephants in a box" ad courtesy of World Wildlife Fund. Illustrations used with the permission of Bristol-Myers Squibb Company and World Wildlife Fund.

8.4. Stock footage ad courtesy of Crosspoint. Coffee ad courtesy of Cityscape Deli.

8.5. Courtesy of Crystal Springs Bottled Water.

8.6. Courtesy of TDA_Boulder.

8.7. Courtesy of Serve Marketing.

8.8. Courtesy of Whitewater Excitement and See of San Francisco.

8.9. Courtesy of McClain Finlon Advertising.

8.10. Courtesy of Pillsbury and Clarity Coverdale Fury. Creative director, Jac Coverdale; art director, Jac Coverdale; copywriter, Troy Longie.

8.11. Courtesy of Mullen.

8.12. Courtesy of Serve Marketing.

8.13. Courtesy of Sawyer Riley Compton. Creative director, Bart Cleveland; art director, Kevin Thoem; copywriter, Ari Weiss.

8.14. Courtesy of BVK.

8.15. Courtesy of Denver Water, March 4, 2012.

8.16. Courtesy of Procter & Gamble.

8.17. Reprinted with permission from Shimano American Corporation.

8.18. Courtesy of Concepts Marketing Group, Indianapolis, IN. Creative director, Larry Aull; art director, Tony Fannin; copywriter, Mark LeClerc; client, Columbus Hockey, Inc., Columbus, OH.

Chapter 9

9.1. Courtesy of Volkswagen of America, Inc., and Arnold Worldwide. © Bill Cash Photography. Used by permission.

9.2. Courtesy of Scott Maney, Founder/ECD, Jones.

9.3. Courtesy of Mars Petcare US, Inc.

9.4. Courtesy of Mars Petcare US, Inc.

9.5. Courtesy of Mars Petcare US, Inc.

9.6. Courtesy of VF/Red Kap.

9.7. Courtesy of Young & Laramore, Indianapolis. Creative director, Charlie Hopper; associate creative director/copywriter, Bryan Judkins; associate creative director/art director, Trevor Williams; photographer, Gary Sparks; typography designers, Yee-Haw Industries.

9.8. Courtesy of Nike, Inc.

9.9. Courtesy of Royal Viking Line.

9.10. "You've taught your kids everything" courtesy of Rethink. "Row, row, row" courtesy of North Carolina Division of Tourism and Film and Loeffler Ketchum Mountjoy. "Spend the difference" courtesy of Black Rocket. "Accepted at more schools" courtesy of Visa.

9.11. Parrot ad courtesy of the Des Moines Register. Cigar ad courtesy of Loeffler Ketchum Mountjoy.

9.12. Courtesy of The Village Voice, New York, NY.

9.13. Courtesy of Reebok International Ltd.

9.14. Courtesy of Clarion Sales Corporation, Gardena, CA, and Stein Robaire Helm, Los Angeles.

9.15. Courtesy of Mullen.

9.16. Courtesy of Millennium Import LLC and Hunt Adkins.

9.17. Courtesy of KVOS TV and Palmer Jarvis DDB.

9.18. Courtesy of the Peace Corps and Backer Spielvogel Bates.

Chapter 10

10.1. Courtesy of Mitsubishi and Chiat/Day.

10.2. Copy of advertisement used by permission of Porsche Cars North America, Inc. Porsche and the Porsche crest are registered trademarks of Dr. Ing. h.c. F. Porsche AG.

10.3. Courtesy of L.L.Bean and Martin|Williams.

10.4. Courtesy of The Nature Company.

10.5. Courtesy of American Honda Motor Co., Inc.

Chapter 11

11.1. © 2012 MINI USA, a division of BMW of North America, LLC. All rights reserved. The MINI and BMW trademark, model names, and logo are registered trademarks. Used by permission.

11.2. Courtesy of DeVito/Verdi, New York.

11.3. Courtesy of Sawyer Riley Compton. Creative director/art director, Bart Cleveland; copywriter, Jackie Hathrimani.

11.4. Courtesy of Jenni Moyer, Senior Director, Corporate Communications, Comcast.

11.5. Courtesy of Keith Gulla, Communications Manager, Converse Inc.

11.6. Courtesy of Bailey Lauerman.

11.7. Courtesy of Cundari and BMW Canada. Copywriter, Brian Murray; art director, Raul Garcia; chief creative officer, Brent Choi.

11.8. Courtesy of Rethink.

11.9. Courtesy of Nestlé Purina PetCare Company and Resource Interactive.

W-11.10. Courtesy of Blue Cross and Blue Shield of Minnesota.

11.11. Courtesy of the Advertising Council.

11.12. Courtesy of United Methodist Church and BOHAN.

Chapter 12

12.1. Courtesy of Martin|Williams.

12.2. Courtesy of DeVito/Verdi, New York.

12.3. Courtesy of McCoy's Building Supply, McGarrah Jessee, and 1080 Productions.

12.4. Courtesy of Rethink.

12.5. Courtesy of Martin|Williams.

12.6. Courtesy of Volkswagen of America, Inc., and Arnold Worldwide. Photography © 2002 Malcolm Venville and Anonymous Content. Used by permission.

12.7. Courtesy of Richter7.

12.8. Courtesy of McGarrah Jessee.

12.9. Courtesy of Richter7.

12.10. Courtesy of Martin|Williams.

12.11. Courtesy of Reason Partners Inc.

12.12. Courtesy of Wolverine Worldwide, Inc.

Chapter 13

13.1. Courtesy of DeVito/Verdi, New York.

13.2. Courtesy of Denver Water, March 4, 2012.

13.3. Courtesy of Reason Partners Inc.

13.4. Courtesy of Black Rocket.

13.5. Courtesy of Borders Perrin Norrander.

13.6. Courtesy of DeVito/Verdi, New York.

Chapter 14

14.1. Courtesy of Fallon McElligott; photography by Rick Dublin.

14.2. Courtesy of Airborne Express.

14.3. UDF truck graphic courtesy of United Dairy Farmers and Snap Advertising. Goodwill truck graphics courtesy of Young & Laramore.

14.4. "Repels all of the above" ad courtesy of Borders Perrin Norrander. Weather Network quotes ad courtesy of Holmes & Lee. "If this bus hit you" ad courtesy of DeVito/Verdi, New York. "Parking. How sad" ad used by permission of BMW NA, LLC. All rights reserved. MINI and MINI Cooper are registered trademarks of BMW NA, LLC.

14.5. Courtesy of Interfaith Airport Chapel.

14.6. Andy Warhol, Self Portrait, 1986 © AWF. Courtesy of The Andy Warhol Museum, Pittsburgh, PA (www.warhol.org).

14.7. Courtesy of Rethink.

14.8. Courtesy of Chipotle Mexican Grill.

14.9. Courtesy of Rethink.

14.10. Courtesy of Ogilvy Brasil and Bar Aurora.

14.11. MINI and MINI Cooper are registered trademarks of BMW NA, LLC. All rights reserved. Ad used by permission.

14.12. Courtesy of Kirshenbaum & Bond.

14.13. Courtesy of The Jupiter Drawing Room, Cape Town, South Africa.

14.14. Courtesy of Rethink.

14.15. Courtesy of Jakpetz.

14.16. Courtesy of Denver Water, March 4, 2012.

14.17. Courtesy of M&C Saatchi.

14.18. Courtesy of Blue Cross and Blue Shield of Minnesota.

14.19. Courtesy of DSW. Creative leader and copy director, Lisa Farina.

14.20. Courtesy of Target. Illustrators: Anna Augul, Matthew Poprocki, Melinda Beck, Oksana Badrak, Rachel Salomon, Robert Risko, and Yuko Shimizu.

14.21. Courtesy of Denver Water, March 4, 2012.

14.22. Courtesy of Denver Water, March 4, 2012.

14.23. Courtesy of Richter7.

14.24. Courtesy of la comunidad.

14.25. Courtesy of Corona, imported by Barton Beers Ltd., Chicago, IL.

Chapter 15

15.1. Courtesy of Schmeltz + Warren.

15.2. Courtesy of Mike Roe and Jason Wood.

15.3. Courtesy of DeVito/Verdi, New York.

15.4. Courtesy of McClain Finlon Advertising.

15.5. Courtesy of Jim Harrington, President, O'Leary and Partners, on behalf of Mothers Polishes–Waxes–Cleaners, 5456 Industrial Drive, Huntington Beach, CA 92649-1519.

15.6. Courtesy of USA WEEKEND and Cabell Harris.

Chapter 16

16.1. Courtesy of Borders Perrin Norrander.

16.2. Courtesy of Borders Perrin Norrander.

16.3. Courtesy of United Hospital and Clarity Coverdale Fury. Creative director, Jac Coverdale; art director, Simon McQuoid; copywriter, Jerry Fury.

16.4. Courtesy of Borders Perrin Norrander.

16.5. "Happy?" ad courtesy of Checkered Past Records. Creative directors, Erik Johnson and Tom Cheevers; art director, Tom Cheevers; copywriter, Erik Johnson; production/printing, John Davis/Colormation. Cigar Attitudes ad courtesy of Craig Mikes, creative director, Smith, Jones & Johnson.

16.6. Courtesy of Christopher Cole. Art director, Christopher Cole; copywriter, Eric Sorensen.

16.7. Courtesy of Advertising Federation of Columbus, SBC Advertising, and Bender & Bender. Photography and imaging, Bender & Bender; concept and design, SBC Advertising.

16.8. Repeal 43 ad courtesy of TBWA\Vancouver. VW ad courtesy of Volkswagen of America, Inc., and Arnold Worldwide. Photography courtesy of © Steve Casimiro and Getty Images and © Bill Cash Photography.

16.9. Courtesy of McGarrah Jessee.

16.10. Courtesy of Statoil Norway; Beril Holte Rasmussen, McCann Oslo; Espen Horn, Executive Producer/Partner, MotionBlur. Used by permission.

16.11. Green Genius ad courtesy of Peter Judd, Director of Design, Hub Strategy. DJ O'Neil and Peter Judd, creative directors; Jason Rothman, designer; Chris Elzinga, writer; Kevin Twomey, photographer. Columbia ad courtesy of Borders Perrin Norrander.

16.12. Courtesy of Bailey Lauerman.

16.13. Courtesy of Kohnke Hanneken Advertising, Inc.

16.14. March of Dimes ad courtesy of Borders Perrin Norrander. "Forty-two percent" ad courtesy of Family Violence Prevention Fund (www.futureswithoutviolence.org).

16.15. Courtesy of GSD&M and the Ad Council.

16.16. Courtesy of Tarzana Regional Medical Center.

16.17. Courtesy of InterContinental Hotels Group.

16.18. Courtesy of the Wisconsin Humane Society and Laughlin/Constable.

16.19. Courtesy of the Wisconsin Humane Society and Laughlin/Constable.

16.20. Courtesy of Bell Sports, Inc.

16.21. Courtesy of Shakespeare Fishing Tackle and Loeffler Ketchum Mountjoy.

16.22. Courtesy of Veritas.

16.23. Courtesy of BVK.

16.24. Courtesy of Gabriel deGrood Bendt.

16.25. Courtesy of Pig's Eye Brewing Company and Hunt Adkins.

16.26. Courtesy of Domtar Inc. and Hunt Adkins.

16.27. © 2004 Chipotle Mexican Grill. Used by permission.

16.28. Courtesy of Brandtrust, Inc.

16.29. Courtesy of Mullen.

16.30. Courtesy of BVK.

16.31. Blood Center ad courtesy of Kohnke Hanneken Advertising, Inc. "Location, Location, Location" ad courtesy of Coldwell Banker® Real Estate LLC.

16.32. Courtesy of Borders Perrin Norrander.

16.33. © 2003 LaSalle Bank National Association. Reproduced with permission. All rights reserved.

16.34. Courtesy of Scott Maney, Founder/ECD, Jones.

Chapter 17

17.2. Courtesy of McCoy's and McGarrah Jessee.

17.3. Courtesy of Power Trip.

17.4. Courtesy of Goodwill Industries and Young & Laramore.

17.5. Courtesy of Stanley Steemer and Young & Laramore.

17.6. Courtesy of Checkered Past Records.

17.7. Courtesy of Jeni Britton Bauer, Jeni's Splendid Ice Creams.

17.8. Courtesy of Michael Cronan and Karin Hibma.

17.9. © 2002 Viva Dolan Communications and Design Inc. Used by permission.

17.10. © 2004, Motorola, Inc. Reproduced with permission from Motorola, Inc.

17.11. Courtesy of Jeff Irish and Revolution Tea.

Chapter 18

18.1. Courtesy of Chicago Creative Partnership. Art director, Michael Dorich; copywriter, Don Dunbar; photography (snake image), Getty Images.

18.2. The words "Pike Place Market" and the Pike Place Market logo are registered trademarks of the Pike Place Preservation and Development Authority. Ad reprinted with permission.

18.3. "28% less" ad courtesy of WCCO Television Advertising & Promotion Dept., Minneapolis, MN. Humboldt penguin ad courtesy of World Wildlife Fund. Guinea pig ad courtesy of Legacy.

18.4. Courtesy of The Gillette Company.

18.5. MINI and MINI Cooper are registered trademarks of BMW NA, LLC. All rights reserved. Bruce Lee ad used by permission. Sir Richard's ad and packaging courtesy of TDA_Boulder.

18.6. Courtesy of Tom Bedecarré, AKQA.

18.7. Courtesy of The Baltimore Sun; Domain, Norwood, MA; and Scali, McCabe, Sloves, Inc.

18.8. Courtesy of Procter & Gamble.

18.9. Courtesy of General Motors Corp./Chevrolet Motor Division and Campbell Ewald.

18.10. Courtesy of Rethink.

18.11. Courtesy of John Taylor, Vice President, LG Electronics USA; Marten Van Pelt, President, Y&R Korea; and Andrew Dowling, CEO, Y&R Jakarta.

18.12. Courtesy of Lowe Roche Advertising Ltd.

18.13. Courtesy of TDA_Boulder.

Chapter 19

19.1. Courtesy of Graphic Traffic Design. Creative director, Mike Bruner; art directors, Dave Kallstrom and Bob Aisenbrey; copywriter, Steve Dolbinski; client, KXMB-TV.

19.2. Courtesy of Fred Goldberg and Jim Noble.

19.3. Courtesy of DuPont.

19.4. Courtesy of McGarrah Jessee.

19.5. Steve McCann ad courtesy of Bell Sports, Inc. Denzel Washington ad courtesy of Boys & Girls Clubs of America.

19.6. Courtesy of Scott Maney, Founder/ECD, Jones.

19.7. Courtesy of Scott Maney, Founder/ECD, Jones.

19.8. Courtesy of Avant Hair & Cosmetics, Inc.

19.9. Courtesy of TCF Bank and Chuck Ruhr Advertising.

19.10. Courtesy of DeVito/Verdi, New York.

Chapter 20

20.1. Courtesy of Martin|Williams.

20.2. Courtesy of Church Ad Project.

20.3. Printed with the permission of Target, Minneapolis.

20.4. Courtesy of Eleven Inc. and Erik Almas, photographer.

20.5. Courtesy of WWF.

20.6. Courtesy of Gibson Guitar Corp., Carmichael Lynch, and Shawn Michienzi, photographer.

20.7. MINI and MINI Cooper are registered trademarks of BMW NA, LLC. All rights reserved. Ad used by permission.

20.8. Courtesy of DeVito/Verdi, New York.

20.9. Courtesy of Denver Water, March 4, 2012.

20.10. Courtesy of Ohio State Athletics and Ron Foth Advertising.

20.11. Courtesy of American Athletic, Inc.

20.12. Courtesy of DeVito/Verdi, New York.

20.13. Courtesy of Reason Partners Inc.

Chapter 21

21.1. Courtesy of Volkswagen of America, Inc.

21.2. Courtesy of Brian Howlett and Axmith McIntyre Wicht.

21.3. Volvo poster courtesy of Veritas. Baby-in-T-shirt ad courtesy of Harley-Davidson and Carmichael Lynch.

21.4. Courtesy of TDA_Boulder.

21.5. Courtesy of The Hardware Store and "Lil-Red" Eden Prairie Grocery. Ad agency, Bozell, Minneapolis; art director, Mike Gustafson; copywriter, Bruce Hannum; photographer, Chris Grajczyk.

21.6. Stop-smoking ad courtesy of Cancer Patients Aid Association, Mumbai, India (www.cpaaindia.org). Diamond ad published with the consent of the De Beers group of Companies.

21.7. Courtesy of Reason Partners Inc.

21.8. Courtesy of Holmes & Lee.

21.9. Courtesy of Duffy Design.

21.10. Courtesy of Barefoot Advertising. Executive creative director, Doug Worple; associate creative director, Jeff Chambers; art director, Carey McGuire; copywriter, Jeff Warman.

21.11. Courtesy of Moffatt/Rosenthal.

21.12. Courtesy of Miller Brewing Company and The Martin Agency.

21.13. Courtesy of Bailey Lauerman.

Chapter 22

22.1. Courtesy of ADC.

22.2. Courtesy of Simon & Schuster. Rex

Bonomelli, art director, Scribner; John Fontana, designer; and Shasti O'Leary Soudant, illustrator. Used by permission.

22.3. Courtesy of Martin|Williams.

22.4. Prickly Pear logotype/symbol courtesy of Richter7. Dogpeople logo/symbol courtesy of Emily Chan and Smog Design, Inc.

22.5. Courtesy of Kohnke Hanneken Advertising, Inc.

22.6. © Children's Defense Fund. Reprinted with permission.

22.7. Courtesy of Scott Maney, Founder/ECD, Jones.

22.8. Courtesy of Borders Perrin Norrander.

22.9. Courtesy of DeVito/Verdi, New York.

22.10. Courtesy of Leo Burnett Madrid and TCM Europe.

22.11. Courtesy of Bailey Lauerman.

22.12. TABASCO ® ad is copyrighted © 2002 by McIlhenny Company, Avery Island, Louisiana 70513, and is used with permission of McIlhenny Company. The TABASCO ® marks, bottle, and label designs are registered trademarks and servicemarks exclusively of McIlhenny Company, Avery Island, LA 70513. American Heritage Dictionary ad courtesy of Mullen.

22.13. Courtesy of Holmes & Lee.

22.14. Jeep ad © 1997. Jeep is a registered trademark of DaimlerChrysler Corporation. Ad used by permission. Snocross ad courtesy of Martin|Williams.

22.15. Courtesy of DHL Vertriebs GmbH & Co. OHG.

22.16. Courtesy of Denver Water, March 4, 2012.

22.17. Courtesy of Spot Design.

22.18. Courtesy of GT SMART and Sawyer Riley Compton. Creative director, Bart Cleveland; art director, Rick Bryson; copywriter, Brett Compton.

22.19. Courtesy of Martin|Williams.

22.20. Courtesy of Rethink.

Chapter 23

23.1. Weather Network ad courtesy of Holmes & Lee. Garden.com ad courtesy of McGarrah Jessee. DSW ad courtesy of DSW; creative leader and copy director, Lisa Farina.

23.2. Honda ad courtesy of American Honda Motor Co., Inc. Porsche ad courtesy of client, Porsche Cars North America; agency, Carmichael Lynch; and photographer, Erik Chmil. PORSCHE, BOXSTER, CARRERA, and the Porsche Crest are registered trademarks and the distinctive shape of PORSCHE automobiles are trade dress of Dr. Ing. h.c. F. Porsche AG. Used with permission of Porsche Cars North America, Inc. Copyrighted by Porsche Cars North America, Inc.

23.3. Courtesy of Patrick Grandy and Zippo Manufacturing Company.

23.4. Courtesy of McClain Finlon Advertising.

23.5. Diamond ad published with the consent of the De Beers group of Companies. Copy of the Porsche ad used by permission of Porsche Cars North America, Inc. Porsche and the Porsche crest are registered trademarks of Dr. Ing. h.c. F Porsche AG.

23.6. Courtesy of Scott Maney, Founder/ECD, Jones.

23.7. © 2004 Chipotle Mexican Grill. Used by permission.

23.8. Courtesy of Richter7.

23.9. Courtesy of John F. Kennedy Library and Museum and The Martin Agency.

23.10. Courtesy of Goodby, Berlin & Silverstein.

23.11. Both ads courtesy of Moffatt/Rosenthal.

23.12. Courtesy of Young & Laramore, Indianapolis. Creative director, Charlie Hopper; associate creative director/copywriter, Bryan Judkins; associate creative director/art director, Trevor Williams; photographer, Gary Sparks; typography designers, Yee-Haw Industries.

23.13. Courtesy of Chrysler Marketing's Visual Asset Management (VAM) team; Tim Curtis, WME Entertainment; and Michael C. Hall. Used by permission.

23.14. Volvo ad courtesy of Veritas. Fishing reel ad courtesy of Shakespeare Fishing Tackle and Loeffler Ketchum Mountjoy. YMCA ad courtesy of French/West/Vaughan.

23.15. Courtesy of Decades Vintage Company and Mark Watson.

23.16. Courtesy of Outward Bound USA and Loeffler Ketchum Mountjoy.

23.17. Courtesy of Tam Airlines and DM9D-DB. Creative team, Mariana Sá, Manir Fadel; creative director, Jader Rosseto/Erh Ray/Pedro Cappeletti; photographer, Manolo Moran.

23.18. Courtesy of Broward County Parks and Recreation.

Chapter 24

24.1. Courtesy of KVOS and DDB Canada.

24.2. Courtesy of Rethink.

24.3. Courtesy of Black Rocket.

24.4. Courtesy of Millennium Import LLC and Hunt Adkins.

24.5. Courtesy of Skydive Twin Cities.

24.6. "Old!" courtesy of Rod Kilpatrick. Red Star Tavern and Roast House ad courtesy of Borders Perrin Norrander.

24.7. Courtesy of Black Rocket.

24.8. Courtesy of Chipotle Mexican Grill.

24.9. © 2003 Wildlife Conservation Society. Used by permission.

24.10. Courtesy of Mullen.

24.11. MINI and MINI Cooper are registered trademarks of BMW NA, LLC. All rights reserved. Ads used by permission.

24.12. Courtesy of Holmes & Lee and Reason Partners Inc.

24.13. MINI and MINI Cooper are registered trademarks of BMW NA, LLC. All rights reserved. Ad used by permission.

Chapter 25

25.1. Courtesy of Goodby, Silverstein & Partners.

25.2. Courtesy of BVK.

25.3. Courtesy of McClain Finlon Advertising.

25.4. Courtesy of BVK.

25.5. Courtesy of Midway Bank and Clarity Coverdale Fury. Creative director, Jac Coverdale; art director, Troy Longie; copywriter, Troy Longie.

25.6. Courtesy of Kohnke Hanneken Advertising, Inc.

25.7. © 2004 Oregon Tourism Commission. Reprinted with permission.

25.8. Courtesy of VF Corporation and The Martin Agency.

25.9. Courtesy of GSD&M.

25.10. Courtesy of Arts & Science Council. Photographer, Jeffrey McCullough; advertising agency, Wray Ward.

25.11. Courtesy of Scott Maney, Founder/ECD, Jones.

25.12. Courtesy of the New Mexico Department of Health and McKee Wallwork Henderson.

Chapter 26

26.1. Courtesy of See of San Francisco.

26.2. Courtesy of The Contemporary Museum, Honolulu, HI.

26.3. Courtesy of Crispin Porter + Bogusky.

26.4. © Rodgers Townsend. Reprinted with permission.

26.5. Courtesy of The J. Peterman Company.

26.6. Courtesy of Viva Dolan Communications and Design Inc. Doug Dolan, copywriter.

Ansel Adams, quoted in Wordsmith, November 15, 1998, http://wordsmith.org/awad/archives/1198.

Scott Adams, "Conversation," *Dilbert: The Scott Adams Blog*, July 20, 2010, http://dilbert.com/blog/entry/conversation (accessed June 6, 2011).

Joe Alexander, "Copywriters (Still) Wanted," *One. A Magazine.* 2010 One Show issue, Summer 2010, 13.

Ron Anderson, "Right On, Ron" (interview), in *Creative Leaders Advertising Program* (New York: *Wall Street Journal*, 1991), 4.

Aristotle, *Poetics,* in *The Complete Works of Aristotle,* rev. Oxford trans., ed. Jonathan Barnes (Princeton, NJ: Princeton University Press, 1984), 2:2334–35.

Matthew Arnold, quoted in Joseph M. Williams, *Style,* 3rd ed. (Glenview, IL: Scott, Foresman, 1989), 1.

David Baldwin, "Nobody Cares That You Only Had the Weekend," *Communication Arts,* January/February 2002, 34.

James Baldwin, quoted in George Plimpton, ed., *The Writer's Chapbook* (New York: Viking, 1989), 126.

Charlotte Beers, quoted in James Atlas, "The Million-Dollar Diploma," *New Yorker,* July 19, 1999, 46.

William Bernbach [p.67], quoted in Bob Levenson, *Bill Bernbach's Book* (New York: Villard, 1987), 116. [p.182], Ibid., 210.

Wayne Best, quoted in Lauren Slaff, "Before You Send Out That Book, Read This," *CMYK,* no. 22, 80.

Alex Bogusky [p. 254], quoted in Warren Berger and Crispin Porter + Bogusky, *Hoopla* (Brooklyn, NY: Powerhouse, 2006), 114. [p. 293], Ibid., 160.

Alex Bogusky and John Winsor, *Baked In: Creating Products and Businesses That Market Themselves* (Chicago: Agate, 2009), 90.

Daniel Boone, quoted in John Mack Faragher, *Daniel Boone: The Life and Legend of an American Pioneer* (New York: Henry Holt, 1992), 65.

Leo Burnett, quoted in *100 Leo's: Wit & Wisdom from Leo Burnett* (Lincolnwood, IL: NTC Business Books, 1995), reprinted in "Wit and wisdom from 'Chairman Leo,'" *Advertising Age,* July 31, 1995, LB-14.

Lewis Carroll, *Alice's Adventures in Wonderland,* in *Alice in Wonderland,* ed. Donald J. Gray (New York: Norton, 1971), 94.

Coco Chanel, "Coco Chanel Quotes," *Goodreads,* http://www.goodreads.com/author/quotes/3004479.Coco_Chanel (accessed December 6, 2011).

Chaucer, quoted in Donald M. Murray, *Write to Learn* (Independence, KY: Wadsworth Publishing, 2004), 264.

G. K. Chesterton, "A Defence of Heraldry," in *The Defendant* (The Literature Network), http://www.online-literature.com/chesterton/the-defendant/9/.

Chuck Close, interviewed by Andy Ward, "What I've Learned," *Esquire* January 2002, 95.

Lee Clow [p.95], quoted in Warren Berger, "By Design, a Company's Culture Goes to the Dogs," *One. Design,* 11, bound in *One. A Magazine,* Fall 2008. [p. 274], Lee Clow, quoted in Teressa Iezzi, *The Idea Writers* (New York: Palgrave Macmillan, 2010), 195.

John Colasanti, "The Simpler the Better," *Adweek,* April 5, 2004, 16.

Billy Collins, quoted in Ben Yagoda, *The Sound on the Page* (New York: HarperResource, 2004), 123.

Sue Crolick, quoted in Sally Prince Davis, *The Graphic Artist's Guide to Marketing and Self-Promotion* (Cincinnati: North Light, 1991), 35.

Laurel Cutler, quoted in "Is any niche too small for U.S. automakers," *Advertising Age,* April 9, 1990, 52.

Leonardo da Vinci, quoted by Jack Foster, *How to Get Ideas* (San Francisco: Berrett-Koehler, 1996), 108.

Miles Davis, quoted in Joel Saltzman, *If You Can Talk, You Can Write* (New York: Warner, 1993), 98.

Edward de Bono [p. 189], *Lateral Thinking* (New York: Harper & Row, 1973), 13. [p. 204] Ibid., 132.

Antoine de Saint-Exupéry, from *The Wisdom of the Sands,* quoted in *Wordsmith,* Sept. 13, 2004, http://wordsmith.org/awad/archives/0299.

Peter de Vries, quoted in Donald M. Murray, *Write to Learn,* 2nd ed. (New York: Holt, Rinehart and Winston, 1987), 210.

Yuri Dojc, quoted in "Fifty Years of Photography," *Communication Arts, Photography Annual 50,* September/October 2009, 84.

Stephen Doyle, quoted in "CSCA, Stephen Doyle, and a Punch," *3rd Thursday,* newsletter of the Columbus Society of Communicating Arts, July 1990, no pagination.

Albert Einstein, quoted in Joseph M. Williams, *Style: Toward Clarity and Grace* (Chicago: University of Chicago Press, 1990), 114.

Peter Elbow, *Writing Without Teachers* (New York: Oxford University Press, 1973), 6.

Shepard Fairey, quoted on NPR's *Fresh Air,* recorded in January 2009, rebroadcast February 26, 2009.

Barbara S. Feigin, quoted in Randall Rothenberg, *Where the Suckers Moon* (New York: Knopf, 1994), 121.

Mark Fenske [p. 192], "How to know when you've done a good ad," print advertisement for ibidphoto.com, *One. A Magazine,* Summer 2002, 24. [p. 254], Mark Fenske, "My Art Center Class in 800 Words or Less," *CMYK,* Fall/Winter 1998, 64.

Craig Frazier, quoted in *Communication Arts,* Design Annual 1989, 143.

Cliff Freeman, "Cliff's Notes," in Maxine Paetro, *How to Put Your Book Together and Get a Job in Advertising,* rev. ed. (New York: W. W. Norton, 2010), 179.

John Kenneth Galbraith, quoted in Donald Murray, *Write to Learn,* 2nd ed. (New York: Holt, Rinehart and Winston, 1987), 53.

Walker Gibson [p. 110], *Persona* (New York: Random House, 1969), 68. [p. 112], Ibid., 51.

Susan Gillette, quoted in Lawrence Minsky and Emily Thornton Calvo, *How to Succeed in Advertising When All You Have Is Talent* (Lincolnwood, IL: NTC Business Books, 1994), 43.

Joy Golden, quoted in Mill Roseman, "Joy Radio," *Communication Arts* January/February 1989, 69.

Jeff Goodby, "The Next Golden Age," *Advertising Age,* February 10, 2003, 23.

Howard Gossage [p. 81] *Is There Any Hope for Advertising?* (Urbana: University of Illinois Press, 1986), xix. [p. 100] Howard Gossage, quoted in Teressa Iezzi, *The Idea Writers* (New York: Palgrave Macmillan, 2010), 27.

Roy Grace, quoted in Lawrence Minsky and Emily Thornton Calvo, *How to Succeed in Advertising When All You Have Is Talent* (Lincolnwood, IL: NTC Business Books, 1994), 93.

Ian Grais, quoted in Joe Shepter, "Online Advertising," *Communication Arts,* May/June 2008, 80.

Tom Grimes, "Workshop and the Writing Life," in Tom Grimes, ed., *The Workshop: Seven Decades of the Iowa Writers' Workshop* (New York: Hyperion, 1999), 10–11.

Nancy Hale, quoted in Donald Murray, *Write to Learn,* 2nd ed. (New York: Holt, Rinehart and Winston, 1987), 53.

Steve Hayden, quoted in *The Copy Book* (Hove, England: Designers and Art Directors Association of the United Kingdom, 1995), 68.

Melvin Helitzer, *Comedy Writing Secrets* (Cincinnati: Writer's Digest, 1987), 37–38.

Mark Hillman, e-mail to author, December 10, 1999.

Sally Hogshead, " 'The Agency with the Best Softball Team Does the Worst Creative' (and Other Unshakable Truths of Advertising*)," One. A Magazine,* Winter 1998, 12.

Claude Hopkins, *My Life in Advertising & Scientific Advertising* (1966; Lincolnwood, IL: NTC Business Books, 1991), 148.

Teressa Iezzi [p. 114], *The Idea Writers* (New York: Palgrave Macmillan, 2010), 103. [p. 135], Ibid., 187.

Harry Jacobs, "Wild about Harry" (interview), in *Creative Leaders Advertising Program* (New York: *Wall Street Journal*, 1991), 19.

Ben Jonson, quoted in Plimpton, *Writer's Chapbook,* 101.

Andrew Keller, quoted in Warren Berger and Crispin Porter + Bogusky, *Hoopla* (Brooklyn, NY: Powerhouse, 2006), 161.

Rob Kitchen, quoted in Ralf Langwost,

How to Catch the Big Idea: The Strategies of the Top-Creatives, trans. Kim Butcher and Denis Buckley (Erlangen, Germany: Publicis Corporate Publishing, 2004), 85.

Theodore Levitt [p. 8], *The Marketing Imagination,* expanded ed. (New York: Free Press, 1986), 135. [p. 32], Ibid., 128.

Marsha Lindsay, quoted in Jeanette Smith, *The Advertising Kit: A Complete Guide for Small Businesses* (New York: Lexington Books, 1994), 255. [Please confirm city of publication.]

Christopher Locke, from *The Cluetrain Manifesto,* excerpted in "Catching the 'Cluetrain,'" *Advertising Age,* March 13, 2000, 24.

George Lois, "Oldest Living Creative Tells All," *Advertising Age's Creativity,* May 1998, 24.

Ed McCabe, quoted in *The Copy Book* (Hove, England: Designers and Art Directors Association of the United Kingdom, 1995), 121.

John Newton, in John Bartlett, ed., *Familiar Quotations,* 16th ed. (Boston: Little Brown, 1992), 327.

Peggy Noonan, *On Speaking Well* (New York: ReganBooks, 1999), 15.

David Ogilvy, *Ogilvy on Advertising* (New York: Random House, 1985), 14.

Charles Osgood, quoted in Bob Schulberg, *Radio Advertising: The Authoritative Handbook* (Lincolnwood, IL: NTC Business Books, 1989), ix.

John Pearson, quoted in Leslie Savan, "Morality Plays on 42nd Street," *The Village Voice Worldwide,* http://www.villagevoice.com (accessed July 13, 1997).

Don Peppers, quoted in Karen Stabiner, *Inventing Desire* (New York: Simon & Schuster, 1993), 179.

P. J. Pereira, quoted in Ralf Langwost, *How to Catch the Big Idea: The Strategies of the Top-Creatives,* trans. Kim Butcher and Denis Buckley (Erlangen, Germany: Publicis Corporate Publishing, 2004), 206.

Mary Pipher, *Writing to Change the World* (New York: Riverhead Books, 2006), 11.

Carl Pope (address), Sierra Club Community Meeting, Columbus, Ohio, May 19, 2004.

Steffan Postaer, quoted in Lisa Hickey, *Design Secrets: Advertising: 50 Real-Life Projects Uncovered* (Gloucester, MA: Rockport, 2002), 29.

Anna Quindlen, quoted in Rose A. Adkins, "Reporting the Details of Life," *Writer's Digest,* March 1993, 36.

Paul Rand, *A Designer's Art* (New Haven: Yale University Press, 1985), 45.

Keith Reinhard [p. 49], "Keith's Beliefs" (interview), in *Creative Leaders Advertising Program* (New York: *Wall Street Journal,* 1991), 40. [p. 52], Keith Reinhard, quoted in David Martin, *Romancing the Brand* (New York: AMACOM, 1989), 92.

Hal Riney, "How Now, Hal?" (interview), in *Creative Leaders Advertising Program* (New York: *Wall Street Journal,* 1991), 42.

Jean Robaire, quoted in Julie Prendiville, "Stein Robaire Helm," *Communication Arts,* May/June 1992, 66.

Alice Roosevelt, quoted in Philip Hensher, "Books & Critics: The Country and the City," *Atlantic Monthly,* September 2001, 31.

Frank Rowsome, Jr., *They Laughed When I Sat Down* (New York: Bonanza Books, 1959), 3.

Michael Schudson, *Advertising, The Uneasy Persuasion: Its Dubious Impact on American Society* (New York: Basic Books, 1984), 227.

Doc Searls and David Weinberger, from Rick Levine, Christopher Locke, Doc Searls, and David Weinberger, *The Cluetrain Manifesto: The End of Business as Usual* (New York: Basic Books, 2000), 113.

Joe Shepter, "The Barbarian Group," *Communication Arts,* January/February 2007, 58.

Mike Shine, "Shine on," *One,* Winter 1998, 8.

Rich Silverstein, quoted in Ralf Langwost, *How to Catch the Big Idea: The Strategies of the Top-Creatives,* trans. Kim Butcher and Denis Buckley (Erlangen, Germany: Publicis Corporate Publishing, 2004), 193.

Jennifer Solow, quoted in Stefani Zellmer, "Visual Metaphor: How Art Directors Articulate the Unspeakable," *Art Direction,* January 1995, 46.

Robert Southey, quoted in Jack Hart, *A Writer's Coach* (New York: Pantheon Books, 2006), 93.

William Stafford, "A Course in Creative Writing," in *A Glass Face in the Rain* (New York: Harper & Row, 1982), 65.

Albert Szent-Gyorgyi, quoted in Jon Steel, *Truth, Lies and Advertising* (New York: Wiley, 1998), 269.

Bob Thacker, "Chewing Gum and Bailing Wire: Big Ideas with Little Budgets" (presentation), Columbus College of Art & Design, Columbus, Ohio, September 21, 2009.

James Thurber, quoted in Thomas Kunkel, *Genius in Disguise: Harold Ross of* The New Yorker (New York: Random House, 1995), 248.

Dave Trott, "They Would Be Better Off Hiring Your Mother," *One. A Magazine,* Fall 1998, 31.

Jack Trout and Al Ries, *Marketing Warfare* (New York: NAL, 1986), 7.

John Updike (address), Thurber House Evenings with Authors, Columbus, Ohio, October 14, 1989.

Voltaire, quoted in John Bartlett, ed., *Familiar Quotations,* 16th ed. (Boston: Little, Brown, 1992), 305.

David Art Wales, quoted in Himpe, *Advertising Is Dead,* 175.

Jeff Weiss, "How Jeff Weiss Gets in the Groove" (interview), *One. A Magazine,* Fall 2000, 10.

E. B. White, letter to Katharine S. White, February 4, 1942, in *Letters of E. B. White* (New York: Harper & Row, 1976), 225.

Chris Wiggins (presentation), Columbus Society of Communicating Arts, Columbus, Ohio, September 17, 2009.

Tracy Wong [p. 169], quoted in Anthony Vagnoni, "The 1995 Obie Awards," *Advertising Age,* May 8, 1995, O-6. [p. 188], Tracy Wong, "Tracy Wong's approach," *One. A Magazine,* Fall 1998, 8.

Virginia Woolf, "The Patron and the Crocus," *The Common Reader* (New York: Harcourt, Brace & World, 1925), 213–14.

James Webb Young [p. 194], *A Technique for Producing Ideas,* (1940; Chicago: Crain, 1975), 35–36. [p. 260], James Webb Young, *Diary of an Ad Man* (Chicago: Advertising Publications, 1944), 68.

Warren Zevon, quoted in Dan DeLuca, "Cancer Claims 'Excitable Boy' 12 Days after Release of Farewell Album," *The Columbus Dispatch,* September 9, 2003, D6.

William Zinsser, *On Writing Well,* 6th ed. (New York: HarperCollins, 1998), 178.1984), 2:2334–35.

INDEX

ABC-TV, 56
Abrams, M. H., 93
Absolut vodka, 267
AC Delco, 30
Ace Asphalt, *57*
Ace Hardware, 51, 146, 226
achievement, consumer desire for, 26
acronyms, 229
Actual Miles, 280–82
Adams, Ansel, 59
Adams, Chris, 97
Adams, Scott, 145
Adidas, 91–92, 170, 226
adjectives and adverbs, 97–98, 121–22, 125
Advertising Age's Creativity (Iezzi), 114, 135
AEG-Electrolux, 131
affiliation, consumer need for, 27
Agee, Bill, 177
AgenciaClick, 297
Agency Communications, *300*
Airborne Express, 167, *169*
Air France, 223
AirTran, 296
Aiwa electronics, *183*
Akroyd, Dan, 205
Alcatraz, *242*
Alexander, Joe, 114
Alibris, 222
Alice's Adventures in Wonderland (Carroll), 118
Alive newspaper, 57–58
Allegra, 229
Allen, Woody, 199
Alreck, Pamela, 26
Altman, Danny, 230
Altoids, 182, 221, 245
Alzheimer Society of British Columbia, *172*
ambient advertising, 173
American Athletic, *252*
American Egg Board, 225
American Express, 30, 35, 225
American Floral Marketing Association, 224
American Furnishings, 27
American Legacy Foundation, 61
American Standard, 63, *64*
American Tourister, 198
Ammirati & Puris, 265
Amster Yard, 13
Amtrak, *82*, 203, 221
Amway, 222
Anderson, Ron, 12
anti-smoking ads, *43*, 61–63, 79, 173, *258, 298*
Apple, 16, 19–20, 26, 49, 72–73, 100, 219, 230, 245–46
Apple Beer, *279*
apps, 134–35
Aristotle, 93, 264
Arnold, Matthew, 120
Arnold Communications, 93
Arnold Worldwide, 61
Arts & Science Council, *296*
Asher, Larry, 146
Asian Branding (Batey), 182
Asics, 207
Athletic Republic, *218*
AT&T, 27
attitude advertising, 55–58
audio
    radio ad sound effects, 165–66
    in television ads, 155–56
    tension between visuals and, 156
Audio Books, 223
Australian Range Lamb, *280*
Aveda, 201
Avis, 182
Axmith McIntyre Wicht, 255

badge products, 52–53
Bailey Lauerman, *269*

Baker's Bourbon, 225
Baldwin, David, 188
Baldwin, James, 120
Baldwin Sport Parachute Center, *289*
Bally, 220
Bamboo Lingerie, *174*
banner ads, 132, 141
Barney's New York, 116
Bartle Bogle Hegarty, 49
Bass ale, 287
Bates, Charles Austin, 174
Batey, Ian, 182
Bauer, Jeni Britton, 75
Baywatch, 111
Bazooka gum, 261
Beers, Charlotte, 54
before-and-after images, 247, *248*
Bell helmets, *211*, 224, 243, *244*
Belushi, John, 205
benefits of products
    consumer's perception of, 35–36
    copy content, 126
    dramatizing, 45
    as focus of slogan, 221
    headline writing, 86
    highest possible, 23
    identifying, for creative brief, 64
    research into, 18–21
    unique selling proposition, 47–48
    visual approaches to depicting, 87
Benjamin, Jeff, 142, 146
Bennett, Graceann, 64
Berger, Warren, 288
Bergstrom, 145
Bernard, Nancy, 99
Bernbach, William, 13, 67, 182, 295
Best, Wayne, *292*
Best Buy, 133
BFGoodrich, 134
Bierce, Ambrose, 201
Big Brothers Big Sisters, 27
Bigg's, 223
Bildsten, Bruce, 160
billboard advertising, 169–72
Birkenstock, 232
Black & Decker, 26, 221
Black Forest Inn, *213*
Bleu Marine for Men, 234
blood drives, *24, 41, 207, 216, 295*
Blue Cosmos Design, 222
Blue Cross/Blue Shield, *177*
BMP, 261
BMW, 124, 131, 137–39, 198, 207
Bodet, Tom, 161
Bogusky, Alex, 18, 50, 78, 133–34, 146, 254, 293
Boks, *108*
Bond, Jonathan, 181–82
Boone, Daniel, 216
Borge, Victor, 195–96
Boston Market, *35*
Boyle, Ma, 75
Boy Scouts of America, *80*, 265
Boys & Girls Club of America, *244*
Bozell & Jacobs, 13
Brainco, 57
brainstorming, 187–88
brand book, 95
branded content, 131
brand image
    addressing weaknesses in, 136–37
    copy content, 126
    creating, 54
    expression beyond advertising, 302–3
    as feature, 20–21
    new media considerations, 132–33, 135–36
    personality in, 5, 52
    social responsibility and, 135–37
    storytelling to create, 5

as strategy, 52–54
symbolism in, 52–53
use of brand history, 136
voice as expression of, 93
Braun, 221, *236*
Britches, *191*
British Airways, 214
Brown, Chip, 124
Brownstein, Alec, 132
Bruegger's Bagels, 222
Brut deodorant, 217–18
Bujutsukai, *215*
Burger King, 129, 132, 142, 180, 230, 245
Burnett, Leo, 40
Burroughs, William S., 226
bus and subway posters, *44*, 170, *239*
business cards, 299, *300*, 303
business-to-business advertising, 42, 167–69
Butch Blum, *55*
Butler Shine & Stern, 45
Butler University, 30
Byrne, Keith, 139

Call of Duty, 222
campaigns, advertising, 58
Campbell, Joseph, 69
Campbell soup, 219–20, 226
Campiello Ristorante, 224
Canada Trust bank, 158, *159*
Canada TV 12, 285–86
Canterbury Cathedral, 234
car buyers, 37–38
Caribou Coffee, 203, 224
Carlile, Brandi, 25
Carmichael Lynch, 59, 63
Carroll, Lewis, 118
Casey, Kerry, 63
categories of product
    competition between, 16–17
    research, 14–15
    strategy based on generic claims about, 45–46
CDP, London, 17
celebrity endorsements and testimonials, 86, 241, 243
Celestial Seasonings, *42*
Cellular One, *47*
Chandler, Raymond, 121
Chanel, Coco, 189
Chaucer, 124
Checkered Past Records, *200, 224*
Chesterton, G. K., 297
Chiat, Jay, 194
Chiat/Day, 194
Chiat/Day/Mojo, 37–38
Chicago Cubs, *43, 244, 278, 297*
Chicago White Sox, 217
Children's Defense Fund, *268*
Chipotle, 18, *172, 214, 279, 290*
Chivas Regal, 295
Chrysler Coporation, 32, 214, 223
Cider Jack Hard Cider, 199
Cigar Attitudes, *200*
Cigna, 207
Cincinnati, Ohio, 224
Cincinnati Academy of Design, *260*
Circuit City, 205–7
citibank, *18*, 184
Cityscape Deli, *84*
cleverness, 8, 12
clichés, 111–12, 215–16, 278
Cliff Freeman & Partners, 13
Close, Chuck, 186
Cloud Star, 220
Clow, Lee, 53, 95, 96, 97, 196–97, 274
Club Med, 274
Cluetrain Manifesto, The (Searls & Weinberger), 144
Coca-Cola, 29, 30, 50, 72, 136, 137, 262

Made to Stick (Heath & Heath), 85
magic store, 189–90
Mann, Charles, 231
March of Dimes, *208*
Marika, 199, 201
Marketing Warfare (Trout & Ries), 49
marketplace, strategic thinking about, 12
market segmentation
  behavioral indexes for, 35–37
  copywriting considerations, 37–44
  demographic, 32–33
  principle of, 32
  psychographic, 33–34
Markham Park Zoo, *284*
Marlboro, 170
Mars candy, 225
Marshalls, 221
Martin, David, 94
Martin Agency, 94, 114, 186
Martin|Williams, 265
Maslow, Abraham, 22
Maslow's hierarchy of needs, 22, 26
MassMutual Financial Group, 223
MasterCard, 221, 223
Masterlock, 156
Matthews, Jane, 231
McCabe, Ed, 16, 121, 167, 293
McCann, Steve, 243, *244*
McCoy's, *151*, 220, *221*
McElligott, Tom, 169
McKee, Robert, 69, 158
McKinney & Silver, 188
M&C Saatchi, *176*
Mellon Bank, *215*
Mercedes Benz, 259
Merkley Newman Harty, 170
metadiscourse, 121
metaphors
  creating, 274–75, 276–82
  definition, 264–65
  in demonstration ads, 149–52
  fused, 265–67
  headlines for, 269
  names as, 228
  personification, 275–76
  pure, 265
  risks in use of, 118
  role of, in advertising, 264, 274
  similes and, 274
  in slogans, 224
  verbal, 274–80
  visual, 87–89, 264–69
  writing, 117–18
metonym, 243
MET-Rx, 224
Microsoft, 29
Midway Bank, *295*
Miller beer, 56, 85–86
Milwaukee tools, *53*
MINI Cooper, *50*, 56, 73, 99, 130, 172, 173, 221, *236*, *250*, *291*, *292*, 299
Ministry of Culture, 180
misdirection, 199–203
mission statement, 95–96
Mitsubishi, 117, 225
M&Ms, 48
Moen, 223
Moler Barber College, 199
Mollá, José, 184
monitoring pop culture, 18
Monkshine, *268*
Monster.com, 224
Mooney, Kelly, 97
Morris, Rob, 169–70
Motel 6, 161, 219
Mothers car wax, *193*
Motorola, *228*
Mount Sinai Hospital, 246, *268*
Movieola, 226
Moyer, Bill, 80
Mroueh, Zak, 179

multicultural advertising, 182–84
Murray's restaurant, 203
Museum of Modern Art, 132
Musgrave, Story, 207
My Life in Advertising (Hopkins), 241
Mystic Lake Casino, 197

names, creating, 227–31
  renaming with metaphor, 280
National Congress of American Indians, *250*
National Pork Board, 224
National Thoroughbred Racing Association, 161–62
Nature Company, *126*
needs, consumers', 22–31
negative features of product, 260–61
negative space, 255–57
New Balance, 214, 221, 234–37
new media, 5–6
  ads as cool things in, 131
  brand awareness in designing cool things for, 134
  communicating with customers in, 133–34
  copywriting guidelines, 130–31
  development of relationship with consumer, 146
  entertainment considerations, 137–39
  fitting message to medium in, 132
  information overload, 148
  lessons from print media, 147
  mobile apps, 134–35
  print media versus, 129–30
  social responsibility considerations, 135–37
  as useful brand extension, 132–33, 139
  writing for, 134–35, 139–44, 146–47
  see also interactive advertising; social media
new product lines
  generic claim marketing strategy, 46
  need for positioning, 50
New Tam Airbus, *284*
Newton, John, 247
New York Aquarium, *290*
NicoDerm, 223
Nike, 23, 26, 39–40, 54, 56, 64, 76, 103–4, 111, 124, 133, 139, 156, 170, 190, 219, 222, 225, 287, 295
Nissan, 37–38, 221
nominalization, 123
Noonan, Peggy, 299
North Carolina Tourism, 178–79
North Face, 29
Norwegian Cruise Line, 29
nouns, 121
novelty, consumer need for, 29
numbers in names, 231
nurturance, consumer need for, 27
Nynex, 223

O'Brien, *56*
Ocean Spray, 225
Odopod, 134
Ogilvy, David, *15*, 52, 90–91, 267, 303
Ogilvy Chicago, 64
Ogilvy & Mather, 23, 52, 54, 66, 73, 86, 105
Ohio State University, *251*
Oil of Olay, 225
Old Grand-Dad whiskey, 234
Old Spice, 203, 221
O'Leary and Partners, 54
online resources for copywriters
  consumer reviews, 14
  library resources versus, 15
Only, 58
OnStar, 225
Ontario College of Art & Design, 227
On Writing Well (Zinnser), 167
opera music, 156
opposition, 204–8
Oreo, 224
organ donation, *217*
Orkin, *138*, *171*, 232

Orlean, Susan, 147
Osgood, Charles, 161
OurHouse.com, 164
out-of-home advertising, 169–72
Outward Bound, *283*
overstatement, 82–83, 110
Owen, Clive, 68, 131
OXO, 73
Oxy 10, 26–27

Pace University, 198
Packages That Sell (Franken & Larabee), 15
packaging, 15
Pafenbach, Alan, 93–94
Pan Am, 259
paradox, 207–8
parallelism, 197–99, 201, 223
Parentsoup.com, 139
Partnership for a Drug-Free America, 208
Patagonia, 96
patent medicines, 19
Patterson, James, 79
Paxton, Bill, 209
Pazzo Ristorante, *268*
Peace Corp, 112
Pearsohn, John, 172
Pedigree, 96–97, *98*, 220
Pentagram, 191
Pepperidge Farm, 75
Pepsi, 50, 72, 136, 137, 262
Perdue, Frank, 75
Perdue chicken, 75, 205
Pereira, P. J., 297
periodic sentences, 203
persona, 93
personality
  adjectives describing, 97–98
  brand image as, 52, 54
  building, 94–100
  profile, 98–99
  voice as expression of, 5, 93
  see also brand image; voice
personification, 275–76
Pete's brewery, *289*
Pike Place Market, *234*
Pillsbury, *88*
Pinter, Harold, 224
Pipher, Mary, 68
PJ's coffee, *53*
PlanetOutdoors, 29
Planned Parenthood, *150*, 198
Playland amusement park, 134, 149–52, *273*, *287*
PMS Escape, 203
Pollan, Michael, 147
Poniewozik, James, 146–47
pop culture, 18, 295–96
Pope, Carl, 68
Porsche, *40*, 117–18, 276, *277*
Porter, Chuck, 182
portmanteau words, 228–29
positioning
  definition, 49
  importance of, 52
  key questions, 51–52
  new product, 50
  power of, 49–51
Postaer, Steffan, 182
postmodern advertising, 285–91
Power Trip, *222*
press releases, 301–2
Prickly Pear, *266*
Prime Suspect, 225
primitive look, 288–91
problem-solving
  lowering standards to enable, 193
  persistence in, 192–93
  products as tools for, 22
  slogan as expression of, 222
  thinking processes and techniques, 186–90
  work routines to foster, 186

product
  assessing consumer's thinking about, 293–97
  benefits versus features, 18–21
  categories, 14–15, 16–17
  as cool thing in new media, 131
  identifying highest possible benefit of, 23
  negative features, 260–61
  research, 13–15, 17–18
  strategic thinking about, 12
  as symbol, 18
  utility, 132–34
  visual approaches to depicting, 86–89
product-oriented strategies
  focus on features, 46–47
  generic claim approach, 45–46
  positioning, 49–52
  types of, 45
  unique selling proposition, 47–49
product placement, 131
Promotion, The, 225
Provost, Gary, 125
Prudential insurance, 76
psychographic data, 33–34
  application of, in copywriting, 37–44
psychological needs, 22–31
punctuation
  in headlines, 92
  of slogans, 225
puns, 212–15
  in product or company names, 230
  in slogans, 225
Purell, 225
Purina, 139, *140*

Quindlen, Ann, 93

Race for the Cure, *206*
radio advertising
  award-winning ads, 166
  challenge of designing, 161, 166
  creating, 161–66
  use of dialogue in, 162–64
  use of voices in, 161–62
Radio Shack, 223
Radio Works, Houston, 161, 162
Raise the Roof, 92
Rand, Paul, 274
Range Rover, 145, 156
recognition, consumer need for, 26
recreational vehicle, *34*
RedKap, *99*
Red Star, *289*
Reebok, 156
Reeves, Rosser, 47–48, 58
Reinhard, Keith, 49, 52
repetition, 197, 203–4
  in slogan, 224
research
  to build brand personality, 95
  for business-to-business advertising, 168
  on competition, 15–17
  on consumer's thinking about product, 293–97
  to create a name, 227
  depth of, 18
  focus of, 17–18
  market segment, 32, 42
  product, 13–15
  writing and, 115–16
resonpartners.org, *253*
Resource Interactive, 97, 139, 143, 195
Rethink, 85, 139, 181
reversals, 254–63
®evolution, *229*
Reyes, Meg, 16–17
rhyme, in slogans, 225
Richards, Keith, 113
Richards Group, 66
Ricoh, 154–55
Ries, Al, 46, 49, 51, 262

Riney, Hal, 42
rites of passage, 35
Robaire, Jean, 7
Robaire & Hogshead, 195
Robinson, Ed, 182
Roces skates, 199
Rockport, 23–25, 190, 197
Roe, Mike, 189–90
Rogaine, 222
Roger, Buddy, 113
Rohöl, *110, 288*
Rolling Stone, 201
Rolls-Royce, 91
Roosevelt, Alice, 215
Ross, Harold, 195
Round-Up, 223
Rowsome, Frank, Jr., 285
Royal golf balls, 262–63
Royal Viking Line, 104–5, 274
Rudkin, Margaret, 75
rule of threes, 224–25
Russell, Alan, 285–86

Saab, 26, 182, 275
Saint-Exupéry, Antoine de, 22
San Francisco, California, *249*
SAS e-Intelligence, 216
Saturn, 222
Scali, McCabe, Sloves, 167, *292*
Schenck, Ernie, 21, 189
Scher, Paula, 191–92
Schiff, Dave, 243
Schudson, Michael, 285
Schwan's Home Service, 27, 216
Schwinn, *60*
Science World, *106*
search engines, 132, 141
Searls, Doc, 144
Sears, 225
Seasons Eyewear, *201*
Seattle Aquarium, 216
Seattle Magic, 189–90
Second Cup, *28*, 162, *163*
security, consumer need for, 30
sequential ads, 253
Seton Hall, 222
Settle, Robert, 26
7-Up, 49–50
sexuality, 27–29
Shackleton, Ernest, 39
Shakespeare Fishing Tackle, *212, 282*
Sharp, 223
Sharper Image, 147
Shedd Aquarium, *233*
Shepter, Joe, 137
Shimano, *91*, 225
Shine, Mike, 45
shouting, 91
Silk soymilk, 36, *38*
Silverstein, Rich, 81, 303
similes, 274
simplicity, 122, 170, 293
Sir Richard's, *236*
slogans
  changing, 222
  focus on product benefits, 221
  good qualities, 219–20, 226
  length, 225–26
  metaphor in, 224
  new media applications, 141
  parallelism in, 223
  puns in, 225
  purpose, 219
  quirkiness in, 226
  as rallying cry, 220
  repetition in, 224
  rhyme in, 225
  spoken language for, 220–21
  techniques for creating, 220–26
  value of, 96–97
Smart Car, 73

Smart Water, 225
Snickers, 16, 137
Snocross, *271*
social media
  definition, 129
  risk of overload, 148
  as useful brand extension, 133
  writing for, 144–47
  see also new media
social responsibility, 135–37
Solow, Jennifer, 265
Sonic, *157*
Sony, 29, 156, 223, 224, 225
Sotheby's Realty, 26
sound effects, 165–66
South Coast Plaza, 170–72
Southey, Robert, 219
special occasion purchases, 35
specificity, 114–15, 116, 147, 210–12, 234, *235*
Spiegel, 243
Spiegler, Eric, 54
split-screen imagery, 87
Sporting News, 51
Sports Illustrated, 201
Stafford, William, 185
Stanislavsky, Konstantin, 218
Stanley Steemer, *223*
Staples, 158, *159*
Starbucks, 175, 199, 224, 226
Starkey hearing aids, *23*
Steelcase/Coach, 198
Stein, Gertrude, 203
Stein Robaire, Helm, 7
Stenz, Leon, *215*
Sterilite, 197
stimulation, consumer need for, 29
Stoddard's fishing store, 214
storytelling
  central image, 76
  characters, 73–75
  consumer's role in, 78–79
  definition of story, 68
  importance of, 5, 68
  length, 79–80
  plotlines, 68–73
  point of view, 77
  power of, 80
  product research for, 68
  quirkiness in, 158–60
  as role of copywriter, 21
  setting, 75
  story elements, 68
  style, 75
  theme, 77
  use of symbol, 76
Stouffer's, 25
strategy
  blending, 58
  continuum of strategies, 58
  definition, 8
  execution and, 8–12
  first steps, 8
  importance of, 7
  kinds of strategic approaches, 45
  objectives, 5
  requirements for creation of, 12
  see also consumer-oriented strategies; product-oriented strategies
Strunk, William, 120
Subaru, 78–79
subliminal advertising, *290*
succorance, consumer need for, 27
Sue Crolick Advertising & Design, 255
Sun Air, 172
Sun Country Airlines, *294*
Super Bowl ads, 288–91
Survivor TV show, 29, 220
Sutton, Dan, 170
Swiss Army Knife, *290*
Sydney Dog Home, *176*